BOUNDARIES
OF COMPETENCE

GWYNNE NETTLER

BOUNDARIES OF COMPETENCE

HOW SOCIAL STUDIES MAKE FEEBLE SCIENCE

Routledge
Taylor & Francis Group

LONDON AND NEW YORK

First published 2003 by Transaction Publishers

2 Park Square, Milton Park, Abingdon, Oxfordshire OX14 4RN
711 Third Avenue, New York, NY 10017

Routledge is an imprint of the Taylor & Francis Group, an informa business

First issued in paperback 2017

Copyright © 2003 Taylor & Francis

Library of Congress Catalog Number: 2003050774

Library of Congress Cataloging-in-Publication Data

Nettler, Gwynne.
    Boundaries of competence : how social studies make feeble science /
Gwynne Nettler.
        p. cm.
    Includes bibliographical references and index.
    ISBN 0-7658-0179-5 (alk. paper)
        1. Social sciences—Methodology. 2. Social sciences—Philosophy.
    I. Title.

H61.N468 2003
300'.1—dc21   2003050774

ISBN 13: 978-0-7658-0179-1 (hbk)
ISBN 13: 978-1-138-50775-3 (pbk)

*"Skepticism is the chastity of the intel-
lect, and it is shameful to surrender it too
soon or to the first comer...."*
George Santayana,
Skepticism and Animal Faith, *1923*

Contents

Preface

At Cambridge University, 1840, William Whewell invented the word, "scientist." He derived the term from the Latin, *scire*, "to know," and intended his neologism to replace the phrase, "natural philosopher." Until then, the latter title had been used to denote those explorers who endeavored to decipher Nature by disciplined reason and diligent observation rather than by unobservant thought and appeal to authority. Whewell's invention was an instant success.

The tools that characterized these intellectual adventurers were publicly verifiable observation and classification, measurement, experiment where possible, and inductive inference. With these instruments, inquirers were expanding knowledge in such diverse domains as astronomy, anatomy and physiology, botany and biology, geology and geometry, chemistry and physics.

At the same time, 1830-1842, the French social reformer, Auguste Comte, published a multi-volume thesis in which he argued that human thought was evolving inevitably toward an overarching science he called "sociology." This progressive mode of comprehending social reality would make possible policies that assured the universal, rational improvement of "the human condition." The implicit logic was, "If Man is part of Nature, and if scientific probes of Nature allow engineering of its parts to fit our desires, then why not a science of ourselves, applicable to the prediction and control of ourselves?"

Comte's invention has been as successful as Whewell's only in the name-game. The word, "sociology," has been adopted by the common lexicon. But Comte's Queen of Sciences has failed to perform as the vaunted "science of the fundamental laws of social relations."[1]

Nevertheless, words propagate, and they often do so by coupling, so that the twentieth century saw the burgeoning of studies bearing the promissory title, "social science." This compound is now attached widely and loosely to assorted inquiries about human action and condition.

Promising a *science* of social action poaches on the success of Natural Philosophers. The honorific title, warranted by college degrees, proposes new techniques for improving upon common sense, adds cachet to the opinions of those who certify themselves as "social scientist," and provokes hostility among other claimants to moral and political authority.

The contest continues. At issue is whether social scientists have contributed to knowledge of human action and, if so, how much in which domains of activity.

Some such contribution is evident, and is cited throughout this exercise. If, to this advantage, we add the works of historians, biographers, biologists, and neurophysiologists, then we assuredly know more today about our nature than we did as recently as ten years ago. But the tools we employ limit the questions we can answer.

Chapters to follow describe some of these limits. They do so by noting major impediments to an applied science of social action. Their message is cautionary, not only for those who produce social science, but also for those who consume our products.

Boundaries of our competence are apparent in three overlapping realms—those of fact-finding, knowledge-creation, and knowledge-application.

Chapter 1 begins the story by grounding knowledge in perception. It shows that a primitive form of "knowing"—the ability to classify and discriminate among objects, actions, and actors—comes with the biological equipment of all organisms. We are *not* born blank slates. A sense of reality is *not* merely socially constructed and therefore malleable according to our desires.

However, language makes a difference. As we graduate from primal perception to conceptions of the world produced with symbols, language not only expands our ability to conceive relations among individuals, things, and events, it also opens doors to delusion.

Chapter 2 describes some of these invitations to folly. They are particularly abundant as social scientists regard the world through symbolic filters that fuzz description with evaluation.

For the most part, students of social affairs work with ordinary language. Unfortunately for science but happily for rhetoric,[2] the terms of a vernacular contain small kernels of denotation embraced by large auras of connotation saturated with moral significance.

Such words can *mean* something without referring to anything observable. They seduce our language-using species into drawing maps of reality with symbols that evoke feelings but lack physical reference. This defect is serious for, in the name of meaningful but empty abstractions, human beings kill themselves and others.

Chapter 3 describes a continuum of perceiving—conceiving involved in different ways of "knowing" worlds. Scientific procedures are but one of these modes with its own powers and limitations. Not all questions we ask are empirical, and not all empirical questions can be answered.

Chapter 4 lays out the requirements of measurement. It argues that assigning numbers to dubious observations gives false assurance that mathematical manipulations, as in "statistics," necessarily represent events.

Chapter 5 continues the argument. It shows that social scientists' most popular tool for finding causes of human action—correlational analysis—has defects. Among these is the likelihood that degrees of association revealed can change with the unit of measurement employed.

Chapter 6 holds that, given deficiencies in knowledge, and perhaps because of the way Nature works, we assess probabilities rather than seek certainties. Four different concepts of probability are described.

Chapter 7 illuminates the difficulty of counting events by noting the difference between "brute facts" that exist independently of our observing them, and "social facts" that depend on agreement among persons. Social facts are invented and employed at varying "conceptual distance" from any brute facts that might anchor them. The greater the "distance," the more likely are quarrels about their existence. As the language we use loses connection with perceptible events, and hence reduces agreement about the denotation of terms, ethico-political interests intrude to distort measurement.[3]

Social facts are slippery, and yet we have to handle them. Therefore, if we are to be rational, we need to measure them. This presents another difficulty: We cannot observe most of the activities that concern us. Instead, we invent indirect probes that, with varying degrees of accuracy, reflect the conditions and actions we wish to gauge.

Chapter 8 describes such "vicarious observation." It shows how these substitutes can yield "findings" that are wide of the targets of inquiry.

Despite the difficulties of accountancy, all of us try to explain events we assume we've classified and tallied. Allaying curiosity is one such satisfaction, and an end-in-itself. Promise of a better world is another, popular kind of satisfaction. In the United States, for example, we give prizes to those whose explanatory schemes fortify hopes.

In the political arena, explanations satisfy insofar as they justify what we already believe, and assure us that means are available with which to attain our desired ends.

In general, and more pragmatically, we look to a science of social affairs to improve anticipation of what may occur, and what may occur if we do, or do not do, particular things. A science of social action, it's been proposed, will increase our power to *predict* events, both those that lie within the compass of our individual lives and those that occur in the lives of others. This aspiration poses three different, and difficult, tasks: "knowing" ourselves, "knowing" others, and "knowing" the likely effects of distant social processes.

Acknowledging this complex of satisfactions, chapter 9 criticizes ways of explaining conduct by *characterizing* actors and their acts, and by *understanding* them through empathy.

Chapter 10 discusses the important, and never-ending, quarrel about causation. It shows that causation is not one idea. In addition, we dispute the *location* of causation (the *what*) and the *style* in which causes produce particular social events (the *how*).

These pages also illuminate the difference between assigning causation and attributing responsibility. It remarks on the difference between the job of doing science, interpreting and administering law, and achieving justice.

Concluding chapters argue that, in social affairs, decision is regularly torn between doing what is effective (rational) and doing what is right (moral). Chapter 11 describes the nature of rational action. Chapter 12 addresses the quality of moral feeling. While rational reasoning weighs means appropriate to ends, morality guides choice of both ends and means.

Given moving mixtures of rational and moral stimulants to action, error-free policies are beyond our powers. Unintended effects are common. Some of these are neutral to our purposes; others are perverse, or what physicians call "iatrogenic."[4] Our predicament is expressed by Garrett Hardin's "First Law of Ecology": We can never do just one thing.

Acknowledgments

Professors F. D. Cousineau, A. R. Gillis, and Robert A. Silverman have read parts of this work. They have encouraged me and cautioned me, and I thank them for their tempering counsel. I am also grateful to friends who have examined my arguments and alerted me to defects: Dorothy Hill, Charles Hill, Rodney M. Quinn, Robert Sykes, Chase Weaver, and Judith White.

Where we disagree, my critics are absolved, of course, of errors in which I may persist.

Gwynne Nettler
San Diego, CA

Part 1

Perceiving and Conceiving

1

Primal Knowledge

*"Even a dog can tell the difference between
being stumbled over and being kicked."*
— Oliver Wendell Holmes, Jr.[1]

Origins

Knowing the world begins with perceiving it. Perception refers to imputed neurochemical processes that organize sensations in such ways that objects and events are differentiated and categorized.

Ability to categorize is a built-in physiological capacity of all creatures. It is a survival process provided—without language or formal instruction—by the perceptual apparatus of organisms.[2]

No "normally developed" organism comes into this world bereft of perceptual—that is, discriminating—ability. ("Normally developed" has to be inserted because some creatures are born damaged. This includes human babies born without complete nervous systems.)

Differentiation and categorization are untrained physiological capacities "to detect recurrences in the environment despite variations in local stimulus energies."[3] The auditory and visual processes, and other channels of the sensorium like olfaction, organize ambiguous stimuli into clusters that exploit certain regularities in the external realm.

Early on, all living organisms exhibit some such talent. Animals "from tadpoles to monkeys [and] bees to ground squirrels" discriminate between kin and non-kin; fur-seals' mothers and their offspring recognize each others' vocal signals; and some birds, carnivores, and primates identify their mates and remain "faithful for life."[4]

A species of ape, the pygmy chimpanzee or bonobo (*Pan paniscus*), demonstrates spontaneous (untrained) comprehension of symbols. These animals communicate their understanding to other apes and human beings, and they refer to "things that are not visible and to activities in which we are not, at present, engaged."[5]

3

We, too, come into this world with the untutored ability to recognize similarities and differences among parts of our surroundings and, of course, "surroundings" includes other living creatures and objects distinguished from ourselves. Such discrimination is the earliest form of "assigning meaning" to "the booming, buzzing confusion" that greets our arrival.

We are biologically programmed "to make sense of"—to classify, and hence to define—reality. We are *not* born "blank slates."[6]

Early Knowing

At eighteen to twenty weeks gestation, the human fetus distinguishes auditory stimuli and "can be calmed by the low frequency sounds produced at the rhythm of the mother's heart rate."[7] Between the thirty-fifth and thirty-eighth weeks of pregnancy, "the fetus is capable of discriminating between familiar and unfamiliar stories (organized sounds) presented to it through speakers placed on the mother's abdomen."[8] Discrimination is demonstrated by changes in fetal heart rate.

Shortly after birth human infants can detect sound groupings (phonemic classes) and ignore "noise" in the speech signal.[9] At one week of age a human baby can distinguish its mother's voice from other female voices, and at two weeks of age it recognizes that mother's voice and face are a unit so that baby perceives the difference between mother and strangers. Human infants also discriminate between (react differently to) their mothers and their fathers.[10] It would not be surprising if other mammals had such capacity, mediated through the same or other sensory channels.

Infantile categorization includes differential preferences for sounds, tastes, and colors.[11] By three weeks of age, human infants integrate sight and touch. "Blindfolded, and allowed to rub its tongue along a toy block, [the human baby] will later gaze at a picture of a block in preference to other objects."[12]

As early as six weeks of age, infants demonstrate ability to perceive environmental contingencies, and at two to three months of age, they show that "both the temporal and physical characteristics of events in a contingency...influence the nature of [their] anticipatory behavior."[13]

Babies exhibit "knowledge of object motion and human action."[14] They demonstrate early numerical differentiation and perceive some kinds of causal connection.[15]

Again, such cognition occurs before language has been acquired and without training.[16] Human beings, and other creatures *perceive* causal links without being able to talk about them.

Hans Furth puts it this way:

> Much verbal behavior proceeds at a fairly habitual, quasi-automatic level. Hence it would seem important not to identify just any verbal behavior with thinking behavior.[17]

Homo sapiens is a talking animal. From our beginnings to our endings, we say much without necessarily knowing, or caring, whether our utterances refer to anything.

At eight months of age, the human infant shows ability to discriminate between strings of three syllables that comprise units and strings in which syllables are jumbled randomly.[18] Babies perform this task without being rewarded or punished. This acquisition is *not* a conditioned response, and learning occurs with only two minutes of auditory input. In brief, human beings have an innate ability to distinguish words from other sounds. Investigators conclude,

> A fundamental task of language acquisition, segmentation of words from fluent speech, can be accomplished by 8-month-old infants based solely on the statistical relationships between neighboring speech sounds. Moreover, this word segmentation was based on statistical learning from only 2 minutes of exposure, suggesting that Infants have access to a powerful mechanism for the computation of statistical properties of the language input.[19]

Import   This brief excursion into the realm of innate abilities strongly qualifies the heedless, but popular, notion that *everything* we perceive and conceive is only a matter of "social construction."

Concepts are important, and they are endlessly invented, but knowing the world is activity performed by human agents whose ultimate test of reality rests on perceptual capacities predisposed to categorize objects and events.

Extensions

> *"Thinking without the positing of categories*
> *and of concepts in general would be as*
> *impossible as is breathing in a vacuum."*
> —*Albert Einstein*[20]

What organisms perceive varies among species, of course, and we humans differ greatly from other animals in our ability to know more than we perceive. We do so by developing concepts, usually with the aid of symbols, but even without them.[21]

We often refer to categories, produced with elaborate symbol-systems, as "constructs." I shall use the terms "concept" and "construct" interchangeably, for variety, but with the understanding that "constructs" are more dependent upon language and work at greater remove from perception.

Ability to structure experience with concepts allows us to generalize beyond the boundaries of individual perception. Conceiving the world, including ourselves in it, is a powerful instrument with which we learn from our pasts and from the pasts of others. Constructs provide ways of knowing that are not constricted by our sense organs.

The distinction between perception and conception is a matter of degrees along a continuum; it does not describe a dichotomy. But, just as we distinguish "hot" from "cold," although temperature is graded continuously, so too we can distinguish between a percept and a concept.

Perceiving and Conceiving

> "*Percepts without concepts are empty; concepts without percepts are blind.*"
> —*Immanuel Kant, 1781*

Jean Piaget offers fourteen criteria by which to distinguish between perception and conception. For present purpose, the most important of these are that:

- Perception is necessarily tied to sensory stimulation, whereas conception is not.
- Perception therefore occurs from the physical position of the observer, whereas conceiving matters can be independent of a thinker's location.
- Perception is "reproductive," whereas conception can be evocative and imaginative.[22]

We *communicate* with concepts, of course, not with percepts. We do this principally with words, but also with other symbols. For example, ± represents a concept.

Since concepts are used for evocative, imaginative, provocative (persuasive), and other purposes, it is important to ascertain whether the terms with which we *conceive* of this, and other, worlds, refer to real objects and energies or only to delusions produced by unfettered "pictures in our heads" and the multiple seductions of language. Thus, in his study of language, Charles Hockett concludes,

> In every language people can talk about things that do not exist and may even believe that they do exist, can say things that are not true and may believe that they are....There is no sharp boundary between acknowledged fictions and talk that reflects mere misinformation or insufficient information.[23]

Humanity has invented a great roster of creatures with personified characteristics that it believes exist, but that cannot be perceived. ET's and other "space aliens" are only among the latest actors in this heritage.[24] Indeed, throughout human history, a majority of our species has conceived of multitudes of quasi-human agents that supposedly control our lives and that are said to require particular activities of us if they are to grace us and do our bidding.

These imperceptible products of our dreams and waking thoughts have differed through time and around the globe. Differing faiths in such powers have been, and are, among the foremost provocations to violence. Fighting and killing for gods have occurred not only *between* human beings who regard themselves as distinctive "kinds of people," but also, to a lesser extent, *among* bands of "true believers" who *kill themselves* in accord with the promises or commandments of their deities.[25]

When we behave as ethnologists and study ways of living among varieties of our species, we come to understand the satisfactions of myth—of stories that are unproved or, more likely, unprovable. On the record, great numbers of human beings appear to be incapable of living happily without the comforts of non-empirical concepts that respond to questions science cannot answer.

Ordinary language carries with it the possibility of framing more questions than any empirical reference can answer. In times of crisis, myth helps people adjust to the accidents and inexplicable injuries that afflict us, including the final insult, death.

And more than that, myth has long served as one of the powerful instruments of social control. Apparently, the human animal is disposed to behave badly, even by its own standards. Many observers of human action have so believed, including the father of psychoanalysis, Sigmund Freud:

> *Homo homini lupus*, who has the courage to dispute it in the face of all the evidence in his own life and in history? This aggressive cruelty lies in wait for some provocation, or else it steps into the service of some other purpose, the aim of which might as well have been achieved by milder measures.[26]

Freud's Latin statement maligns wolves, but it acknowledges that *Homo sapiens* is a predator, and one that attacks its own species as does no other animal.

In recognition of this possibility, mankind has for centuries invented stories and accompanying rituals that promise punishment in other worlds, if not also in this one, when we do wrong. The control-function of myth has long been acknowledged, a fact that says nothing about the efficacy of the effort:

> Since the masses of people are inconstant, full of unruly desires, passionate, and reckless of consequences, they must be filled with fear to keep them in order. The ancients did well, therefore, to invent gods, and the belief in punishment after death. (Polybius, ca. 125 B.C.)

> Religion and morality put a brake on nature's strength, but they cannot destroy it. (Voltaire, 1764)

> A nation must have a religion, and that religion must be under the control of the government. (Napoleon I, 1801)

> No state is ever without religion, nor can be without it. (Mikhail Bakunin, 1871)

> When religion is banished, human authority totters to its fall. (Pope Benedict V, 1914)

In similar fashion, some modern scholars argue for the controlling value of faith in supernatural powers. A few criminologists, for example, can be heard prescribing religious instruction in schools as cure for crime.

Nevertheless, however valuable non-empirical belief may be—for consolation and control—the agents conceived by myth cannot be those of science. The claim of science to provide *knowledge* rests on constructs that can be "related to" observations that are public and reliable. Private insights don't count.

Despite the many disorders that distort perception and reason—and that we recognize as "illusions" and "delusion"—*if* we are to work with the desiderata of science, then tests of hypotheses, framed with clear concepts, come down to *replicable perception* of objects and events.

Concepts in Science

By both definition and promise, *all* social "science" claims adherence to the model of *scientific* inquiry. In this enterprise, the *concepts* employed must satisfy at least three criteria as philosopher John Mackie describes them:

1. Concepts should be coherent—that is, clear and precise. Mackie refers to this quality as "the internal health of a concept." I translate this to mean that a concept must have unitary reference.
2. Conceptual clarity requires clear meaning, in the sense that it should refer to, "What we ordinarily mean by a certain word or words [and] whether it is *the* concept or *a* concept that we actually use in certain fields of thought."

   Mackie inserts this criterion because almost all the concepts employed in the attempted sciences of human action are elements of "ordinary language," and, as we shall see (ch. 2), the evolved vernacular is full of traps laid by the multiple uses of its terms.

   Psychometricians call this desideratum of their measuring instruments "construct validity." Such clarity of reference is *not* a criterion of clear thought that politicians adopt when they are caught in embarrassing situations. In power struggles, the fact that many words in common use have rubbery referents or no clear reference, gives advantage to lawyers, but it is an obstacle to science and search for truth.
3. Concepts must have *empirical referents*. They should have well-defined utility in aiding the *reliable* observation and measurement of aspects of reality.

   This requirement assumes that there is something to be experienced "in the world—as contrasted, perhaps, with our established ways of thinking and speaking about the world—which conforms to that concept, or which we have reason to believe conform to it."[27]

   Psychometricians refer to this quality of a measuring tool as "predictive validity." As we shall see in the next chapter, we distinguish that use of "prediction" from a different, and more difficult, meaning of "ability to predict."

The requirement that a science employ clear, empirical concepts rests, of course, on the assumption that there is a reality to be known that exists independently of our conception of it. This has to be said because some people, some of the time, deny this requirement, even though no doubters can *act* consistently in accord with their avowed skepticism.[28]

Assumption: An Independent Reality

> *"Any healthy person who is not an inmate of an insane asylum, or in the school of idealist philosophers, [holds to] naive realism, [a belief which] consists in this, that he believes reality, the environment and the things in it, to exist independently of his perception."*
> —V. I. Lenin, né V. I. Ulyanov (1870-1924)[29]

We *test* claims to knowledge by observing what happens when we *act* in accord with any of the multitudes of propositions that human beings utter and that compete for our attention. But, if the tests are to allow verdicts of probable, improbable, or not proven,[30] then some conditions or events must be observable, independently of our "stations in life" and our hopes and desires.

Without such reality, all knowledge-claims become matters of opinion, faith, preference. And, in such cases, debate becomes logomachy: a fight with words divested of reference.

A generation after Lenin made his famous pronouncement, philosopher C. I. Lewis confirmed the necessity of assuming an independent reality.[31] He based his argument on three assumptions:

1. "The givenness of what is given; our realization that we do not create the content of experience and cannot, by the activity of thinking, alter it."
2. An independent reality means that we can state "if-then" propositions, and that "the content of the 'then' clause and the truth of the proposition as a whole, are things with respect to which the knowing mind is not dictator, but dedicated to."

Lewis adds,

I may confront the given with different attitudes and purposes; I may be differently active toward it and starting from it, I may proceed into the future in different ways. *But what I should then find*:; what eventuations of experience are genuinely possible, that is something independent of any purpose or attitude of mine. (Emphasis his)[32]

3. The assumption of a reality outside our skins means that we can ask *empirical* questions that can be answered by finding out whether....

If this were not possible, then contestants in academe and other political arenas would become nothing more than propagandists or visionaries.

Lewis writes,

> In terms of experience this means that, starting from the given in certain ways, I can safely predict the accrual of *something* the particular nature of which I cannot now determine. For example, if I examine the contents of this drawer, I either shall find a piece of chalk or I shall find none. So much I know; but I do not know—and cannot discover merely by taking thought—*which* of these alternatives I shall find true. There is that in the object which I do not know; I know something to be determined in reality which is neither implicitly nor explicitly determined in my knowledge of it. This, and all similar questions I could ask and could not now answer, witness the independence of my object. (Emphasis his)[33]

The many ways in which these criteria are applied help us distinguish among the many combinations of feeling, imagining, believing, and reasoning that have been titled "knowing." These processes deserve discrimination if we are to think clearly about possible differences in the *powers* of ways of comprehending worlds.

Succeeding chapters describe some of these powers, as well as the limitations, of a *scientific* way of finding out what occurs, and how, in the realm of social life.

Kinds of Knowing

> *"It would be possible to describe everything scientifically, but it would make no sense. It would be a description without meaning—as if you described a Beethoven symphony as a variation of wave pressure...."*
> —*Albert Einstein*[34]

When we attempt to know how the world, including ourselves, is, and how it comes to be as it is, we do not leave our bodies. Thinking is physical activity. It moves, somewhat, with changes in our physical condition that, in turn, varies with states of our internal organs and external circumstances. As a cardiac patient once told me, "After a good bowel movement, I'm an optimist again."

We start life with sets of interacting nerve fibers that *sense* changes in our innards and changes in energies external to us that affect us. The organs with which we apprehend events within and outside our bodies are so organized as to yield percepts, and it is reliable perception, I argue, that constitutes *test* of claims to knowledge, as that ability will be defined.

Because perception works with sensation, it is useful to acknowledge that a primitive kind of "knowing" is that given by neural tissue, with little or no awareness of how the feeling of knowing is aroused. Emotions "tell" us things, and it is only with difficulty that we try to insulate their messages from the more refined processes called "reasoning."

Emotions are products of the multiple systems of nerve fibers that inform us of the locations of our body parts and that allow purposively directed action upon our environments. These aggregates of neurons are differentially tuned to receive signals from within our bodies and from our surroundings, without the intercession of language and learning.

While the mammalian brain, especially its cerebral cortex, is the principal organ of thought, it is strongly affected by how it is composed, fed, exercised, and organized. This means that it is subject to change by emotions and the glandular secretions associated with them, by the effects of experience on neural connections, by ingested chemicals, and by the destructive effects of age and injury.[35] (For an easy test of part of this proposition, drink a few ounces of that most popular of anesthetics, ethyl alcohol, a chemical cousin of ether and chloroform.) And, in all of this, *individuals*—both the human kind and less brilliant creatures—differ remarkably.

Feeling-Thinking-Believing-Knowing

> *"Man, if you gotta ask, 'What is it?', you ain't*
> *ever gonna git to know."*
> *—Louis "Satchmo" Armstrong,*
> *responding to an intellectual who*
> *asked him to define jazz.*

Without being able to measure the many causes of feeling, thinking, believing, reasoning, possessing know-how, having knowledge-of, and their mixtures, we concede that we experience percepts that we cannot communicate with words or other symbols. This is particularly the case in our relations with other organisms, most notably, people.

America's first philosopher-psychologist, William James,[36] argued that emotions are part of the instrumentation of perception. In the vernacular, affected individuals often call this sensibility, "chemistry," and they acknowledge such empathy between human beings and between people and their animal pets. Thus, trainers of seeing-eye dogs are said to match the temperaments of their clients with those of their canine guides.[37]

Some aspects of our environments are appreciated only emotionally, and their enjoyment is destroyed by "thinking about them." To convert "dancing for joy" into instrumental action—that is, trying to make it rational—kills joy. This is true of *all* pleasures—in the arts, in physical exercise and play, in "communing with Nature," and loving.

Such delights are not to be questioned. They are ends-in-themselves, not means toward ends. In such cases, asking "why?"—"Why do you thrill to Mozart?", "Why do you spend time and money to ski deep powder?"—are useless queries. They can be answered only with utterances called "reasons" that yield no causal knowledge.

Valuing the pleasures is the good sense of Louis Armstrong's reply to his intellectualizing inquisitor. Attempting to rationalize joys—of affiliation, for example, or of destruction—is futile. And the unrequited suitor who asks, "Do you love me?", has his answer in his need to ask the question.

Deficits

This much is admitted. Yet there are shortcomings in the information that emotions transmit. "Feeling," undisciplined by attempts to reason—that is, to relate concepts to observations—is inarticulate. The messages conveyed by emotional expression alone tend to be simple, subject to incorrect translation, and usually limited to what we can perceive.

In addition, as thinking becomes heavily emotionalized, it loses predictive power. Normal foresight, always limited, becomes clouded; passion trumps reason; and belief turns indomitable—resistant to correction by argument or experience.

Thus, we say, "love is blind," and so too are commercial, religious, and political zeal. "Irrational Exuberance" is the title an American finance minister recently applied to money-marketers.[38]

Antidote

This is our predicament. We look to education to temper feeling with knowledge. Universities commonly have "truth" in their mottoes: Harvard's *Veritas*, Yale's *Lux et Veritas*, Alberta's *Quaecumque Vera*.

We want to know how better to achieve peace, equality, justice, health, wealth, and happiness—to name only the Big Desiderata. And if such abstractions refer not to achievement, but to the results of evolutionary processes—like emergents—then how do these come about? But we also want to *feel*—to enjoy risk and challenge, to love and be loved.

We are not made of one piece, and long schooling gives no guarantee of internal or external harmony. The idea of a "learned fool" has substance; much theory is gray, as Goethe's *Faust* declares; and our exercise here offers only prudential counsel against faith in omniscience.

Nay-saying is an important defense against folly. Our work begins with examination of the traps ordinary language sets for reason. Argument follows. It questions our ability to measure everything we wish to count. It cautions, then, against undue confidence in public numbers, authoritatively proclaimed.

2

Linguistic Follies

*"If names are not correct, language will not
be in accordance with the truth of things."*
                    —*Confucius, ca. 470 B.C.*

The Language Trap

No one who reads this book is an intellectual virgin. We've all been had, and one of our masters is ordinary language.

As we graduate from perceiving the world to conceiving it, concepts are denoted by symbols—for most of us.[1] The earliest symbols were voiced, and only later organized as spoken words.[2] These signals were followed by marks—glyphs, hieroglyphs, pictograms, and more recently, lexigrams.

In modern times, the most popular kind of symbol is the word. Words are usually voiced or graphed, but they are also sub-vocalized. They are indicated visually, aurally, and tactually—usually with alphabets, but also with ideograms, patterns of binary digits, photographs, and with shorthand signs such as dots-dashes (aural, visual, and tactual), conventionalized squiggles interpreted phonetically, and with gestures with fingers, hands, arms, and faces.

Number, organized in the languages of mathematics, is probably the second most popular kind of symbol.

When symbols receive *some* conventional use—always time-and place-bound—and are regulated by a logic (syntax), they constitute a language. However, at least three difficulties afflict attempts to think about ourselves, and an assumed reality "out there," with ordinary language.

One trouble arises as we learn more about the anatomy, chemistry, and physiology of the nervous systems (plural) with which we apprehend the nature of ourselves and our worlds. This knowledge suggests that the terms of folk psychology such as "mind," "belief," "desire," "intention," "will," "know," and more do *not* describe accurately what goes on in our sensing, perceiving, and reasoning equipment as we experience self, others, and circumstances.

If such words describe anything reliably discernible, they refer to activities whose sources are inaccessible to actors. Nevertheless, for scientists, these sources must be physical processes. There are no minds without bodies, and our physiologies do their work without our having to direct them.

Moreover, difficulty compounds as we reason beyond our individual, local experience and attempt to expand its lessons with instruction from our reading of history and from current experts. Physiologies guide us, willy nilly, and ordinary language misleads as well as helps.

Students of neural activity advance this charge *against* the use of evolved languages—our "native tongues"—as distinct from invented symbol-systems such as musical and mathematical notation. Such investigators show that far more occurs within our neural apparatus than we are aware of, and can be made aware of.[3]

The words of a vernacular come to us with checkered careers. Thus, we have little reason to believe that they must map realities accurately—neither maps of the motors of human action nor maps of events in worlds.

This is one reason why it would be more accurate, although awkward, to speak of "feeling-thought." The compound acknowledges that, as we employ our so-called "voluntary" nervous system to manipulate images of things and actions, emotions accompany these representations. Reasoning is suffused with feeling.

A second trouble occurs because ordinary languages change. The changes involve movements of meaning with use and abuse.[4] Promiscuous use infects cores of reference with parasitic connotations.

Words thus become fickle, and their inconstancy requires revisions of dictionaries that attempt to fix their reference. They can do this, but only for a time and within the boundaries of disloyal dialects.

More than this affects linguistic change and poses a third hurdle to the indicative use of ordinary language. Science is also at work, and not only in studies of human neurophysiology, but also in representations of worlds external to us. Thus we no longer use the idea of "phlogiston" to explain chemical processes or *élan vital*—the "vital spirit"—to account for biological functions. Many spooks and ad hoc hypotheses vanish.

In this manner, Albert Einstein's hypothesized special theory of relativity forever changed concepts of time, space, mass, energy, and other familiar physical terms. It did so, at least, for educated persons while leaving the mass of Earth's near-six billion persons content with their commonsensical ideas, habituated by folk speech and reinforced by social commerce.[6]

In sum, ordinary language lays obstacles to the development of *science. For this purpose*, deficiencies of the vernacular provide good reason to translate, where possible, ordinary-language concepts into mathematical symbols, and to use the latter as the language of reason.

The numbers of mathematics—not to be confused with the numbers called "statistics" (ch. 3)—are relatively sanitary. They remain clean despite the fact

that some "spiritually" inclined persons have tried to attach religious significance to particular figures and their combinations. But in mathematical employment, numbers do not carry the emotional baggage that loads common
speech with feeling, preference, wish.

Indeed, mathematician-physicist John von Neumann (1903-1957) argued
that the mathematics "inherited from the classical Greeks had been crucial to
the development of civilization." He added that this symbol-system did its
distinctive work *because* it was "free from emotional content, free from ethical content, and free from political content."[7]

Particular Traps

"There is no point in using exact methods
when there is not clarity in the concepts and
issues to which they are to be applied."
—John von Neumann,
on the failure of mathematics to make a
science of economics.[8]

Von Neumann's complaint about economics applies to all attempts to construct a science of social studies. We are hindered at the outset by the fragility
of the conceptual tools with which we work.

A prime object of *science* is reasoned judgment in answer to *empirical*
questions. Improved judgment requires, then, that we be able to tell the difference between empirical queries and other kinds.

After we have done this, scientists can search for pattern in the stream of
information deemed appropriate to their inquiry. Later chapters describe the
cognitive tools that scholars invent in their search for regularities among
social activities. Here we address the barriers to clear thinking set by the
principal instrument with which we reason—ordinary language.

One of these obstacles is imposed by the human brain that employs the
common lexicon to manufacture more question-like utterances than it can
answer—*empirically.*

Many of these non-empirical queries puzzle people:

- How many angels can dance on the head of a pin?
- What is God's will?
- Was this war necessary?[9]
- Was it right for her to have an abortion?
- Is electricity fire?[10]

At an extremity, majorities of modern populations agree that some such
phrasings are nonsensical. But other of these factually neutered interrogations are regarded as important, and people grow angry when they are not
answered "in the right way."

In this manner, morally "significant" questions that have *no empirical answer* stimulate shunning, banishment, and murder. Believers kill their heretics. Ideas, even crazy ones, *do* matter for some people at some times and places. Modern times are not immune. (Cf. chs. 11-12).

This fact intrudes upon all public debate. Many quarrels turn on interpretations of words. The contests can be momentous for citizens as well as for the combatants. They affect how power is obtained and maintained, and thereby how wealth is distributed. The inefficient election of an American president, 2000, provides but one illustration.

Recognizing this, one of Queen Victoria's prime ministers, Benjamin Disraeli (1804-1881), noted, "It is with words that men rule the world." Words can be weapons.

Logomachy

Logomachy—fighting with words—is the practice of lawyers. It is not the vocation of scientists, but it is the seductress of students of social affairs.

For example, during a recent presidential scandal, the American citizenry and its legislators debated the meaning of words in the United States Constitution that attempt to define actions of "the president, vice-president, and all civil officers of the United States" that justify their removal from office.[11]

The same document stimulates a parallel, hostile struggle concerning the meaning of its Second Amendment:

> A well regulated Militia, being necessary to the security of a free State, the right of the people to keep and bear Arms, shall not be infringed. (Capitalization in the original)

Is the phrase "the people" to be interpreted collectively or distributively? Does it refer to some organized cluster within each state's population or to individuals within it? The Founding Fathers did not say, and today citizens and their judges fight about this wording.

Semantic quarrels of this nature have no "objective" resolution because even facts can be differently colored with words. This tactic is now so common among politico-legal combatants as to have been given its own neologism, "spin."

With "spin," debates are turned from possible empirical issues into ethico-political ones. They are therefore not settled by reason alone, much less by science. They are "resolved" by compromise, neglect, deceit, or domination. And domination is exercised with votes, fraud, threats, or guns and bombs—to the extremity of homicide.[12]

Such debate is satirized truthfully by Lewis Carroll when he has his Alice walk through the looking glass into a perverse world where she engages in her famous quarrel with the original egghead, Humpty Dumpty:

"When I use a word," Humpty Dumpty said, in rather a scornful tone, "it means just what I choose it to mean—neither more nor less."

"The question is," said Alice, "whether you can make words mean so many different things."

"The question is," said Humpty Dumpty, "which is to be master—that's all."[13]

Mimicking Humpty Dumpty in real life, 1998, an American president—like most such officers a lawyer—instructed his people, and much of the rest of the world, in how to employ a "legal definition" of an act to distort, and trump, any commonsensical, clinical, or dictionary definition of that event.

The president's performance, and similar acts, suggest a rule: *The more law and litigation a jurisdiction allows, the less useful do contracts, dictionaries, oaths, and the vocabularies of specialists become.*

Empirical Query

"Words are but wise men's counters, they do but reckon with them, but they are the money of fools."
—*Thomas Hobbes (1588-1679)*[14]

To approximate a science of social action, it is important to understand when—in principle at least—questions are such that *observations* can resolve them. Questions of this kind, phrased as hypotheses, allow reliable perception to affirm their proposals with some degree of probability, or to refute them, or with some inquiries, to acknowledge that they are beyond our current ability to test—even though we can know what kinds of observed events could answer them.

In the last type of inquiry, we are compelled to admit that the best verdict thus far is the Scottish one: *Not proven.* This inference does not say "yea" or "nay" to an empirical hypothesis, nor does it mean, as some American students believe, "hung jury" or "acquitted." It means what it says: Thus far, available data cannot answer the question.

It's a fair bet that the Scottish verdict applies to more propositions in the social studies than scholars are willing to acknowledge.

In Sum Empirical questions are those that can, in principle, be settled with repeated, independent, and public recording of events "relevant" to them, as "relevance" is defined below.

Reliable and valid observations generate statements of *facts*. When these are organized with the aid of logic in service to pattern-recognition, they constitute a science.

In this enterprise we are, to repeat, burdened with the defects of common speech. We are trapped by having to use ordinary words as the very tools with which to criticize them.

Before we can legitimately apply numbers to our observations (chs. 3-4), the best we can do is to heed von Neumann, and Confucius long before him. Both remind us that recognition of the difference between empirical and non-empirical questions, and discovery of answers to empirical queries, depend on the *clarity of the concepts* with which we frame inquiries of Nature.

All this is relevant to a would-be social science because what we *call* actions and things affects what, and how, we attempt to measure them. Dependable inquiry needs sanitary language; it is corrupted by terms of moral significance.

We are therefore handicapped by the necessity to work with a popular vocabulary. Such employment makes it difficult to maintain antiseptic linguistic conditions because ordinary language is a multi-purpose tool.

Consider: We employ the same vocabulary—

- to express emotion;
- to transmit these descriptions and evaluations to others;
- to move ourselves and others to act, and also to inhibit action;
- to insulate ourselves and others against the inevitable accidents, insults, and injuries we encounter;
- to comfort ourselves and others after such damaging events;
- to define the causes that presumably produce "acts of God" and of humans; and
- to provide delight through entertaining stories and play with words.

Such mixtures of functions build particular traps. A few of these include: (1) scholars' entanglement with popular, but empty questions; (2) love of metaphor that often leads ordinary-language users into category mistake; and (3) the common tendency to reify abstractions.

1. Empty Questions

Language distorts inquiry when it tempts us to pose questions for which no facts can give answers. Arguably, this is the case with moral queries. But, without resolving that argument here, it is notable that social-scientific investigators, like everyone else, can be lured into asking non-empirical questions.

If we regard empirical interrogations as those that can be distinguished, in principle, by their reference to valid observations, then we can log an enormous quantity of linguistic arrangements that sound and read like legitimate questions, but that are something different.

To escape this language trap, we distinguish vacant questions from substantive ones, and allow a possible fuzzy frontier in which we are not clear about the cognitive status of an apparent query. We do so by noting the kinds of utterances, phrased as questions, that can *not* be satisfied with facts:

- "Why don't you watch where you're going?"
- "Who do you think you are?"
- "Why don't you do right?"

Sensible people, but not concerned ones, are able to recognize these queries as complaints. They are not empirical questions.

If individuals respond to such expressions with words, as the talking creature is prone to do, the responsive words constitute reasons, but they probably do not describe causes, and they regularly fail to satisfy inquisitors.

Similarly, many verbalizations, formed as questions, ask for no facts. They are lamentations:

- "Why did this have to happen to us?"
- "Why my child?"

Literate auditors understand that such utterances are not empirical questions. Such verbalizations do not ask for information. They request solace, and can be soothed with "verbal massage."

We placate one another with words that need not refer to anything observable. We often accompany such solemnly pronounced terms with appropriate gestures, music, scents, and lights that comfort sorrow and allay anxiety. Ritual is emollient.

Other kinds of apparent questions are products of excessive cogitation and semantic constipation:

"Professor, professor, how do I know I exist?", the eager student asks Morris Cohen.

"Who's asking the question?"

Philosophy is full of such vacant questions. Even esteemed practitioners of the search for wisdom are not immune. Thus Immanuel Kant (1724-1804), who himself wrote about "pseudo-questions," was nevertheless prompted to pose some:

"How is space possible?"

"How is Nature itself possible?"

David Stove[15] provides these and other examples of philosophic lunacy in a work that stimulates its philosopher-reviewer, Simon Blackburn, to admit:

Most philosophers hate philosophy some of the time. You try to think moderately sensibly about mind and matter, knowledge, meaning, rationality, truth, and become fatally entangled in a jungle where any motion is impossible. Good strategies include rhetoric (shouting that you are free when you are not), illogicalities engendering an illusion of movement, and, best of all, denial that there ever was a jungle in the first place.[16]

If, in reply to queries, there is nothing to be observed—even in principle— then the questions we ask about ourselves and Nature require no research to settle.

In Sum: Ordinary language is a vehicle with which we confound empirical and non-empirical questions. The practice allows us to believe much that we do not know. It tempts us to ask questions, and to respond to them, without knowing what we're talking about.[17]

Thousands of people now make their livings asking strangers questions, and *Homo sapiens*, the habitual talker to itself and others, obliges with answers. To do so is polite; silence is sullen.

But many of these interrogations are vacant. They ask about matters that respondents cannot know.

"Sting operations" give one demonstration of this possibility—as when Henry McCord induces one-third of a sample of American citizens to "remember" having voted in a non-existent election, and more than half to "recall" the non-existent "Taft-Johnson-Pepper bill on veterans housing."[18] McCord's experiment has been repeated many times with different topics and similar results.[19]

Why?

Among all empty queries asked about human action, probably a majority begin with the awesome word "why?".

"Why did you do it?" is a common interrogatory, thrust particularly at "bad actors" and more forcefully at "good people" caught in wicked deeds. This question is frequently useless—apart from making the interrogator feel important. (I'd like to say it's mostly useless, but no one has counted this.)

The query stimulates people to "say something," and inquisitors are frustrated when they are met with the child's "just because" or the psychopath's "because I felt like it." More customary responses state *reasons.*

Reasons will satisfy inquirers *only if* they are deemed "good reasons." Good reasons are pre-judged by investigators' notions of human nature and their ideas of how people do, and should, behave. Reasons are thus evaluated by empathy (ch. 9), not by any objective process.

This fact, and additional defects noted below, advise us *not to confuse reasons with causes.*

Reasons' Defects: Reasons are not to be confused with causes, first, because they "too often" *justify* actions. How often this is so is an empirical issue that has not been addressed. But, insofar as reasons are used to vindicate actors, it becomes improbable that they specify causes. If that were the case, everyone would be pardoned.

Second, people no more know "why" they behave as they do than they know how they acquired their native tongues or moral sentiments. We have abundant evidence that these important abilities and dispositions are acquired without individuals having been consciously trained or taught.[20]

Indeed, psychologists demonstrate that they can manipulate some range of the causes of decisions *without* their subjects' awareness. But when individuals are asked, after they've made their directed choices, "Why did you choose that?", they regularly make statements. They talk, and their words constitute *reasons*, but they seldom identify the *causes* of their decisions.[21]

When we are asked to explain ourselves, language is our only instrument. But to accept words as indicators of causes is, as mathematician Alain Connes puts it in another context, "[to] confuse the tool with the reality that it's being used to study."[22]

Third, in Judaeo-Christian lands at least, when the "why?" question is put to wrongdoers, their answers are accepted if they admit guilt and "sincerely" express repentance and request forgiveness. Here again, a kind of *reason* is allowed to substitute for a *causal* reply to "why?"

Known contingencies influence this substitution. These conditions include whether the wrongdoer is regarded as "one of us" or as a different "kind of person," and whether we imagine his/her offense to be something we also could do or as something alien to our possibility. (Refer to ch. 9 on explanation with empathy.)

Meaning without Reference

Nonsensical questions are asked repeatedly. One cause of this nuisance lies in the possibility that symbols to which we are habituated can *mean* something without their pointing to any discernible object, or activity, or relationship among humans and other creatures.

What words *do* to us, and for us—such as arouse emotion and move us into action—is not to be confused with what words *indicate*. Symbols can *mean*, in the sense of having causal power, independently of whether they *refer*.

Following Gottlob Frege (1848-1925), linguists and other philosophers commonly distinguish between the *sense* of a word and its *reference*.[23] The sense of a symbol is noted by its relationship to other symbols. By contrast, a symbol's reference, if any, is an indicative relationship between a term and some set of reliable observations of physical items, persons, circumstances, or kinds of activity.

Conceiving of a symbol's reference is an attempt to escape the circularity of defining words with words. It is an effort to rid ourselves of the common confusion of words' *effects* upon us with what, if anything, words *indicate*.

The distinctions between sense and reference attempts the difficult task of clarifying *how* we employ symbols by testing their *reference*—that is, by noting whether, and how accurately, symbols point to definable objects, events, and interactions among organisms, human and other.

Without a pointed sense of reference, there is no end to quarrel about whether the way symbols make us *feel* demonstrates the *reality* of the pictures-in-our-heads they evoke. Images of nonexistent organisms and territories are common, including Santa Claus, Uncle Sam, unicorns, centaurs, devils, ghosts, gods, heavens and hells.

As ordinarily conceived, science requires that its indicative language be cleansed of terms that are diffuse. Science can't work with symbols that are promiscuous, each one accommodating a wide range of reference. We find such employment among the many meanings of "meaning," such as:

1   A *linguistic concept*: In this sense, what a word or proposition means is known by its translation into other symbols in the same or different languages. Science can operate with this idea of meaning.
2   An *interpretive—inferential—concept*: In this usage, an auditor or reader infers a propositional content extended from, or different from, that intended by an author as in, "She claims X, but that means Y."
3   An *empathetic concept*: Social scientists who adhere to the Weberian mode of explanation through "understanding" others do so by looking for the "meaning" that these others assign to their conduct. Such explicators then find this kind of "meaning" in what individuals *intend* to achieve. (ch. 9).
4   An *institutional concept*: "Meaning" is attributed to, and known by, social practices—in particular, by those activities that are conventional, ritualized.
5   A *cognitive concept*: "Meaning" is said to reside in a postulated "mental content," like an image or other symbols.
6   A *logical positivist* (aka "logical empiricist") *concept*: A statement is considered "meaningful" only if what it predicates can, in principle at least, be verified or falsified.
7   A *pragmatic concept*: The "meaning" of a term or proposition is said to lie in the consequences that result from acting on it.
8   A *metaphysical-spiritual-religious concept*: "Meaning" is regarded as that which gives *value* to living. This is usually assumed to be a relationship among human beings and/or fulfillment of the *purpose* assigned our lives by a great teacher or supernatural being.

Present purpose suggests yet another meaning of "meaning," one that is not found in dictionaries of philosophy. It is *emotional response* to a conditioned symbol. It can be called (9) *psychological meaning*.

Emotionalized responses to habituated symbols are usually reflexes. They are involuntary, unconscious, and products of repeated associations with other symbols and their accompanying practices.

With conditioning—both classical (Pavlovian) and instrumental (oper-ant)—words that *refer to nothing* can "ring bells" in the nervous systems of attentive persons, and the changes can be measured.

For example, repeatedly uttering or hearing nonsense syllables associ-ated with "good" and "bad" words produces changes in the galvanic skin reflex, a reliable indicator of emotion.[24] In this fashion, *nonsense gains mean-ing*.

This is also the process by which words formerly considered "dirty" lose their shock value, as some "foul-mouthed" comedians promised (viz., Lenny Bruce). Succeeding generations then invent new terms of abuse.

All language is employed in more and less emotionalized contexts. The more popular the linguistic items, the more likely they are to be saturated with psychological meaning. Attachment of emotional response to com-mon symbols is a *background constant* of language use. It cannot be avoided, but we can become aware of its contamination. Emotion-laden association remains a potential source of defect in reasoning with ordinary words.

Ability to "think straight" can be bent when "hot" concepts are injected into argument. For example, a simple test of this possibility demonstrates that ability to "solve syllogisms" is reduced when words of emotional (moral) significance are inserted in place of neutral symbols. That is, while the *form* of the "logic-problem" remains the same, but the *content* changes from neutral (indifferent) to emotional (significant), individuals' ability to reason deteriorates.[25]

In Sum: The sight and sound of conditioned symbols—songs, rhythms, colors, flags, as well as words—are well-known generators of feelings and actions. Political and religious symbols are among the most forceful of these movers. The colors and insignia of sports clubs are also potent. Under their banners, enthusiasts joyously fight and sometimes trash their cities.

These many emblems of distinction do more than elicit emotion. They can also provide solace, offer promise, guide conduct, give "purpose" to life, and stimulate people to both loving and hostile action.

By contrast, a science must eschew such distorting symbols. Its indicative language must approach neutrality as regards moral and political interests. But the social studies are so heavily invested in matters of ethics and power as to have difficulty meeting this requirement (ch. 11).

Without the possibility of symbolic neutrality, claims to knowledge often reduce to logomachy—linguistic warfare.

2. Metaphor and Category Mistake

Besides encouraging us to pose hollow questions and to respond to them, ordinary language sets another trap. It produces metaphor.

Metaphor draws comparisons between two or more objects or events.[26] It is employed to clarify an unusual concept by showing its similarity to familiar ones.

Metaphor makes things clear by analogy, but at the risk of obfuscation. Everything depends on the appropriateness, *for some purpose*, of its comparisons. For example, metaphor is the heart of poetry, and many persons enjoy both its sounds and its allusions while more literal individuals find the load of information it yields slight relative to the quantity of words.

The risk we take when we play with words is that figurative speech is mistaken for literal utterance, and that improbable associations of concepts become "meaningful"—emotional—even though they are nonsensical.

Alice in her looking-glass world illustrates this possibility. There she encounters a poem written in *Jabberwocky*. It starts:

'Twas brillig, and the slithy toves
    Did gyre and gimble in the wabe,
All mimsy were the borogoves,
    And the mome raths outgrabe.[27]

Years after Alice's adventure, Hollywood film writers elaborated on *Jabberwocky* with their game of "Double-Talk." This sport consists of inserting made-up non-words into ordinary speech for the pleasure of mystifying audiences. We now have numerous demonstrations that even "intellectuals"—professionally thoughtful persons[28]—as well as other long-schooled individuals can be suckers for gobbledygook.[29]

However, despite our enchantment with the sounds of words, augmented with inflection and gesture, there is among all peoples a tail of the distribution of silly speech and inappropriate action at which individuals are deemed to be psychotic—"possessed" was a pre-medical term.

At an extremity—varying with *how much trouble strange persons cause their neighbors*—a people develop some consensus about disturbed, and disturbing, talking-acting, and especially so when others' utterances make large "category mistakes."

Category mistake—aka "type-confusion"—is a concept philosopher Gilbert Ryle concocted to describe a not uncommon habit—the custom of applying an attribute pertinent to one kind of thing or event to a different kind.[30] This error resides in metaphor.

Thus it is un-sane to interpret my statement, "metaphor is the heart of poetry," as signifying that poetry possesses an organ identifiable as a "heart." But type-confusion is ubiquitous and, given the persuasive power of metaphor, difficult to combat.

Category mistakes range, then, from the clearly lunatic to the contestably sane. The gradient occurs because analogy comes naturally; words are slippery; and abstraction—although convenient and necessary—is also dangerous.

Qualities of Lunacy

An important, but unresolved, debate concerns the varieties of lunacy and the boundaries between being crazy and being sane. To some untallied degree, this quarrel flows from linguistic invention and the promiscuous use of words that refer to nothing observable, but that create feeling-meaning.

Thus, students of schizophrenia—the most common psychosis or consortium of disaffections—have long noted the type-confusions and weird verbal connections that characterize this *moving balance* of mostly unhappy thoughts and feelings and irrational action.

Swiss psychiatrist Eugen Bleuler (1897-1939) termed such confounding of concepts, "associative loosening."[31] Years later American psychologist Paul Meehl confirmed this trait among schizophrenes, and referred to such linguistic anarchy as "cognitive slippage."[32]

Slippage is exhibited both as category mistake and bizarre association:

- "Why are you growing your father's hair?"
- "What color is justice?"
- "How does it feel to be five?"—referring to the number, not one's years.
- "What are we going to do about the three B's?", a patient asks.
  "The three B's?"
  "Yes, you're wearing a blue suit, your office is on Bedford Drive, and then there's Aunt Beulah."

An unknown quantity and degree of lunacy is "normal." That is, it is demonstrated by large numbers of individuals who "get along" despite their episodic and departmental exhibitions of improbable beliefs and incompetent thought-feeling-action.

The previous chapter calls attention to this proposition as George Santayana affirmed it.[33] And Paul Meehl's study of the roads to schizophrenia lends substance to Santayana's thesis.

Normal madness occurs, and persists, because we are potentially divided creatures. We repeatedly display conflicts between our appetites and distaste for their consequences, between rights and other values, between our urgencies that translate easily into "needs" and thence into "rights," and between our vaunted rationality defeated by the actions we take to satisfy them.[34]

In social action as in medicine, iatrogenic effects are real, although we prefer not to count them because doing so is apt to deflate our zeal as well as our bank accounts.

Ideals clash, and so do notions of "human nature," as we see in struggles between equality and freedom, justice and law, compassion and merit, causation and agency. We resolve these, and many more tensions, with a variety of tactics. These devices work more and less well, usually unconsciously, to help keep us somewhat sane.

The thesis here is that ordinary language produces, reflects, reinforces, and sometimes allays the segmentation that afflicts "self." And in this uncharted fashion, *people who are deemed crazy are not necessarily crazy all the way, every day, in every way.*

The dignified and long-suffering woman who asked me the non-empirical question about the "three B's" often functioned medium-well, was only episodically lunatic, and felt she could "let herself go" into insanity if she wanted to. She reminded me of Shakespeare's *Hamlet* who assured his friends

> I am but mad north-north-west, when the wind is southerly, I know a hawk from a handsaw.[35]

Possible segmentation of the perceiving-conceiving-appetitive "self" is acknowledged insofar as we distinguish between dimly defined but presumed processes called "reasoning" and those called "desiring." Both concepts take on further partitions.

"Reasoning" rests on neural activity that can be called "thinking," but not all thinking is thoughtful, that is, reasoned.[36] To "reason" implies possessing information relevant to an empirical query and having the ability to manipulate symbols representing that information according to rules of a logic.

"Taking thought"—as distinct from the thinking-feeling-imagining that is a constant of living—is *work*. The effort is expended *for a purpose*, even when the end sought is satisfaction of "idle" curiosity. More accurately, since we seldom, if ever, act from a single motive, reasoning is work employed to satisfy several ends, not all of which need be conscious. Hence, reasoning can be said to serve desire.

And "desire," too, is a composite of appetite, wish, and hope so that an intermittent warfare occurs within our cognitive equipment between "thinking straight" and being an active, desiring person. The tension produces shifting balances and degrees of sanity and lunacy.

Arthur Koestler provides a prominent illustration. Koestler was a journalist-essayist whose political commitment got him sentenced to death when he took the losing side during the Spanish Civil War (1936-1939). His life with revolutionaries and his close escape from a firing squad confirmed for him Santayana's thesis about "normal lunacy." Koestler writes,

> The hot steam of belief and the ice block of reason are packed together inside our skulls....The human mind is basically schizophrenic, split into at least two mutually exclusive planes. The main difference between "pathological" and "normal" schizophrenia lies in the isolated character of the irrational component in the former, as opposed to the collectively accepted irrationality of the latter. [N.B.!] Typical examples of socially approved split-mind patterns are the Astronomer who believes in both his instruments and in Christian dogma; the Army padre; the Communist who accepts "proletarian millionaires"; the Psychoanalyst who gets married; the Determinist who abuses his opponents.[37]

Recognition of such tension flavors my thesis. The potential conflict is encouraged by the follies induced by ordinary language, including the language with which we initiate research and conduct it.

Among the follies is our tendency to enlarge the scope of abstractions, and thereby to employ them carelessly.

3. Abstraction: Necessary, Useful, Reified, and Airy

> *"There is only one step from the sublime to the ridiculous."*
> —*Napoleon Bonaparte (1769-1821),*
> *after his return to Paris from the debacle of*
> *his Russian campaign, 1812.*

If we think of sanity-lunacy as describing a continuum rather than as impermeable categories, we then conceive of even "normal" emotion-thought-action as vulnerable to "dys-association." This disposition affects attempts to construct a science of social affairs that, like all science, employs abstract concepts.

To *ab-stract* is to select from particular things, events, or processes aspects of their individual exemplars that, *for our purposes*, seem similar, and then to educe images of what has been selected. These conceptions are, in varying degree, distant from anything perceptible.

They are nevertheless useful, *if employed with care*. They are also necessary, in the sense that the human organism produces some abstractions physiologically, without trying.

The Risk of "Thing-ness" Abstraction carries with it the risk of reification. To reify (from the Latin) or to hypostatize (from the Greek) is to regard a concept of non-material reference as though it signified a directly perceptible object or process.

As is their wont, social theorists stretch this idea. For example, in Marxist metaphor, "to reify" is to depersonalize, as when bosses treat their workers as things.

Reification is a likely possibility whenever we use high-level abstractions. It becomes tempting to treat them as though they readily and reliably point to actions and conditions we perceive rather than to construed complexes of things and events. In this manner, some philosophers, by awesome extension, *assign agency* to concepts with uncertain referents.

This is one of the sins of social science, examples of which are given on subsequent pages. Philosopher Simon Blackburn describes their tone with such hypostatized propositions as "thinking of beliefs as in the head, or numbers as large spatial objects, or God as a person, or time as flowing."[38]

Our difficulty is that, despite the necessity of abstraction, at some end of the spectrum of this selective, combinatorial process, inquirers quarrel about the reference and utility of particular concepts. Since abstractions lack spatio-temporal properties, scholars argue about the legitimacy, *for our ontology*, of specific "pictures in the head"—notions of what things or kinds of activities must be supposed to exist.

For example, as regards economics, Daniel Hausman shows that

> In macroeconomic theories one finds many quantities—such as the rate of unem-ployment or inflation, the level of prices or inventories, or the state of consumer confidence—that are certainly not directly observable. But these should not, I think, give rise to empirical qualms....the macroeconomic quantities are all averages of some sort, and although averages are not observable, they can be defined in terms of observables. The average height of the students in a particular lecture hall cannot be observed, but the height of each individual student can be, and the average can be calculated.[39]

Hausman is correct. Abstractions can be useful in drawing maps of reality. But this utility is not to be confused with their employment as comforts when people are hurt by realities.

However, the descriptive value of abstractions rests on our ability to indi-cate the empirical components to which they refer—activities or things that can be reliably categorized and observed, and accurately measured.

For example, it can be useful to think with "averages," as Hausman argues, but only if those who employ this word know how they are using it. This kind of knowing is different from what the term "means" to them.[40]

On the Idea of "Believing"

We are reminded that perceptual processes are cognitive processes, and that percepts—observations—work at some remove from necessary, but in-sufficient, sensing.

The neural assemblies that produce cognition are tuned to symbols. They can be said to have been affected—changed—by "meaningful" associations encapsulated in popular abstractions. We are at risk, therefore, of employing words on the unexamined assumption that they reliably refer to empirical elements.

Habit conceals risk, and the hidden assumption of empirical reference becomes misleading when comfortable words are inserted into proposed ex-planations of human action.

For example, the concept of "preference," commonly employed by econo-mists to *explain* "choice," draws a circle when given that job. We can never *know* another's "preference" if it is assumed to be *only* something in her head or a disposition in his heart. And many of us have learned better than to rely *solely* on others' words as signals of their choices (ch. 8).

Similarly, a popular way by which we "explain" others' conduct, and some-times our own, is to place a mental process called "believing" in the engine-room of the causal train and human action in the cars hauled along: "They do Y because they believe X."

It does not deny the frequent value of this shorthand style of explanation to suggest its limitations. At minimum, it quiets curiosity.

For the human performer, sets of acts called 'believing" are *medleys* of utterances and other behaviors. (To utter a word is, of course, one kind of behavior.)

For us (ignoring for the moment other intelligent creatures such as the great apes and our animal pets), to "believe" something refers to *a compound of purposeful acts* associated with "appropriate" verbalization, and often accompanied by "appropriate" gesture.[41]

With the talking animal, a conjunction of "right" symbol-use *and* other actions is required before we attribute "believing" to actors. Without such union, we are hesitant to apply the abstract idea, "belief."

We hesitate in this employment not only because *Homo sapiens* and other creatures act deceptively at times, but also because the human actor is a babbler. We say much that communicates feelings *without* utterances being directed toward attainment of any other interpersonal objective.

Mature human beings, and children and apes, talk to themselves. In addition, and to repeat, talking is sociable, silence is sullen. The anthropologist Bronislaw Malinowski called this bonding activity, "phatic communion." It is produced "automatically," without instruction and without other motive than to affiliate.

The requirement that, among human beings, other acts accompany words as attest of 'belief" is further demonstrated by the skeptic's challenge when others make unduly firm assertions, "You don't *really* believe that?!" And this exclamation is correctly interpreted to mean, "If you had to put your money where your mouth is, you'd back down."

It is an empirical hypothesis whether, and to what degree and under what contingencies, people invoke "belief" to *explain* conduct unless others' words are appropriately associated with their deeds. Insofar as this hypothesis proves correct, *explaining* why individuals and groups behave differently, as they do, by injecting "belief" into the formula becomes circular.

The insertion satisfies inquirers who have been habituated to the word, "belief," and who thereby regard whatever that term refers to as some kind of *agent* inside actors, like a non-material "mind," that works *independently* of the actor's constitution and the acts to be explained.

The idea of an immaterial "mind" that constitutes us, and that serves as motor of our acts, is embedded in religious assumption. With increased knowledge of the nervous systems, many of us no longer adhere to this "spiritual" belief. Rather, whatever feelings-thoughts are attributed to "mind-work" are regarded as products of physical functions. In brief, *matter makes minds.*[42]

Nevertheless, "belief" remains a troubling abstraction, and particularly so for an aspiring social science that would explain our activities.

A Philosopher's Beliefs about Belief. The American philosopher Willard Quine claims that "belief" must refer to propositions that "a reasonable person" holds to be true. He adds that "experience has taught" this imaginary "reasonable person" that "some of his beliefs...will turn out to be false."[43]

Quine wins his argument by begging the question. He does so by appealing to the undefined qualifier, "the reasonable person," an abstraction whom we regularly meet in courts of law.

Whether particular individuals are deemed to be "reason-able," and how often under what circumstances, will depend on tests of ability "to listen to reason." And more than that, to appreciate others' reasons.

One conceivable test of this ability, and yet a difficult test, applies "the Rapoport debate" (after its inventor, Anatol Rapoport, 1974). This procedure requires disputants to repeat accurately their opponents' arguments *before* they present their own counter-arguments. It takes the heat out of quarrel, and works toward mutual comprehension—if that is sought—by forcing me to restate your thesis satisfactorily before I rebut it, and vice versa.

Given the demand for time-compression, a Rapoport Debate is not likely to be witnessed on television, now our major source of news, information, and entertainment. However, with or without such test of 'being amenable to reason," we note that not every experience that falsifies what one believes is accepted as a corrective.[44]

Experience is filtered by priors—prior investments of time, money, and energy, prior commitments to intimate others, and prior compounds of ego-laden statements and activities—and these filters can produce resistance to truths.

For one impressive demonstration of the persistence of belief despite evidence that it is false, see Festinger, 1956. How frequently such immunity armors humanity against facts is an empirical issue that has not been adequately addressed.

However, Quine's argument raises another question, "When is it rational to be unreasonable?"

A strong argument can be made that there are occasions when survival is aided by being unreasonable. There are times when acting unreasonably gives power.

This possibility raises an additional issue. It's a lively hypothesis that the performance called "believing" is never known from actors' utterances alone. We attribute the status, "believing," to human beings principally when their repeated statements "accord adequately with" the actions we are trying to explain. But notice that we readily assume that our mute animal friends also "believe" when a pattern of their behaviors indicates purpose in their movements.

We are thereby lured toward redundancy. We explain others' conduct by reference to a mental state called believing. But we assume that others' beliefs cause their behaviors only when they also *behave non-verbally* in patterns "concordant with" an assumed cognitive status.

Given the possibility of such circularity, inquirers who are less addicted to the drugs of words find many "belief-explanations" unsatisfactory. When, for example, they are told that, "the Wallonians behave that way because they believe a, b, c," skeptics reply, "Possibly, but how did they come to believe THAT?"

This response is particularly noticeable when others behave in ways that are unacceptable to our group's belief-practices.

In Sum: Abstraction serves to provide *summarizing concepts* that constitute "as-if's." These work as convenient, albeit seductive, fictions.

Abstractions operate as generalizing constructs. Tacitly they say, "Let us consider the term 'Gronik' to represent behavior of type x, y, z."

In actual research, words such as "belief," "preference," "expectation," "discrimination," "intelligence," "justice," "opportunity," "power," and more perform as the imagined "Gronik." There is nothing incorrect about this manner of abbreviated summary *as long as we recognize what we're doing*.

Damage results from reifying such encapsulating symbols, and thereby failing to appreciate their redundancy when they are invoked as *explanatory concepts*.

For example, consider use of the word, "culture." In its ethnographic mode—as distinguished from its evaluative application, sometimes pronounced "kul-chah"—this concept refers to what Blackburn calls.

the way of life of a people, including their attitudes, values, beliefs, arts, sciences, modes of perception, and habits of thought and activity.[45]

As ethnographers use the term, that is what "culture" means with an assumption added. The assumption is that cultural practices are *learned*. They are assumed to be transmitted from one generation to another without intervention or selection by genetically transmitted constitutions.

With this premise added to the definition, the concept of "culture" refers to the entire spectrum of human activities that Blackburn and others have listed. There is, then, no value to invoking the word to *explain* any of the elements to which it refers.

The exercise that uses "culture" to explain itself is pretentious and uninformative. It employs one part of a *web of life* to explain other parts. But the *explanandum*—that which is to be explained—cannot be contained within the *explanans*—that which does the explaining.

Despite the circularity of this practice it is popular among journalists and social scientists. If such application were to be useful, it would have to indicate that "culture" is a force—a cause—*identifiable independently* of how its carriers behave. To repeat, a presumed effect cannot be the same set of events as its nominated cause.

But with such popular usage, the abstract concept, "culture," becomes a vacuous *explanatory* device. Except as the term is applied to infants, no such force works as something separate from the conduct of the people who exhibit its tastes and practices.

Among newborns, of course, "culture" can be used as an abbreviated term to refer to the characteristic practices of their caretakers, under the assumption that "culture" constitutes a cause of how children are shaped, but not totally formed. Viz.:

• "If babies are reared by Inuit-speakers, they think-speak in Inuit."

  But

• "Your honor, I do everything I know how to control him, but he just won't obey me."[46]

Apart from this qualification, "culture" serves as a contracted word that tries to *describe* how a people distinctively conduct their lives. And such *description*, put into service as *explanation*, not only draws a circle, it also generates failures, as when "having a culture" cannot explain defection from one's origins and conversion to another people's way of life.

Sociology provides additional examples of the careless wielding of abstract concepts. This is particularly apparent as sociologists and their allies in social work address "social problems."

In this occupation, affection strongly imputes undesirable conduct to "fundamental sources" that are presumably imposed upon people rather than produced by them. These nominated "root causes" are conceived as "forces" beyond the control of those whom they affect. They constitute environments that others have created and by which those who behave badly are compelled to do as they do. Wrongdoers are thereby exculpated.

Later pages provide experimental evidence that individuals' likes and dislikes tend to attribute causation in asymmetric fashion so that people whose "side we're on" have their disapproved activities attributed to their circumstances, while people whom we dislike have their disapproved activities attributed to their characters (ch. 10).

Of course, an attempted *science* of social action cannot look for causes in locations assigned by our affections. The causal ship of science cannot be boarded and disembarked at morally congenial ports.

Nevertheless, reified abstractions find employment in service to ideological preferences, and particularly so when the subject of inquiry is wrongdoing, as in the domain of criminology.

Criminology is a lively employer of unexamined abstractions. In one example, Robert Sampson and William Julius Wilson attempt to explain *some kinds* of larceny and violence by referring them to "root causes." They attribute differential commission of these selected crimes to "*structural social disorganization* and *cultural social isolation*, both of which stem from the concentration of poverty, family disruption, and residential instability."[47]

Postulating "structural social disorganization" sounds as though it refers to some condition *observable independently* of its nominated sources: "poverty, family disruption, and residential instability." It does not.

"Social disorganization" serves as a reified abstraction; it only summarizes the complex of behaviors it attempts to explain. Similarly, to live "that way" *is* to be "culturally socially isolated."

When investigators accord a select trio of sources the status of "structural" cause—*external to* and *independent* of how people behave—their assignment adds no information to the description. Their attribution is rhetorical and redundant.

Moreover, the few causes of "disorganization" and "isolation" that Sampson and Wilson name, and that, in turn, are presumed to generate *some kinds* of criminal activity, are incomplete.[48] To this *web of life*, other researchers add a vast inventory of causal candidates. Among these nominees, many scholars emphasize lack of education—despite the availability of free public schools; lack of vocation—a function of poor education and differential interest; and irresponsible reproduction—regarded as both effect and cause of these deficits.

In addition, it is questionable whether "criminal activity" of certain sorts can be usefully extracted from a way of living and called "effect" of all else that goes on among a self-identified people. With greater detail, later pages argue for a more integrated conception of how people come to act as they differentially do.

However, locating causation in "structures" *outside* actors performs ethico-political service. It converts agents to victims, shifts the burden of responsibility, and justifies one kind of political policy: State support of criminals as victims.

The risk of such transformation is that all of us can claim some kind of victimhood.

Caution: Argument against the employment of reified abstractions as names of causal factors does *not* deny that human action is responsive to, and restricted by, environments. Rather, this argument alerts us to explanatory circularity.

It acknowledges that all activity is situationally circumscribed, but it also recognizes that neither individuals nor self-identified "tribes" respond in the same way to the same circumstances. It notes, too, that *some parts of the environments to which people respond are their own product.*

In Sum: To abstract is to classify. As with all systems of taxonomy, the utility of the differentiation and grouping depends on the clarity and stability of the defining criteria, *and* on what working with one set of abstractions rather than another allows us to do better.

Utility is, of course, a function of purpose. Abstract terms that help us persuade one another are *not necessarily* those that are descriptively accurate, nor need they be aids to causal analysis, foresight, and improved control.

There is no end to the abstracting process—not even to the reification of summarizing concepts. However, would-be scientists of the social need to know what they're talking about if they are to observe reliably and measure accurately. They need to know what, if anything, can be perceived and reliably counted as indicators of their abstracting terms.

Herein lies the double bind of a would-be science of social events. All social inquiry and its findings have moral and political significance. Since we are said to be both moral and political creatures, it requires effort to work also as truth-seekers and truth-tellers.

Socrates advised, *Gnothi seauton*—"know thyself." To engage in this vaguely phrased pursuit requires at least that we "know *what* we're doing."

To follow this instruction puts us at risk. We are in danger of being revealed as ideologists masquerading as truth-aspiring inquirers.[49]

A partial antidote to this schizoid condition prescribes caution when handling morally infected language. This prescription refers to how we classify and count events, the topic of following chapters.

3

Varieties of Knowing

"There are three principal means of acquiring knowledge: observation of nature, reflection, and experimentation. Observation collects facts; reflection combines them; experimentation verifies the result of that combination. Our observation of nature must be diligent, our reflection profound, and our experiments exact."

—Denis Diderot[1]
(1713-1784)

To "Know"

All attempts to perform in a scientific manner are efforts to *know* something other than what untutored experience teaches. It is important, then, to distinguish among kinds of "knowing," that is, to separate ways in which that word is used. A suggested set of distinctions is based on the different *powers* to which ways of "knowing" refer.

For Example:

1. One meaning of "knowing" is *to admit, to confess*, as in, "Do you know who killed him?"
2. A second, popular but multiple, roster of meanings employs the phrase, "*to understand*."

The flexible reference of this concept permits several kinds of performance to be included under its umbrella (chs. 9, 10). A common confusion muddles the affectionate idea of "liking" the other person with different meanings of "knowing." "Do you understand Jill?" often translates as, "Do you appreciate her, do you look upon her favorably?"

Further to confuse matters, "understanding" others is often used to indicate the ability to decipher other persons' motives or traits from their conduct.

Such comprehension is daily practice. Unfortunately, this way of knowing people is entangled with our affiliation with, or dislike of, the persons to be so understood. When, as is usual, affection is blended with attempted comprehension of others, it does not yield accurate prediction of their behavior. Folk wisdom recognizes this confounding when it says "love is blind," but it might as well include other passions that distort predictive "understanding."

Additional confusion occurs when "to understand" refers to ability to comprehend a symbol-system, as in, "Do you understand French?" or "Do you understand quantum physics?"

In these cases, the appropriate test of "understanding" is ability to decode one set of symbols and encode them into another set without loss of information.

3. *To be acquainted with* signifies familiarity. Its major sign is recognition, as in, "Do you know John?"

4. *To have information* is a kind of "knowing" indicated by ability to state a fact.

4.1. The word "fact" comes to us from the Latin *facere* meaning "to make, or do, or produce." With use, the term now refers to several ideas. *The Oxford English Dictionary* lists these: (a) "truth or reality," (b) a state of affairs "known for certain," (c) "a thing assumed or alleged as a basis for inference," and (d) in law, "events or circumstances distinct from their legal interpretation."

4.2. Among facts that count as information are *definitions*. Definitions become factual as they approximate those that say, "According to such-and-such dictionary, THIS word means THAT."

Private definitions are acceptable as "provisional facts," when they refer clearly to new ways of thinking about a much-used term such as "morality," or "crime." Otherwise, private definitions are not considered even as candidates for factuality. Such personal usage may communicate— feelings, for example, or their author's trustworthiness or lunacy—but they do not predicate states of the world external to participants in a dialogue. (Refer to Humpty Dumpty's argument with Alice, p. 16-17).

4.3. A class of facts included in the idea of "being informed" is the ability to identify and communicate the cues to which one is differentially responding.

4.3.a. The distinction between "having information" and any form of "receiving communication" is required by the fact that persons can "know" without being aware of their ability. That is, they can make differential discriminations *without* being able to specify the signals that guide their perceptions.[2] In common parlance, we do not call the ability to discriminate "being informed" unless the response can be accompanied by a statement that indicates the cues that guide the differential action.

The fact that we regularly distinguish among changes in the energy fields that bombard us *without awareness* that we are doing so is one good reason for doubting that people can always accurately answer the popular and difficult question, "Why did you do that?"

4.3.b. It is this definition of "being informed" that justifies the assumption that we can reliably catalogue and communicate "data."

By contrast, non-informative messages contain signals with unclear (unconventional) codes. Thus it can be argued that music and art "communicate"—that is, they arouse feelings, attitudes, insights—without claiming that they inform.

4.4. Among scientists, common use regards "facts" as sentences of *empirical predication* for which, within some context, there is public warrant. The qualifier, "within some context," is required because all knowledge is time-and-place bound.

Public warrant refers to the quality and quantity of evidence—that is, to observations that have been reliably replicated. Here again, individual intuition does not count, except as a source of empirical hypotheses to be subjected to multiple, repeated test.

5. *Know-how* denotes skill of various kinds and degrees. As chapter 1 indicates, know-how is not to be confused with having knowledge as that power is defined below.

5.1. In tongues other than English, "know-how" can include the behavior of inanimate as well as animate objects. For example, C. F. Hockett remarks that in Chinese "one can say that high wind *whei* (here perhaps 'is apt to') blow down a tent, or that an electron *whei* behave in accordance with the equations of wave mechanics."[3]

5.2. When "know-how is attributed to persons, the phrase refers to a range of actions from those that are largely combinations of reflexes to those that involve the conscious exercise of technique. The term is usually reserved for application against some standard of competence.

Thus surgeons and dentists acknowledge that their colleagues can have equal knowledge-of without having equally good "hands and eyes," i.e., "know-how."

5.2.a. Examples at the reflexive end of the range include knowing how to swim, play tennis, type, and speak a language. Notice that children do not acquire the ability to construct meaningful sentences by being told how to do it. They are not taught a recipe for linguistic competence. Rather, children are "adhesive." They learn the vocabulary and syntax of their mother tongues by hearing and seeing language *practiced in activities*. Similarly, insofar as they learn a morality, this is how they acquire it (ch. 12).

5.2.b. Examples on the more consciously adaptive end of the spectrum include knowing how to influence people, build a house, conduct a battle.

5.3. The range of reference of "know-how" and its lack of a separate lexical indicator in Germanic and Romance languages enlarge the risk that

Westerners will confuse habit, skill, and some styles of physical ability with having knowledge (ch. 1).

The confusion should be avoided. It allows citizens to be gulled by celebrities whose qualifications as entertainers do *not* certify their expertise in public policy.

5.4. Know-how includes what some anthropologists call "practical knowledge" or, in classical Greek, *mētis*.[4] This kind of knowing derives from apprenticeship. It can come only from working with those who already know-how.

Mētis in this sense is the mode of knowing embedded in folklore. It is local, particular, and reckoned in the difference between acquired skills and abstract principles. Those who possess such know-how need *not* be able to reduce their art to textbook formulae. James C. Scott explains:

> *Mētis* is most applicable to broadly similar but never precisely identical situations requiring a quick and practiced adaptation that becomes almost second nature to the practitioner. The skills of *mētis* may well involve rules of thumb, but such rules are largely acquired through practice... and a developed feel or knack for strategy.[5]

Mētis can be, and is, destroyed, and Scott describes some of the conditions of its loss. A prominent cause of decay is expansion of centralized government and its bureaucratic powers that work to apply administrative formulas to distant situations. Given the value of local know-how, Scott cautions against application of "imperial knowledge."[6]

When today's social scientists adopt the compound ambition to be both truthful and ethico-politically useful, they generate conflict for themselves and become enemies of *mētis*.

6. *To have knowledge* is a different kind of knowing. It is ability to state a non-tautological empirical rule.

6.1. The idea of "rule" means that a statement refers to more than one instances of ....

6.2. One kind of empirical rule that we seek, and consider to be "scientific," states a reliably observed regularity, such as a timed succession of independently observed events—e.g., the earth's rotation on an imagined axis and the appearance of light and dark called "day" and "night."

6.3. Another kind of empirical rule, desired but difficult to attain, states more than the expected schedule of successive events. It asserts a probability of an identifiable kind of occurrence, *conditional* upon human activity of a specified sort.

This valuable kind of knowledge says, "Given conditions a, b, c, if we *do* X, in such-and-such amount, then evidence d, e, f indicates that Z is likely to occur with probabilities ranging from x to y within time q to t."

Such is the type of knowledge that can guide know-how. It is a combination that we expect of physicians and dentists, and that variety of engineer who works in domains such as civil, mechanical, chemical, electrical, aeronautic, and cosmonautic practice.

> Propelling people and things into distant space and retrieving them in a designated location at a specified time is a wondrous example combining knowledge with know-how. Thus on 14 July 2001, a dummy warhead fired from Vandenberg Air Force Base in California was shot down by a missile launched from the Marshall Islands 5,000 miles away—"a bullet hitting a bullet"—each traveling at 16,200 mph.

In the social realm, expertise of this sort is not to be expected—for the many reasons given in these pages. This does not mean that we know nothing about ourselves. It means that our "laws" of human conduct are conditional and probabilistic, with the requisite conditions often unknown and the probabilities unspecified.

6.4. Nevertheless, social scientists look for some kinds of regularity. Among the regularities we conceive, we acknowledge that they propose *degrees* of "rulefulness," and these vary. They vary because empirical rules receive more and less warrant.

"Warrant" is a synonym for evidence pro and con the validity of an asserted connection. In turn, evidence is judged by the quantity and quality of observations adduced in support of, or in contradiction of, an empirical proposition. Such judgment is unstable because, in tests of hypotheses, investigators often disagree on the *relative weight* to be accorded quality of observations and their quantity.

Later chapters demonstrate that, in the social studies, much evidence brought to bear as tests of empirical relationships are of poor quality. Indeed, some published research is so weak as to be fraudulent.

Apropos of this argument, a program titled "meta-analysis" has gained popularity as a method of weighing the quantity and quality of socially relevant findings so that we can extract "sense" out of voluminous publications.[7] However, this procedure runs the risk of pooling faulty research with sound inquiry. Demographer-statistician Kenneth Wachter reminds us of this possibility. "In science," he writes, "a single good study ought to be able to stand against any number of weak ones."[8]

Contrary to the assumption that knowledge is easily generated by right method and right thought, the history of all sciences shows that they rarely give us absolute assurance. Findings are subject to modification, and the best that attempts at rational ways of knowing can yield is greater and lesser degrees of probability. Science works by building "cases" for and against empirical hypotheses, step by step, and out of medleys of controlled observations, revised theories, and more observations.

For those who seek certainty, this is not good enough. Nor is it good enough for those who need, or want, ACTION NOW.

But, for individuals who can live with probabilities, and even with "chance" (ch. 10), and who are gifted with open, but not draughty, intellect, the scientific way of knowing is the best procedure yet devised for developing *knowledge-of*.

To repeat, this kind of knowing need *not* provide *know-how*, and especially not in studies of human action. In moderation of the common claim that "knowledge is power," knowledge-of does not guarantee power-to-do, nor need it answer every question we ask.

Boundary

The many kinds of knowing described have nothing to say about *non-empirical questions*. It will be argued throughout our exercise that human beings ask more questions that science can answer. These range from the silly to the important. Among the *important, non-empirical questions* are those that ask about the perennial issues of *what should be valued*. Not what *is* valued, but what *should be* prized and why.

These queries are phrased in various ways: "What is the purpose of life?" "What is the good life?" "What is right and wrong?" "What is true happiness?"

About these questions, *empirical* science is silent.

Against Tautology

In addition to the restriction listed above, the scientific enterprise has to winnow possibly informative propositions from circular statements. Knowledge claims are to be *non-tautological*. Since politics and the social studies are vulnerable to such puffery, would-be scientists need to be alert to this kind of redundant reasoning.

The idea of tautology assumes the reliability of systems by which we classify things and events. These organizing principles constitute "taxonomies."

To construct useful taxonomies of actors and actions, we have to be able to specify patterns of objects and events that are independent of each other. Some of these arrangements are themselves matters of definition—of convention—as chapter 7 shows. Other categories are built into our physiologies (ch. 1).

If we are able to identify independent kinds of things and activities—without which there is nothing to be scientific about—then a tautological statement is one in which what it proposes repeats what it is talking about, but with different words.

More formally, a tautology is a proposition or argument in which its predicate (*explanans*) is included within its subject (*explanandum*). Or, when a proposition is expressed as a conditional, a tautology is a statement in which the conditional repeats the proposal so that, while it can appear informative to the unwary eye, it yields no information.[9]

Tautological reasoning ranges from simple sentences to entire arguments (theories). Because these redundancies are common and persistent, and because they camouflage nonsense with the appearance of knowledge, it is important to recognize how statements can be persuasive while composed of non-informative utterance.

The examples that follow can be expanded, of course. They range from the obvious to the contestable.

A Sampler of Tautologies

"You won't get bald if you don't lose your hair." (My first mother-in-law).

"When many men are out of work, you have unemployment." (U. S. President Calvin Coolidge, ca. 1929).

"We can't make peace until we end violence." (U. S. President Bill Clinton, 17 December 1996).

"Why didn't your opponent win the election?", a journalist asks former Chicago Mayor Richard Daley. "He didn't get enough votes."

"A low voter turnout is an indication of fewer people going to the polls." (U. S. Vice-President Al Gore, cited by David Horowitz, November, 2000).

"It isn't pollution that's harming the environment. It's the impurities in our air and water that are doing it." (U. S. Vice President Al Gore, *ibid.*).

"It's a higher cost of living caused by the falling value of the dollar." (Former Prime Minister of Canada P. E. Trudeau, explaining inflation, CFRN interview, 28 December 1978).

"Insomnia deprives us of sleep." (David R. Burke, psychiatric counselor, 31 October 1977).

"[C]ongestion reflects the fact that so many of the region's roads are carrying heavy volumes of traffic." (*The Washington Post*, 16 December 1999).

"Americans can outproduce, outcreate, outeducate any people on earth, if we'd just do it." (U. S. Senator and presidential candidate John Glenn, "Good Morning, America," ABC-TV, 30 January 1984).

"It is a characteristic of people that they want more of those things they deem desirable." (Economist Willard R. Allen, 1983).

"In order to prevail, you have to have staying power." (U. S. Secretary of State George Schultz, "Good Morning, America," ABC-TV, 6 February 1984).

"[A]ll other things being equal, *the larger the number and the greater the diversity of the perspectives of a group of units, the more difficult it is to achieve a consensus*." (Sociologist Amitai Etzioni, 1968, emphasis his).

"This faith expresses the Darwinian certainty that no species can in the long run behave contrary to the conditions of its survival." (B. Caton, 1985).

"Increased employment in British industry resulted in no increase in output because of low productivity." (James Callaghan, former British Prime Minister, 1985).

"The more rewarding (valuable) to one man is the action of the other, the more often will the first perform the action that gets him the reward." (Social psychologist George Homans, 1967).

"Good fellowship springs from friendship." (Aristotle, ca. 320 B.C.).

"Species, people, and cultures all perish when they cannot cope with rapid change." (Psychologist B. F. Skinner, 1981).

"The so-called sexual revolution has changed the way people behave both in the bedroom and on the street." (Sociologist Peter Berger, 1988).

"Nothing can have value without being an object of utility." (Social theorist Karl Marx, 1867).

> This statement is either a definition, in which case it only proposes a synonym, or it is an alleged fact, in which case it is false.
> As employed in Marx's materialism, "use" refers to means for producing food, shelter, health. However, human beings *indicate by their deeds* that they value much more than such "use." They also prize risk, change, liberty, *dolce far niente*—"sweet doing nothing"—the "useless arts," and silence.

"To escape isolation a person must be able to become a member of a group." (Social psychologist George Homans, 1950).

"An individual who is not integrated into the group will not conform to the demands of the group." (Criminologist C. R. Jeffrey, 1959).

"A single homogeneous population is less likely to exist [in a complex society] because there is generally too much variation in the group social attributes." (Sociologist S. E. Singer, 1981). Or, "A heterogeneous population is heterogeneous."

"The greater the cohesiveness of the group, the greater the ability of the group to influence its members." (Sociologists L. Broom and P. Selznick, 1955).

"Predictably, much resistance is encountered from the community [to inmates released from "mental hospitals"]...and stigma presents itself as a major explanatory variable." (Psychologist Amerigo Farina, 1987).

"In order for arms control to have meaning and credibly contribute to national security, it is essential that all parties to agreements fully comply with them." (U. S. Senator Malcolm Wallop, 1987).

"[T]he child usually orients to those people who possess physical or psychological attributes he admires." (Psychologist J. Kagan, 1971).

"The meaning of an object resides not in the object itself but in the definitions brought to it." (Symbolic Interactionist Norman Denzin, 1969).

> Q: Is the meaning of an object something different from its definition?

"If men define situations as real, they are real in their consequences." (Social psychologists W. I. and D. S. Thomas, 1928).

> Among theorists who call themselves "symbolic interactionists," this statement is repeated like a mantra. However, it yields no information with which to improve foresight.
> Moreover, in an uncounted number of events, acting upon beliefs—"definitions of the situation"—does *not* generate the results desired. Such "definitions" often produce effects other than what was intended.
> It is also true that, if we do *not* define situations as real, consequences can still be real, and contrary to what believers desire. Military history is full of failures produced by incorrect "definitions"—i.e., *denials* of "facts of the matter."
> And, if Symbolic Interactionists defend their central hypothesis by translating it to say, "beliefs have consequences," their slogan becomes a truism. By definition, "beliefs" have consequences (pp. 28-31). The important question is, "What consequences follow upon which beliefs in which circumstances?"

"Crime is normal because all of us commit so much of it." (Criminologist Harold Pepinsky, 1988).

"When asked how they were affected by inflation, most of those who believed they were affected said that it reduced the value or purchasing power of their incomes." (Statistician M. R. Gainsbrugh, 1962).

Import

"I've studied now Philosophy and Jurispru-
dence, Medicine—and even, alas! Theology—
From end to end with labor keen; And here,
poor fool!, with all my lore I stand, no wiser
than before."

— *J. W. v. GOETHE*[10]
(1749-1832), Faust

The beauty of tautology is that people can sound knowledgeable when they are not. In this manner they can prove persuasive—making others feel good—without being informative. Our brief exercise in redundancy alerts us to a common predisposition to circular utterance—even among scholars who should be able to recognize the difference between a stipulative definition and an empirical proposition.

Against this tendency, we work to develop knowledge. However, when the topics of inquiry concern social action, the difficulties of our enterprise draw boundaries to our competence. It is important to know what we don't know.

Public expectation that justifies direct and indirect expenditure of tax dollars for "scientific" social studies assumes that, as per self-advertisement, social scientists can, and should, be able to do more than "merely" describe how things are—a work that is also engaged by novelists.

In addition, claimants to knowledge of the social are expected to be able to explain how matters come to be as they are, and to be able to provide improved ways of scanning the world for signs of future events.

Efforts to foresee outcomes of events-in-the-making are as old as human history. These activities range from the purely reflexive— physio-logical "knowledge"—to conscious work at prognostication. When anticipation is attempted consciously—by "taking thought"—it asks two kinds of ques-tions: "What is likely to happen regardless of how we behave?" An example is weather forecasting. And "What is likely to happen if we *do* X?" This is sometimes an easy question to answer accurately and, at other times, a formi-dable query.

These questions are addressed with different kinds of cognitive procedure.

Modes of Anticipation

"It was ordained in the beginning of the world
that certain signs should prefigure certain
events."

— *Marcus Tullius Cicero*
(106 B.C.-43 B.C.)[11]

"A fixed image of the future is in the worst
sense ahistorical."

— *J. Mitchell*[12]

We believe Cicero and attend to Mitchell. But when we believe Cicero, we confront difficult questions:

- What are the premonitory signs of which kinds of events?
- How shall we weigh these several omens?
- How valid (accurate) are these cues, assuming that they are reliably weighed?

Despite these nagging questions, people spend enormous amounts of time and money on the assumption that Cicero was, and is, correct. They also make money by proposing (pretending) that they have formulas with which to foresee others' destinies. These alleged algorithms range from the patently superstitious to the contestably rational. And, as always when people need hope, fraudsters enter the game of promise.

Descriptions of the major procedures for judging what is apt to happen are offered on the twin assumptions that *there is no error-free method* by which to improve foresight beyond short-range, physiological anticipation, and that some ancient methods are worse than some recent guides.

Three Conceptual Styles

"Life is short and the art long, the occasion fleeting, experience treacherous, and judgment difficult."

—*Hippocrates, ca. 380 B.C. to neophyte physicians.*

We are born with the capacity to *perceive* changes in events that our sensoria apprehend (ch.1). Our physiologies categorize as aid to here-and-now foresight. The process is initially unconscious, untutored, and the most common mode of short-time forecast. A reflex eye-blink is one example. So is the fact that a lioness chasing her prey runs, not to where it is, but to where it will be if it continues a trajectory. This ability can be trained, of course, but it forms the basis of foresight.

However, all of us engage in longer-range estimates of futures. We do so when we decide how to spend a holiday, in which stocks to invest, or whom to marry. In these situations, we do not perceive events-in-the-making, we imagine them and *conceive* them (ch. 1). The conceptual effort yields less accurate judgment than "seeing" events as they unfold, and it involves more than one style of reasoning—that is, of manipulating symbols according to a logic.

For convenience, these major operations can be called "prophecy," "forecast," and "prediction," but the distinctions to be offered are not given in most dictionaries. They are stipulative terms, justified by their pointing to different processes and powers.

1. *Prophecy* is probably the most popular way of imagining what is likely to happen. Employers of prophecy defend their preferred auguries by citing "authority." However, the defining characteristic of prophecy is that it has *little or no empirical basis.*

The authorities to whom prophets appeal for justification are of three general sorts: Sacred books, teachers (gurus) who have *private* modes of divination, and practitioners who "know how" to interpret *public* signs per some formula, the more ancient, the better.

Some of these sources overlap in technique. Some gurus allege that they have a special way of reading a holy book so that they have privileged sensitivity to premonitory signs. Others offer projections of futures from indicators that are public in the sense that formulas for their interpretation can be transmitted.

Historically, these signs have varied greatly. They include "reading" crystal balls, shuffled cards of special design, animal entrails, creases in people's palms, and horoscopes.

When prophets make pronouncements from public cues, their judgments of futures are sometimes difficult to distinguish from empirical forecasts or predictions. A strong indication that we are attending to a prophet rather than a forecaster is the guru's penchant for uttering vague estimates—the kind that "come true" whatever happens.

Other indications that some employers of public omens are prophetic, rather than knowledgeable, are their failure to keep score, their low "hit rate" of successes to failures when they or others do keep score, and their lack of a well-validated theory connecting the cues they use to the events they "foresee."

Utility ≠ Validity, One More Time: Astrology is a prime example of old and persistently popular prophecy from public cues *that have no empirical warrant.*[13] This pretender to science assumes that its maps of human destinies, called "horoscopes," when "correctly" interpreted, allow its practitioners to foresee the character of adult personalities and their careers from positions of heavenly bodies at times of clients' birth.

Astrology is most accurately regarded as "superstition," that is, false belief. Nevertheless, it has its uses.

In Western lands, astrology columns appear in many newspapers and slick magazines. It is taught in some community colleges, and as many people are said to study astrology as study psychology.[14] While some communist countries have declared astrology to be a form of "feudal superstition," and therefore criminal,[15] the practice remains legal in more open countries because few complain of its harm, and because the sincerity with which its practitioners sell their product absolves them of fraud.

However, sincerity is no substitute for knowledge, and the utility of astrology lies in its giving comfort, not in its accuracy in diagnosing personalities or its powers of foresight. Experiments have demonstrated that consumers of astrology can be made happy with analyses from other peoples' horoscopes as well as from their own.[16]

Continuity of Superstition: We seek knowledge in service to more than one purpose. Allaying curiosity and providing solace have long been two of the uses of beliefs that lack empirical support. Against such uses, education is hard work. And it is hard work not just because of the difficulties of generating information and translating data into valid precepts, but also because knowledge does not answer all the questions about ourselves that human beings ask.

The uncertain gain from scientific efforts to know the social, when compared with the satisfactions of assured belief, guarantees the continuity of superstition. The utilities of false belief are powerful enemies of the cautionary and imperfect results of the would-be sciences of human action.

More than this fights against education. Prophets are believed, and will continue to be trusted, because consumers of their stories don't keep records of their successes and failures. Gullibility also persists because, once consumers have been blessed with a few successful auguries, they are prone to become devoted disciples who then discount—explain away—their gurus' errors.[17]

This is why observers who *count* events are skeptical of prophecy. They call it "the seer-sucker" theory of prediction: "For every seer, there is a sucker."[18]

By contrast with prophecy that makes no attempt to test its conjectures empirically, "forecast" and "prediction" are efforts to judge the likelihood of future events by using *public signs* whose indicative value is suggested by a theory—a set of assumptions and facts that is never assumed to be complete and that is amenable to empirical test. Empirical testing means that someone keeps score, that the scores are themselves tested for reliability (pp. 65-68), and that we *count our failures as well as our successes.*

Failures of foresight are important. For scientists, they suggest revisions, and sometimes abandonment, of theories. For all of us, failures should teach humility.

2. *A forecast* is a statement about the likely course of events, made on the basis of *public* evidence, and tested for contingent accuracy.

Contingency refers to recognition that all attributions of futures are made within some set of assumed conditions, and that these are subject to change.

Moreover, the indicators used for forecasting need not be causes of the events anticipated. The signs are just what they are—presumed portents. They may, or may not, also constitute causes, but their validity is only as cues prognostic of events to come, just as the epileptic's aura is a portent of a seizure *without* being the cause of that occurrence.

But, whether or not the public cues used in forecasts are assumed to be causes, forecasters ordinarily cannot manipulate them. (Exceptions occur when investors try to "corner a market").

In addition, forecasts can be made either on the assumption that we are ignorant of the causes of the occurrences that concern us, or that the events being foretold are generated by random elements. In the latter case, we attempt to use statistical procedures that accept the inevitability of error, and we try to be comfortable with mistake even as we work to reduce it.[19]

The usual method of forecasting is to look for patterns in the past and to project them into the future, adding qualifications about the assumptions made when pasts are extended into the unknown. An example is meteorologists' anticipations of changes in the weather. (Notice that we do not speak of "weather prediction"). Forecasts are also made when demographers use data to project population growth, when speculators rely on "market indicators" to bet on changes in commodity prices, and when clinicians employ "background factors" to identify which convicts may succeed on parole.

In these kinds of work, the cues used are public and their empirical foundations are testable. But, however valid these signs may be, they need not be causes of the events being foretold, and their control is beyond the skills of forecasters.[20] This means that, even when prognosticators are mostly correct, the indicators they use need not tell us *why* events occur as they do.

3. *Prediction*   The Latin roots of this term, "pre-dict," mean "to say in advance." But everything depends on *what* we wish to fore-tell, and *with what signs* for *what span of time*.

Our predicament is that we can know only pasts. We can, and do, estimate futures, and we do so with a variety of cues, variously counted and combined, and with assumptions, implicit and explicit, about the *continuity* of particular pasts into futures at varied distance.

It is small wonder, then, that social scientists so often appeal to the *caeteris paribus* clause—"everything being equal"—and social workers resort so frequently to the adverb, "hopefully."

Nevertheless, most of us engage in some kind of prediction for some sorts of events. The characteristic of a prediction that distinguishes it from a forecast is ability to state, with some empirical warrant, that certain events in the publicly observable world constitute the *efficient and sufficient causes* of particular happenings.

These causal nominees need *not* be the *necessary* causes of the predicted events. This is to say that the outcomes that interest us can be generated in more than one way.[21]

Unfortunately, "prediction" is another of those useful words that is employed with a range of reference. In a weak, and popular, sense, "prediction" refers to theory-testing. It proposes a match between theory and data. It signifies that a set of empirical propositions *implies* something yet to be discovered.

This quality of prediction states a deduction of the form, "According to our theory, we should expect to find X when we make such-and-such observations." It need say nothing about a temporal arrangement of events—which comes first and which after—nor need it specify what causes what to what degree. It can be silent about the *powers* of the nominated causes.

Nevertheless, theory-testing statements of this nature can suggest the likely effects of interventions, always assuming the validity of the data manipulated and that the correlations discovered in some past among particular people will persist in some future among these and other people.

In sum, this style of predicting is heuristic. It is suggestive without being conclusive.

By contrast, a more difficult sense of predicting requires ability to discern sequence and to specify *the kinds and quantities of power* needed to move nominated causes.

To predict in this strong manner is to be able to manipulate causal candidates, and to do so "in the right way." "In the right way" poses additional requirements, including knowledge of correct portions of causal nominees to be applied with least damage from side effects and perverse effects.

It is useful to distinguish this mode of anticipation from other means of foreseeing. I call it "temporal, instrumental prediction" (TIP).

TIP requires a difficult mixture of information and power. It rests on knowledge of the *sequence* of relevant events, the *timing* between causes and their effects, the relative *powers* of correctly identified forces (this is like knowing correct dosage), plus *ability to manipulate* these forces efficiently. "Efficiency" refers to a relationship between the costs of trying to move the probable causes and the conceivable benefits of doing so.

To repeat, TIP is the kind of predictive performance we expect of dentists and physicians, of cosmonautical navigators, of plumbers, carpenters, and electricians, and of technicians who operate, maintain, and repair motor vehicles, aircraft, television and electronic devices.

TIP is not an expertise for which governments can certify scientists of social action.

By contrast with the somewhat knowledgeable practitioners of engineering, medicine, and mechanics, students of social activities regularly nominate *competing lists of candidates* as causal agents. And, since these lists are chosen for their ethico-political desirability as well as for their practical potency, we need to be able to test for "dosage effects" and for benefits net of costs among varied combinations of causal nominees. This makes a social engineering difficult, if not impossible.

In brief, scientific foresight of the TIP variety, that would inform public policy in the social realm, requires both empirical *knowledge* and *power* exercised within a *moral* context.

Boundaries of Competence

"To know yet to think that one does
not know is best;
Not to know yet to think that one knows will
lead to difficulty."
　　　　　　　　—LAO TZU, 6th C., B.C.[22]

Lao Tzu, founder of Taoism, was probably correct. Calling social studies "sciences" arrogates to its practitioners more skill than we possess.

This does not mean that we know nothing or that there has been no advance in knowledge of ourselves. It means that all claims to knowledge of social action are to be tested, and that we know something about the requirements of adequate testing.

Succeeding chapters describe these demands and thereby circumscribe our competence. Preliminary to that work, a brief summary of some of the contingencies that affect foresight is appropriate. Our ability to foresee social events varies with:

1. What we attempt to foretell. It is easier to predict changes in the behaviors of "lower" (simpler) organism than changes in the actions of "higher" (multiply moved) creatures.

2. Time span. Extrapolation from the past to the future tends to be more accurate the closer the future is to the present.[23] We do better, too, the more repetitive a pattern has been in the past (assuming that there is a pattern), and as we predict with the least number of qualifying assumptions added. The trouble with adding many qualifications is that the events they refer to are variables, and this means that they can change without our knowing how they will fluctuate.

3. The reliability of taxonomies of actors and events. Accurate forecast and prediction depend on a reliable system for classifying objects, persons, situations, and incidents. The reliability of such a system is judged by the degree of inter-personal agreement among those competent to perform the required categorization of acts, actors, and the products of action.

Competence is required because the application of some taxonomic criteria has to be learned—how to "read" an X-ray, for example.

"Products of action" refers to such "results" as "gross national product," "crime rates," "traffic crashes," "death rates," and other such "effects" that both describe our lives and influence them, but that no single individual can observe directly. (Notice the causal assumption embedded in use of such words as "results" and "effects," and refer to ch. 10.)

As has been argued (ch. 2) and is further demonstrated (chs. 5-8), attempts to classify actors and acts with morally saturated terms reduces the reliability of taxonomies.

4. Accuracy of tallies. Reliable taxonomy is required, but so is accurate record keeping. Indeed, these two requirements interact: Without reliable means of classification, records are worthless, and without clean recording of events, nothing can be measured.

5. The standard of accuracy. If there were a strong science of social events, we would expect its practitioners to be able to improve estimates of futures above commonsensical judgment or chance.

"Improvement over chance" refers to the degree of accuracy in foresight added by knowing something more than just the *base rate* of a class of events. "Base rate" is the proportion of a defined population that exhibits the activity of interest.

A base rate of some kind of social event gives us information—assuming requirements item 3 and item 4 above have been met. But what we expect from prognostic experts is that they develop data, and ways of using them, that increase predictive accuracy beyond that given "merely" by a base rate (cf. item 8 below).

This is difficult work, for reasons to be amplified in later pages. However, insofar as we have tallies of expertise in economics, psychology, criminology, and other social sciences, when there is improvement beyond chance, it is modest.

6. Knowledge of the system in which action occurs. All causal attribution assumes contexts in which nominated causes do their work (ch. 10, "Causation").

In the social studies, this limitation, and those mentioned in preceding sections, are neither fully acknowledged nor well described.

7. Prediction of the temporal-instrumental kind is improved by feedback. One element of experience that keeps us from being more stupid than we might be is feedback—particularly "negative feedback."

As its title implies, "negative feedback" says "nay." It tells us when doing X to obtain Y does *not* work.

It provides one good reason for holding individuals responsible for their actions. Responsibility in its moral sense means that persons experience the consequences of their conduct. Responsibility teaches.

Put the other way about, relieving people of personal responsibility infantilizes them. It allows them to be less intelligent than they otherwise would be.

It is this kind of divorcement that makes politicians dangerous. "Too many" legislative acts *force* others to experience the consequences that policy-makers escape.

8. The method with which we manipulate information. Despite these many limitations to our prescience, we do know something about how to improve foresight. Such improvement rests, to repeat, on reliable categorization of events and their accurate tally. Given these combined desiderata, plus dependable record keeping, psychologists have devised techniques with which to make better judgments of what is likely to happen.

A first improvement comes from employing actuarial (mathematical) methods of weighing prognostic signs rather than relying upon individual (clinical) insight. Chapter 10 cites evidence of this phenomenon and concludes that, "numerical formulas for *combining cues* allow more accurate forecast of others' actions than do clinicians' judgment. 'Objective ordering' of premonitory signs trumps experts' 'intuition'" (pp. 180-190).

Given such measurement, we can better assess the likelihood of some kinds of events with a procedure of signal-detection-evaluation called ROC— "receiver operating characteristic."[24] This method involves counting ratios between "hits" and "misses" for *each range* of test scores—such as medical diagnostics, aptitude indicators, interests, and more.

This information can then be plotted with curves that describe the relationships between premonitory signs and "outcomes" (actually, correlates). Such graphs allow estimates of the ratios between "false negative" diagnoses and "true positive" diagnoses. That is, we can calculate how many "misses" we make using particular cues (test scores; diagnostic signs) compared with the "hits" we make with them. We tally failures against successes.

"False negative": We say persons do *not* have a particular disorder, or will *not* perform a kind of act, but they do.

"True positive": We say persons suffer from a particular disorder, or are likely to do X, and they do.

Caution: Inventors of ROC are well aware that all diagnostic and prognostic procedures assume that test scores are reliable and valid (ch. 4), and that "outcomes" have been accurately recorded and tabulated.[25]

One is reluctant to appear unduly skeptical, but "data mining" is not an unheard-of phenomenon. Enumerators who wish to obtain particular results can, and do, add and subtract "information" so as to produce desired tallies. This is dangerously true of those brokers who count money,.[26] and those military authorities who count bodies.[27]

The possibility of "interested scoring" pertains to activities of *all* bureaus that have the task of obtaining, recording, and reporting the courses of events. It occurs among corporations' reports of their finances, registrars' tallies of votes, clinicians' assessments of their interventions, and government statements about the efficacy of crime prevention programs, traffic safety devices, job training, drug therapies, and more.

The practice of having "interested parties" count the effects of their work is like asking foxes to count the chickens in the hen-house.

For example, those of us who have suffered iatrogenic effects of medical care wonder how frequently physicians *report* (as distinct from *record*) the damaging consequences of their treatments with medicine and surgery. In this regard, admitting *null results* is not the same as confessing *perverse effects*. The latter admission takes more courage.

The Asymmetry of Knowledge-Power

Some studies of social action have attempted to *count* what it is that we can foresee most accurately with our instruments and, as the foregoing attests, how best to improve judgment.

From a sample of these studies, two tentative principles can be adduced:

1. "Bad" signs are more prognostic of "bad" events than "good" signs are of "good" events. (For "good" and "bad" substitute less morally tinctured terms such as "desired-undesired," or "happy-unhappy," or "fortunate-unfortunate").
2. Hindsight yields higher correlations between nominated cues and outcomes than does foresight.

On the first generalization, we have evidence from such realms of conduct as:

1. Ominous cues are more indicative of adult criminality than beneficent cues are of freedom from later criminal activity.
2. Early mental disorder, drug abuse, and serious juvenile delinquency correlate more closely with adult violence than does their absence with freedom from adult violent behavior.
3. Early indicators of marital discord more assuredly foretell marital breakup than do early signs of marital bliss foretell later marital happiness.
4. Poor youthful schoolwork is more closely associated with low occupational achievement in adulthood than is successful early schoolwork with successful adult vocational careers.
5. Low juvenile IQs more accurately indicate poor adult college achievement than high early IQs assure later school success.
6. Ominous scores on psychological tests are more accurate signs of poor "mental health" than beneficent scores are of sound psychological functioning.
7. Overweight more accurately foretells shorter life expectancy than "normal" weight guarantees longer life.
8. Positive—that is, "bad"—signs on neurological tests more accurately indicate brain pathology than negative ("good") signs indicate freedom from such disorder.

In brief, for these kinds of important courses in human lives, early ominous cues more accurately foretell undesirable outcomes than favorable cues assure later happiness.

This finding does not say that "bad" portents are error-free, nor does it depreciate the good luck of joyous portents. This warped relationship is comparative, and the comparison is significant.

"Bias" in our knowledge-power comports with the direction of our curiosity and differential demand for explanation. We are not so surprised when bad starts yield bad results as we are when good starts also end up badly. Surprise is indicator of our preconceptions of causation and our flimsy knowledge of the causes of conduct.

Elsewhere I present evidence of the *degrees* to which this asymmetry occurs, and note that the *extent* of such lopsidedness is not known.[28] That is, we have not tested for this possibility among every kind of career.

However, one cause of this imbalance between precursors of human events and later measures of their validity is that many of the ominous signs tend to be *disabilities*. "Disabilities," be definition, describe limited possibilities, and limitations narrow the range of action, thus permitting greater prescience.

By contrast, abilities represent expanded possibilities that may or may not be used. Hence our lesser assurance that talents will be used, abused, or neglected.

The second of our anticipatory principles claims a lopsided relationship between knowledge from hindsight and its application to foresight. It can be called *"Dawes's rule of basic asymmetry."*[29]

Psychologist Robyn Dawes demonstrates that we obtain higher correlations when we reason "backwards" from an event regarded as an effect to its possible causes than when we reason in the opposite sequence from nominated causes to possible futures.

Moreover, says Dawes,

[t]his asymmetry is exacerbated when the investigator is free to search for antecedents [possible causes] in a situation involving multiple potential antecedents. [And] this asymmetry is exacerbated to an even greater extent when the investigator relies on memory [as in "self-report" studies described in ch. 8] rather than recorded observations in this search.[30]

Unfortunately for a would-be science of social action, these two additional limitations characterize much social research. Other boundaries to our competence are apparent when we examine the requirement that a science be able to measure what it talks about.

Part 2

Knowing with Numbers

4

Measurement

"He who begins to count begins to err."
                    —Scholastic proverb

*"The government are very keen on amassing
statistics. They collect them, raise them to the
nth power, take the cube root and prepare
wonderful diagrams. But you must never
forget that every one of these figures comes in
the first instance from the village watchman
who just puts down what he damn pleases."*
                    —Josiah Stamp[1]

Tallies and Errors

The Scholastic proverb cited above "swings" better phrased in its Latin original: *Qui/numerare incipit/errare incipit*, but what it says is true in either language. Our trouble is that the opposite is also true. If we cannot count, we cannot "know" much.

"Primal knowledge," yes. Many kinds of "know-how," yes. But "conceptual knowledge," little.

All knowing, even primitive perception, is subject to error. It is a glory of our self-knowledge that we have become increasingly aware of this, and of some of the sources of delusion and illusion. But major tasks of those who would be scientists of the social persist: To discern how much error resides in our "information"; to locate the origins of such distortion and, if that assignment can be fulfilled, to learn how to reduce mistake.

This work is difficult for all the reasons listed here and in preceding and succeeding chapters. Our occupation is made additionally difficult insofar as social scientists advertise their expertise, and thereby promote the expectation that we have answers to most of the questions the citizenry ask about their lives.

Judging with Numbers

This expectation was given impetus by the Belgian astronomer-statistician Adolphe Quetelet (1796-1874). His *Essai de Physique Sociale* (1835) proposed that human action *in the aggregate* could be described by eternal laws.

Just as entomologists can discern pattern in swarms of insects, and biologists can observe order among schools of fish and flocks of birds—*without* attending to characteristics of their individual members—so, too, Quetelet reasoned, social scientists should be able to identify regularities in human social activities when the appropriate gathering is noted and its conditional behavior recorded.

This assumption is not all wrong although, to date, eternal laws of social action are scarce, and theory-laden plans to increase health, wealth, and happiness around the world are not notable for their success. Indeed, during the twentieth century such plans produced great epidemics of immiseration and intentional killing.

Nevertheless, Quetelet's promise continues to animate social scientists. We believe, with good reason, that we have improved upon common sense concerning some interpretations of action, even though our conceived regularities are highly provisional—that is, local, temporal, and hedged about with contingencies.

We know *what* is required to test a limited range of empirical hypotheses, particularly those that tally results of legislation and other interventions in peoples' lives. It should be clear, however, that knowing these requirements is not the same as having power to perform the requisite operations. It is also a different function from ability to develop novel theories that increase temporal, instrumental predictive power (TIP).

To assume possession of such skill is to raise the risk of a promissory science of the social with its accompanying hazard of converting scholarship to propaganda.

Numbed by Numbers

In modern times we are not so much eloquent with numbers as bombarded by them. Inescapably, we are consumers of "statistics" that purport to inform us of a grand list of "things that exist and occur": The numbers of persons in territories, the proportions of "kinds of people" and their conditions and activities in those spaces, the "state of the union," the "state of the world," and the quantified risks of everything that conceivably concerns us and more that does not.

Under this onslaught of "information," the burden we bear is unmeasurable error and anxiety. We can only sample this load without measuring its extension, duration, and intensity.

But the barrage of figures, many of them "official," pummels their consumers into believing that what "the statistics" say must be true. Contrary to this assumption, public numbers range widely from the contingently accurate—"good enough for some purpose"—to tallies of the unknowable and enumerations that are outright fraudulent.

No one has scored all official and unofficial numbers issued by governments and independent investigators, ranked for their accuracy net of their errors. But the fact of error generates cautionary advice:

1. To expand your experience, peruse a starting inventory of doubtful data.[2]
2. Do not confuse statistics with mathematics.
3. Be chary of journalists' and politicians' use of scientists' research.
4. If a particular set of figures is important to you, ask, *"Who counted what, how, and with what reliability and validity?"*

Comments on this advice follow:

Mathematics ≠ Statistics: Although statistics are stated with numbers, and many of the symbols they use look like those employed in mathematics, the two uses differ in an essential way.

Mathematical numbers, and other of its symbols, are manipulated according to the rules of a logic. Compared with uses of ordinary language, says mathematician Alain Connes, "Mathematics is a more rigorous language—no more, no less."[3]

If one accepts the rules of mathematical logic, as most of us do, then its numbers are precise. Moreover, Connes adds, they are "absolute, universal, and therefore independent of any cultural influence."[4]

By contrast, numbers assigned to empirical things and events are always liable to err. Their abstraction from, and application to, "real" objects and occurrences are subject to "the gravity—the pull—of ideology."

This difference points to an additional source of deception. If the original observations from which enumerations are made are not reliable, then statistical manipulation of those figures cannot reveal what we want to know from our research. More will be said about this in later chapters.

Second-Hand "Information": Journalists and politicians who insert public numbers into their arguments are frequently more interested in proving points than in enlightening the citizenry. In an age that urges "activism" to address our multiple concerns, and that muddles news with entertainment, a reportorial bias favors raising alarms.

When professional researchers check many of these frightening figures, they regularly find discrepancies—some of them huge—between what journalists and "public-interest" groups tell the public and what scientists say (cf. item 3 above).

As a recent example, Robert Lichter and Stanley Rothman were interested in the "information" that journalists and "environmental activists" disseminated about just one of the many hazards that assail us—cancer. They compared the beliefs of these reporters with those of professional students of the disease—M.D.s specializing in oncology.

A vast majority of journalists—85 percent—think that Americans suffer from "a cancer epidemic." This majority drops to about two-thirds among "activists" and to a minority—30 percent—of oncologists. Similar differences characterize these occupations' beliefs about the *causes* of the various cancers.[5]

In addition, popular interpreters of others' data find it necessary to simplify. This means that they omit researchers' qualifications. It means, too, that some common words as used by scientists—"probability," for example—are given an unrefined usage different from that employed by scientists, who themselves sometimes use more than one conception of likelihood (ch. 6).

These are only some of the difficulties that trouble us. We are restricted to a limited competence because the *scientific way of knowing depends on measurement.*

Measurement

> *"When you cannot measure it, when you cannot express it in numbers, your knowledge is of a meager and unsatisfactory kind."*
> —*Lord William T. Kelvin, mathematician-physicist, 1824-1907*

Lord Kelvin's motto is chiseled in stone over the entrance to *The Social Science Building* at the University of Chicago. Many of us agree with this British scholar and yet, as with many maxims, Kelvin's dictum allows modifying verdicts. Thus two of the university's prominent economists qualified the aspiration expressed by the physicist's prescription.

Jacob Viner commented, "Even when you can measure a thing, your knowledge will be meager and unsatisfactory." And to this, his colleague Frank Knight added, "...what Kelvin's dictum came down to, at least in the social sciences, was, 'If you cannot measure, measure anyhow.'"[6]

As we shall see, Knight's description remains accurate. It is particularly apt when social scientists place their trust in strangers' reports of their conduct as measures of their behavior (ch. 8).

Requirements

Measurement may have a physiological basis—a basis in perception (ch. 1)—but measuring becomes more extensive and useful with constructs, starting with the fundamental idea of "number."[7]

Archeological studies suggest that the notion of number evolved about 10,000 years ago from early tallies of things—sheep, goats—and led to the realization about 5,000 years ago that *numbers can be independent of the things counted.*[8]

Measurement, then, starts with counting. Counting assumes clean classification of objects or events observed. In mathematicians' language, measurement requires that the things or happenings tallied be *homogeneous.*[9] That is, it requires that an attribute observed of any single instance of a "class" of objects or events must be true of all cases in that set. This is the meaning of a *unit*.

Applying the cardinal numbers to things and acts assumes dependable identification of units. Moreover, there must be justification—by preliminary theory at least—that the units selected for tabulation are the *appropriate ones* with which to answer an empirical question.

This requirement arises because statisticians frequently work with numbers that they themselves have not generated. They regularly use figures produced by government agencies, whether or not the collections of people and acts enumerated can be regarded as unitary (homogeneous) *for investigators' purposes*.

As a consequence, developers of public numbers are sometimes correctly accused of "putting together things that are actually quite different."[10] This practice is facilitated by the use of fuzzy vocabulary, as chapter 2 argues.

For example, the United Nations Children's Fund (UNICEF) recently issued a report on the amount of "child poverty" in the world's twenty-three richest countries.[11] "Poverty," of course, is a shock word. It creates images of squalor, hunger, filth, sickness, misery, ignorance—a picture of subsistence-level degradation.

Unfortunately for investigators and consumers of their studies, "poverty" refers to no singular condition. The word is not specific.

If pollsters could have their informants "freely associate" to that word, it is a safe bet that the preponderance of their respondents would think of "poverty" as depicted above. But inquirers for the United Nations did not measure such a condition. Instead, they counted *inequalities within populations*, and designated "households" with "incomes" less than half of the median national "income" as "living in poverty."

For the moment, ignore all the defects of counting "household income" by asking people about it. Ignore, too, whether such wealth is counted before or after taxes, and whether "income" is supplemented by transfers and other wealth. Comparison among countries as diverse in their economies and wealth, culturally habituated practices, territorial and population size, and ethno-racial homogeneity as Canada and Norway, the United States and Finland, Denmark and Turkey, Sweden and Mexico leads unwary consumers of United Nations "information" to *equate* the lives of "poor" children among these disparate lands.

These categories are not unitary. The "things" counted within them are not homogeneous.

If one regards the United Nations calculators as earnest truth-seekers, their use of slippery language is innocent error. If one regards these enumerators as ideologists, their choice of words serves propaganda.[12] In any event, measuring inequalities in "incomes" among "households," and calling a division of their ranges "poverty" misleads. Once again, statisticians can be charged with "putting together things that are actually quite different."

Definition

> "Nothing can be measured for which there exist no good concepts, and concepts, no matter how precise, are of little practical value if the corresponding measurements cannot be performed."
>
> —Oskar Morgenstern[13]

Before we can measure, we must define the objects or actions to which we wish to assign numbers. This necessity returns us to the argument of chapter 2.

If concepts have no fixed borders, if taxonomies of things and events are permeable, nothing can be counted with assurance.[14]

In keeping with Morgenstern's statement above, we can draw a sensible circle. Before we measure, we have to have a clear idea of what we are attempting to tally. But if, given that, we have no way of counting what a term clearly indicates, then the concept itself can have no *scientific* utility, although it can have aesthetic, moral, and rhetorical value (ch. 2).

Morris Cohen and Ernest Nagel put the binding requirement this way:

> We...employ counting to make precise our ideas, *subsequent* to our having acquired sufficient knowledge about a subject to permit us to distinguish various features in it.[15]

Clear concepts organize matters in such a way that "adequately equipped" observers can agree on what they refer to. "Adequately equipped" is a necessary qualifier. We do not ask blind persons to classify colors, and one has to learn to "see" through a microscope and to "read" an X-ray chart.

Additional Requirements

Assuming that we have defined sets of events or conditions *homogeneous for our purpose*—a fragile assumption in "the moral sciences"—then the process of measuring is a rule-ful way of ordering things or happenings so that real numbers can be assigned quantities of them. Mathematician S. S. Stevens puts it this way: "Measurement is the assignment of numerals to aspects of objects according to rules...."[16]

Among these rules is the requirement that the units designated by our scales be fixed, that the intervals they mark off be equal, and that they do not change their calibration when employed by different individuals who are assigning numbers to presumably the same things, conditions, or actions. It is also assumed that the cardinal numbers we attach to sets of particulars are of the sort that allow us to manipulate them according to the rules of arithmetic: addition, subtraction, multiplication, and division.

Moreover, measurement is considered to be either "fundamental" or "derived." It is fundamental when its ordering of things or events does *not* depend on other measurements. It is derived when it rests on vicarious tabulations, as when we measure "intelligence" with a standard set of tasks or "temperature" with a "thermo-meter" composed of a column of mercury in a tube.

Thus several scales of temperature, and ways of gauging its quantity, have been invented. Each device refers to a different range of heat, and scores it with different degrees of accuracy.

The differences are sufficiently great as to permit calling what they measure different "concepts" of heat. In this manner, what we *do* to calibrate a conceived process can change its definition—what we call it.

Philosopher Carl Hempel further refined the idea of derived measurement by noting that some instruments grade *novel* quantities made up of numbers already known. He termed these indicators "stipulative derived measures," as when we conceive of, and calculate, a new kind of condition, activity, or process from numbers produced by other measurements.[17]

Such composition is illustrated when we invent IQ, net reproduction rate, gross domestic product, the poverty ratio, quality of life score, and similar "manufactured" gauges. These quantified concepts, and more like them, combine two or more *separately tabulated* values. In this, lies opportunity for mischief.

All measurement expresses a relationship, and all such expression is subject to error, as our opening proverb states. But probability of error compounds as we fuse numbers from "village watchmen" of varied temperament and interest whose job it is to count *presumably* homogenous kinds of events and conditions at different sites.

For example, think of highway patrol officers who are asked to "observe," *after events*, a suggested roster of the probable causes of crashes, and to describe these "factors" in terms of the conditions of drivers and passengers, the weights and speeds of vehicle at impact, point of impact, use of safety devices, and more, with these ticks on a report-sheet to be transformed into numbers that Departments of Transport calculate *in terms of* fatalities and injuries per passenger miles traveled, with these *unknowable* numbers derived from other sources that have tabulated them *independently*. Such chains of derived figures increase opportunity for error and raise doubts about their accuracy.[18]

Most citizens—probably the vast majority—do not realize, or care, that the persons who make the initial observations of social activities, and who record them with ticks on a reporting sheet, are not usually the same persons who sort these marks according to a coding scheme, and who, in turn, may, or may not, be the same individuals who assign numbers to what has been coded, with these tallies delivered to actuaries-statisticians who manipulate the numbers for meanings to be given writers who compose "summary reports."

Social statistics are socially processed and, with such filtered transmission, become ripe for error. Succeeding chapters give examples. To make the point here, one instance suffices:

A Tale of Two Cities

Criminologist Robert A. Silverman[19] became intrigued by the fact that two large Canadian cities, Calgary and Edmonton, located only 180 miles apart in the same province, operating with the same coding rules, and with no remarkable difference in their population composition, listed consistent differences in crime rates between 1969 and 1975.

Edmonton repeatedly showed 1½ to 2½ times the number of rapes that Calgary reported, 1½ to 2 times the number of assaults, and 2 times the number of robberies.

After interviews with officers in charge of records and tests of coders' reliability (consistency), Silverman concluded that much of the variation in reported crime between these cities resulted from *different ways of processing information.*

This does not mean that either police department was "doing something wrong." It means that social events are complexes of action, and that the title given an occurrence depends on a host of variables, including *which part* of an action sequence one attends to and the *subjective importance* attached to elements in the happening.[20]

In this vein, Silverman notes that sex offenses are particularly difficult to classify:

> The meanings of rape, indecent assault, and "other sex offenses" seem to baffle police, classifiers, and many other participants in the criminal justice system. This results from the concepts of sexual morality that underlie these offenses.... The nature of the offense and the cultural meanings we give to those offenses can make it unclear whether a rape, an indecent assault, or an act of gross indecency has taken place.[21]

Similarly, it is sometimes difficult for police and crime-coders to distinguish between "assault," "assault occasioning bodily harm," and "wounding." Furthermore, "assault with intent to steal" may be counted as an "assault" in one city and a "robbery" in another.

Broadening the classes of acts increases reliability in coding at the cost of "refined" definition and description.

The upshot is that, while trend lines can be drawn in crime rates for a jurisdiction that does not change its coding practice, comparisons between cities, and even more between countries, that use different coding rules have *no known* validity.

Socially processed "information" is open to miscalculation. Error is stimulated by the handling of records by multiple processors and by social scientists' efforts *to measure much that they cannot observe.*

All manner of events, variously defined and hence variously classified, occur "out there." But we do not perceive them, do not control them, do not uniformly evaluate them, and can only infer them and try to reconstruct them. Little wonder, then, that a vocation that would count them is fraught with mishap.

We shall not abandon the gathering of social statistics. But in environments congenial to error, what we desire of public numbers is *not* ordinarily provided. What we desire is assurance that socially significant measurements are reliable and valid.

Reliability and Validity

If social studies were to approximate a science, they would not only have to work with clear concepts but also their processes of observing, recording, and measuring would have to be open to public review, replicable, and accurate.

Statistician Louis Guttman makes the point:

> The essence of science is replication: a scientist should always be concerned about what will happen when he or another scientist repeats his experiment [or observation and measurement].[22]

Unfortunately, in studies of human activity the ideas of being reliable (dependable, repeatable) and being valid (accurate, true) become concepts with many referents. Thus Arthur Reber's *Dictionary of Psychology* lists three types of "reliability," to which more have since been added, and twenty-two kinds of "validity."[23]

Some of these meanings are useful for particular purposes; others are so employed as to give a false impression of the fidelity of measurements.

The "reliability" that concerns us here is warrant that a measuring device, designed to gauge some kinds of objects or events, always within the limits of appropriate conditions, scales these things or actions uniformly upon repeated use. It is guarantee that we are not measuring with an elastic meter-stick.

The "validity" we need is assurance that a measuring tool accurately grades what we wish to count. The idea of validity is that of correct reference. Psychometricians call this quality "the *object* of measurement.[24]

Options: Psychometricians who develop tests by which to judge particular abilities—in reading, writing, and mathematics, for example, and the general ability to learn called "intelligence"—think of "reliability" as the degree to which the scores persons obtain on such tests indicate the assumed "true score" for each individual who responds to that probe. That is, *this kind* of "reliability" grades *how well* the score one receives on a test represents the score one could be expected to receive under all "appropriate" conditions— like no headache that morning.[25]

This "classic" conception of reliability has recently been expanded, and enhanced with a computer program, under the title, "generalizability theory" ("G-theory").[26]

G-theory equates reliability with dependability. It offers procedures for *generalizing from a sample* of persons' behaviors, depicted by a single test (measuring device), to the likelihood that other samples of their performance on the same task—spelling, high-jumping, doing algebra—taken by the same instrument, under a variety of "suitable" circumstances, will yield a score "truly representative" of their skill.

A popular psychometric textbook describes this conception of "reliability" thus:

> Dependability, then, refers to the accuracy of generalizing from a person's observed score on a test or other measure (e.g., behavior observation, opinion survey) to the average score that person would have received under all the possible conditions that the test user would be equally willing to accept.[27]

There are, of course, different ways of assessing the reliability (dependability, generalizability, faithfulness) of a measuring tool, and it is the job of psychometric textbooks to describe these methods, their assumptions, and their uses.

Here it only needs reminding that the choice of a measuring instrument, and justification of its use, depends on our purpose: What is it we can do better with that device (procedure) than without it?

This theme will be repeated. It will be joined with arguments that social scientists collect more data than they properly analyze, that much of it is skimpily, if not inaccurately, descriptive, and that it is questionable how much social-scientific information improves the quality of our explanations of human action and increases our ability to predict it.

Meanwhile, it is important to recognize that, while validity assumes reliability, the reverse does not hold. Reliable results—in the sense of repeated "findings"—give no assurance of truthfulness. Just as an individual can deceive us consistently, so too a measuring device can generate popular and replicable numbers that are either vacant or false. By "vacant," I mean that we don't know what, if anything, the numbers refer to.

Conceptual Varieties

Testing the trustworthiness of inquirers' observations and their measurements is costly. In lieu of this expense, social scientists invent substitutes so that, as we've seen, the ideas of reliability and validity take several meanings. By this tactic, the same word, as spelled and pronounced, is employed to refer to *different processes* and, hence, to different qualities of a measuring instrument.

Consumers of statistics, innocent of these many modifications, are thereby misled into calling a purported gauge of some social activity "reliable" without knowledge of its worth as a stable indicator. Thus are words borrowed and corrupted to add gloss to dross.

For example, a common, and cheap, practice assesses "reliability" by calculating the "internal consistency" of a set of responses to tasks or questions, and to do so with data from a single trial on a single sample of individuals. This popular procedure yields only an indication of how people respond to tests or questions, phrased in a particular way, on a particular day. It is a gauge of verbal—or, if you prefer, logical—congruence.

If social scientists were subject to a *truth-in-labeling* law, they would be required to call their indicators of "internal consistency" just that, to distinguish this quality of a measure from the repetitive consistency we require of our instruments.

A "one-shot" test of "internal congruence" does *not* tell us what we want to know. We want to know how well a measuring device reports similar results when we gauge the same kind of activity repeatedly under similar circumstance, and when it is used by *different investigators* on comparable samples of humanity.

For example, we want to know how consistently individuals reply to questions when we ask them about the *same content* of their activities or conditions *repeatedly*, and preferably in response to different interrogators employing a different ordering and wording of questions probing that content.

In a lovely essay titled, "What Is Not What in Statistics," Louis Guttman makes the point:

> When calculated from a single trial on a sample, an estimate of a reliability coefficient for the population is generally inconsistent....Item analysis for internal consistency does not analyze items. It merely attempts to 'test' the—challenging!—hypothesis that all inter-item correlations are zero, and usually by an incorrect item-total score correlation technique. It is a way of trying to avoid the basic problem of definition, and involves wishful thinking that correlations should determine content.[28]

Of course, the requirement that a measuring tool give reliable results applies only on the assumption that the type of behavior we study has not changed. This assumption *must hold true* when investigators ask strangers to tell of their current status and past activities.

It need not apply when we study individuals' expressions of opinions, feelings, or desires because these attributes are known principally by what people *say* they are! Psychologists who try to measure such fluctuating moods can offer no assurance that their findings are stable.[29]

As regards the omnipresent polls of public *opinion*, we have abundant evidence that their "findings" are wobbly. What people tell pollsters is strongly affected by the timing of surveys, their question-wording, question-order, context, acquiescence bias (tendency to be agreeable), and by the oft-ignored distortion produced by a "social desirability" factor (tendency to present oneself as a good person).[30]

In brief, the requirement that a measuring device be reliable is *not* satisfied by many gauges of social events. It is notably lacking when investigators rely on what strangers *say* as indicator of what they have done or experienced.[31]

The concept of "validity" is even more distorted and neglected than that of "reliability" because, to repeat, we wish to study much that we cannot observe. This raises the probability of error and the cost of inventing ways of assuring the accuracy of our instruments. Here again, students of social activity accommodate by proposing more than one notion of veracity.

For example, some investigators claim *face validity* for their instruments, if a panel of experts agrees that the content of their scale refers to the *idea* of the activity being tallied.

A cousin of this procedure attributes *construct validity* to a probe of behavior when its elements—such as questions or tasks—seem to gauge the degree to which these samples fairly represent a *hypothetical trait* like "dominance" or "intelligence."

Other qualities of "validity" have been nominated. However, the idea of accuracy that concerns most lay persons, but not all professional inquirers, is variously known as *empirical, criterion-related,* or *predictive validity*.

The difference among these sorts of accuracy is a matter of timing. Every empirically accurate test is but a cheaper, shorter way of assessing what people have done, or are likely to do, than directly observing a large range of many individuals' actions over time.

An *empirical, or criterion-related,* instrument rates the degree to which its scores correlate with a sample of *non-test* records of the activity of interest. A common example is a set of questions with which to measure "delinquent disposition." If its scores are "satisfactorily associated" with other records of "delinquent" conduct, such as police logs, then the scale is regarded as "valid."

The effort to gain *predictive validity* also works with some measure of co-relationship, but with the added utility that the measurement can be used to *increase foresight*. The increase in fore-knowledge is, of course, about a particular quality of future action assessed within some range of probabilities.

For example, this type of validity is sought from measures of likely academic achievement and job performance. Its correct use requires repeated testing, large bodies of data with which to construct a "track record," and attention to revision as times, people, and targets change. And again, one should employ the results of such tools only as range concepts, not as point predictors.

The Ideal: Multiple, Independent, Convergent, "Blind" Test

We approach truth about some domain of human action by developing multiple, independent probes of each well-defined kind of activity.

In this regard, the difference between a scientist and a layperson is that the ordinary individual is more easily satisfied with a small slice of experience, with early judgment, and with stable opinion sometimes called common sense or faith.

The scientific attitude assumes that, insofar as we can construct several, different ways of gauging a distinct type of action, and insofar as we find that they yield similar results, we gain assurance that each mode of inquiry is accurate. Psychologists Donald Campbell and Donald Fiske term such happy congruence *convergent validity*.[32]

Searching for regularity among conditions and actions with multiple, independent, converging probes is costly. But it is what *scientists* do, and it is our best defense against error.

Necessity: Science acknowledges the omnipresence of bias. Call it what you will—interest, preference, taste, or value—bias operates as a disposition—a pull or push or blinker.

While it is comforting to regard bias as the other person's tendency, it is both the pleasure and the burden of every caring individual.

Expectations influence judgments. They do so on a continuum that ranges from fully conscious likes and dislikes through degrees of awareness to unconscious leaning. *Placebo effects* are among these expectations. They are real, and they can be induced and directed.[33] The common mixture of wish and preference in thought is our reason for speaking of feel-thinking, rather than one or the other.

An early case illustrates the ways of bias and a procedure for defending against its operation in the enterprise of science.

Example: The United States of America exhibits a long-standing concern about its ethno-racial divisions, with Americans still unable to agree about how best to live as many peoples in one polity. Against this background, a quarrel in the human sciences demonstrates the necessity of sanitized observation and recording.

At the opening of the twentieth century, a professor of anatomy in a southern university became wary of the "findings" of one of his graduate students who had measured the cranial capacity of Negroid and Caucasoid skulls. The premise of the study held that cranial size was indicative of brain size and hence of "intelligence."

Student R. B. Bean reported "significant" racial differences.[34] His mentor, F. P. Mall, suspected prejudice in his apprentice, and particularly so when he noticed that Bean had labeled each skull by race. He had performed his measurements "sighted."

By contrast, Mall repeated the study with the same skulls, but he did so "blind." He identified the crania by number rather than by title, and obtained a much reduced result.[35]

Common assumption sees bias only in wicked people, but not in good persons. This assumption is incorrect. Goodness biases. So does Evil, of course, but Goodness has preferred status. It presumes its innocence and thereby its correctness. However, some research indicates that, for accurate depiction of some kinds of social events and conditions, the Evil Eye is more accurate than the Benign Eye. At least, we should not presume that only good intention sees events accurately.[36]

Error is inevitable, but it can be reduced without being eliminated. Unfortunately, the putative social sciences have been reluctant to acknowledge the need for tighter control of the observation-recording process. The urge to be useful stimulates enthusiasm, and enthusiasm trumps diligence.

The lesson of *Mall v. Bean* continues to be ignored. Here, for example, is a brief list of actual practices that should *not* be followed, if we desire accurate measurement:

- Teachers should not be the only judges of their pupils' skills.
- Psychotherapists should not be trusted to gauge changes in their clients' conduct. Neither should the intimates of clients, aware of their friends' therapy, be used as assessors of personality change.
- After having applied one of the fashionable new treatments, reformatory custodians should not assess the behavior of their wards.
- Highly propagandized—that is, prejudiced—highway patrol officers should not be expected to correctly classify causes of death and injury in motor vehicle crashes.
- In brief, "interested parties"—those who have an investment in a particular finding—are not trustworthy recorders or reporters. (What interested parties *record* and what they *report* can be different matters.)[37]

This principle has long been recognized, but it continues to be violated. The costs of such motivated assessments are immeasurable. A recent financial fiasco illustrates the potential damage.

Late in 2001, America's seventh largest corporation, Enron, collapsed. By early 2002, it had filed for bankruptcy protection and thousands of its employees had lost their pensions.

There are always steps toward such disasters, but a major misstep occurred when external accountants audited the reports of the corporation in which they themselves had financial stakes.

At this writing, the debacle involves lawyers as well as accountants and corporate executives in what appears to have been a variation of the Ponzi tactic. Pages 122-123 describe this age-old scam.[38] It's a fraud that governments also commit, and one that justifies the prison inmates' maxim, "You can steal more with a pen than with a gun."

In Sum: If studies of social events were to approximate the rigor of science, they would have to employ language that denotes clearly. This requires careful surgery on moral concepts.

Moreover, clarity would have to be attained whether social scientists use ordinary words, as is their habit, or stipulated, derived concepts.

In addition, tallies of social conditions and activities must prove reliable and valid. Responsibility for giving assurance of such qualities of measuring instruments falls on their employers, not on their critics.

Unfortunately, "reliability" and "validity" are frequently claimed for social scientists' figures without their consumers having been told which types of these guarantees, if any, are offered.

Given the recent embarrassments of governments and corporations by their flexible figures and outright deceits, journalists have concocted a new term for lying; it's called "spin."

What follows is the ancient Roman advice: *Caveat emptor.* The warning to know what you're buying applies to modern consumers of public numbers. Citizens who are prone to trust official statistics are reminded that everything begins with "the village watchman."

No statistic is worth more than the procedure by which events have been observed, classified, and transformed into numbers.

This statement of value refers to "contribution to knowledge." It does not deny the *political utility* of arcane statistics.

Scholars who claim the authority of social scientist are "too often" remiss in fulfilling their duties. Of the several sources of their deficiency, succeeding chapters attend to their having to work with "social facts," "vicarious observations," and contentious units.

Their competence is also bounded by their assumption of an impoverished notion of causation, and by their semi-aware acceptance of a rationalist political philosophy.

5

Units and Correlates

"Everything correlates with everything."
—Statisticians' Maxim

Association as Causation

Chapter 2 began our consideration of the possibility of a science of social activities. It showed that ordinary language makes observation and measurement of human action contestable. These difficulties are elaborated in this and succeeding chapters.

Here we note that social scientists search for causes principally by calculating and interpreting co-relationships. They try to measure what-goes-with-what as a potential sign of what-causes-what. Tallies of association—and there are several—constitute the most popular tool used by would-be scientists of the social. Common use promotes misuse.

In adopting the instruments of correlation, we immediately confront the statisticians' suggestion cited above. To illustrate the actuality of this possibility, economist George Marshall once calculated an association between annual death rates in the state of Hyderabad, India, from 1911 to 1919, with annual membership in the International (solely American) Association of Machinists from 1912 to 1920. Marshall discovered an unusually close relationship, a product-moment coefficient of +.86.[1]

This is a higher degree of association than most of the vast mass of presumed connections produced by social scientists. Fortunately, no one has bothered to argue that death rates in a faraway place somehow cause membership to vary in a labor union in the United States one year later.

More recently, Douglas Mould repeated the Marshall exercise relating a different set of events. He calculated the association between tallies of rape in the United States and variations in membership in the Southern Baptist Church and found a correlation of +.96! Mould correctly notes that "the incidence of rape will correlate positively with any variable that also evidences an increase over the same time period."[2]

If not everything correlates with anything, at least so much in the worlds of human action can be found to be "associated" that psychologists have dubbed the phenomenon "the crud factor." *Viz.*, Jerry Bishop reports studies of "risk factors" associated with coronary heart disease that yield 280 such correlates, including poor dental health and *abstention* from alcohol.[3]

In addition to these warnings, one should note that what are correlated in the behavioral studies are always *measures* of the activities of concern. And these are usually "indicators" that stand at some observational and recording "distance" from actual events.

The enormous number of conceivable, but silly, correlations that can be found between facts moves instructors to caution beginning students that "correlation does not prove causation." However, this wisdom is commonly forgotten as teachers themselves use causal language to interpret the correlations they report.

Social scientists repeatedly demonstrate this leap in logic. They do so by their common reference to a selected variable in a correlation matrix with such phrases as "influenced by," "the result of," "as a consequence," and so on, when all that is displayed and known is a correlate—a number representing a degree of associated change as recorded by a mathematical manipulation. Their graphs contribute to this delusive work when they refer to variables on the x-axis (abscissa) and y-axis (ordinate) as "independent" and "dependent," respectively. Such labeling begs the question. It assumes what needs to be known. These terms suggest more than "vary together in some degree." Implicitly, but rarely explicitly, such titles connote, "we can change the one by moving the other to the degree indicated and as measured in a particular way within a local context."

This linguistic trap is reinforced by our daily immersion in correlations. Some of these cannot be known, but are believed. This is especially the case with the great quantity of connections that human beings assure us were revealed to them or their Great Teachers by supernatural agencies.

Such promised associations are rife in folk knowledge. Confidence in their veracity is expressed in the numerous charms, costumes, gestures, and practices designed to bring luck and ward off evil. The latter superstitions— guarding against harm—are formally titled "apotropaic." One can observe their persistent popularity by attending to televised news and, particularly, its sporting events.

And then there are those myriad relationships that are conceivably empirical, but that prove false when tested. Some of these false beliefs have ancient lineage to which authority is added with formulas and charts. Their alleged connections gain credence by promising "scientific" guidance, and, in "enlightened" lands, they are widely disseminated and consumed. Even some prominent world leaders and their influential wives have been (are?) avid consumers. Astrology remains popular among long-schooled people.

Judgment

Reading social science to gain knowledge calls into play that fine balancing act among feeling, imagining, and thinking with symbols and evidence known as "judgment." The balance is always tentative, and vulnerable to the passions. However, reading to comfort preconception is easy.

Earlier pages describe difficulties in defining the actions and circumstances that concern us. To calculate correlations among records of these events/situations assumes, at minimum, that the numbers being manipulated accurately represent these actions/conditions. This means, in turn, that the objects of interest must have been well defined, a requirement that is easier to satisfy in the affectionately neutral physical sciences than in the morally saturated studies of human conduct.

But even if this difficult minimum were satisfied, other obstacles slow the advance of knowledge of social activities. Some of these impediments arise as inquirers invent and employ an impressive array of mathematical tools with which to assay causes from correlates.

To this pursuit, present purpose adds four hurdles, incumbent on those previously described. These obstacles lie in the logical assumptions underwriting correlational techniques, the choice of units to be correlated, deficits in counting "results,"[4] and the winnowing of research by "peers" who are themselves contaminated by ethico-political interest.

We shall be left with the necessity of "sound judgment," an ideal toward which we strive with limited success.

Shapes of Relationships

> *"Mathematics deals exclusively with the relations of concepts to each other without consideration of their relation to experience."*
> *—Albert Einstein[5]*

No mathematical procedure operates free of assumption. If we are to judge what social scientists report to us about their correlations—presumed to demonstrate causation—we need to understand the assumptions involved in their manipulation of numbers.

Computer-power with its disks of "programs" for transforming numbers into relationships, allows students to ignore, if they ever knew, the premises underlying their programs' devices.

This is not a statistics textbook, so I describe only some of these assumptions, sufficient to local purpose. These "basics" are important because they are supposed to reflect how the world "really" works, and because they are frequently neglected by professionals and their publics.

Variation: In the first place, there would be no point in calculating how much one thing, X, is associated with something else, Y, if neither of these measured events/conditions varied.

If everyone were equally brilliant or equally rich, there would be nothing to co-relate between IQ and wealth. Similarly, it is useless to quarrel about what "predicts" school "achievement" when the latter is measured by school grades, and school grades are inflated so that they don't vary much among students. Thus no pre-college "aptitude" test can be expected to forecast college grade-point average if everyone is deemed "excellent." (One of my former university colleagues gave all registrants in his classes "A's." Another allowed his attendants to grade themselves. Enrollees in these classes cannot be called "students" because they didn't have to learn anything.)

Second, and as part of the requirement of variation, *restricting the range* of difference reduces the likely degree of association to be found. So, too, does *limiting the number of "data points,"* that is, the number of cases/instances being co-related. For example, it is difficult to assess the risks of new surgical procedures if both the range of results observed and the number of operations evaluated are limited.[6]

Configuration: Third, social scientists "too often" neglect, and don't report, *the shapes of the distributions* of the quantities they test for correlation. Shapes matter. The mathematical tools employed to discern association assume that *particular forms* exist in the distributions of the units that have been measured. These are not known prior to data-collection, and they have to be inspected before applying a mathematical manipulation.

As the preceding chapter notes, we conceive of different patterns in the associations from which we derive causal inference. Reality is not necessarily linear, as though connections occurred in a straight line. Not all co-relationships accord with the popular Pearsonian assumption that events are so ordered. If they were, it would mean that increases (or decreases) in units of X are accompanied by proportional increases (or decreases) in units of Y. But Nature probably portrays a host of different and changing relationships, as Hayward Alker, Jr., notes,

> The simplest form of mechanistic assumption we can make about human behavior is that it obeys linear additive determinative relationships—in fact, we assume this, at least approximately, every time we calculate a product moment correlation coefficient and impute to it causal significance. Much more closely corresponding to the insights of biological and cybernetically oriented theorists is the idea of contextually contingent determinative relationships which themselves may evolve or devolve through time.[7]

Partial Remedy: A prudent, but less than certain, remedy is available. Data should be examined not only for quality, as Chapters Six through Eight recommend. They should also be represented visually.

Independently of one another, William Cleveland and Edward Tufte have shown how some kinds of visual display can illuminate relationships more accurately than mathematical calculations of association among numbers.[8] These images can be heuristic—suggesting causal connections—as well as confirmatory, lending evidence to inference.

Nevertheless, judgment remains necessary, and is not to be displaced by "automatic," computer-driven manipulation of numbers, with or without charts and graphs. We are reminded that we can lie with maps.[9] Thus Tufte concludes one of his exercises in visual depiction of correlation with this warning:

> There are right ways and wrong ways to show data; there are displays that reveal the truth and displays that do not.[10]

In Sum: Patterns of relationships are not necessarily simple or uniform. For example, configurations can be curvilinear, as in a parabola, or sinuous, with bulges and contractions appearing throughout the ranges of X and Y.

Cascades occur—plateaus where no association appears—followed by leaps up or down in either variable, to speak, for the moment, of bivariate correlation.

"Dosage effects" illustrate this shape. They signify that *thresholds of efficacy* pertain—a reality commonly ignored by social scientists when they prescribe policies from modest correlations.

These possibilities mean that no mathematical manipulation of numbers, nor any representation of numbers in diagrams and scatterplots, excuses us from using our heads. Finding causes by calculating degrees of association demands, at minimum, assurance of the *quality of content* of measures being correlated and of the *integrity of the patterns* revealed by them.

"Quality of content" refers, again, to the validity of measures (ch. 4). It asks about the accuracy with which numbers represent the quantities of objects, conditions, and actions counted and graded.

However, accurate measurement can be made of irrelevant things and events. Indeed, economist Peter Bauer criticizes his colleagues for allowing their devotion to mathematics—"econometrics"—to contribute to their

> disregard or neglect of evident reality. Their use [of mathematics] has led to unwarranted concentration in economics on variables tractable to formal analysis. As a corollary, it has led to the neglect of influences which, even when highly pertinent, are not amenable to such treatment. Similarly, it has encouraged confusion between the significant...and the quantifiable (often only spuriously quantifiable)....[11]

To repeat, the "relevance" of procedures of data manipulation is to be judged by the purpose of inquiry: What "satisfaction" does one seek from knowing?

If the purpose of a social science is to develop knowledge that yields improvement in temporal, instrumental prediction (TIP), then its practitioners have to be clear not only about the assumptions underlying their mathematics, but also about what is to be regarded as a "unit."

Units

> "Social statistics promised...methods that, under explicit and often plausible assumptions, but not in every circumstance, converge to the truth..."
>
> —Clark Glymour[12]

All measuring devices count units of something (ch. 4). Social statistics sometimes tally individual persons and their actions as units, but it is their nature also to move beyond individuals and to enumerate collections of individuals as constituting *unitary* categories.

Social categories are, of course, social facts; they are multiply conceived (ch. 7). But whenever we count kinds of people and their activities, we assign *unity*, of some sort, to such abstract aggregates.

In two of its definitions of "unit," *The Oxford English Dictionary* makes the point:

1.a. *Math.* A single magnitude or number regarded as an undivided whole and the ultimate basis of all numbers, *spec.* in *Arithmetic*, the least whole number, the numeral 'one', represented by the figure 1.

2.a. A single individual or thing, regarded as a member of a group or number of things or individuals, or discriminated from these as having a separate existence; one of the separate parts or members of which a complex whole or aggregate is composed or into which it may be analysed.*

In these definitions, the phrase "regarded as" points to difficulties in the measurement of social facts. One difficulty concerns the justification of aggregation, and it becomes more acute as we move conceptually "up" the abstraction ladder and put "cognitive distance" between what is phrased as concept and what can be reliably observed as its exemplars.

This trouble raises at least these questions: When are aggregates units? How best can we use numbers representing collections? What errors of inference can mislead us as we move measurably "up and down" the abstraction ladder?

---

*Reproduced by permission of The Oxford University Press from *The Oxford English Dictionary* (2nd edition).

How Unitary are Social Aggregates?

We have little trouble *perceiving* human beings as singular objects, even though we are bundles of organs, and organs are collections of cells. But we are obviously social, dependent on others for survival at the same time as we remain perceptible singulars.

However, scholars take the fact that we are social as ground for studying human action, not merely as a linear product of discrete individuals, but also as an *emergent consequence* of the behaviors of numbers of persons— numbers that range from twosomes to multitudes.

More than that, many of these conceptual groupings involve "high-level" abstraction. That is, they refer to presumed collective entities "joined" by something they exhibit in common that is not shared with other human clusters.

These aggregates are believed to generate social relations—regular ways of behaving—that are *not* the product of individual intention. Such supra-individual effects are assumed to organize themselves as units, open to discernment and measurement by especially disciplined students. This kind of study is the chosen work of some biologists and historians and of an unknown portion of economists, ethnographers, political scientists, social psychologists, and sociologists.

These occupations have their troubles, some of which are the object of this book. Among these troubles is the fact that we can, and do, *describe* human action as occurring among units of varied size and degree of abstraction.

Thus we speak not merely of individuals, but also of cohabitants and married couples, of teams that range from doubles partners to forty-man football squads, of platoons and brigades, and on to such grand "units" (?) as nations and civilizations.[13] Stock market prices are also used as units, the consequence of many anonymous persons' bids.

Quarrels about the use of such gatherings concern at least these questions: How clear are the boundaries of each nominated unit? How unitary are these composites and by what criteria? How, if at all, can their quality be measured?

These issues are of no moment when we are not employing such collections to construct a science of conduct. They become worrisome when we try to use such variously conceived "wholes" as *actors* in events assumed subject to causal analysis:

- "Why did Team-Alpha win and Team-Beta lose?"
- "Why did the British and Prussians beat the French at Waterloo?"
- "Why did the American economy grow, 1920-2000, while the Russian economy faltered?"

"Why?" questions of this nature ask for causes, and our examples illustrate how they are posed at different "levels" of aggregation and abstraction.

Levels

The idea of "level" is employed to refer to two different ways of thinking about collections of objects and persons and their actions: "Level of aggregation" and "level of abstraction."

Level of aggregation refers to quantity. In the social studies, the notion of "level" points to the number of "things"—persons or their enumerated conditions and activities—*considered to be sufficiently of one kind*—a "unit"—to permit assigning a single, descriptively useful number to each category of collective.

Levels of abstraction can be roughly classified, but without assigning numbers to them. This concept of "level" defies measurement. It refers to "conceptual distance" between an abstract name for a category and anything observable as its exemplar.

For example, the idea of "national spirit" is more abstract than the notion of "the Blasters" hockey team, and both are more abstract than "James Jones."

The "national spirit" is an abstraction at such a high level as to move it beyond the assignment of numbers. By contrast, "The Blasters" can be counted and their players named, but they change personnel more easily and frequently than "James Jones" changes his "selves."[14]

Nevertheless, *within* any conceptualized strata—whether aggregates of identifiable individuals or airy abstractions—researchers who would measure with these concepts assume that their tallies of persons, or populations, or activities constitute reliably observed units. *Without discernible units, no measurement* (ch. 4).

Example: The U. S. Census Bureau publishes figures on the distribution of annual "income" in the population. What, then, shall count as "income" and as an "income unit?"

The Bureau reports its numbers as relationships between the proportions of the total population, classified as fifths (quintiles), and the proportion of the total "pre-tax money income" received by each of these fifths. According to the Bureau's accounting for 1997, the lowest quintile earned only 3.6 percent of such "income" while the highest quintile took home 49 percent of such receipts.[15]

("Money-income," of course, does not represent non-cash income and other resources received by individuals and families each year, nor does it count wealth possessed. In addition, this tally does not include differences in hours worked nor does it discount for the equalizing effects of taxes.)

But, apropos of our current concern, the Bureau defines its unit as "households." This category contains varying numbers of *individuals* who work. The result is that quintiles of households do *not* represent equal proportions of income-earners. Thus, while the poorest quintile of households contains about 15 percent of wage-earners, the richest quintile represents about 24 percent of such workers.[16]

Correcting for undercounts of the numbers of workers, and for inadequate tallies of income and taxes, the bureau's publicized "gap" between top and bottom quintiles of nearly 14 to 1 reduces to a ratio of about 4 to 1. Furthermore, when "the fact that working-age adults in the top quintile work almost twice as many hours, on average, as those in the bottom quintile," the "income-distance" between top and bottom quintiles reduces to about 3 to 1.[17]

From these facts, we draw a twofold lesson: Not only does counting different units "of the same thing" matter, but also the figures that the news media report about American "income inequality" are wide of the mark.

Fallacies: We obtain different pictures of the distribution of material wealth when we count wages rather than all income, and when we count aggregates of persons as income-units rather than individuals as units.

Such alarming differences point to two common fallacies that occur when we uncritically assume that the characteristics of individuals apply to the characteristics of the clusters into which *we group them*, and vice versa.

The first error is called *the fallacy of composition*. It is the mistake of assuming that what is true of the individual components of a collection must be true of the aggregate. It is as if, when each individual soldier is strong, the army of which he is part must also be strong.

The converse error is called *the fallacy of division*. It is the mistake of assuming that what is true of a cluster of persons must apply to each "member" of that gathering.

These fallacies intrude upon ways in which social scientists interpret their correlations. A prime mistake has been termed "the ecological fallacy," but it is more accurately labeled "the aggregative error."

The Aggregative Error: Abbreviated Statistics

The aggregative error is the mistake of assuming that numbers that *summarize* activities or conditions in collections of people—numbers such as averages and proportions—necessarily yield correlations that accurately describe what-goes-with-what among individuals in those populations.

The error is produced by the use of *single numerals* to represent behaviors or situations descriptive of kinds of people. Such numbers tell us something about a nominated population, but in abbreviated fashion. For example, an average, in its arithmetic sense, reports, with a single cipher, the "central tendency" of activity-X within a selected group.

Such abbreviated statistics abstract. They summarize much with little. They *omit information* about the components of the aggregates described by one number. As philosopher Simon Blackburn reminds us, "the average person has one testicle and one breast."[18]

Employing such summarizing statistics is common, and it is satisfactory as long as we are clear about how we are using such "shorthand" numerals. Purpose determines appropriate use.

For example, attempts to estimate probabilities *rationally* rest on tallies of collections of events, actions, or categories of people. There is no "probability" of a unique event (ch. 6). Thus, numbers descriptive of aggregates can be aids to foresight and are required for the reasoned judgment of risks in all domains of human activity.

However, trouble develops when we try to locate the causes of kinds of activities *generated by, or characteristic of, individuals* by calculating degrees of association between abbreviated statistics that skimpily describe the clusters into which we have subsumed them.

This is the basis of the aggregative error. It arises, in part, because governments and other agencies typically report their "findings" with summarizing numbers. But the mistake is also stimulated by recognition that human action, like much mammalian behavior, occurs in groups. ("Aggregate," from the Latin, *grex* = "flock")

This observation leads readily to the assumption that individuals are less important than the social and geographic habitats in which they form, develop, and continue to act—a premise that underwrites a "sociology."

About the time that Auguste Comte (1798-1857) was inventing the term "sociology," and promoting it as Queen of the Sciences, the German philosopher-biologist Ernst Haeckel (1834-1919) conceived the idea of "ecology," a term he used to refer to the study of how physical and social environments influence the behavior of organisms.[19]

American sociologists picked up Haeckel's reasonable hypothesis and his terminology, and an extensive literature grew, descriptive of the activities of large congregations of humans who live in degrees and kinds of proximity— the so-called "ecological niche."[20]

But we run into difficulty when we search for causal patterns in human action by describing conditions or activities within collectives with *single numbers*, and then calculate correlations with such compressed representations among aggregates of varying size.

Since at least the early 1930s, we have known that the degree and direction of association between variables can change when information about the same phenomena are differently grouped and expressed by summarizing statistics. Since then, many mathematically inclined scholars have noted the likelihood of this confusion and how it arises.[21]

However, American sociologist William Robinson gave this misleading use of statistics its clearest demonstration with his seminal paper on what he called "the ecological fallacy."[22] Robinson adopted this title from Haeckel because his units were populations defined by area. However, "ecology" is

now a term confused with other issues and, for current purpose, is best re-
placed with more pointed terminology.

The argument concerns, again, what should be regarded as a unit. It becomes important as we note what happens to measurement when human conditions or actions are represented with numbers that *abstract* from aggregates
of different sizes. Given continuing misrepresentation of this deceptive use
of numbers, Robinson's demonstration merits summary.

Robinson showed that relationships calculated with numbers representing proportions or averages of behaviors in collections of persons do *not*
necessarily hold when correlations of the same behaviors are computed among
individuals in those clusters.

Moreover, the size of the collection of persons affects the size of the correlations calculated. In general, the larger the population from which a summarizing figure is extracted, the higher the computed correlation, and the further
that calculation is from the truth about what-goes-with-what among individuals.

Illustratively, Robinson demonstrated that the percentage of black persons in the U. S. Census Bureau's nine geographic divisions, 1930, correlated
+.946 with the percentage of illiterate individuals in those areas. But when he
reduced the size of the aggregate from nine geographic zones to the then
forty-eight states, the aggregated correlation fell to +.773. And, most important, a recalculation of the association *among individuals* in the same populations yielded an association of only +.203, a correlation about *one-fifth* the
size of the computation aggregated by census area.

In an additional demonstration, Robinson tested the hypothesis that Americans born in foreign countries were less literate than native Americans. In this
test, the correlation obtained among individuals *reversed* the sign of the
association found among aggregates.

Computing the association between the proportions of foreign-born persons and rates of illiteracy for the Census Bureau's nine geographic areas
yielded a negative correlation of -.619. Such an association suggests that
foreign-born Americans were *more literate* than native citizens..

When Robinson reduced the size of aggregates to states, the negative
association remained, but was lowered to -.526. However, when he calculated
the association between foreign birth and illiteracy individual-by-individual,
the sign of the relationship was reversed to a slightly positive +.118.

Error

Laypersons, including jurists and legislators, are largely ignorant of the
aggregative error, and, when told of it, have difficulty understanding how it
can occur. "If," they ask (often in anger), "areas containing larger proportions
of Alphas exhibit more Y, on average, than areas with larger proportions of
Betas, doesn't that mean that Alphas do more Y than Betas?"

The answer is: Theoretically, it's possible. Actually, computing correlations between averages or proportions usually draws a false picture of which *individuals*, in what conditions, displaying what dispositions, do more and less of what. Moreover, the picture is likely to be more incorrect the larger the aggregates that are compared and the less frequent the behavior among them.

For example, concerning research on the consistency with which individual personalities behave in different situations, Seymour Epstein writes,

> One can obtain any amount of consistency with sufficient aggregation, given some consistency to begin with...Where initial correlations are high, a relatively small amount of aggregation can produce very high correlations.[23]

Why? Abbreviated measures provide a partial picture rather than a large-screen, high-resolution photograph. They show nothing of the range and distribution of conditions-activities within populations. Correlations calculated from such information-poor data do not indicate which individuals in those aggregates, and how many of them, distinguished by what attributes, do how much of what interests us.

Uses of Multitudes

Our exercise with aggregates is *not* to be interpreted as denying the value of measures of multitudes. For some purposes, such studies are not just useful; they are required.

For example, all judgment of the risks of activities, including legislation, requires comparison among collectives that describe gatherings of persons, conditions, and/or actions. In this employment of aggregates, the issue concerns the size and nature of the base of rates (ch. 6).

But there are other satisfactions in attending to multitudes of things and events. Simply to know that the population of an area called "China" contains more than one billion persons is interesting on its own. And so are stories that describe smaller clusters of human beings: husbands and wives, tribes and nations. Biographies of individuals are also pleasurable in themselves, although there are times when we extract cautionary advice from them.

Then, too, we study collections of individuals to ascertain how their different *modes of organization* affect particular "outcomes." We do this, for example, in evaluating the activities of work teams and sports teams, armies and economies.

For some inquiries, it is appropriate to work with data descriptive only of aggregates. For example, macro-economics poses questions about the connections between the manufacture of money and credit, prices, and the production of wealth. Answers to such queries do not require inspection of the individuals who constitute the workers in such systems.

Choosing Units: Of the many conceivable ways of defining units, choice of appropriate category depends on the question asked of research.

For example, what we believe about the conduct of persons deemed to differ as "social classes"—defined by their incomes, vocations, and levels of skill and schooling—can vary, depending on whether we tally the behavior of individuals who "possess" these "class characteristics" or work with numbers abstracted from collections of persons.

Thus Charles Murray's studies of "the underclass" in Britain and the United States reveal that figures that *summarize* behaviors in congregations differ from those calculated among individuals within those populations.

Concerning one marker of difference between "social classes"—reproductive practice as gauged by births-out-of-wedlock—Murray writes,

> [A] gap between low-skilled working-class and upper-middle-class *individuals*...is already much greater than the gap between lower-class and upper-middle-class *communities*...the relationship between socioeconomic class and illegitimacy becomes stronger as the focus shifts from communities to the individual.[24]

Here Murray shows the obverse of Robinson's finding. Murray reports a connection that is *stronger among individuals* than is revealed with abbreviated statistics from collectives. It does so because the congregations employed as units contain mixed "kinds of persons." They are not actually "communities."

However, the research by both Robinson and Murray indicates that *information is lost* as we move from tallies of actions among individuals to calculation of correlations between averages or proportions among clusters of persons.

A study in a different domain of action-condition illuminates the nature of the aggregative error. This example points to the necessity of appropriate conception of causal location *prior* to inquiry.

Who or what develops lung cancer? In a report that seeks to vindicate research with pooled data, Robert Zajonc and Patricia Mullaly describe studies that presumably find associations among the behaviors of aggregates *not* discerned by studies of the individuals who comprise them. As an important illustration of this phenomenon, these psychologists state,

> Smoking, too, shows strong consequence for lung cancer when analyzed in the aggregate but shows little when individually distributed chances of lung cancer are calculated for smokers and nonsmokers.[25]

Contrary to Zajonc and Mullaly, I've seen no research that reveals a higher correlation between smoking tobacco and lung cancer when one compares smokers and nonsmokers in cohorts than that which is reported from comparisons among individuals.[26]

However, if contrary to available evidence, Zajonc and Mullaly were correct, it would provoke a puzzle: "Who or what suffers cancers of the lungs, proportions or persons?"

To speak of proportions as "having" disease is to speak metaphorically. Only individuals have lungs.

Meaning: If we were to pool data on nonsmoking, smoking by degree and duration of inhalation, and the incidence of lung cancer from which *abbreviated statistics* were extracted, and if such correlated numbers were to indicate closer connections than is found with individual-level data, then we should expect, from previous experience with grouped information, that as cohorts of kinds of smokers and nonsmokers increase in size, the correlations between smoking and lung cancer increase. In such case, the aggregative error is probably operative.

If the aggregative error were at work, it would mean that investigators had been fooled by their manipulation of numbers. But, in addition, it is always possible that more than one road leads to any terminus in a career—vocational, marital, criminal, or medical. The issue again is: "What's the question? What do we wish to find out?"

As concerns the tobacco-cancer question, we want to know how the probability of developing lung cancer changes with increase in degrees and duration of smoke-inhalation, holding constant other possible causes of this disease. We know how to calculate changes in the odds of events, conditional upon the presence or absence of other behaviors-circumstances.[27]

To ascertain the likelihood of contracting this malignancy, and after examining the hints provided by epidemiology (aggregated data), what is required is information about individual careers.

More Hurdles: In addition to the many impediments to a science of the social thus far described, two more obstacles intrude. Both are erected by "prejudice," where this pejorative term applies to pre-judgment, unfairly made and held. In a socio-psychological sense, prejudice refers to a preconception that is both inaccurate and resistant to change with information. It is ignorant pre-judgment.

Prejudice is, of course, a frailty to which all of us are vulnerable, and the more so as we "take sides" in our inquiries of human action. Two origins of prejudiced information include the effects of prejudice on observation and publication.

Prejudice I: Observational

> "Deep-seated preferences cannot be argued
> about—you cannot argue a man into liking a
> glass of beer."
>
> —Oliver Wendell Holmes, Jr.[28]

We have known for a long time that preconception affects perception.[29] Expectancies affect nice people with good intentions as they do wicked people with evil intentions. The popular idea that "prejudice" is only malevolent is incorrect. One can be prejudiced *for* as well as *against*, and benevolence also stimulates bias.

If a "bigot" is a person whose opinions are obdurate, impervious to reason, then there is bigotry for goodness' sake as well as for service to evil. Indeed, in the social studies it is a lively hypothesis that good-hearted intention exceeds by orders of magnitude mean-spirited attitude in distortion of evidence.[30]

I offer this possibility as a corrective hypothesis, subject to empirical test. But regardless of the balance between distortion by morally approved observers and morally disreputable investigators, a science attempts to counteract the known, misleading effects of preconception. The story about the measurement of "racial crania" told in the preceding chapter is but one of many examples.

Implication: Scientists have long recognized the tug of anticipation upon observation. It is a distortion that does not dissipate with awareness of one's preferences. The "pull" is subtle.

Against the common disposition to observe results favorable to our preconceptions, scientists employ several remedies. One requires multiple replication of tests of hypotheses performed with different modes of observation. Another procedure requires double- and triple-blind counting, where possible (cf. pp. 69-71).

In addition, a lesson from Chapter Four merits repetition: The pervasive effects of prejudice upon observation and recording justify the demand that interested parties *not* assess their own work. Administrators of meliorist programs are *not* to count the results of their projects; political advocates are *not* to measure the "outcomes" of their policies.

Apropos of the need for independent assessment and repeated measurement, a seventeen-month investigation of New York City public schools discovered that, in thirty-two schools, teachers had taught their students to cheat on standardized tests. In some cases teachers themselves completed the examinations.[31]

Science requires *disinterested* auditing, judging, counting, and other forms of evaluation. If it is difficult or impossible for social studies to meet this requirement, we have yet another reason for drawing tighter the boundaries of social scientists' competence.

Prejudice does not end at the observational level; it also intrudes upon dissemination of information.

Prejudice II: Editorial

Editors of scientific journals have the daunting job of sifting well-conducted studies from the mountains of documents that cross their desks. For example, Richard Horton, editor of the British medical journal, the *Lancet*, reports that his office receives annually more than 6,000 papers of which it publishes only about 400.[32]

In doing their work, editors rely on "peer-reviewers." But both editors and the experts they select to assess submissions are frequently motivated by more than disinterested science.

Horton illuminates this prejudicial possibility. Apropos of current debate about the health hazards of genetically modified food, Horton writes,

> Peer review can only elicit comments about what is written—the importance of the question being posed, the description of the study's design, execution and analysis, and the scientists' interpretation of what they have found. It can say nothing about the validity or "authenticity" of the experimental findings themselves. Indeed, peer review is often prejudiced, unjust, incomplete, sycophantic, insulting, ignorant, foolish, and wrong....
>
> Peer review...is simply a way to collect opinions from experts in the field. Peer review tells us about the acceptability, not the credibility, of a new finding.
>
> Still, it remains the best method editors have for filtering the enormous amount of research they receive.[33]

Insofar as Horton accurately describes the sometimes-biased process of winnowing research in such science-based disciplines as anatomy, biology, chemistry, cytology, neurology, and physiology, we should expect a much stronger pull of prejudice in the heavily moralized and politicized social studies.

Indeed, social-scientific bias is apparent. When ethico-political attitudes are gauged repeatedly, and by different kinds of measures such as party affiliation, voting record, publication, and self-identification, professors of the humanities and social studies display a consistent leaning to the Left. In this they are joined by journalists and disseminators of opinion via the arts. Only economists show a semblance of balance among ideologies, with an approximate 3:1 split, Left v. Right.[34]

(As employed here, "Left" refers to preference for more centralized power to direct more aspects of individuals' lives. My usage ignores, for the moment, the many other nuances of ethico-political allegiance.)

In brief, vocationally employed students of social life do not represent the full spectrum of moral and political sentiment to be found among their colleagues or the citizens who pay their way.[35] Given editorial and peer-prejudice, this means that some unknown quantity of contra-convenient information does not appear in major journals of the social sciences.[36]

Given the difficulties of counting and correlating much that interests us, scholars have recommended that we reason with probabilities rather than certainties. Chapter 6 describes the nature of different uses of this concept.

6

Probabilities

Certainties?

We entertain arguments about whether the sun will rise tomorrow only
when we have time to talk to philosophers. Qualifying Einstein, most of us
believe it is certain that Earth revolves around Sun with measurable regularity.[2]

We also know some things about ourselves with certainty. We know that
we have been born, and that, as we read and write, we exist. We are also sure
that we will die.

But at the sub-atomic level, physicists assure us that we can know events
only as probabilities.[3] Similarly, generations of inquirers who have become
statisticians tell us that, with the exception of such mortal certainties as noted
above, our attempted rules of human action are best regarded with degrees of
probability rather than with certainty.

Social scientists have taken this advice. Today the practice of assigning
numbers to our activities, and to those of other animals, is widespread, and so
normal we scarcely notice it. With this practice, we propose empirical hypotheses to be tested with information drawn from the past—recent or at
various degrees of temporal distance—and organized with several types of
mathematics.

In doing this work, we recognize that we engage daily in the task of estimating the likelihood that certain events will, or will not, occur, and with or
without our doing some particular thing. (Forecast is *not* temporal-instrumental prediction—TIP, ch. 3.) It is relevant, then, to consider varieties of
probability, with our attention directed to those versions that affect social
scientists' efforts to reduce the uncertainties of their promissory propositions.

However, description of kinds of probabilities, and their values and deficiencies, does not allow us to escape the philosopher's web. We reason probabilistically on the basis of contestable assumptions.

Our Limitations or Nature's Disorderly Behavior?

"Probability" is a concept, a human product. Like all symbolic messengers, it has evolved so that we now possess more than one idea of "the chances that...."

Some scholars contend that competing concepts of probability involve different realms of discourse—the *ontological* and the *epistemological*. On the ontological issue, debates concern what *exists* and what *must be*. On the epistemological issue, quarrels persist about what we can *know* and how we can *know* it.

In these long-running debates, a tangle of questions ensnares us:

- Is judgment difficult because of limitations of the human brain and its neural attachments, or
- because of the opacity of Nature, at least in some of its "departments," or
- because Nature "really is" more disorderly than we wish it to be, or
- because the languages with which we think, including mathematics, may not accurately represent Nature, or
- because of some awkward mixtures of these impediments, varying with the questions we ask?

Attitudes toward these intertwined queries affect how we use the several conceptions of probability. They also affect whether, and how, we invoke the related notions of accident, fate and fortune, luck and chance (ch. 10).

More than these questions disturb our inquiries. The knowledge-enterprise rests on assumptions, and assigning probabilities is no exception. We estimate the likelihood of various kinds of events with at least these suppositions:

- that empirical inference is possible,
- that Nature is at least somewhat orderly,
- that probabilities are contingent,
- that no one idea of probability is appropriate for every occasion,
- that, in its ideal form, no concept of probability is attained in practice,
- that the purpose of inquiry defines appropriate use of a concept of probability, and
- that judgment is never a matter of mathematics alone.

Following pages amplify these assumptions. They tell us that rationality is circumscribed.

Assumptions

1. Empirical Inference is Possible

All of us infer. This statement includes other animals and even organisms without brains. Neurophysiologies do the work. Perceptual-motor systems sense, and respond to, signals from external worlds *as if* they indicated that some kinds of events were in the making and likely to occur.

Signs serve as *portents*. Predators, including *Homo sapiens*, have to know how to "read" the messages.

We also infer in reverse, from current signals to past events. We "read" *traces*.

Of course, *Homo sapiens*, with its ability to abstract and symbolize, performs the tasks of inference over greater spans of time—past and future—and over larger quantities of events than other creatures. And we may be as accurate in interpreting traces as we are in employing portents to guide us.

The practice of conceiving probabilities, and differentially attributing them, is an attempt to formalize reasoning that extends what is perceptible into what is conceivable. We do this over varying periods of time, of course, and with application to a huge inventory of conceptualized kinds of activities.

In an attempt to discern "what happened," we infer, deduce, reconstruct, guess with information of varied quality, based on our own and others' readings of traces. This is historians' work, but it is also the job of detectives and some kinds of lawyers, and of medical and engineering diagnosticians.

Astronomers infer what is likely "to be there" from light that their instruments record, and that was emitted from stars zillions of years ago. Astronomers infer from what they have seen to what Vera Rubin says:

> [W]e know must be there. Based on 50 years of accumulated observations of the motion of galaxies and the expansion of the universe, most astronomers believe that as much as 90 percent of the stuff constituting the universe may be objects or particles that cannot be seen.[4]

We also readily construct and interpret portents in the never-ending effort to guess what might happen among events we can, and cannot, control.

While such inferential work seems obvious, philosophers are rightly critical of attempts to reason from the here-and-now backwards and forwards. Given the time and money spent on gazing into futures, philosophers are particularly critical of portent reading. They call this *the problem of induction*.

Their originating authority is the Scottish philosopher David Hume (1711-1776) who argues that futuristic induction cannot be *logically* justified. Nevertheless, and happily for our enterprise, philosophers who teach this doctrine do not practice it. Hume himself joins the rest of us in assuming that experience warrants some degree of confidence in reasoning from pasts to futures. For example, in his *A Treatise of Human Nature*, 1739-1741, he writes:

Generally speaking, the errors of religion are dangerous; those in philosophy only ridiculous.[5]

Of course, the word "dangerous" makes a prediction. This is an activity that Hume's logic will not allow, but that his experience validates.

To repeat, our nervous systems infer. They do so most accurately, and fortunately, at near distance and through brief periods. But our thoughtful equipment goes beyond such boundaries, and we regularly estimate what has happened, and what is likely to happen, at greater ranges in time and space from our current situations. Induction is both practiced and justified, and philosophers provide us with several ways of doing this work.[6]

What is at issue among would-be scientists of the social, and indeed among all persons with the time and interest to consider how we reason, is the accuracy of our expectations and the relative utilities of different ways of improving judgment. (ch. 3). Inductive practice need not assume that the future will always be like the past—if we reason with *conditional* probabilities and *ranges* of likelihood. The limits of our experience, and the fragility of our reasoning from what we have experienced to what is likely to happen, suggest prudence in theory building. This returns us to additional assumptions underlying kinds of probabilities.

2. Nature is at Least Somewhat Orderly

> *"There's always the unexpected, isn't there?"*
> *—Major Warden[7]*

Mathematician-electrical engineer Petr Beckmann interprets the assumption of an orderly Nature to mean that "under exactly the same circumstances, the same event will happen."[8]

Without this assumption, Beckmann believes, scientific research is futile.

However, some scholars read Beckmann's interpretation to signify that each kind of event must have the same kind of cause. This goes beyond what Beckmann says. It reverses the direction of attention—from present-to-future to from present-to-past.

Beckmann doesn't know, and doesn't say, whether the "same event" can be differently caused. Nor does his premise allow the popular mistranslation, "The future will be like the past."

Preceding chapters, and pages to follow, ask how well these linked assumptions about "order" apply to human action. With corrections of mistranslations of Beckmann's statement and of others' assumed regularities, my argument is that there can be "many roads" to apparently similar social events.

This thesis discomforts those journalists and politicians who believe there must be a singular explanation of their conception of a distinctive "kind of event"—a schoolyard shooting, for example, or an economic depression. Such thinking leads to a common error in logic.

Judgmental Asymmetry Again (Ch 3.). Reasoning backward from an event to what might have presaged it or caused it makes one vulnerable to the fallacy of "affirming the consequent." This error can be phrased abstractly as:

> If P, then Q
> Q
> Therefore, P

The mistaken reasoning is that, whenever Q occurs (is "affirmed"), then P has been verified. Such logic ignores the possibility that other combinations of preceding events may also presage Q or cause it.

Reminder: Cues that indicate an event is likely to happen need not be causes of that occurrence. The epileptic's aura is not the cause of his seizure. Forecasts, to repeat, are not temporal, instrumental predictions (TIPs).

We debate how best to weigh evidence pro and con. In this contest, it is easier to ascertain what did *not* happen according to our hypothesis than to learn from what *did* happen whether its cause was P, as per our hypothesis.

Our knowledge, and our reasoning with it, suffer from asymmetrical values. Falsification of a favored hypothesis *should have greater persuasive force* than confirmation, particularly in judging the relative risks of doing or not doing some important thing like marrying or otherwise investing one's resources.

Example: When we consider whether to undergo serious surgery, rational judgment multiplies the *chances* of improvement, null effects, and perverse effects—*if these can be known!*—by the *values* (to us) of the consequences of each possibility.

Pages 100-110 describe difficulties in estimating "the chances that...." Here we notice that we make these estimates from *reports* of successes, zero effects, and iatrogenic (harmful) consequences. Of course, these reports need *not* include all records. (p. 50-54, 70).

In the sciences, fudged reports are not unheard of. One stimulus to such error is the fact that records of the damaging effects of acting upon a favored hypothesis are less congenial to therapists and meliorists than reporting null effects or successes.[9]

3. Assigned probabilities are always contingent

They are not pure. They are stated with conditionals, and they assume contexts, whether or not these are stated. Among the conditionals we find the frequent question-begging *ceteris paribus* clause—"other things being equal."

4. No one idea of probability is appropriate for all judgment

Each idea, described below, is used, but some are more useful than others in particular circumstances.[10]

5. No concept of probability, in its ideal form, is attained in practice[11]

Difficulties in reliably observing and counting the events that interest us assure imperfection.

6. The purpose of inquiry defines appropriate use of a concept of probability

When employing any one of the several notions of probability, it is advisable to ask, "What can we do better—for our purpose—with this conception of probability rather than with another or none?"

Of course, the *doing* in this question does not refer to one kind of activity. The "doing better" that we expect from a *science* can differ from the "doing better" that satisfies curiosity, or provides comfort, or supports ideology. Within their domains of research, we expect scientists to develop an increase in prognostic accuracy.

To repeat, calling activities "scientific," as in "social science," promises knowledge. It is the kind of knowing that improves foresight when we have no control over events and temporal, instrumental predictive power when we do.

7. Judgment is never singular

While we debate specific issues—"Will this legislation do that?" "Will treatment Y cure X?"—the judgments we make are produced in bundles of preference, belief, and unstated assumption.

Numbers may inform judgments. By themselves they do not create them. Personalities produce these complexes of knowledge, evaluation, and disposition-to-act. Temperaments select philosophies, and education is thereby difficult.

In brief, a well-reasoned assessment of probability in aid of rational policy is always modified by the fact that we judge ends and means in moral contexts. This background is characterized by conflict. Conflict is generated not only within us—by our limited knowledge and contradictory desires—but also between us and others whose desires differ.

Nevertheless, probability remains an important idea, frequently used and often abused, and we need to know its meanings and their values.

I offer four major conceptions of probability, about which much has been written, and that need only be summarized here. For convenience, I call these different uses of the term "subjective," "logical relations," "classical," and "relative frequency" probabilities.

1. Subjective Probability

> *"Coins don't have probabilities; people have probabilities."*
> —*Persi Diaconis*[12]

In this statement, statistician and professional magician Persi Diaconis expresses the ontological premise of subjective probability, illustrated by his *ability to control* the results of coin-flips—events that are classically considered to be "random." With such demonstration, Diaconis argues that "a probability is a measure of someone's *degree of belief* in an outcome...."[13]

This conception of what-is-apt-to-happen turns our attention from "how things are" to how the human mind works. All "probabilities" are, of course, products of human intellect, but the subjective idea excuses itself from statements about Nature—that is, about ontology.

The subjective, or "personalist," concept covers a range of belief. At a "lower" extremity, it refers to an individual's expression of belief stated with minimum assurance. At its "higher" elevation, it refers to an individual's ability to give "good," but not conclusive, "reasons" for believing that....

While such a range-concept allows one to make rough comparisons among peoples' judgments of what is likely to occur, or to have occurred, numbers cannot be assigned these statements except in circular fashion. Circularity is apparent, for example, when psychologists ask individuals to rate the confidence with which they hold beliefs, a request that validates words with words, and assumes a close correspondence between self-ratings, intentions, and particular kinds of deeds.

A stronger, and yet imperfect, test of subjective probability is the amount one is willing to wager on a conjecture—in the manner of the folk challenge: "Put your money where your mouth is!"

This test is less than satisfactory because its results vary with factors other than confidence in belief. Results also depend on how much money persons feel/think they can spare and on individuals' taste for risk, a personality trait that can be distinguished.[14]

Nevertheless, subjective estimates of probabilities are everyday events, and liable to err. Preceding chapters have described some of these error-making influences. They include faulty observation, the "pull" of emotion on logic, and the omnipresent confirmation bias—the tendency to seek "proof" of what one already believes and to ignore evidence that contradicts one's beliefs.[15]

In addition, *the nature of the risk* affects estimates of the probability of outcomes. "Nature of risk" includes the *ethical* as well as the monetary value of a desired objective, and *the amount of control* decision-makers feel/think they can exercise over the relevant events.

In this scenario, judged probability is infected by fear and desire. Wants and costs affect visions of futures.

Such interweaving of judgment with preference explains how it is that judicial decisions can violate logic and scientists' conceptions of probability. The courtroom is not a site of disinterested inquiry. It is an arena in which adversaries fight—mostly with words. In that venue, *greater allegiance to justice* than to truth warps judgment of likelihood.[16]

It is thus that courts of law employ a different interpretation of probability from that used in other fields of action.

2. Logical Relations

A "logical relations" conception of probability attempts to weigh evidence in justification of inference. It proposes that a *logical* connection be established between grounds for belief and a hypothesis under test. In courts of law, this effort is routine, and its application comes in two versions.

A "necessary" or "objective Bayesian" definition[17] considers "probability" to be a measure of

> the extent to which one set of propositions, out of logical necessity and apart from human opinion, confirms the truth of another....[Probability, then refers to] the extensions of logic, which tells when one set of propositions necessitates the truth of another.[18]

A second, "softer" application of this idea holds that it is commonplace and rational to judge the likelihood of events, past and future, by the *quality of evidence* brought to bear upon a proposition.

Jonathan Cohen shows that this notion of "probability" is entrenched in our culture.[19] It is employed in everyday argument as well as in the practice of law. It proceeds by reasoning about "degrees of provability," says Cohen, and it avoids the many difficulties of the popular relative frequency definition of probability, to be described below.

In brief, this kind of probability involves reasoning about the logical relationship between evidence and argument.[20] It necessarily includes dispute about *what* constitutes "evidence," and *how well* available evidence tests a hypothesis.

The connection that is sought when one applies this idea of likelihood is one of "quasi-entailment." It is expressed in the proportional syllogism offered by philosopher John Mackie:[21]

x% of As are B.
C is an A.
Therefore, C is B.

Given such evidence, says Mackie, we can justifiably—that is, logically—infer "that these premises probabilify to degree-x this conclusion."[22]

Several difficulties trouble this work. One concerns the idea of "total evidence." Mackie's syllogism is persuasive only in the absence of contravening evidence. This opens the door to argument for something that can never be known: "total evidence."

For example, responding to my criticism of a professor's use of a highly politicized textbook in social psychology—one that claimed that Gestalt theory "proved" the scientific rationale of communism and foretold the "inevitable" success of Soviet communism—she challenged, "Is all the evidence in?"

Of course, "all the evidence" is never in, and we have no way of knowing what it would look like were we to approach it. Thus, in legal attempts to resolve conflict, judges and juries "finally" have to decide, and they do so through their judgment of the *quality* of evidence presented as well as its quantity. But, again, such judgment is always bent by attitudes towards the contestants.[23]

In Sum: Moral conflict biases judgment of the quality of evidence. Given such bias, the relevance of evidence to hypothesis fluctuates. Judgment moves with ideas of "justice," as well as, or even more than, with rules of logic.

And, like all moral concepts, "justice" is not one idea.[24] Legal service to any one of the several conceptions of justice is *not* the same as drawing an inference from evidence, nor is it the same as demonstrating a particular style of causal connection.

The "logical relations" definition of probability serves more as an ideal than as a description of practice in courts of law.

Law, Justice, Truth: The principal function of law is to resolve conflict. This is why Ortega declares, "Law is born from despair of human nature."[25]

The resolution of conflict need not yield justice, nor need it adhere to truth.[26] For example, Sheila Jasanoff's excursion through changes in law with changes in technologies, and her description of the tensions between law and science, provide illustrations of conflicts among uses of the law.[27]

Law is an instrument of combat with means short of violence. *But force always sits behind law.*

Law's force is most effective when it is validated by a people's morality. It is less effective when a citizenry is morally fragmented, as are most modern "multi-cultural" jurisdictions. Nevertheless, the power to coerce is implicit in both the enactment of law and its implementation.[28]

Example: The celebrated 1946 trial of famed movie star Charlie Chaplin reveals the *always-possible* battle between truth and justice, and the rubbery quality of a "logical relations" conception of probability.

Joan Barry claimed that Chaplin had fathered her child, born October 1943. Joan's mother filed a petition for funds for her daughter and grand-daughter.

Chaplin admitted having had sexual intercourse with Joan in 1942, but denied he could have produced her baby. Blood tests supported him, and demonstrated that he could *not* be the child's father.

Nevertheless, a jury voted 11:1 to *hold* the actor responsible. (Notice the verb "to hold." It indicates a difference between "is" and "is deemed to be".) The court then *ordered* Chaplin to pay money in support of Joan Barry and her daughter.[29]

Journalists' post-trial interviews with jurors showed the negligible impact of a "logical relations" link between evidence and hypothesis. Many jurors disliked the actor because he had amassed a fortune from his work in Holly-wood, but had remained a British subject. In addition, some jurors felt/thought his remaining an alien was doubly unfair because they also believed he was a communist. But the most damaging "evidence" against Chaplin was the fact that he was rich and his "victim" poor. Therefore, jurors' *sense of justice* deemed it fair that he pay for his pleasure, whether or not it had produced a child.

In evaluating this "solution," Jasanoff believes that

> [T]he jury's refusal to accept the scientific denial of Chaplin's paternity could prop-erly be characterized as social wisdom rather than scientific illiteracy.[30]

Thus, with the State's awesome force behind it, law can "resolve conflict" without achieving a uniform ideal of justice, without adhering to truth, and without applying any notion of the "logical relations" between evidence and hypothesis.[31]

QED

Other conceptions of probability are less emotionally charged.

3. The Classical Idea

> *"A random selection requires that each*
> *member of the universe shall, in the long run,*
> *be selected equally often."*
> —*Deborah Bennett*[32]

A classical definition of "probability" refers to the proportion of events favorable to a bet that *can occur* in a "field" of *equally likely* possibilities. It is a tally of the number of ways your chosen event—your bet—can happen *in relation to* all the possible events that can occur in a "closed system" in which *all possibilities are known and random.*

Everything that can occur is known in advance of play and is equally likely—within a "universe" as Bennett calls a closed system. *Combinations* of such events change them from "equally likely" to a different arrangement of possibilities (see below in re the difference between casting a die and casting dice.) Nevertheless, all possible combinations are known *before* one enters a casino.

A "closed system" is a domain of activity—like a game—in which all possible outcomes are not only known in advance of action, but also are not subject to influence by factors outside its realm. Some kinds of gambling provide an early, and continuing, model of this sense of likelihood.

"Games of chance" involve happenings when we play with *inanimate* objects whose structures allow reasonable estimates of how to bet on risky events that occur in realms of *known, random* possibilities.

Notice that under this definition, horse race betting does not qualify. Horses, riders, trainers, and bettors are obviously animate variables, unlike dice, cards, or roulette wheels-and-balls. And with pari-mutuel betting, payoffs change as bettors differentially choose horses. This makes betting on the horses more risky, and more fun, than pulling the handle of a slot machine.

But consider dice. Here we know *in advance* of the toss of a "fair" die—of which there are only approximations—that the likelihood of any one of its six pips showing, over some unknown but "sufficiently long" run, is 1/6. Hence the probability of throwing a double six, or a double four, is 1/6 x 1/6 = 1/36.

Each face of a fair die has an equal chance of appearing. But when one throws two or more dice, the combinations of possibilities are not equal. With two dice, for example, there are more ways to produce a "seven" than a "four." (Count them.) And in a game that accords a win if one tosses a "seven" on the first throw, but a loss with a "seven" on succeeding throws, gamblers are tempted to beat the odds. In a short run, they can, but casinos are betting on a long run. They never close, and they're open before and after gamblers leave their money.

Such "closed system" games work with one kind of "relative frequency" notion of probability. However, this concept differs from a separate idea of "relative frequency," described below, in that, in closed-system plays, "relative frequency" refers to "action" among *inanimate things* whose physical properties *fix the number of possible combinations of events*.

In games of this sort, the kinds of *possible results* are not only *known* before we enter a casino, but this number *does not change* with how people bet, or how many bet, or by any "run of luck." Dice, cards, and roulette wheels-and-balls have no memories, and they don't care how they have "behaved" prior to a particular toss of dice or hand of cards.

It is a sad commentary on human judgment that many (most?) citizens of compulsorily schooled countries do *not* believe this fact. It is popularly assumed that a "run of luck" in such games *changes the probability of events* for the next toss of dice or turn of a wheel. It does *not*, and to assume so is to commit the "gambler's fallacy," a.k.a. the "Monte Carlo fallacy." What dice and cards and wheels-of-fortune have been doing does *not* affect the probability of what they will do.

It is these facts of life—about how games of chance are structured and what people believe—that ensure that the "gaming" industry—never to be known as a "gambling" enterprise—remains profitable.

A different employment of the "relative frequency" concept does *not* involve closed systems, inanimate objects, and known distributions of possible outcomes. It more closely mimics human action.

"Relative frequency" as indicator of "probability" is common in commerce, medical research, and the social studies that aspire to scientific status. It is more subtle and more demanding than the classical idea about the likely turn of events, and hence more vulnerable to abuse.

4. Probability as Relative Frequency

> *"The concept of probability is an unusually*
> *slippery and puzzling one. [It hovers]*
> *uncertainly between objectivity and subjectiv-*
> *ity [and] in this uncertainty...probability*
> *resembles moral concepts such as goodness*
> *and obligation."*
>
> —*John Mackie*[33]

Decisions are about futures. They therefore *prophesy*—if you believe they're based on wish, hope, hunch, or false authority—or they at least make a *forecast*, and possibly a *prediction*—if you believe your decisions have empirical foundation (ch. 3).

Thus, the aspiring sciences of the social, like some physical sciences, try to improve foresight by estimating empirical probabilities, where choice of the ground from which to project a forecast is supposedly justified by "an adequate causal theory."

Hence, the most popular, most useful, and yet imperfect procedure for accomplishing this feat of prognostication estimates a "probability" of what *will happen* from the *frequency* with which a kind of event *has happened in some past relative to* a "base" of events or conditions assumed to be "relevant" to the production of what is being foretold. In the many worlds of decision, the pasts from which frequencies are counted vary. Spans of time range from months and years to centuries. In addition, the bases of these fractions also vary.

More is troublesome. Use of such a probability assumes, again, that the future being estimated will be like the past from which we gathered the experiences (data) with which to judge what is likely to happen. As we shall see, the worlds of social activities sometimes violate this fundamental premise.

Judging what might occur with a relative frequency notion of probability trusts that, if we can reliably count what has been happening— always in the context of other kinds of events or conditions that seem "relevant" to the object of our inquiry—then we have a better estimate of the future than we can get from guessing or intuition or common sense.

The relevant context, the *base* of the fraction, is presumably chosen according to some theory of causation. It may consist, then, of a tally of kinds of events, or conditions, or of kinds-of-people-in kinds-of-conditions. The base chosen is one that seems either to constitute some of the causes of the activities we're trying to foresee, or seems at least to be "relevantly associated" with them. More informatively, the base should consist of conditions or actions that are *necessary* for the events we are trying to anticipate.

From this practice, we have the title, "relative frequency."

Qualification: Reliable Taxonomies

This brief description requires amplification. For example, consider the requirement that the number placed in the numerator of a rate must refer to a homogeneous set of events.

For the purpose of making fair comparisons among different jurisdictions, or to make such comparisons before and after an intervention, or to increase foresight, it is improper, and downright silly, to construct a numerator that includes, for example, "all violent acts"—forcible rape, domestic punchouts, gangland "hits," terrorist bombings, and schoolyard killings.

To do so is to assume that each of these kinds of violence varies with the same set of conditions, and therefore that the events they describe are equally likely whatever base of the rate has been calculated. Nonsense!

Contrary to this unfortunate practice, we require a reliable taxonomy of the events tallied in the numerator. And this pertains to all estimates of conditional probabilities—of roadway crashes and their effects, criminal activities, lovers' fights, workplace injuries, climatic disasters, stock market crashes, diseases, and other unpleasant events we wish to understand, anticipate, and either accommodate or control.[34]

Base of Rates: It is also important to attend to the quality of the denominators tallied for rates. The most useful base of rates consists of events *necessary* for the occurrences tallied in the numerator. "Necessary" means that the denominator should refer to circumstances *without which* the events in the numerator could *not* happen.

For example, if one can't bear a child without being a woman of certain age—a condition no longer exact—then a reproductive rate should count births *relative to* the number of women within a population who are of fecund age.

And, since people can't get "divorced" without being married, a proper divorce rate must show a relationship between its numerator—divorces granted during a year—and a denominator that includes *all* married couples, and *only* those couples, during that time. It should *not* refer to the number of marriages during a year, as is sometimes reported by journalists and sociologists.

However, these necessary conditions need *not* be the causes of the events that concern us—except among comedians:

- "Why did they divorce?"
- "Because they were married."

These comments illustrate again the difference between a forecast and a prediction (ch.3). While refined rates improve foresight, they need *not* increase temporal, instrumental predictive power (TIP). The latter mode of anticipation requires something additional: The ability to specify causes of the events tallied in the numerator, including their styles and powers, *and* ability to manipulate them correctly (ch.3).

In Sum: Probability, in its relative frequency mode, expresses a relationship between the *actual* and a *potential*. It reports an association between a number of reliably tallied events *of one sort* and another number that represents *in summary fashion* the conditions, or kinds of people, or kinds of people and their distinctive dispositions that are at least correlated with or, better, are the cause of or, better yet, are *necessary for*, whatever has been counted in the numerator.

This fraction states a *rate*—the amount of change in what's been counted for the numerator to be expected with some quantities of change in what's been counted for the denominator. *Everything depends* on the quantity and quality of experience that has produced the numbers placed in such a fraction.

Apropos, such rates, popularly consumed, use figures that come from different sources. The individuals who count whatever appears in the numerator are *not* usually the same persons who produce the numbers placed in the denominator. Again, the careful inquirer looks at the *quality* of *both* sets of tallies. To say, as many citizens do, "statistics show" is to beg the important question: *"Who counted what, how reliably, and how appropriately for our purpose?"* (ch. 4).

Moreover, if, in our search for the causes of a kind of event, we wish to compare its incidence at different times, or among different populations, then *the bases of the rates must be identical.*

This seems commonsensical, but it is a requirement frequently violated. For example, on the assumption that the mixtures of ethno-racial peoples in populations affect, say, their robberies, and for the purpose of comparing the efficacy of police policies or welfare practices in changing such activity, it is unfair to compare numbers from ethnically homogeneous Sweden, as some commentators have done, with numbers from ethnically heterogeneous United States.

This is the well-known issue of "adequate controls." Somewhere in the research process, rates must be refined to meet the requirement of identical bases of rates.

Population Term

Another qualification affects how we use a relative frequency conception of probability. "Relative frequency" is a *population term.*

This concept of probability refers *only* to the number of times a kind of event occurs *in some aggregate* during a period of time. The aggregate forms the *base* of the rate and, in the social realm, it can include kinds of people, or conditions, or both, but it is nevertheless a *cluster* of some "things."

Many interpreters of the relative frequency idea have difficulty with the significance of "population term." They wrongly assume that the frequency of a type of event in a collective can be translated as "the chance that" a particular individual in that group will experience whatever has been tallied in the numerator. *It cannot.*

For example, if within a specified time period, 50 percent of American women of a certain age have induced abortions, this proportion can *not* be converted to a 50-50 likelihood that an individual woman has such a "chance." *Such translation makes no sense.*

Fifty percent of what? Of her "due" menstrual periods? Of the times she has sexual intercourse? Of her pregnancies?

"Relative frequency" refers *only* to a number of events *within an aggregate* of some kind during a period of time. Hence, we have to know *what collective* is appropriate for estimating the risk of what we are counting in the numerator. *A cluster of persons does not translate into a cluster of events for an individual.*

There is, of course, such a possibility as a cluster of events *in the careers of individuals.* It is on this basis that we conceive of people as "personalities."

The idea of "personality" means that we identify individuals by some *continuity* in the patterns of their tastes, interests, talents, emotional responses, and "personal signatures," such as their idiosyncratic ways of speaking and moving.

But this is a side issue to that of the legitimacy of translating percents of events in populations to an individual's chances-of....

Many literate people have trouble comprehending this fact. I've experienced college-schooled editors—competent in literature but uncomfortable with numbers—who doubt me, check my statements with their experts, confirm that I'm correct, and then continue to publish "an individual's chances-that" inferred from relative frequencies *known only* for some aggregate of persons.

Language deludes (ch. 2). Thus citizens and their scholars slide easily from chances in a population to using the same numbers to judge chances for an individual. Even geneticists who know better fall into the trap. Thus Matt Ridley informs us that

> A person who has watched her mother die of Huntington's disease knows she has a fifty percent chance of contracting it. But that is not right, is it? No individual can have fifty percent of this disease. She either has a one hundred percent chance or zero chance, and the probability of each is equal. So all that a genetic test does is unpackage the risk and tell her whether her ostensible fifty percent is actually one hundred percent or is actually zero.[35]

Two paragraphs later, Ridley contradicts himself. Referring to inheritance of the same disorder, he criticizes textbooks that say, "Half your children may suffer." "Not so," responds Ridley, "each child has a fifty percent chance, which is very different.[36]

Once more, words set the trap. Language can obstruct comprehension as readily as it facilitates it (ch. 2).

The trap is set by the phrase, "the chances that...." As we've seen, this wording can be interpreted in at least three ways. In the classical sense, it refers to the odds for and against an event that occurs in a closed system of possibilities in which each event is equally likely. A second interpretation assigns a subjective probability—a person's guess about the future, tested, sometimes, by the odds one will take on a bet as indicator of the confidence of her belief. And a third meaning reads "the chances that" as a relative frequency probability—the number of times event-X occurs *given some collective of potentials*.

Muddling Probabilities

The citizenry is inundated with forecasts that some event will occur "with an x-percent chance." The likelihood of climatic change—of wind, rain, earthquake—is familiarly reported this way, and so, too, are the chances of changes in social affairs—the outcomes of battles, the hazards of medical procedures, the risks of motoring injuries, the effects of laws on behaviors, and the expected results of political policies.

When political promise is expressed as a *numerical* "probability," the literate public—unless deluded by enthusiasm (an unfortunately common occurrence)—recognizes such "statistics" as figures of speech—hopes, invocations, inspirations. But when scientists make public pronouncements about "chances," lay consumers of their numbers can't tell whether such "scientific probabilities" refer to a known frequency with which some kind of event occurs *relative to* a base of necessary conditions (relative frequency probability), or whether the figure cited is a "professional estimate" (subjective probability), or some combination of these "chances."

One example of the many that are available tells the story of "muddled probabilities":

On 19 October 1992, geophysicists with the United States Geological Survey issued a public warning that the San Andreas fault near the central California town of Parkfield—then the most closely monitored fault segment in the world—had "a 37-percent chance" of a major slippage—an earthquake of magnitude Richter 6.0+—"within 72 hours."

Depending on the amount of error one allows in judging foresight, this forecast can be said to have failed. A lesser, 3.9 quake did occur *one week after* the promised Big Shake. But what is pertinent to our concern with "official statistics"—and particularly those announced about social events— is that consumers of such authoritative numbers are ignorant of their basis.

I wrote one of the seismologists involved in the Parkfield study and asked him four questions:

- Are you estimating a relative frequency probability or a subjective probability?
- If the former, what is the "37 percent" a percent of?
- If the latter, how do you and your associates arrive at subjective estimates?
- And, in either case, what justifies the precision: 37 percent, not 35 percent or 40 percent or 35-40 percent?

The geologist did not answer all my questions, but he did kindly reply:

Good questions. The answer is both. We strive for quantitative, but given the small samples and dearth of models, we settle for subjective.[37]

According to news broadcast 19 March 2000, the U. S. Geological Survey has increased the number of its sensors in California, and now believes it can give warning of earthquakes of various magnitudes within thirty seconds of their occurrence. Such warning, a spokesperson for the Survey said, will allow elevators to be calibrated to return to floor-levels and children to hide under school desks.

Given the likely mix of repeated experience with the new sensors (relative frequency) and seismologists' interpretations of the timing and gravity of their forecasts (subjective estimates), one wonders how much error the citizenry will accommodate before people exhibit the "cry wolf" response.

This question persists even as earth scientists attempt to augment the relative frequency component of their forecasts and reduce their subjective element. Thus Tom Parsons and associates estimate the "odds" (N.B.!) of large earthquakes near Istanbul, Turkey, from historical records of damage over the past 500 and 1,000 years. In their study, these geologists "depart from current practice" by including measures of stress along fault-lines on the assumption that "faults with increased stress will fail sooner than unperturbed faults.[38]

Combining historical records with measures of changes in stress through time, the Parsons team foresees a 62 percent probability of "strong shaking" near Istanbul during the next thirty years and a 32 percent probability of such movement during the next ten years.

On the assumption that earthquakes in this area, graded by their severity, form a unimodal and symmetrical distribution over the times of their records, these seismologists reckon that their probabilities represent a one standard deviation plus and minus 15 percent for the longer period and plus and minus 12 percent for the shorter span. This means that about 2/3 of their calculated "chances" of a destructive quake, within the next decade, range between a 20 percent and a 44 percent probability.

We have here several transactions:

- *projections* of pasts into futures;
- *blending* of relative frequencies, estimated from pasts of varying periods, with recent calculations of changes in probable cause (stress);
- *translation* of this blend into subjective probabilities that might better inform public policy.

To derive policy from the geologists' model requires converting an element of relative frequency, qualified by estimates of the magnitude and timing of events and recent measures of stress, into a subjective probability. And, again, a strong test of this kind of conjecture is how much one is willing to bet for and against the events of interest.

In the Istanbul situation, the earth scientists' stated probabilities and their ranges of likelihood translate into wagering odds that vary between 4 to 1 against a major quake during the next ten years to almost even odds against it (1.1:1).

What citizens and governors can do with such odds is another matter. Like other residents in trembling areas, those who live in North Anatolia already know that they are subject to great shakes. So, too, do the millions of persons congregated around "the ring of fire" that encircles the Pacific Ocean.

In addition, and with or without human intercession, Nature itself moves— in geologic time—with "sudden, abrupt, and enormous" changes in the Earth's climate. These shifts occur, says geologist J. A. Rial, "within the span of just a few years and *without demonstrable cause*.[39]

Questions, then, follow: when and how much should seismologists' models affect judgment of what-to-do? If denizens of such quivering zones are rich, they can build safe edifices or move. They can try to restrict immigration. But hazards will persist. Alarms will be raised, and forgotten. People return to disaster areas. And we remain open to the possibility that Nature may be less orderly than some scientists believe—not because we are ignorant, but because that's the way she is (ch. 10).

Meanwhile, as long as scholars and ideologues muddle probabilities, we shall be swamped with awkward mixtures of "the chances that...."

For example, recent journalism (27 March 2000) tells us of a relatively new childhood "disease" called Attention Deficit Disorder, given an acronym, ADD, and "measured" with a questionnaire that asks parents whether their children are "easily distracted" or "fidget with hands and feet or squirm in their seats."

Chapter 8 discusses the risks of such tallies in which we cannot know whether we are counting parents' reliable observations, or their emotionally affected interpretations, or children's actual behaviors. Nevertheless, on the basis of such unknowns, the U. S. Surgeon General announces that 21 percent of schoolchildren suffer some type of "mental disorder."[40] (Notice, again, the persuasive, and questionable, precision of an "irregular" figure: 21 percent.)

Notice, too, that "finding" ADDs has been stimulated by the Special Education Law, 1991, through which the U. S. Department of Education gives schools extra money for each child so "diagnosed."[41] Surprised?

Muddled probabilities are common; some are fraudulent.[42]

Implications

"Everything is deemed possible except that which is impossible in the nature of things."
—*California Civil Code* [43]

From the many meanings and uses of "probability," we draw some inferences.

1. Many important decisions have to be made without knowledge of the frequency of specific outcomes relative to known conditions and, worse, relative to circumstances *that change as we act*. It is not unusual, for example, for public predictions to change the course of events we wish to foresee. Stock market prices are an instance.

Politico-military decisions are another common example. For illumination, read *The Kennedy Tapes*, a work that describes deliberations by the President of the United States and his advisors during the 1962 "Cuban Missile Crisis" with its potential for starting World War III.[44]

To live is to risk. There is no such condition as hazard-free life—not for other organisms and not for us.

Sophisticated persons find this statement trite. It merits saying, however, because meliorists talk as if risk could be abolished. In this manner, the U. S. Consumer Product Safety Commission asserts its task to be protecting us from "the possibility of any injury" from things we use.[45]

2. Social scientists have not been able to demonstrate that the bulk of their statistics can be converted—by well-verified theory or formula—to relative frequency probabilities about the results of programs they advocate.

This statement refers to futures; pasts, of course, are what we enumerate.

Some clinical formulas improve foresight (pp. 50-54). Nevertheless, they leave room for error, and a persistent question asked of policies is how much error one is willing to pay for.[46]

3. Even when decision is bolstered with numbers, subjective inference intrudes. It does so because the *value* of a result is personal. The surgeon who assures patients that procedure-x for condition-y is "highly successful" cannot judge for each patient the value of a successful outcome, a null result, and a perverse effect.

No one knows everything, and we are forced to trust some authorities about some things. But, to know what we're doing is to acknowledge that there can be a difference between what our experts *believe* and what they *know*. For expensive decisions, second and third opinions are advisable.

Apropos of this caution, and contrary to popular impression, the *confidence* with which advisors assert their prescriptions *says nothing* about the *accuracy* of their advice.[47]

Power stimulates arrogance. Knowing what we don't know, and admitting it, is difficult, but important.

4. Whenever experts advertise *exact numbers* where only a range of likely outcomes can be warranted—and these results are based principally on personal opinion—citizens, and social scientists in particular, should be alert to the possibility of con-artistry.

No one has counted this, but I notice that promoters of products and policies usually cite "odd" probabilities—37 percent rather than 40 percent, or 21.5 percent rather than 20-25 percent. It would satisfy curiosity if someone tallied the kinds of proportions commonly given to justify public promises.

Presumed precision can be persuasive while it spreads baloney.

5. If we assume that all major social events represent the node of many causal influences, not all of which are known or can be known, then prudence trumps zeal.

Ideas have consequence, and their effects range beyond their objects. Insofar as this is true, grand theories of social action are to be questioned. (See the "Summing Up," pp. 237-241).

Laws of human conduct, improving upon tempered judgment, are rare, if not non-existent. This does not invalidate all specialized competence. It acknowledges that expertise is bounded.

6. The intellectual exercise in this chapter confirms philosopher Ludwig Wittgenstein's contention that, "Names creep on from subject to subject, until all traces of a common meaning sometimes disappear."[48]
Wittgenstein's statement accords with his philosophically popular notion of "family resemblance," namely, that words are *used* with the assumption that their different meanings—like those of "probability"—carry only overlapping similarities, not identical referents.

7. With the possible exception of "logical relations" probability, all other estimates of likelihood are calculated from pasts and used to guess futures. So stated, the project is obviously hazardous, but it's the best we can do.
Everything depends on the accuracy of our tallies, a premise that is challenged throughout this book. In addition, the construction of probabilities assumes that we can discern order in apparent disorder, that past experiences (our data) will characterize futures, and that interventions do not disturb such order as we've conceived. In short, it's assumed that the world remains as we tentatively know it to have been, changing in the same way, and changing in that fashion regardless of whether we do, or do not do, some specific things.
This is an awesome bundle of assumptions. Failure of any one element can be disastrous. An expensive case illustrates the danger of assuming more than we can know in "open systems" of events.

Model Failure: The shocking collapse, September 1998, of a Connecticut-based "hedge fund"—Long-Term Capital Management (LTCM)—is instructive.
This program (betting system) was guided by "geniuses of finance" who employed probability theory to devise a fail-proof method of judging market movements. The team included Harvard economist Robert C. Merton and Stanford economist Myron C. Scholes. Only one year earlier, these men had shared the Nobel Prize in economics for their work on the pricing of financial instruments. Merton and Scholes joined prominent Wall Street traders, including David Mullins, once the number-two economist to Alan Greenspan on the Federal Reserve Board, and John Meriwether, who had enjoyed "legendary" repute as a Wall Street bond trader.
These students of monies and their proxies had developed mathematical models with which to engage in arbitrage, betting on price spreads among government and other bonds in different markets. Their novel idea borrowed from the work of Japanese mathematician Kyoshi Ito who had shown how to calculate the trajectory of missiles in "continuous time," that is, with infinitesimal gaps in graphs of ballistic objects hurtling across the sky. With the Ito

Calculus applied to "dynamic hedging," LTCM's economists "believed," Merton said, "we could eliminate all the risk."[49]

For the first three years of their application, the economists' bets, spread over individuals, markets, and time, produced handsome profits: 20 percent, 43 percent, and 41 percent annually. In their fourth year, other traders adopted similar techniques and LTCM's profit fell to a still comfortable 17 percent. Then the unexpected happened.[50]

Asian markets collapsed, followed by Russia's default on her debts. And, as Scholes put it, "All the relationships disappeared."[51]

LTCM began losing hundreds of millions of U. S. dollars a day. In one day, it dropped US$500 million. During a five-week period, it lost an estimated *four billion* U. S. dollars. The *Economist* called this collapse "one of the greatest financial failures of all time."[52]

By September 1998, the foolproof betting program was in debt an estimated US$1.25 *trillion*, a sum equal to the annual U. S. budget. The debacle threatened comparable losses among internationally linked investments and the demise of world financial systems. Only an unprecedented intervention by fourteen private American banks rescued worldwide funds from bankruptcy. George Melloan explains:

> [LTCM's] high-powered brain trust, working with a computer model, simply had not allowed for the possibility that high-priced Treasuries [bonds] could go still higher, while the relatively lower-priced securities that they were betting would rise, wouldn't perform as expected. Past behavior of markets, as captured in their computer model, did not predict what would happen when investors started fleeing from emerging markets.[53]

In the social arena, every cause can be assumed to operate in a web of causes. Each cause is subject to change in its power, and even in its direction—stimulating or inhibiting—with changes in everything else that goes on in a *conceived system*, and with more outside the model that can intrude.

Even *chance* is regarded as a possible part of the causal complex. Analysts of LTCM's demise include "colossal bad luck" as a source of model-failure.[54]

Philosophers who assume that chance is actual, rather than a filler for our ignorance, give it a formal title, *Tychism*. Chapter 10 discusses this idea.

Words and numbers are principal tools for enlarging knowledge beyond our immediate experience. At the same time, their powers create delusions.

This is our predicament. A major task of education is to reduce delusion with expanded knowledge. This means tempering enthusiasm for *Grand Theories of Everything Social* with recognition of the contestable assumptions with which we study ourselves. The result sought by this balancing is neither nihilism nor apathy, but modesty.

In this effort, social scientists suffer additional handicaps. We are limited by our inability to *observe* most of the events that interest us. Chapters 7 and 8 describe this disability.

Part 3

Limited Vision

7

Social Facts

The Real and Quasi-Real

If facts only came to us clean, a product of pure perception, we would have less to quarrel about in science and politics. But we work necessarily with mixtures of what philosopher John Searle calls "brute facts" and "social facts." The difference, he says, is that:

> [Brute facts] exist intrinsically or independently of human observation and conscious attitudes....[It is] the distinction, in short, between features that are observer-independent and those that are observer-relative.[3]

The term "brute facts" refers to things or processes that are "there," regardless of our preferences and whether or not we know them. For example, "night and day" and "the seasons" are brute facts. They occur whatever we call them and whether or not we know what produces them.

Social facts emerge as mutually reinforcing clusters of individuals try to live "together" in some continuing relationship. The facts termed "social" are empirical as distinct from supernatural; they are available for observation. But they owe their "reality" to agreement among "a people."

Thus "marriage" and "murder" are social facts. Events so named can be observed. In the case of "marriage," we can directly perceive the activities given that title, and indirectly notice them through attendants' reports and written records.

In the case of "murder," it is possible to perceive some of these acts directly, but we most often know them only indirectly, through a trail of indicators. However, in both instances, the definition of such activities, and attention to them, are matters of consensus within a culture. Both definition and importance vary at different times and among different nations.

Unconscious Efficacy

Agreements that lubricate social relationships—indeed, that make social life possible—have usually evolved without plan. And it is likely that they do their jobs better as unplanned understandings than as inventions proposed to achieve some local purpose.

An advantage of social processes that are evolutionary, or that have attained honored, habitual practice as "institutions," is that their agents need not know the roles they play either in continuity or in change of ways of life. Social institutions—ritualized patterns of "getting things done"— are friction-free to the extent to which they seem "natural" to their participants.

Therefore, we commonly legitimize our practices—administering "justice" or getting "married"—with faith that they are founded in Nature or through Reason or by Divine Decree.[4]

Rebellion and Renewal

While modes of human association have a physiological basis, they do not operate like instincts. Institutionalized practices are not programmed into our physical constitutions and, for better or worse, tribes and larger gatherings experience individuals among them who are more and less compliant.

In today's huge populations, inaccurately but hopefully called "societies," disgruntled individuals and iconoclasts are not uncommon. Their Western versions often call for destruction of "The Establishment."

Whichever side we take in such local contests, we are inevitably confronted by the *brute fact* that social interactions are always regulated, and ordinarily through hierarchies of power. In various forms, sooner or later, "Establishments" return. They do so via naked force and/or modules of cooperation, and often by an unplanned process of "self-organization."[5]

"Self-organization" among clusters of individuals is discernible in Nature. We are part of Nature, of course, and similar processes work among us.

They are particularly apparent when relatively isolated gatherings must interact frequently and intimately.[6]

However, we are spared repetitive reorganization by memories, lessons, habits embedded in what is called a "culture." We do not start social lives anew with each generation, but we have no knowledge of the extent to which our current activities and our inventions—physical and social—are producing changes in our social arrangements, and thereby in our social facts.

Thanks to our relatively large, multi-folded cerebral cortex, we pride ourselves on our species-adaptability. And therein lies one good reason why students of the social have no formulae with which to calculate the direction or extent of our evolution. Futurism is fun, but it's not science.

Contestable Facts

The social-scientific vocation must work, then, with social facts that are variously linked to brute facts. Such fragile data are always subject to modification. They can be challenged by changed circumstance, by iconoclastic ideas, and by rare events for which adequate titles are lacking. Social-scientific work is vulnerable to surprise.[7]

An additional complication arises.

Whenever several nationalities reside within a jurisdiction that claims legitimate power to produce and administer law, it is to be expected that some social facts will be contested. The contest will be most fierce as practices are assigned differential moral weight by ethnic enclaves.[8]

By contrast, social facts facilitate interpersonal transactions, and allow their observation and measurement, insofar as few of the persons they affect care much about what social arrangements are called. What matters for social practice is that "understandings" are accepted regardless of how tightly they are tied to brute reality. Viz.:

- On which side of the road shall we drive?
- How shall we reckon time?

But as moral attitudes intrude upon social facts, the "reality" accorded such "facts" dissolves, and lawyers gain work:

- Was the killing "intentional" and "justified," and therefore "execution" or "war"; or was it "intentional but "unjustified," and therefore "murder"; or was it "accidental" or "defensive," and therefore "excusable" or "justifiable?"
- Do the rights and duties of "marriage and family" pertain only to heterosexual couples, or also to homosexual pairs, and possibly to polygamous units, permanently or temporarily "united?"[9]

In ignorance of the *gradient* of distinctions between brute and social facts, and our changeable degrees of acceptance of the latter, a comforting intellectual fashion has contaminated academic discourse, particularly within Western universities. In the spirit of many hopeful faiths, a "social constructionist" movement argues as if Reality were *nothing but* a matter of what we choose to call things and events.

Implication: Social Constructionism

Truth is what is useful to humanity; falsehood what is harmful.
—Commissar Gletkin, instructing the condemned revolutionary Rubashav[10]

If there is no "state of Nature" independent of our knowledge of it, and if what seems to exist, and appears to occur, are only products of how we choose to regard objects and events, then, per the "constructivist" thesis, we are free to create a world according to our wishes.

In opposing this academically popular idea, critics do not deny that we function with social facts. Nor do they deny that this category of reality moves with human conception. Moreover, critics are well aware that ideas and their symbols wield power, whether or not they describe truths.[11]

But skeptics contend that social constructionism commits error as it slides from the fact that *knowing* "reality" is a human activity—"it's up to us"—to the *facts* that what we *call* events affects *how* we respond to them, and that both naming and responding fluctuate, to the false inference that *everything* we know can be differently construed, and that we can, with such verbal manipulation, shape human activity in desired directions to suit our pleasure—"it's up to us."

As inquirers slip happily and thoughtlessly down this slope, an attempted social science risks becoming a version of Christian Science.

Conceptual Distance

Most concepts common in the social studies and everyday life indicate a *range* of "conceptual distance" between what they advance as organizing ideas and the possibility of observations that might allow measurement of their referents. Think of "crime," "discrimination," "exploitation," "justice," and other such morally saturated terms.

"Conceptual distance" is a metaphor. It suggests the likelihood that many terms popular in the social sciences are either so vague, or their referents so hidden from observation, as to make them resistant to measurement.

With this possibility, it is proposed that the "distance" between concepts employed in the social studies and what can be reliably observed and accurately tallied as their referents varies, not only with consensus about classification, but also with:

- the number of gatherers and handlers of the relevant information,
- the degree to which these original collectors and coders "possess" their data,[12]
- their ethico-political interest in finding preferred results—many investigators begin their studies knowing what they want to discover, eager to "prove-that" rather than "test-whether," and
- the moral content of the concepts with which they work.

The greater the moral input of concepts, the greater their probable "distance" from either coherent social facts or brute facts.

Why? This hypothesis is justified because morals are commandments with special force. (ch. 12). Moral commands are prescriptions or proscriptions to *counter* what we currently do or are prone to do. For a long time, philosophers have agreed that morals and their laws represent efforts to control ourselves.

Moralists by vocation are, therefore, more concerned with how we *should* behave, and with attaching penalties to our misbehavior, than with finding and describing the sources of our conduct.

By contrast, the job of scientist is to find out *what* and *how*: *What* is "it"— that is, what is its material make-up, its constitution, knowledge of which allows us to identify "it," and *how* does "it" come to be, behaving as it does?

Finding the likely sources of human action is the job taken by anthropologists, economists, historians, psychologists, psychiatrists, and sociologists *when* they move beyond "mere" description to causal analysis and prescription. Although this work can be stimulated by moral concern as well as by relatively dispassionate curiosity, the vocation of social *scientist* is supposed to be devoted, first, to truth-seeking and truth-telling.

Among the truths we seek is clear statement of the nature of *a kind* of human activity, a statement clear enough to allow accurate enumeration of "it" in its varying contexts. This search includes ascertaining pattern, if there is such, in the realm of human action that interests us.

Only latterly are we allowed to be practical in service to some good end. This priority holds because we advertise ourselves as counseling from knowledge rather than from wish. That is, when we do-good as part of our occupation, it is assumed that we do so with truth. Doing good with lies and bullshit is other peoples' work.

Psychologist Paul Meehl illustrates this point in preface to his theory of schizophrenia:

> ...the explicit aim here is theoretical understanding, finding out about the way schizophrenia works, if we can, rather than helping schizophrenic patients. There are many interventions, even in organic medicine, that are not theory based and that are helpful;

and there are true theories which, at a given stage of technology, do not lead to prophylaxis or cure.[13]

The range of concepts more or less tightly tied to brute facts is large. The examples to follow are, of course, not exhaustive. They have been selected only to demonstrate morally induced variation among constructs in their amenability to reliable observation and accurate enumeration. As indication of *differential moral saturation* and its "pull" on conceptual clarity, we examine the ideas of "time," "money," and "suicide."

Time or Timing

Rotation of Earth, presenting different faces to Sun, produces regular changes in light and dark upon the surface of our sphere. It does so without our wishing it, whether or not we understand the process of production, or what we call it.[14]

This is a brute fact.

However, attempts to measure variations in light and dark, and their correlates, require calibrating the rhythm. In this sense, "time"—or more accurately, "timing"—was invented.

The fact that we count time with sixty "seconds" comprising one "minute," and so on, is a social product. It is a convention, and no one cares much whether we tally time as we do, or with a decimal or other scale.

Similarly, the practice of "zoning time" is a modern social invention now employed, with few exceptions, around the globe. Indeed, we admire the person who was the principal inventor of "standard time," Sir Sandford Fleming (1827-1915). Fleming was a Scotch engineer who surveyed the route for the transcontinental Canadian Pacific Railway. Working across this vast expanse from the Atlantic to the Pacific Oceans, timing as the sun "moved" was awkward.

Fleming suggested calibrating timing devices as 24 "time zones," each corresponding to $15°$ of longitude (another recent invention), and with an origin at a "prime meridian" in Greenwich near London, England. Dates would change at an International Date Line drawn through relatively unoccupied areas of the Pacific Ocean. Fleming's ideas were adopted as recently as 1884 during a Prime Meridian Conference in Washington, D.C.[15] In the spirit of Victorian progress, his contribution was hailed as further evidence of human ability to impose order on unruly Nature.

Here we have a social fact that rests on a brute fact. Compared with many other social facts, the conceptual connection is close.

Money

Money [is] a fiction, an addiction, and a tacit conspiracy.

—Martin Amis[16]

"Money" is also a social fact. Whatever "it" is, its "reality" resides in *agreement among a people*, and when one kind of money dies, another is born. Thus we have allowed a variety of things and beings to serve as money—carved stones, salt, cigarettes, animals, gold, silver, nutmeg, pieces of printed paper, squiggles on ledgers, and imprints on silicon.[17]

Notice, please, that even this short list of what is, and has been, money demonstrates a *range* of connection to wealth (see below) and brute fact.

However, with agreement about what constitutes money, we can tally its quantity with sufficient reliability to serve several purposes. Yet the reliability of money-measurement is not fixed.

Reliabilities change as we count locally—in our pockets and neighborhood banks—and as we try to count "money supply" nationally. In the latter case, economists invent different gauges, nominated with various "M's," and referred to as "M0," "M1," "M2," "M3," and more.

Like other common concepts, "money" loses its reference with fights about it. Enlargement of its meaning makes tallies of it less reliable, and even unreliable, for business and bank decision.[18]

What is at issue is the "conceptual distance" between a social fact and any brute facts that might permit use of the social notion *in a science*.

The concept of "money" needs ventilation because, implicitly if not explicitly, it is involved in discussions of other social facts such as "income," "wealth," "poverty," and "social class." These several concepts, and others, are regularly invoked in efforts to explain human action. Their kinship to "money" draws attention to what money "is."

Money Trouble

A difficulty with the concept of money is that it, like other popular terms, refers to more than one use, and hence possibly to more than one thing. In addition, its basis is psychological. What money *is*, is "up to us."

Introductory economics texts usually call money, "a measure of value, a medium of exchange, and a store of wealth," but this definition puts at least three distinct functions into one blender.

What is used as a *standard* by which to calculate *value* for the purpose of *exchanging* things, rights, and services need not itself constitute *wealth*. And what is accepted as an *instrument* with which to facilitate exchange of goods, rights, and services need have no intrinsic value. Such instruments, by themselves, can be worth little or nothing, as is true today of much coined money and the paper rightly called "currency."[19]

But neither of these meanings of money—that it is used as a *unit* for measuring value or as a *medium* of exchange—defines everything that is meant by *wealth*. Therefore, whether and when money constitutes a "store of wealth" is a matter for inquiry.

Wealth

"There is a gigantic difference between earning a great deal of money and being rich."
—Marlene Dietrich, German-born American actress (1904-1992)[20]

Wealth is an important idea, and a vague one. It is commonly regarded as the same as having much money. But this conception confuses a local and always fluid condition with all else that human beings seek and appreciate.

Economists sometimes speak of "wealth" as "assets" that have the *potential* of producing "income." But this is a narrow notion and un-psychological.

Wealth is part of a family of ideas, all of which reduce to what people *value*. However, as the term is ordinarily used, it tends to be restricted to "the good things" that people value. It tends to be so limited because "wealth" is an intellectual cousin of concepts of "well-being," "health," and "being whole." Indeed, it is often said that health is the *sine qua non* of everything that is regarded as wealth.

Given the composite nature of "wealth," the concept can never be employed without open or hidden reference to individuals' preferences. Wealth and value form an equation. One is identified by the other.

We recognize wealth as that which is currently appreciated by self and others, and that which can, within some *individually valued span-of-time*,[21] produce objects, conditions, and psychological states desired by self and others.

Value is Not Intrinsic

It can be known (and tentatively counted), not so much by what people *say* they desire before they act, but better by what they have paid for, with payment made in mixtures of time, services, objects, and currencies.[22]

Value, of course, has different aspects. It can be observed in the possibility that some form of wealth provides for *exchange* with others for their goods and services, or in the *utility* that an object, attribute, or skill has for its "owner."

Utility also comes in packages. It can reside in *practical* use—as when a shovel is an asset—or in the *potential* of a thing, process, or personal quality to give pleasure. In this sense, wealth can be accorded a book, a recording, a painting or sculpture that entertains, refreshes, and yields aesthetic delight.

Ideas, too, have value—aesthetic as well as practical. Beauty in things and persons is a multi-faceted "utility." Practically, beauty yields power; aesthetically, it is its own joy—for both its possessor and its observers.

Prestige and honor, privacy, silence and solitude are also treasures of great value.

In Sum: Values are assigned to multitudes of things, conditions, services, and social relationships. These kinds of wealth are motors of action within persons and between them, and they do their work in *moving hierarchies.* The rankings of "things" valued do not hold constant.

This fact makes exchange possible and life interesting. It means, too, that individuals who own large quantities of money can be rich in that storehouse of wealth and poor in other kinds of wealth—particularly in health, physical and mental.

Poverty in mental health is indicated by moneyed people who, lacking purpose, are bored. A sign of this malaise is the killing of time with such anesthetics as booze and other narcotics.

What we desire changes as we get more or less of what we want.

When is Money Wealth?

Among huge populations that live under one jurisdiction, confusion arises because citizens are unclear about the distinction between wealth and money and the related concepts of "rich" and "poor."

This confusion infects universities and legislatures when their members assume that a State, claiming a monopoly in the manufacture of money, can produce wealth by fabricating money and distributing it.

It is not that this can never occur. It can—for a short run and under certain conditions. These conditions include the work-skills and habits of a people. But such a brief process—deficit-financing, pump-priming—moves to a limit as more money is manufactured than the wealth it helps produce.

Nevertheless, the possibility of creating wealth by fabricating and distributing money generates a temptation. The lure is for agencies with a monopoly of power—that is, governments—to borrow wealth with which to pay for promises, with the debt to be repaid with money. This exchange creates an always-temporary advantage for debtors and disadvantage for creditors.

Against this temptation, many states have restricted "money" to that which is itself some kind of wealth. This occurs, for example, when cattle are standards of value, instruments of exchange, *and* wealth. But, in our multi-product, rich populations, it is awkward to move cattle and convenient to reckon accounts (exchanges) with "money" that is variously minted, printed, and registered as "zeros" and "ones" in silicon.

When Lydians first coined money during the seventh or eighth centuries B.C., their units were composed of an alloy, *electrum*, and their value judged by weight of the coins. With such mintage held roughly stable, money approximated at least material wealth, as it does when tokens are composed of rare gems or metals. Coinage of this sort is linked to a variety of wealth, and it retains that kind of value. And so too with paper that is guaranteed by—is convertible to—gold or silver held by a state.[23]

But money divorced from any form of physical wealth *rests on faith*. Hence we now have "fiduciary" ("trustworthy") coinage and "fiat" ("mandated") currency. It is appropriate, then, but disconcerting, that American paper money bears on its obverse the prayer, "In God We Trust."

Trust is indeed the cement of any aggregate of individuals that would constitute a "community" or "society."[24] But trust is eroded in mass democracies insofar as we manufacture kinds of money that have no anchor in material wealth.

The impulse to fabricate money, and to invent novel forms of it, creates risks. The various risks can be assimilated to one general hazard: That of distancing social facts from any brute facts that might discipline dreams with doses of reality.

The American president, Richard Nixon, accelerated the process in 1971 when he "closed the gold window." After this decision, every major country adopted a paper (fiat) standard. Nobel laureate economist Milton Friedman declares that "such a worldwide fiat monetary system has no historical precedent."[25]

Trusting in the Silicon Economy

As money is transformed from things, and precious gems and metals, and coins and currency, to credit and information—meaning marks on someone's ledger—it becomes free of guarantee that it represents any quantity of wealth. It becomes more of a social fact and more distant from any brute fact. And, as credit itself constitutes exchange power, divorced from its classic foundations in collateral (material wealth) and trust ("know those who borrow from you"), it becomes stimulus to fraud. The ease of transaction that credit permits encourages borrowing wealth on trust, consuming it, and repaying lenders with lesser wealth or not at all.[26]

A psychopathic client once told me that he had long wanted to die with a few million dollars in his bank account. He later experienced a "revelation" that this was irrational. His revised ideal was to die *owing* several million dollars because that would represent wealth he had enjoyed without earning it.

In a parallel ploy, governments and their citizen-subjects engage in the swindle known eponymously as the *Ponzi*. This is a form of "pyramid scheme" in which early lenders to "Ponzi" are repaid with high interest from the deposits of later investors, without the circulatory process producing any other wealth than gratification for those "first on board."

The charm of this crime is that it never ends. The infection spreads from con artists to states, and its damage gets morally attenuated, normalized, and excused.

As one illustration, Risa Kugal claimed bankruptcy in Brooklyn, 1991, because she was unemployed, separated from her husband, supported by her mother, and in debt some $75,000 via her credit card charges.

It took Judge Conrad Duberstein less than three minutes to excuse Kugal's burden under federal bankruptcy law. In this manner, the psychopath's ideal was realized by a legal form of theft that leaves debtors richer and creditors poorer.

When asked how she had managed to rack up so much debt without re-sources, Kugal gave a Ponzi-type reply, "I used one [card] to pay off an-other."[27]

Lessons

Money is a social fact. Ontologically, it's not "real." Epistemologically, it possesses varying qualities of "reality."[28]

Money does not exist in Nature; it exists as we create it, nominate it, and agree upon what represents it.

The point here is that the social fact works. People historically, and around the globe, know what serves as money, in their time and place. Even the most devout social constructionist refrains from quarreling with his bank manager about the quantity of "the stuff" in his account.

Other lessons follow. One refers to what economists call "the money illu-sion" (actually it's a delusion). This is the error of feeling-believing that receipt of a greater number of fiat units means that one has grown in wealth. It is the mistaken assumption that currency translates uniformly into a quantity of wealth. Sometimes this happens; many times it does not.

A related lesson is that, when we live among large masses of strangers, reliance on social facts, conceived at great "distance" from any brute facts, incurs costs.

Fraud

It is thus that a trade-off occurs between the mobility credit allows and the opportunities it creates for theft by deceit. Fraud is probably the most lucra-tive of all styles of larceny, only exceeded on occasion by military looting.

It is a mode of stealing practiced by persons who wear the mask of honesty, and who are equipped with moderate to high schooling and social status or, put negatively, who are *not* unschooled, poor, and stupid. In brief, this style of theft refutes the popular idea that taking other peoples' wealth is mainly a crime of deficiency, motivated by *lack* of money, education, and intelligence.

Fraud's instrument involves a complementary meeting of swindlers' tal-ents and victims' wants. Fraudsters' talents include ingenuity, confidence, and persuasive promise that fits victims' ignorance, desire, and faith. With such conjunction of abilities and appetites, great quantities of wealth are transferred from one set of accounts to others.

During the 1980s and 1990s, such transfers have no longer been limited to thousands of U. S. dollars, but now amount to millions and even billions. In the recent chronicle of mega-buck swindlers, one of these grand thieves stole an estimated $915 million from some American insurance companies and perhaps *two billion* dollars through a religious charity.[29]

Money is what people think it is. As official money becomes represented by credit, and as individuals and corporations can borrow more with little collateral—i.e., little wealth—faith in the value of money moves from what it represents to what it promises. Debt exceeds promised value. The practice is called "leverage"—a little lifts much. (Note that the verb "to lift" is slang, meaning "to steal.")

In an exuberant financial climate, promissory instruments are invented, accountants' terms of reference are blurred, and bubbles of wealth—inflated with trust—burst.

John McKinnon and Gregg Hitt describe one such tactic:

> In 1993, Goldman Sachs & Co. invented a security [N.B.!] that offered Enron Corp. and other companies an irresistible combination.
>
> It was designed in such a way that it could be called debt or equity, as needed. For the tax man, it resembled a loan, so that interest payments could be deducted from taxable income. But for shareholders and rating agencies, who look askance at overleveraged companies, it resembled equity.
>
> [This invention allowed Enron] to borrow more and more without making clear what it was doing.[30]

Faith works miracles, for fraudsters as well as for honest folks.

A summary lesson enlarges those adduced about flexible money and fraud: The greater the separation of social facts from brute facts that might underwrite them, the more contentious and fragile do social facts become.

"Fragility" refers to open borders around the referents of concepts. As concepts become porous, taxonomies of social conditions and activities expand and contract with ethico-political interests. *Elastic systems of classification make it difficult to measure the indexed terms and, hence, to gauge their associations with their proposed causes. A science of the social becomes impossible.*

In qualification of this argument, "open concepts" can be useful in the exploratory stages of inquiry, when we are trying to ascertain what kinds of observation, if any, allow test of our hypothesis.[31] But, as we garner information, we narrow the domain of things and activities that can represent the concept(s) with which we examine Nature.

At some stage, then, a system of classification must work with categories that *exclude* observation of some kinds of events; otherwise we have no

taxonomy. A promiscuous concept that accepts all candidates has value neither for common-sense rationality nor for science.

This defect—"flaccid taxa"—affects many attempts in the social realm to
know what we're talking about. For example, it intrudes upon the practice of
officially classifying "causes of death" and, in particular, its morally offensive style called "suicide."

Death

> "So ingrained is the human capacity and
> propensity for classifying, so central is it to all
> argument and exposition, that scholars in
> various disciplines find it easier to dismiss the
> activity as Scholasticism than to analyse its
> pervasive occurrence in their own and others'
> work."
>
> —Bennison Gray [32]

Death is both a brute fact and an idea to which moralities, through the ages
and around the world, have assigned various meanings. Humans have located
death at different times in the process of "ceasing to be," and at different
locations within bodies and in "the scheme of things."

Thus in western nations today we have such concepts as brain death, cardiac death, cellular or biological death, partial death, and acute and chronic
self-destruction, to name some prominent conceptions of termination.[32]

Along with these categories, death has been feared, hated, and embraced.
It has been imposed, honored, and denied. And when human beings inten-
tionally kill one another—as we have done and continue to do from earliest
record—we respond to these endings with joy, pride, gratitude, satisfaction,
sadness, rage, repugnance, indifference, and lust for revenge.[33]

Such a shifting melange of emotions accompanying various sources of
death encouraged America's first newspaper columnist, Ambrose Bierce (1842-
1914?), to define "homicide" as

The slaying of one human being by another. There are four kinds of homicide:
felonious, excusable, justifiable, and praiseworthy, but it makes no great difference
to the person slain whether he fell by one kind or another—the classification is for
advantage of the lawyers.[34]

Despite such actual difficulties, a terminus of human beings *on Earth* has
been acknowledged everywhere, at all times, and thereby merits the category
"brute fact." ("On Earth" is emphasized because unknown millions of human
beings assert belief that they possess an immaterial identity that persists in an
"after-life," as per Arthur Koestler's suicide note below.)

However, our interest here is not in measuring the degree to which moral
feelings affect observation and measurement of all conceivable styles of death,

but rather in employing suicide—intentional self-destruction—to illustrate the likely distortions of public numbers when investigators attempt to count social facts that bear strong moral significance and flexible links to brute facts.

Suicide

> "I wish my friends to know that I am leaving
> their company in a peaceful frame of mind
> with some timid hopes for a depersonalized
> after-life beyond due confines of space, time,
> and matter, and beyond the limits of our
> comprehension."
>
> —Arthur Koestler,
> suicide note [35]

"Suicide" is one word, but more than one act. It is an ending toward which people travel by many routes, impelled by a variety of motives, in differing "states of mind," and with varied consequences for those left behind.

Indeed, the many demographic variables that social scientists employ as possible correlates of suicide in their search for its causes—such as age, sex, marital and financial status—do *not*, as far as we can tell, bear a constant relationship to self-destruction.

This inconsistency is in part a function of classification error (see below), but it is also a likely result of the many qualities of psychologically differentiated acts called by a single name.

In the naming game, religions and their moralities intrude. Some kinds of self-willed, but socially impelled, endings are termed "martyrdom." These forms are honored by colleagues-in-faith.

Other types of voluntary "dying-for-others" are sometimes regarded as heroic and sometimes as deplorable; at other times and places, self-sacrifice is recommended and even required.

Sociologists often employ the term, "altruistic suicide," as a general phrase for voluntary "dying-for-others." They borrow the locution from one of the fathers of their discipline, Emile Durkheim (1858-1917), who made a special, but defective, study of suicide.[36]

Since Durkheim calls suicide a "problem" about which "society" should do something, it is not clear whether he would also have deemed all "dying for others" as worthy of public remedy.

Nevertheless, many nations have praised particular styles of "killing oneself for others." It has been reported among the Inuit whose infirm old used to accept the "long sleep" on the unprotected ice, among Hindu widows who incinerated themselves on the funeral pyres of their husbands (*suttee*), among Buddhists who also burned themselves to ashes for a "good cause," and among Japanese gentlemen who committed *hara kiri* (*seppuku*) when dishonored.

Fighters, past and current, who serve as human bomb-delivery systems, have been, and are, regarded variously as "terrorists" or "martyrs," depending on who kills whom and with what justification, as with Japanese (*kamikazi*) and Muslim warriors.[37]

Filtered Facts

"There are three kinds of lies: lies, damned lies, and statistics."
—Benjamin Disraeli [38]

A variety of observations assures us that some styles of self-termination are voluntary. They are deliberate, desired, chosen, and therefore, within some religio-political jurisdictions, qualify as "suicide."

If this is acknowledged, then we begin study of suicide as an officially recognized category of death, at least within Western countries. That is, such a category of death exists, but it is tied only loosely to any brute fact. Looseness is generated because killing oneself is variously honored and dishonored.

Among nations that partake of a Judaeo-Christian conception of life and death, self-destruction is immoral, and illegal for those who facilitate it. Although "suicide" is commonly recognized, we classify such "unexplained" deaths, not to serve the interests of scientists, but for moral and legal purposes.

Suicide, then, is a social fact. And when scholars examine the process by which official categorizers of death label endings, they uniformly find the diagnosis of "suicide" to result from a parley among workers. This is a conversation, not always cordial, that generates the public numbers we consume. Such social filtering does *not* yield tallies sufficiently reliable for a science.[39]

For example, sociologist Ian Ross worked in a medical examiner's (coroner's) office in a Canadian province where he observed how death-defining practitioners assign cause of death. In agreement with other investigators, Ross notes that the diagnostic work is not a straightforward matter of discovery. Rather, it involves negotiation among officials of varied background, interest, training, and expertise who employ movable criteria in fitting corpses to categories.

Thus, while physicians recognize more than 100 "causes" of death, officials work with only four legal kinds: "natural death," "accident," "suicide," and "homicide." Such reduction simplifies the diagnostic task, but the ethico-political consequences of causal assignment remain as sources of flexible numbers. Ross comments,

These [official] categories of death are matched with corpses on the basis of some combination of medical and non-medical evidence usually derived from physical and social circumstances at the scene of the death. There are *no universal criteria* for assessing the precise significance of social and physical evidence nor can finding of pathological alterations always be used to infer the mode of death.[40]

Neither Ross's research, nor that of any other "external" examiner of death-classification, can assign a validity score to coroners' work. No one *knows* the actual number of suicides per jurisdiction.

The value of studies by Ross and others lies in their description of *how* causes of death are officially defined. Where inconsistencies are found between styles of assignment, as they often are, investigators can then suggest some of the sources of unreliability among reporting agencies. In addition, since most of these origins of error are not readily repaired, "external audits" demonstrate the hazards of social scientists' theorizing about the causes and prevention of self-extinction. Durkheim's famous study of suicide provides no information useful for public or private policy.

A sample of evidence confirming these conclusions illuminates both the likely sources of inaccuracy in corners' data and the difficulties of doing science with social facts that are distant from reliable observation.

However, what is useless for a social science can be useful for ethico-legal purpose. A social practice does not have to be veridical in order to "get a job done."

Confirmation

Other research supports Ross's findings. A sample gives their flavor:

1. During the nineteenth and early twentieth centuries, several European countries changed their methods of collecting information about their suicides. The revision resulted in a jump in their rates by as much as 50 percent.

In German-speaking territories, Catholic priests and Protestant ministers had filed reports of suicides from their own constituencies, while government officials did this among Jews and religiously unaffiliated persons.[41]

Transfer of data-collection from religiously interested reporters to more neutral actuaries apparently effected a dramatic change, not in the unknown actual rates of self-destruction of course, but in the numbers classified and recorded as suicides—that is, in social facts.

2. A Swiss demographer, Pierre-B. Schneider, notes parallel findings. During the first half of the twentieth century, Catholic cantons listed disproportionately more accidental deaths than did Protestant cantons, while Protestant cantons reported disproportionately more suicides than did Catholic units.[42]

3. A team of investigators of American suicides examined the characteristics of personnel in 191 coroners' offices in 202 counties in eleven western states. Their interest lay in the reliability, and hence validity, of official certification of suicide.

They tested *consistency* among the 191 agencies by noting the degree to which their reported rates of self-extinction cohered with demographic variables suggested by socio-psychological theories to make a difference in disposition to suicide—factors such as age, sex, marital, financial, and occupational status.

This is a weak test of reliability since we cannot know the extent to which variations in counties' descriptions of the correlates of their listed suicides reflect real differences in rates of self-execution by "kinds of people" in these varied locations, or whether they demonstrate inconsistencies in styles of classification among agencies.

These investigators assume the latter. With this assumption, multiple manipulations of their data suggest variations among these definers of death that Nelson and his colleagues say "call into question the validity and comparability of reported suicide rates."[43]

Origins of Error

"Only the cleverest of animals err."
—Georg Lichtenberg,
German physicist
(1742-1799)[44]

Two facts make it difficult to count suicide with precision. One, to repeat, is saturation of the concept with moral meaning. The other is the related difficulty of identifying "cause of death" from among the many candidates we and our officials nominate in circumstance and individual career.

These facts work in concert. They color all other considerations of the likely sources of error in detecting self-termination. Viz.:

1. *Moral attitudes* affect interpretations of many social activities, not just suicide, and as they do so, they move our selection of causes (pp. 442-445).

In Western cultures, this movement applies *a fortiori* to identification of suicide, an act condemned by both law and religion. Condemnation is applied with consequences meant to deter self-destruction and likely to impede its recognition. Among most of the people with whom we live, suicide is taboo.

2. *Projection and the Achensee Question.* As the nineteenth century gave way to the revolutionary twentieth, Sigmund Freud and his best friend, Wilhelm Fliess, attended a scholarly conference at a resort by the Achensee. During public discussion, Fliess happened to ask the "analyst of others' souls" a question subversive of Freud's declared vocation: Psycho-analysis. "Whose mind," Fliess wondered, "does the mind-reader read?"

For the would-be reader of others' minds, the question is, of course, unanswerable. We cannot shed our own "minds" as we try to interpret those of others.

This embarrassing conundrum broke the heretofore cordial alliance between Freud and Fliess. It did more than that for us latecomers. It alerted us to the fact that we have no resources other than our own feelings/thoughts with which to interpret others' conduct. Moreover, this remains true regardless of how well, or ill, we have been educated.

"Projection," the unwitting disposition to assume that others share our values and emotional responses, is a source of error in "reading" others. But it is also a "normal" process and desirable.

It is popular because it is probably a physiologically built-in mode of appraising others. It is desirable because such extension of self "into" others is the foundation of empathy and hence of morality.

Nevertheless, we pay a price for this virtue. To assume that others feel-think as we do is a common source of error. We are not identical to everyone else.[45]

Those who have the job of certifying cause of death are thus trapped. To diagnose "suicide" requires identification of others' intentions.

Sometimes this is easy, as when we have known the deceased for some time, and that person has not only given us signs of world-weariness, but has also left a declarative adieu.[46]

But in the less intimate relationship between coroner and stranger, deciding about decedent's intention can be tricky. It is particularly so in cases of death by drowning and when the deceased has had a history of risky conduct. Financial and political factors also play a role in assigning cause of death.

3. *Equity.* Examiners of coroners' procedures note that their feelings of fairness sometimes affect diagnoses of manner of dying. Concern for the reputation of decedents and for the viability of insurance claims by their survivors have altered definitions of modes of death.[47]

Similarly, the "integration" of decedents with their communities, including its officials, exerts a "pull" on diagnoses. Jack Douglas writes,

> All students of suicide have known that there are many individual cases of attempts to hide suicide, and all students of suicide have likewise assumed that many cases are successful.[48]

4. *Politics.* The difficulty of identifying cause of death becomes most apparent when important persons die under "mysterious" circumstances. Thus, doubts persist about whether 36-year-old actress Marilyn Monroe killed herself of whether she died from an accidental overdose of barbiturates or was murdered.[49] Questions also surround the official diagnosis of "suicide" in the death of the forty-eight-year-old White House lawyer and "First Family confidant" Vincent W. Foster, Jr.[50]

Detectives who work for insurance companies suggest that some unknown portion of suicides and murders are not counted because they are "covered" as "accidents." Economist Oskar Morgenstern arrived at this assumption from his study of detectives' techniques in one of North America's largest insurance companies:

> Accidents are another case where often great doubts prevail as to cause and effect. Probably most murders go undetected. [Sic!] For example, a very large proportion of hunting accidents are apparently murders; an investigation showing this was suppressed, however.[51]

In Sum: The point of this exercise has been to call attention to fragile facts that emerge when officials and academics try to count events they have not observed and that have ethico-political significance.

Chapter 8 continues discussion of the hazards of observation through social filters.

8

Vicarious Observation

"In the Tractatus I was confused....
I thought at the time that there is a connection
between language and reality."
　　　　—*Ludwig Wittgenstein (1889-1951)[1]*

"Although we think we govern our words...
certain it is that words, as a Tartar's bow, do
shoot back upon the understanding of the
wisest, and mightily entangle and pervert the
judgment."
　　　　—*Francis Bacon (1561-1626)[2]*

Proxies

Outside laboratories where we can control stimuli, record responses, and make reliable measurements, those of us who try to expand knowledge of social worlds beyond our individual experiences confront a grand obstacle: We cannot observe most of the activities we wish to study.

We rely instead on "indicators" that are supposed to represent accurately the activities to which our concepts refer. For example, these concepts include economists' ideas of "price," "value," "expectation," "productivity," and more. They include psychologists' notions of "reward," "punishment," "motive," "frustration," and sociologists' categories of "crime," "exploitation," and "social class."

The proxies we use to "stand for" these conceptual organizing terms always bear a fluctuating relation to the conditions and activities we wish to record, count, and translate into assured regularities.

Nevertheless, from the torrent of substitute observations, social scientists extract numbers, treated as measurements useful for some purpose. We do so extensively, confidently, enthusiastically, with diligent attention to the fairness with which we sample populations, but with floating attention to the reliability and validity of our tools.

It merits reminding that the authentic meaning of "validity" refers to the accuracy with which proxies depict what we assume we're measuring (ch. 4). Of the many substitutes that social scientists employ, the most common is words standing in for deeds—past or future.

Trust in Utterance

"Words, as is well known, are the great foes of reality."
—*Joseph Conrad (1887-1924)*[3]

"Never bet on anything that talks."
—*Gambler's maxim*

Man is the talking animal, and proud of it. But pride is misleading as well as encouraging. Social scientists' great folly is their trust in words.

No one has counted the nature of all data published by students of the social, but probably the single most observed datum is words—words voiced or written, or represented by ticks on paper, or with key punches. It is safe to claim that social scientists more frequently observe words than the acts to which they presumably refer.

A short sample of inquiries gives the flavor of social scientists' reliance on what others tell them as indicators of how they behave.

1. Brown and Gilmartin counted the kind of information reported in a major sociology journal, 1969, and found that more than 90 percent of its "data" consisted of what people say.[4]

This tally deserves enlargement and modernization.

2. During the *ten years* preceding his review of research on "personality," Jerome Kagan found that inquiry relied principally on individuals' responses to questionnaires.[5]

3. In their summary of research on "alcoholism," intended to ascertain which "kinds of persons" respond favorably to what kinds of therapy, Babor and colleagues discovered that "the procedure of choice" had been to *ask* people about themselves and their behaviors.[6]

Talking and Other Actions

"The most immutable barrier in nature is between one man's thoughts and another's."
—*William James*[7]

Putting questions to others (as well as ourselves) has many uses, but asking people what they have done, and have experienced, and want to do, and feel/think is never a straightforward procedure. The process is never guaranteed to give either reliable replies or truthful ones.[8]

Much verbal exchange is ceremonial:
"Good morning, how're you?"
"Fine, thanks. How're you?"
When this common practice is not merely customary, it yields variable results. It yields unstable results when it occurs between loving persons; it probably produces less stable results when it occurs among strangers.

Talking is a form of behavior, of course, and our species exhibited this ability long before we learned to write.[9] However, we have also long recognized differences between speaking, writing, and the actions and conditions that words and pictures represent.

It is popular to say, "Promises are not performances," and "Words are not deeds," by which we mean that "mouth morality" is not to be mistaken for the conduct we think important. Good advice, because the relationship between the morality one talks and the morality one does is far from perfect; some would argue that it's negligible.[10]

More than that: Even when we remain on the verbal level, and question people about their moral convictions, many individuals find it difficult to give logically consistent replies.[11] As we shall see, moral beliefs are often held contingently depending upon....

Therefore, some logical contrariness in ethical expression does not alarm us. But what is novel is the extent to which social scientists employ symbols to extract symbolic behavior as *a way of measuring* others' non-symbolic activities.

This proxy for observation is often called "self-report," and is usually collected in "surveys." The practice rests on a multiplicity of assumptions. At minimum, it assumes:

1. That respondents think-speak in the same idiom as their interrogators.
2. That strangers are attentive to the same events as those that concern their inquisitors.
3. That people truthfully report their feelings, experiences, and activities to unfamiliar others.
4. In turn, this assumes that people accurately "know themselves." And to "know oneself" entails what is *not* always true: That individuals never deceive themselves.
5. That persons can accurately recall particular events.
   (Assumptions 1 through 5 are sometimes valid, but they are always subject to varying degrees of invalidity).[12]
6. "Surveys" assume, too, that informants' opinions, preferences, and reports of their conduct hold constant regardless of who asks whom about what and when.
   Such stability is questionable.[13] It requires testing with each object of a survey.
7. Observation-by-interrogation assumes that respondents are free of the unconscious "pull" of a host of well-known contaminants.

For example, accuracy of self-report varies with the topic of inquiry, with the wording of questions and their level of abstraction, with their positions in a series of queries, with the degree to which they depend on memory, and, as per item 6 above, with the relationships between inquirer and respondent.[14]

Accuracy also varies with a personality trait called "acquiescence bias." This is the disposition to agree with the inferred request of the interviewer by saying "yea" rather than "nay," by appearing "positive" rather than "negative."[15]

Acquiescence is an aspect of a more general "social desirability" distortion (*SD bias*). SD bias is the tendency to describe ourselves in better light than we behave.[16] As we shall see, this contaminant, like self-deception, is often good for our mental health. Knowing how we actually behave may not support our self-esteem.

8. Last, "scientific" employment of verbal instruments requires that investigators themselves do not give false impressions of the meanings of their surveys by attaching promissory titles to what they've collected.

When researchers say, for example, that their sets of queries measure "attitudes," "beliefs," "preferences," or "values," such rubrics signify that their results have *predictive utility*.

Applying these labels to verbal tools carries an implicit promise: That what is measured is a *disposition to act* in a particular way in particular situations.

Put the other way about, if "valuing" or "having an attitude" tells us nothing about the likelihood of respondents' future action of a distinctive sort, measuring "it" only adds decoration to argument.

Unless we have "adequate evidence" of the validity of people's reports of their pasts, tabulated by categories of action/condition, we remain at the mercy of others' and our own, reconstructions of what happened from fragile memories (pp. 140–144). And unless responses to verbal scales can be validated by non-verbal performances in the temporal-instrumental-predictive sense described in chapter 3, *we do not know* what respondents' utterances portend for their future deeds.

To validate, by our definition, means to give sound grounds for accepting social scientists' reports as legitimate measures of the activities—past or future—in which we're interested.[17]

This requirement asks for more than concordance of words with words. The requirement applies *because* social scientists who use "self-reports" want us to believe that these indicators refer to non-verbal activities and objectively discernible conditions.

Burden and Resistance

"Every man who attacks my belief diminishes
in some degree my confidence in it, and

therefore makes me uneasy; and I am angry
with him who makes me uneasy."
—*Samuel Johnson*[18]

To state the assumptions listed above is to challenge those who employ them. As per Samuel Johnson's sentiment, their mention makes devotees of self-report both uneasy and angry.

Nevertheless, the *burden of proof* that numbers, derived from questions-and-answers, bear the meanings their publishers attribute to them rests on those who produce them. It cannot be said that social scientists have adequately fulfilled this responsibility.

One cause of this default is clear. From beginnings in government censuses and, later, in "public opinion polls," a huge industry has developed. It employs hundreds of thousands of workers worldwide, and its product relies largely on what people tell strangers.

Money and repute are at stake, and calling caution becomes unwelcome. Indeed, criticism often incites odium.

It is necessary to emphasize, then, that inquiring about the *conditional utility* of strangers' responses to verbalists' questions does *not* assert that no one tells the truth about anything, ever. Nor does it say that we can never use queries about others' opinions or, with more risk of error, about their conduct and intentions.[19]

A fair-minded inquirer treats the issue of the accuracy of such vicarious observation as an empirical question. This attitude assumes that tests of the validity of what people say about themselves will exhibit *degrees of accuracy*. These tests assume, further, that the quantity and quality of error in self-reporting is *contingent*.

A Brief Résumé

"Let's not confuse the tool with the reality it's
being used to study."
—*Alain Connes*[20]

A huge library of research acquaints us with some of the distortion in others' reports of their circumstances and activities.

We know, for example, that pollsters can get people to express different opinions about the same topic by wording their questions in different ways.[21] Respondents will even offer opinions about legislation that doesn't exist and events that never happened.[22]

Such "deception" is not necessarily purposeful; it need not be lying. It is also careless, obliging, playful, and unconscious. On occasion, we even deceive ourselves.[23]

Moreover, as regards some truths about ourselves, it can be wholesome *not* to know them and *not* to reveal them. The popular prescription to "express yourself" to "let it all hang out," is not necessarily healthful.[24]

As per the SD bias, attempts to verify the answers given to registrars' questions find that respondents are most accurate about innocuous topics—like having a telephone and owning a house—and least accurate about prestigious topics and their intimate lives.

Thus a considerable proportion of American adults does *not* accurately state its age, income, occupation, military service, race, citizenship, use of hospitals, receipt of welfare assistance, housing characteristics, and voting record.[25]

Again, we expect reliabilities and validities to vary with time and place as well as with topic. For example, the pervasive and intrusive pre-election polls suffer from disagreements among themselves. Their discordant reports are multiply caused. One source of error is low response rate that, in turn, can be a function of the citizenry's satiety.

During the race for the American presidency, 2000, eight major polls received responses to about *half* their inquiries. Some of this reluctance is attributed to too many pollsters ringing our telephones as we sit for dinner.[26]

In Britain, Andrew Cooper shows that a major survey agency, MORI, has been consistently inaccurate in national elections between 1992 and 1997, and on various topics. He writes,

> Like opinion polls in general they consistently exaggerate Labour support, consistently understate Conservative support, and consistently fail to predict how well either party will do in national elections.[27]

Cooper attributes the source of error to "the spiral of silence" in which "many of the people who are disinclined to give their views to pollsters...are more likely to vote conservative."

Regardless of Cooper's explanation, we have here another instance of a weird kind of "reliability"—consistency in error (p. 136).

SD bias is also at work in United States' census enumerations. Regarding tallies of "income," Melis-Wright and Associates describe how the "pull" of social desirability distorts strangers' reports of their financial status:

> Money equates with respect, authority, one's self-concept and autonomy [and] the silence about money appears to be a social mechanism for insuring one's privacy. While...money may have religious significance, albeit unconscious, it may also signal an unstated dichotomy between a work-ethic mentality and the potential evil, corruptive influence of money. The fact is that survey researchers *know almost nothing* about how our respondents mentally construct their answers to the income question. While it is curious that some respondents presented a "bravado" about the topic and were eager to have their views represented, other respondents were quite angry and adamantly told us that this was "none of the government's business."[28]

SD bias is also apparent when prospective jurors are asked whether the race of defendants and victims will influence, or did influence, their decisions. Only naive lawyers accept jury-candidates' conventional protestations that they are innocent of prejudice.

In the climate of a spate of race-infused criminal trials in Los Angeles County during the 1990s, Jeffrey Toobin comments,

> American jurors have a long and still flourishing tradition both of taking race into account and of denying that they are doing any such thing.[29]

So, too, while Americans (at least when polled) say that "they don't object to racially mixed schools...nevertheless [they] move to and live in exclusionary areas...."[30]

Therapeutic Cautions

Verbal surveys are not only a widely approved way of "observing" human action and condition, they are also political tools. Their importance merits therapeutic reminders of the hazards of asking others for information about themselves.

This reminder does not, to repeat, argue that there is never concordance between what people say about their lives and how they are and what they do. It argues that there is enough discrepancy between utterance and other activities to call caution to those who use the former as indicator of the latter.

This gap is contingent, not absolute. Many of these contingencies are sufficiently well known to require modification of research methods. Modification includes tempering presumption about who can usefully ask which questions of whom.

Such caution prescribes responsibility. In particular, it urges that those who would *measure* action by attending to their subjects' words have an obligation to inform consumers of their studies of the *reliability* and *validity* of their instruments.

Moreover, these reliabilities and validities should be the kind that literate persons can comprehend. (It would make an interesting project to ascertain what, if anything, the publics that pay our way understand by a measuring instrument's being "reliable" and "valid.")

It is misleading to substitute unusual sorts of "reliability" for assurance that an index or scale maintains *constant reference* upon repeated application. This is the *useful* meaning of dependability. (It assumes, of course, that what is measured doesn't change between trials.) This is a possibility that seldom characterizes opinion polls and uncertainly characterizes stories about our pasts. Pages to follow give examples of errant memories.

Against this requirement of a measuring tool, it is a poor, but common, practice to declare "reliability" when all a researcher has done is evaluate the *internal consistency* of one's instrument—that is, that respondents give the same answer *at one time* to different questions about the same acts. Such inter-item concordance—"internal coherence"—does *not* guarantee *replicable reference*.[31]

Similarly, the kinds and degrees of validation required of a vicarious gauge will vary with what one is measuring and for what purpose. Examples that follow illustrate this point.

Varieties of Error

Trust in utterance is, we've said, popular. Such popularity among those who propose a science of the social makes it advisable to describe some domains of action and condition to which the self-report tool has been applied and how it can err.

Since asking people about their past activities is a major employment of questions put to them, memory is basic. A brief account of the vagaries of memory is followed by depiction of possible gaps between the stories respondents tell investigators and what other modes of observation reveal.

The illustrations given below are not intended to be encyclopedic. No one has assessed the quality of social scientists' tools for every realm in which they have been applied. Examples can be illuminating without being comprehensive.

Memory

"Imagination and memory are but one thing, which for divers considerations hath divers names."
—*Thomas Hobbes (1588-1679)*[32]

Hobbes was correct. Memories are not photographs of pasts. They are retrievals from various "distances" filtered by individual temperaments. They are reconstructions, and the word, "memory," serves to include such different neurophysiological processes as recognition, recall, and the unconscious accumulation demonstrated by the "savings test" (p. 144).

Remembering is the work of the nervous systems that vary with those enduring dispositions we term "personality." For example, among "mentally healthy" individuals, memory tends to forget the unpleasant. By contrast, neurotic personalities are prone to recall the unpleasant.[33]

Such chronically unhappy persons find it rewarding to regurgitate troubles. They "enjoy" reminding themselves and loved ones of miseries that others have allegedly put upon them. They expect the worst and their attitude sometimes produces the events they protest they do not desire. This activity has been called the "nocebo effect," the opposite of the well-known "placebo effect" that occurs when expecting a benefit (cure) helps create it.[34]

In this respect, psychopaths seem healthier than persons burdened with remembrance of wounded pasts.

In Sum: Recall is influenced by the kind of activity to be retrieved, by an individual's current psychophysical condition and enduring temperament, by image of one's self, by the relationship between inquirer and informant (including their personality traits),[35] and by a variety of expectations, including those produced by the unstated "theories" that each of us bears concerning how "things" are supposed to be connected.

For example, religions provide powerful stories about what makes us and our worlds, and why events occur as they do. With these "theories," some people become more superstitious than others. They remember more peculiar associations, and coincidence becomes meaningful correlation.

Then, too, memory degrades with age.[36]

Particulars

1. Depressed patients tend to report that their parents were "aloof, indifferent, and demanding"—a picture that accords with current theory about why people "get the blues." But these patients produce such memories *only when* they are "down," not before or after their dispirited periods.[37]

Depressed patients have "better" memory for unpleasant events than for pleasant ones. As might be expected, the relationship between emotional tone and memory is reversed when happy events are recalled.

For example, when college students are asked to recall their high-school grades, the higher their actual grades, the easier they are to remember or, at least, to report.[38] (SD at work again).

In sum, personality traits, the emotional flavor of events to be recalled, and acquired assumptions about the causes of one's current thoughts/feelings affect people's answers to others' questions. How much these effects vary with the intimacy of relationships between interrogators and respondents is not known.

2. Timing also makes a difference. Individuals questioned intermittently for fifteen years *incorrectly recall* in 1982 that they had always been as much in favor of equal rights for women as they had been when questioned in 1957.[39] We prefer to regard ourselves as consistent and, of course, as beneficent.

3. Similarly, defects in memory are revealed by the inconsistent reports individuals give epidemiologists concerning their childhood experiences, political activity, and medical-hygienic conduct.[40] When these investigators attempt to estimate hazards to health by asking questions of the citizenry, some of them now admit limits to this favored and faulty procedure.[41]

It is important that they do so because efforts to weigh the relative risks of the numerous conceivable causes of disease have expanded in recent years. These inquiries have extended from the realm of pathogen-induced illness into the boundless area of "mental disease/disorder," supplemented with newfound causes that might affect the "quality of our lives."[42]

In this spirit, epidemiologists have "tested" for the possible carcinogenic effects of the many possible hazards that surround us—in our "environments." They have inquired about the materials we eat, drink, and smoke. Under the awkward rubric, "lifestyle," they have asked us how we live, including questions about the quantity and quality of our exercise, sleep, and sexual activity.

With the aid of journalists who barrage us daily with new "findings" and "unfoundings" about the dangers that beset us, epidemiological work has produced what physician Lewis Thomas regards as "an epidemic of anxiety."[43]

Multiple difficulties confront researchers who would extract one or a few possibly damaging factors from what is probably a dense web of causes in which our health is shaped. Prominent among these impediments is the same obstacle that afflicts social scientists: Our inability to observe directly the activities we wish to test for *causal power*, and our consequent reliance on talk with its dependence on fragile memory. Inaccuracy of recall and report is to be expected.

Examples

Underweight individuals tend to overreport their intake of fat while overweight persons tend to underreport their intake, according to epidemiologist Ross Prentice. Similarly, Walter Willett notes that "people may recall their past intake of fat differently if they have just been diagnosed with breast cancer than if you pluck them out of a random sample, call them up out of the blue over the phone, and ask them what their past diet was." In this vein, the relationship between *self-reported* [female] breast implants and connective-tissue disease [principally cancer] was challenged by a validation study that revealed that what women said about their suffering from such disease could be confirmed by their individual medical records in *less than one-fourth of those who claimed such disability.*[44]

Comparable error occurs when investigators, testing the efficacy of anti-tobacco therapies, *ask* addicts about their smoking. What such persons say yields poor results even when their memory is aided with hand-held computers.[45] So, too, we cannot trust what young people tell us about their use of cocaine and heroin. Urine tests find large gaps between self-reports and actual indulgence.[46]

4. Our memories are not as accurate as we like to believe. We often say more about our pasts than we know.

For example, on the morning after the space shuttle *Challenger* exploded on launch, 28 January 1986, psychologists Ulric Neisser and Nicole Harsch had 106 university students write freely about how they had heard the news. They followed this memorial with a questionnaire that asked,

> What time was it, how did you hear about it, where were you, what were you doing, who told you, who else was there, how did you feel about it, how did the person who told you seem to feel about it, what did you do afterward?

Two and a half years later, in the fall of 1988, these psychologists found forty-four of the individuals who had completed the "morning after" questionnaire and had them respond to the same questions along with assessments of their confidence in their memories. They call these vivid recollections "flash-bulb memories."[47]

The investigators then calculated a weighted score of accuracy of recall between the first and second interrogations that allowed a top score of seven. Among their forty-four respondents, the average score was just under three.

> What makes these low scores interesting, the researchers conclude, is the high degree of confidence that accompanied many of them....Two subjects...exhibit an entirely appropriate relation between confidence and accuracy—they had none of either.... In the rest of the group there seems to be *no relation* between confidence and accuracy at all.[48]

As chapter 6 indicates, considerable additional research finds that the confidence with which people make statements is of *no value* in assessing the accuracy of their assertions.

This replicated result is relevant to judgment of politicians' "facts" and the validity of eyewitness testimony.[49]

5. Fragility of memory is further attested by the fact that we can be led to believe imagined events and stimulated to "unearth" activities that never happened.

For example, adults can insert false recollections in children who come to believe, sometimes firmly, that others did "bad things" to them. Zealous social workers and other "experts" have encouraged exaggerated reports of child abuse and have thereby assisted in modern "witch hunts."

Such counselors, many of them state-licensed, have done immeasurable damage with their practice of "guided imagery" and "memory work" that is presumed to "uncover" repressed memories of childhood molestation.

With authoritative stimulation, people will "recall" events that never occurred.[50] And it is not only children who are so suggestible. Women encouraged to "recover" memories of sexual abuse in their childhoods are prone to conjure up false images.[51] Just imagining such untrue events can "implant false memories."[52]

Moreover, experiments demonstrate that such false memories can be more durable than true ones, and we now know how this comes to be.[53]

None of these frailties of memory denies the fact of valid memory. Nor does it deny the demonstrable phenomenon of "memory trace." These are like sediment m early events in one's life, unavailable to recall, but observable as "savings."

"Savings" refers to reduction in time, trials, or both required to learn a novel performance when the aptitude has been conferred by infantile training that *cannot be known* to the trainee.

For a remarkable demonstration of such unconscious learning, read psychologist Harold Burtt's reports of his experiments with his son.[54] These trials extended from the boy's fifteenth month, with intervals, until the lad was eighteen years old. They show remarkable savings in memorizing Greek (nonsense to the child) between infancy and eight and a half years with a declining savings during later periods of the boy's youth.

Such "hidden competence" in no way validates claims to unearth from the unconscious accurate memories of early events in one's life. The "savings test" describes a singular process. Recovering memories under "professional" guidance is a quite different phenomenon, and one to be questioned.

Work, Wage, Income

Social scientists and their governments attempt to define "work," and then to count who works at what, with what result in producing wealth and distributing it.

This assignment is difficult. It arouses passions. Political struggles ensue. And, if opponents remain civil, they try to advance their positions by citing numbers. But when these numbers derive from interviewers talking to strangers about their "work," "income," and "wealth," gaps open between what people report and how matters are with them.

Tallies vary, then, with *who defines the units* with which we converse, and how units are conceived (ch. 5). Categories such as "family," "work," and "income" seem commonsensical. They are nonetheless subject to manipulation.

Thus the Canadian government recently changed its definition of "work" for census and tax purposes. One angry woman, Carol Lees, demanded, with threat of boycott, that census questions about "work" be revised to recognize that caring for a household and rearing three children was such an activity that qualified her family for tax reduction.[55]

In addition, it is not unusual to find differences between what people tell tax-registrars about their earnings and what other indicators reveal. For example, when Americans' statements about their "incomes" were checked against other databases between 1950 and 1980, citizens failed to report between 11 and 13 percent of their probable money income. Christopher Jencks summarizes:

> asking respondents to report household members' money income before taxes simplifies the respondent's task, but it yields a measure that does not necessarily move in tandem with the respondent's material standard of living.[56]

A parallel discrepancy between what people *say* about their work and wages and what payroll records show became apparent during an American debate on the likely effects of a federally mandated minimum wage increase.

Economists David Card and Alan Krueger tested by *telephone survey* the hypothesis that minimum wage rise would diminish "entry-level" employment in New Jersey. They report, "...no evidence that the rise in New Jersey's minimum wage reduced employment at fast-food restaurants in the state."[57]

Economists David Neumark and William Wascher tested the same hypothesis on an overlapping sample of fast-food restaurants and found that

> ...our estimate using *payroll data* implies that the minimum wage increase led to a statistically significant 4.6 percent *decline* in employment.[58]

Beyond the argument whether to seek information by questioning people or by other means, such a discrepancy is important for other social scientists. For example, several prominent students of crime advocate that governments should *raise* minimum wages as a means of *reducing* criminal work.

This prescription is made in ignorance of dosage effects. It is made without knowledge of *how much more* low-income persons would have to be paid to reduce their incentive for which kinds of criminal activity.

Moral Beliefs

Earlier pages commented on the well-known difference between "mouth-morality" and moral conduct. It deserves repetition that moral beliefs, like other "facts" about ourselves, reveal different pictures depending on the wording of questions, who asks the questions in what situations, and whether the queries are framed as generalizations or as specific issues.

Simple, specific moral questions are easier for most people to answer. By contrast lengthy questionnaires, with items variously phrased and dispersed produce contrary and contradictory beliefs for as much as one-fourth of the material.[59]

Social Status

When American schoolboys are asked to indicate their parents' socio-economic status, agreement between what they say and independent assessment of parental status is high among white seniors in high school, lower for younger white boys, and of modest validity for black boys.[60]

In parallel with this discrepancy between utterance and reality, when interviewers asked Australian fathers about their principal occupations and then inquired about their sons' work, they drew different maps of social positions from those derived by asking sons about their own principal occupations and then about their fathers' work.[61]

While fathers used language to close the social distance between their own and their sons' status, their sons' descriptions tended to distance themselves from their fathers.

The authors of this research cutely title their report, "Is it true what they say about Daddy?" Their findings were extracted from a democratic populace.

Family Scenes

In keeping with the Australian study of fathers and sons, interviews with 1,669 American high-school seniors and their parents find wide differences in their assessments of one another's attitudes, values, personal traits, and behaviors.[62]

Similarly, when mothers and fathers use a Child Behavior Checklist to describe their children, ages three to thirteen, mothers report more undesirable conduct than fathers do, and they disagree with their husbands about the occurrence of particular children's behaviors about *two times* as often as they agree.[63]

These parents agree most about their children's characteristics when their behaviors are specifically described and when parents consider their children's conduct to be "disturbed."

It is not known whether it is words that make the difference in how "loved ones" describe each other, or faulty observations, or both, but additional evidence confirms the large zones of inaccuracy in familial evaluations.

Fifty-nine American couples rated themselves and their spouses on twenty-two dimensions of personality. Their degree of agreement ranged from low regarding being "secure" ($r = +.14$) to modest regarding "emotional stability" ($r = +.64$). As regards who has "power" in the family, spouses *disagree* more often than they agree ($r = -.43$).[64]

The low order of these correlations challenges easy assumption that intimate aspects of domestic relations can be known by asking questions of strangers.

A Canadian study verifies this difficulty. *Independently of one another* individuals in 321 married couples in Toronto answered six questions about their private lives.

These "middle-class" spouses seldom agree about whether "lack of privacy ever prevented intercourse" ($r = +.15$) and about "who gets his/her way in a dispute" (r = +.22). This is yet another indicator of *lack of agreement* about that sensitive question, "Who has power?"[65]

These couples concur moderately about the number of hours they spent together the day before the interview (r = .40) and how frequently they fight (r = .46). They agree best about how many times they had sexual intercourse during the four weeks preceding interrogation (r = .68).[66]

Josefina Card substantiates these Canadian findings with her test of agreement between one hundred Filipino couples and fifty Caucasian spouses in the San Francisco Bay area. Card reports that these married individuals agree in their statements about demographic variables, but, again, disagree about their attitudes and activities. As regards their attitudes, the average correlation between Filipino couples was .25 and for Caucasians, .45. Concordance concerning activities in which they had jointly participated again averaged .25 for Filipino spouses and only .38 for Caucasian couples.[67]

Similar low to modest levels of agreement appear when researchers ask individuals who live together about their domestic violence, and do so by interviewing participants *independently of one another*. For example, investigators had 103 American married duos respond privately to the Conflict Tactics Scale (CTS)—a popular measure of marital brawling. Spouses agreed about their fighting only a little better than by chance—that is, what we would expect if we flipped a coin to assign their answers.

Worse than that, these persons agreed *less* than by chance when they were asked about "severe fights." And, when they were asked about "having beat him or her up," *no couple agreed*. This means that when a husband admitted he had "beat up" his wife, she did not record the incident, and conversely, when a wife said she had been "beat up," not a single husband agreed.[68]

Scholars who review confessions of marital violence conclude,

> Couples exhibit little agreement in reporting the occurrence of acts in which both were allegedly involved, and self-reported acts sometimes fail to differentiate the behavior of groups known to exhibit huge differences in the perpetration of violence.[69]

Many (most?) inquirers concerned with domestic violence and the distribution of power among cohabiting intimates have failed to check the validity of the responses they receive to their questions by the simple tactic of interrogating married couples and other household residents *independently* of one another, and comparing their assertions for concordance. The research by Booth and Welch in Toronto, Card in the San Francisco Bay area, and Szinovacz's tallies of marital fighting are the only such comparisons I've been able thus far to find.

Against such caution, Murray Straus, advertised as 'the foremost researcher on family violence in the world," informs me that, among the more than 9,000 families he has studied, he has *not* tested for the congruence of reports received from members of these units.[70]

What Goes On?

No one who has survived a contested divorce, and no attorney who has attended such, believes that the stories failed lovers tell will agree. Nor do they believe that outsiders—friends, kin, counselors—can ascertain which of the antagonists, if either, is giving an accurate description of their domestic life.

Tears won't tell, and neither will a polygraph reading—popularly and misleadingly called a "lie-detector."[71]

For those who resist this information, videotherapy is prescribed in the form of motion pictures: the famed Japanese film *Rashomon* or its remake as an American-Western story, *The Outrage*. In this ancient drama, three participants in a killing, and possible rape, give their interpretations of events. Each tale is plausible; none accords with the others. Therefore, if there is a "whole truth," we can only guess which rendition, if any, tells it.

What applies to fighting families is relevant to investigation of apparently pacific units: Presentation of a favorable self constitutes formidable defense against hurtful veracity. It is a healthy type of self-deception, and an impediment to those who seek the truth about intimate activities by asking questions of their participants.

Sexual Activity

> *"Sex as an institution, sex as a general notion, sex as a problem, sex as a platitude—all this is something I find too tedious for words. Let's skip sex."—Vladimir Nabokov (1899-1977) author of* Lolita, *a money-making love story, reproduced in two film versions, that some critics condemn as pedophilic-sexual.*

Apropos of differences in lovers' reports of their intimate lives, and indicative of Americans' ambiguous interest in others' use of their genitalia, the latest in a long list of surveys quizzing people about their erotic pleasures promises to be "definitive."[72]

At great expense ($450 per interview), and with assurance that they had sampled a representative segment of American adults, investigators used a ninety-minute interview and a four-part self-administered questionnaire to ascertain what their informants had done "sexually" *with others* over the past year, past five years, and during their lifetimes (!). (Refer again to the earlier section on memory.)

Asking strangers questions about how they've used their genitalia, and other erotic parts, alone or with others, in what fashion, how frequently, and with what satisfaction, yields replies that *cannot be validated*. In the realm of Eros, and with wild assumptions about individuals' capacity for self-revelation, everything depends on the contingencies listed on pages 135-144. In particular, everything depends on persons' use of language, on the diligence of their attention during passion, the accuracy of their memories, and the honesty of their assertions.

Laumann and associates admit as much. For example, with regard to self-reports of homosexual activity, they write,

> The widespread strongly negative view of homosexuality shapes both behaviors and our attempts to measure them. While we have attempted to be nonjudgmental in our inquiries, many respondents are likely to have been reluctant to report behaviors and feelings that they think might reflect badly on them in the eyes of the interviewers or the researchers. The estimates derived from survey data on socially stigmatized sexual behaviors and feelings, whether they be masturbation, homosexual relations, anal sex, or extramarital affairs, are no doubt lower-bound estimate.[73]

In Sum: SD bias is admittedly at work. And it can also work in another direction. Thus, with regard to respondents' statements about the *duration* of their sexual intercourse, social desirability can stimulate bragging.[74]

Given the moral significance attached to uses of what were once called our "privates," it is no surprise to hear scholars and legislators complain about such research. Some of the criticism is scathing, on both moral and technical grounds.[75] The issue, then, is not only about the dependability and validity of such studies, but also about their utility: In addressing any particular "sexual problem," what can governments do better with the results of self-reported activities than without them?

Against criticism, and given social scientists' vast investment in interrogation, it is also not surprising that some psychologists and sociologists defend asking strangers questions about their private lives. Their defense claims that such inquiry is valuable. It allegedly yields accurate information important for public policy, and it is said to be especially germane for programs designed to prevent the spread of diseases such as AIDS.[76]

Further to their defense, Laumann and his colleagues propose that the agreement between their findings and those of some other surveys of sexual practices—three in particular—assure the reliability of their data.[77]

With some divergence among them, studies of self-reported sexual activities draw similar maps of who does what with whom, how frequently, and with what satisfaction. From such verbal concordance, the 1995 investigators suggest that their measurements are generally valid, and valid not only for the persons sampled, but also for the American population at large. Their data, they say, "are as accurate as the communication between researcher and respondent can sustain at this time."[78]

The unresolved debate concerns the degree of credibility to be accorded results of these many inquiries, with allowance for the possibility that questions about some domains of sexual practice may be more accurate than others.

If such investigators of our sexual lives could have questioned partners as well as respondents—*independently of one another* as did studies of cohabitants—credibility would have been enhanced. Lacking that, belief in the accuracy of such surveys remains a function of temperament modified by personal experience.

With apology for personal reference, and with no knowledge of the "normality" of my own experience, contestable memory advises me that I could not answer many of the sex-surveyors' questions—either for my privy self or for their interrogators. Accuracy would vary with age, with time-of-life queried, and with such easily revised variables as the quantities and qualities of pleasures remembered.

Many such questions—not always, but often enough—strain attention and memory and, as a consequence, appear hollow at best and naive at worst.

For example, I doubt that interviewers' judgments of the "frankness" with which strangers answered their queries have any value—as Laumann et al. take time to report—and I doubt the tallies that respondents "remember" concerning their *partners'* orgasms.

Skepticism about these and other "facts" is induced by a central question that Laumann and associates asked of their respondents—a query about "having sex." President William J. Clinton later fortified this doubt with his famous (infamous?) reply to questions about his "sex life" during 1998 impeachment proceedings. At that time, the president vigorously denied having had "a sexual affair," "sexual relations," or "a sexual relationship" with a young White House intern. In his lexicon, fellatio did not count as "sexual activity." And apropos of his interrogation, the president, in correct and lawyerly manner, questioned what the word, "is," meant.

The president's evasiveness parallels the sociologists' slippery language. Their 1995 survey's definitive question tells respondents

...by "sex" or "sexual activity," we mean any mutually voluntary activity with another person that involves genital contact and sexual excitement or arousal, that is, feeling really turned on, even if intercourse or orgasm did not occur.[79]

Replies to this question and projections from similar surveys allow Laumann and associates to find that an estimated 45 percent of men between the ages of eighty and eighty-four have "sex partners." While journalists gave this "finding" cheerful publicity, less than ten percent of women of like age report having such company.

A Personal Note

I am a male octogenarian and multiply fractured lover (b. 1913). I was therefore intrigued by sociologists' revelation that so large a proportion of us oldsters are enjoying "sex partners"—a vague phrasing that some journalists translated as our "having sex,"

I therefore share with readers a more private and intimate inquiry than the sociological staff was able to conduct.

I belong to two athletic clubs where, at the time this survey was published, I had known men over a span of five to twelve years. These men range in age from their late twenties to their late eighties. They do not constitute a representative sample of American manhood. They are not poor. I don't know how their health compares with all men of like age, but they are probably no less vigorous than others of similar vintage.

The older segment of these acquaintances—most of them in their sixties and seventies—includes retired military officers, former executives in commerce and industry, professional workers at medicine, law, accounting and engineering, small-business proprietors, and, including myself, two emeritus professors.

Undirected banter with these men in sauna, hot tub, and locker-room conceivably yields more honest admission about our "sex lives" than individuals' responses to strangers' ambiguous questions, particularly when we confess to loss of power.

When I told my audiences about the national surveys of our sexual activities and the alleged pre-Viagra vigor of us male octogenarians, I was greeted with hoots, ribald comments, and impolite doubts about the probability of such delight for men of such seniority. Allowance was made that there might be a few gray studs who still stood for conjugation, but *almost half* of men in their early eighties?

A lawyer in his late seventies, alert to question-wording, asked, "If I snuggle with Emily [his wife], does that mean I have a 'sex partner'?" I contributed the consoling words attributed to Johann Wolfgang von Goethe when he found his sexual appetite waning, "FREE at last!"

Of the five men in my age-cohort, born between 1910 and 1914, none of us was having penile-vaginal intercourse. At the end of one bout of raillery, an eighty-year-old engineer asked, "What difference does it make?"

Knowing Alien Others

Similar difficulties arise when we try to understand exotic peoples whose language and manner of conversation differ. Like detectives, cultural anthropologists (ethnographers) must make decisions about the trustworthiness of their informants. Such decisions can, of course, be in error—error produced by differences in the social standards of signal-senders and receivers, or of preconceptions (desires) on either side of a communication, or of innocent misunderstanding of the meaning of signs.

Instance

For example, in recent years ethnographers confronted a challenge to one of their prominent colleagues, the late Margaret Mead.

Over seventy years ago, Mead had depicted an idyllic life among Polynesians for whom "coming of age" was a transition without stress and where sexual freedom before marriage was allegedly enjoyed without shame, jealousy, or violence.

Mead reports that her discovery of a people who share a "carefree" (her term) and sexually easy adolescence on one of the Samoan islands is based on interviews with twenty-five girls whom she "studied in detail [and] who had passed puberty within the last four years but were not yet classed by the community as adults.[81]

On this island, no English was spoken and Mead was not fluent in Samoan. Moreover, the two Samoan women on whom Mead relied were hardly "girls." They were, at the time, Mead's age, twenty-four years old (see notes 83, 84).

Antithesis

Mead's *Coming of Age in Samoa* has gained high repute. Thus, sixty years after its publication, a guide to "cultural literacy," listing "what every American needs to know," includes her research for having "revolutionized the field of anthropology."[82] Long before receiving this eulogy, Mead herself had described her book as "a classic scientific study."[83]

Australian anthropologist Derek Freeman disagrees. In a series of publications, Freeman argues that Mead was hoaxed by her joking respondents—in particular, the two upon whom Mead had relied.[84]

In defense of Mead, several American anthropologists have offered other interpretations of her work—its methods and results. And at the annual business meeting of the American Anthropological Association, 1983, the Association voted unanimously to condemn Freeman's publications as "...poorly written, unscientific, irresponsible, and misleading." Freeman has responded and produced additional information lending credence to his critique.[85]

Among his rebuttals, Freeman claims greater intimacy with the people Mead had studied. He was adopted by them and arguably has greater knowledge of their practices in general and language in particular. To repeat, Mead had no command of Samoan.

In addition, Freeman extracts from Mead's unpublished notebooks statements that contradict her published description of a people who, she alleges, had no strong convictions, no interpersonal hostility, and no experience of rape and murder. Against this portrait, Freeman refers to *court records* of assault, rape, and murder, inclusive of the time when Mead conducted her study.[86]

Urban Sites

Difficulties of observation and communication do not disappear even when ethnographers and their informants come from nearby venues and speak somewhat similar languages. Thus when a succession of "urban anthropologists" visits poor enclaves in the West's large, rich cities, readers of their reports often receive conflicting pictures of how these others live and, more strongly, why they live in ways their visitors find unpleasant.

For one such contest of interpretations, read Katherine Newman's depiction of life among poor workers in New York City and Heather Macdonald's contrary portrayal.[87] Then compare these portraits with a few that other observers of "the culture of poverty" have developed.[88]

In company with different samples of people, and their actions "observed," and *reliance upon utterance*, inquirers' preconceptions probably work to produce some of these differences. Nevertheless, in moderation of the aspiration to be scientific in studies of social conditions/events, it bears reminding that the heart of science is multiple, independent tests of data derived from several modes of "observation."

Convergence among findings lends credibility, but not certainty, to hypotheses. Divergence among results validates the Scottish verdict, "Not proven," meaning either "not adequately tested" or, perhaps, "not testable."

Criminal Activity

Criminologists have been enthusiastic consumers of verbal reports. They were driven to this substitute for observation by their obvious inability to observe most criminal events in their making and consummation, and by their recognition that police records are necessarily partial. Police work is largely reactive—responsive to citizens' calls. It therefore counts only a ridiculously small portion of all offenses.

For example, criminal homicide—murder and manslaughter—is presumably the most thoroughly pursued and recorded of all crime in rich countries. However, such killing probably occurs in large numbers *not* "known to the police," and, even when recorded by police, are *not* "cleared by arrest."

According to a recent tally, the nine American cities with more than a million inhabitants "clear by arrest" an average of about 60 percent of criminal homicides. Proportions range from the mid-40 percents in San Diego and Chicago to a high of 78 percent in Dallas. In Washington, D.C., only 30 percent of such killings result in arrest, meaning that, in 70 percent of re-corded criminal homicides, no one is indicted much less convicted.[89]

With such gaps between the numbers of homicides committed and those reported, and those reported that result in arrest, indictment, and conviction, it is likely that the numbers of lesser crimes—all the assaults, arsons, and thefts—far exceed the number we produce. Official tallies are local and lim-ited, and need not give an accurate picture of who does how much of which kinds of offense in large populations.

And what is true of the size of the gaps between crimes committed and crimes counted in wealthy lands must be exceeded by orders of magnitude in poor countries. Ethnographic studies suggest as much.[90]

For this reason, criminologists have supplemented their use of police records by asking citizens whether they have been victims of crimes and, alternatively, by asking them to confess their own offenses. Neither supple-ment is complete, and neither is error-free.

The first of these vicarious observations is called "victimization surveys"; the second, "self-report surveys." Governments in several prosperous lands regularly conduct the first type of inquiry; the second is usually conducted by academics among captive audiences in schools, prisons, and reformato-ries.

Victimization surveys question samples of populations about their having suffered assault, forcible rape, robbery, and "personal larceny"—considered to be crimes against *individuals*—and about theft of automobiles and auto parts, burglary, and "household larceny"–considered to be crimes against *households*.

These surveys generally do *not* count arson, murder and manslaughter, nor do they inquire about crimes committed by, within, or against organizations—commercial and governmental.

Such interrogations also do *not* record offenses against children under 13 years of age, although independent tallies in some American states indicate that perhaps one-sixth of individuals reported to be victims of rape are such youngsters.

Moreover, interviews do not count serial victimizations, so that "if a woman can't recall precisely the number of times her husband beat her, the survey counts just one crime.[91] In addition, questions are not asked of the *millions* of persons in jail, prison, hospital, asylum, shelter, and the military who are vulnerable to attacks on body and property.

Like every other attempt to count crime, surveys omit much. For example, in rich lands, the most expensive style of thievery is fraud—theft by deceit. It is committed by and against individuals, and by and against commercial, industrial, religious and political organizations. Neither the frequency with which theft-by-fraud occurs within populations larger than a face-to-face commune nor the quantity of wealth stolen can be counted.

Confessing Misconduct

*"We only confess our little faults to persuade
people that we have no big ones."*
—Francois, Duc de la Rochefoucauld (1613-
1689)[92]

An immense inventory of confessions of delinquent and criminal activity has accumulated over the past three decades, most of it gathered from young people in captive clusters. This library of research cannot be said to have dramatically changed the picture of criminal careers obtained from police work.

That common portrait of the uneducated, anti-social tough has been altered more by unobtrusive observations, including "sting operations." These "sneaky" tactics have expanded information, not so much about who attacks whom, but about who lies, cheats, and steals, and in which ways and under what circumstances.[93] From this expanded base, one general lesson can be drawn: Outside small communities, *a quantity of wealth left unguarded will be stolen.*[94]

Nevertheless, criminologists persist in using self-reports, with slight attention to the quality of the information obtained, and despite early research that showed race and sex to make a difference in the accuracy of American youngsters' admissions of misconduct. Early on, Hindelang and his associates found that, when they checked their subjects' admissions of delinquencies against their police records, about two-thirds of white boys and half of their black boys were accurate while their young women were less candid—about half of their white women and only 30 percent of their black women were accurate.[95]

Undeterred by this poor start, optimistic inquirers continue to believe that the question is a powerful instrument with which to discern truths about others' private lives. Thus social scientists have spent time and money asking people in prison about their criminal careers.

Honesty among Inmates

We imprison bad actors with several justifications that sometimes reinforce one another and sometimes conflict.

We incarcerate persons because they deserve it and because their victims want it; these are ways of "doing justice."

We also wish to impose pain and shame on offenders in order to deter those who might be tempted to commit their crimes and, sometimes, as a means of reforming the criminals themselves. But the most immediately practical reason for imprisoning individuals is to protect ourselves from them.

To estimate how much crime-reduction is produced by the expense and damage of incarcerating persons, criminologists need to know how much crime, of what sort, current inmates might have committed if they'd been free.

They call this number *lambda*, and they've been sufficiently bold, or naive, to try to calculate this figure by asking questions of prison inmates!

A series of studies have employed both interviews and questionnaires. They work, of course, with the hopeful assumption that what concerns academics also concerns inmates.

On this assumption, researchers interviewed forty-nine men imprisoned for robbery who had at least one prior felony conviction. Limiting their inquiry to these convicts' adult offenses, investigators found gross *underreporting*. These men recalled roughly *half* of their officially recorded arrests and convictions.[96]

A second survey among 624 male felons in five California prisons used anonymous questionnaires that allowed only restricted checks against official records.[97] However, less than half of these men (47 percent) submitted usable questionnaires! Of the remaining inmates, 13 percent denied having committed any of the eleven crimes about which the researchers inquired. Six percent of respondents denied having committed any crime, including the offense for which they had been imprisoned, and half of convicted rapists denied that they had raped.[98]

A third survey of more than 2,000 male inmates in jails and prisons in California, Michigan, and Texas produced response rates that ranged among institutions from 49 percent to 82 percent.[99] In this study volunteers from prison populations were asked to complete signed questionnaires that reviewed the two years (!) of their careers prior to their current incarceration. They were asked to indicate the number of offenses they had committed while "on the street" and the distribution of their crimes month by month!

Such interrogation flatters inmates' attention and memory. It unduly trusts their diligence, and it bespeaks academic projection—the assumption that convicts care about the events that their inquisitors study.

Nevertheless, for the 1,214 of these men for whom tests could be made of their *demographics*, some three-fourths were deemed correct on 85 percent or more of the "quality checks" that applied to them. But for the nine types of *crime* about which they were quizzed, *mismatches* were made between self-reports and official records by 28 percent of respondents concerning their *arrests*, 24 percent concerning the number of their *convictions for felonies*, and 26 percent concerning *the crime* for which they were imprisoned.

Sixteen percent misstated the number of prison terms they had served and 43 percent could not recall, within a two-year span, their age at first arrest. For the two years prior to their current incarceration, between 24 percent and 36 percent of all convicted robbers denied having robbed and 30 percent of convicted burglars denied having burglarized.[100]

These large "errors" were made where respondents knew their veracity could be checked. Current literature suggests that criminologists may now have abandoned their search for *lambda*.

Confessing Delinquency

The accuracy with which youngsters confess their misbehavior is no greater than that of inmates' confessions. A team of social scientists [101] interviewed 930 young men and women in peaceful Dunedin, New Zealand, and 430 boys in urban Pittsburgh, Pennsylvania, with what is probably the most respected self-report tool for assessing youthful misconduct, the National Youth Survey.[102]

Scores on this measure were compared with police records, court convictions, and parents', teachers', and friends' ratings. All six modes of inquiry point toward the same kinds of persons as more and less delinquent. However, the relationships among these indicators range from near zero to mostly modest.

For young men, the correlation between their self-reported misconduct and their *police records* is "statistically significant," but moderate: $r = .41$ to .44. The association between their delinquency scores and their *convictions* is lower: $r = .35$ to .36.

The young women in this study, like those in California noted above, are *less candid* than the men concerning their receipt of police attention. Their self-reported delinquency correlates only .21 with *police records*. But they produce the same low order of honesty as their male counterparts in admitting their *convictions*: $r = .35$.

These loose relationships mean that only between four and 18 percent of the variation in self-reported delinquency is associated with variations in police contacts and criminal convictions. From these weak connections, supplemented with ratings by parents, teachers, and friends, investigators compute no formula that increases their ability to foretell which of these youngsters will become serious adult offenders.

Here, again, social scientists' difficulties are illuminated. Lacking ability to observe the many influences that channel lives, we rely on talk. And with this reliance, we do mischief.

Embarrassment

Criminologists have tried to count crime by *asking* people about their victimization or their commission of offenses, in order to correct the admittedly deficient police tallies. Given this purpose, it is not known how much concordance, if any, to expect between what police logs show, what victimization surveys indicate, and self-reports reveal. In this uncertainty risks abound, not only in the hazard of publicizing "funny numbers," but also in the possibility of producing injustice.

For example, one of America's premier criminologists published an essay in which he praised self-reports for giving him "evidence" that police arrests were biased. In particular, the bias was said to disqualify police records as indicators of the likely honesty of job candidates.

The late Marvin Wolfgang testified in *Gregory v. Litton Systems, Inc.*, a 1970 civil suit involving equal opportunity law, that measures of "hidden delinquency [by self-report] reduced to insignificance" police figures that showed a criminal arrest record for blacks that, at the time, exceeded that of whites by four times.[103]

Of course, the value of comparing *admissions of delinquencies* with *arrests for crimes* assumes that the events counted by these different sources are the same: Does the delinquency scale inquire about the same offenses for which adult Americans are arrested?

Despite the patent weakness of this assumption, Wolfgang reports that he found a study by Chambliss and Nagasawa "particularly useful" because it included whites, blacks, and Japanese, and allowed the inference that the wide gaps in arrests between these ethno-racial categories of young men were reduced, but not eliminated, by their self-reports.[104]

The sadness of this example of social science-in-use is that the peer-reviewed study that Wolfgang found helpful in court is flawed. Indeed, it is so defective it should never have been published.

It asked samples of white, black, and Japanese boys in Seattle eight questions. These questions were *not published* in the research-article, and no comparison was made between the offenses for which young men were arrested and the behaviors listed on the sociologists' questionnaire.[105]

More than that. To the faulty notion that the criminologists' measurement gauged the same activities to which police attend, these investigators added another week assumption. They decided, on no ground other than "flip judgment," that those boys were "delinquent" who scored above the median on their unvalidated scale. There is no basis for this cutting-point and, of course, one can obtain different proportions of "delinquents" by moving it.

Such expert testimony perpetrated injustice because the court did not know it was based on "junk science." Judge and jury had only the criminologist's *authority* with which to assess the quality of his "evidence."

The hazards of finding out how people live, and what they do and have done, persist when we inquire about who they "are."

Ethno-Racial Identity

Like all other creatures, *Homo sapiens* has long clustered as "kinds." Humanity recognizes differences among its species, prefers its own, defines some kinds as allies, some as indifferent, and others as enemies, and fights for separate territory.

Throughout the animal realm, recognition is based primarily on physical characteristics, secondarily on behavioral traits, and among human beings most elaborately, but not alone, by distinctive symbols.[106]

We insert such signals into our bodies—as designs in scars and tattoos. We paint them on flesh, hair, fur, and nails. We display our distinctive signs by costume, coiffure, and colors, by song and dance, gesture, dialect, and diet, and by the additional banners and manners we prize as markers of difference, pridefully called "identity."

Today these badges are regarded as both pleasant and healthful and evil and dangerous, depending on who evaluates whose affiliation.

For example, among some scholars, it is now deemed morally offensive and physically inaccurate to regard varieties of humanity as "races." Many cultural anthropologists and some geneticists decry the concept as invalid— that is, as being non-taxonomic of "fundamental" attributes of the human species.[107]

In this vein, physicist Philip Morrison refers to "race" as "an old and wicked idea."[108] He also deems this concept unsatisfactory because "people vary genetically within groups more than they vary from one group to another."

This popular statement assumes, of course, that human "groups" can be, and are identified, whatever we call them. It ignores the fact that small differences in origins can make large differences in consequences, and that, no matter what title we give "kinds of people," Morrison's criticism can be applied to *every classification* of human "families" and their relatives. Variation among identifying markers can be greater within nominated clusters than between them.

As a suggestion of this possibility, geneticist Matt Ridley shows that, *chemically*, we are "to a ninety-eight percent approximation, chimpanzees," and vice versa, "they are...human beings." He adds that, "in genetic composition, we are more like chimpanzees than gorillas are."[109]

The clarity of the clusters—the presumed taxa—by which we nominate people as 'types" will vary with the size of the "groups" being compared, the criteria by which we identify them, and the shapes of the distributions of the traits by which we classify them as distinct.[110]

However, the idea of "race" is additionally called "wicked" because it has lent itself to "racism," an ideology that ranks varieties of humanity along a gradient of superiority-inferiority, stimulating hatred of the different and justifying their exclusion and even their extermination.

But what is said to be wicked about classifying people by "race" applies as well, and with a *longer history*, to such currently acceptable nominations of persons as by their "religion," "nationality," "ethnicity," "color," "social class," and, according to the U. S. *Census 2000*, their "ancestry," a novel rubric under which it counts 604 "kinds."[111]

These, and other markers, have long been used to justify claims to difference and distinctive rights, and to stimulate and rationalize hatred, enslavement, expropriation, exclusion, and extermination. This statement applies in the twenty-first century as in the past.

Nevertheless, and in contrast to tallies in most European lands, the United States *Census* specifically labels categories of its population as "races." And some associations of American scholars do as much, but employ euphemisms such as "color," "ethnicity," and "origin."

Recently, the Hawaiian legislature considered a law that would grant special privileges, including shopping discounts, to those of its residents who could document possession of "50 percent or more Hawaiian blood." If enacted, this law would provide identity cards to such distinctive persons, in keeping with practices in the former Union of Soviet Socialist Republics and Nazi Germany.

In parallel, the Republic of Fiji moves in this direction. Its politically inspired impulse to categorize its population by ethno-racial types is a consequence of struggles for commercial and political power between its "people of color"—"native Fijians" and fourth-generation "Indians" (Hindus).

In such fluctuating manner, "race" is ousted by the front door and admitted by the rear.[112]

What also offends critics of the "race" concept is its correlative assumption that differences between kinds of people are genetically based and transmitted. For many consumers of public opinions, this suggests, *incorrectly*, that if a distinctive disposition is inherited it is incorrigible.

By contrast, when differences between "groups" appear to have been learned-in-situations, many scholars and their publics assume—again *incorrectly*—that such behaviors are therefore malleable according to our desires. This mistaken interpretation offers hope of correction by State power when others' activities are unpleasant, and it thereby becomes ethico-politically acceptable among meliorists.

This optimistic thesis is explicit in the work of some biologists who wish to liberate us from "oppressive forms" of genetic determinism so that we shall be free "to create...a more just—a socialist—society." In their "struggle to create that society," these professors believe their opponent to be "much of today's science [that acts] to preserve the interests of the dominant class, gender, and *race*"[113] (emphasis added).

Although these privileged academics oppose the notion of "race," they cannot avoid using it when they wish to refer to their despised kind: *White* men who, like themselves, are relatively rich.

Our concern here is not with the nature-nurture debate that changes, as it should, with knowledge. Nor is it simply to doubt the ability of biologists and their preferred politicians to *create* a "more just society" according to plan. Our attention is directed toward fluctuations in the ways people identify themselves, and towards the effects of *purpose* and *language* upon modes of classifying our nature and self-regard.

With this turn of concern, we notice that American hospitals, and some in Europe, now sort applicants for service by ethno-racial "kinds." Without calling these clusters "races," "ethnicities," or "nationalities," hospitals assign titles for their own use. They do so in recognition of the *fact* that some kinds of people carry differential, genetically transmitted vulnerabilities to disorders. The categories are for preventive use by physicians and, thus far, they offend few.

I've not seen studies of the criteria by which hospital officials perform their sorting. However, upon a recent admission for surgery in a California hospital, I counted 14 ethno-racial types prominently displayed on the entry-office wall. Since I was not asked to associate myself with one of these hyphenated classes, I assume that physical features are used as a first screening cue. Such distinction is, of course, biological, not cultural. (I didn't learn my skin-color, hair covering, or nasal and cephalic indices, and it is doubtful how much of these indicators have been shaped by my nurturing environments.)

In a practice similar to that of modern hospitals, American census enumerators first began the task of racial identification by judging the *appearance* of the persons they counted. Today the Bureau of the Census depends on *self-reports*, and it asks separate questions, both of which are to be answered, concerning ethnicity and race.[114]

Census 2000 increased the number of racial categories from five in 1990 to sixty-three. In addition, as Eduardo Porter notes, the new classification "system" allows Americans to combine these sixty-three nominations with ethnic titles to produce 126 "kinds of people":

> This [enumeration] included the six single races, 15 possible combinations of two, 20 combinations of three, 15 of four, six combinations of five, and one grand mix of all six main categories....[so that] the census produced a matrix of 126 total combinations of race and ethnicity.[115]

However, with its large, heterogeneous, and mobile population, now the third largest aggregate after China and India, the United States cannot satisfy all its claimants to ethno-racial distinction with a "mere" 126 niches.

During the 2000 tally, thousands of persons who speak some variant of Spanish ticked "Other" as their race, and some Arab-Americans, German-Americans, Cape Verdeans, and Creoles lobbied unsuccessfully to be named as separate *races*.

The Melungeons, a clan that resides principally in the Appalachian Mountains, appear "neither all white, nor all black, nor all Indian." In the census of 1820, they were titled "free persons of color."[116] How they classed themselves in 2000 is not known.

But in the same census, some Americans of Arab descent wished to be listed as "middle Eastern" rather than "White," and the Association of Multi-Ethnic Americans and Project RACE ("Reclassify All Children Equally") demanded that future tallies include a category, "Multiracial."[117]

Similar contention and obscurity occur in other lands populated by persons of varied ethno-racial mixture. In Brazil, for example, its citizens recently "offered 135 different descriptions of their skin tones."[118] The Republic of South Africa lists its Negroid people as "African," while "black" refers to "all people of African, Indian, and mixed-race origin."[119]

Fickle Words, One More Time

Given what we know about the contingencies that affect emotionally infused utterance, we should not be surprised when persons give themselves different ethno-racial titles depending on who asks them questions and under what circumstance.

Thus when the same or "matched" individuals are asked about their "ethnic origin" on successive population surveys, as of 1970 *one out of every three* [Americans] gives different responses from one year to the next."[120]

Demographer William Petersen notes, "If asked about race first, some Mexican Americans might have designated themselves as 'Indian,' and some Puerto Ricans might have checked 'black'."[121] Another demographer, Tom Smith, adds that an estimated 10 to 15 percent of adult "White" Americans either do not know their ethnic identity or express nonesuch and that, among the 35 to 40 percent who list two or more ethnic origins, about 12 percent cannot choose a principal ethnicity.[122]

Similarly, during the 2000 U. S. census, a family of six whom I've know intimately, denoted themselves as "Mexican American," but in reply to the race question, one individual called himself "White," while the rest of his family did not, and probably could not, answer this question.

What is also striking about this recent American tally is that the "racial group" (sic!) Called "White" is treated as one kind. Contrary to such unitary categorization, Caucasoid-type people in the United States, and around the world, recognize differences between their tribes, sometimes in physical appearance, but more consistently in cultural practices.

Thus, in Northern Ireland, kinds of Christians, all "White," have been killing, maiming, and torturing one another over the past 300 years.[123] English, Scotch, Welsh, and Irish peoples take pride in their differences. So, too, do the "white" English and French clusters that struggle to maintain their distinction while residing in a fragile union called "Canada," from a native Indian word for "community."

In the United States, Iranians, Arabs, Assyrians, Chaldeans, and Jews—mostly "white"—set themselves apart as they do in the Near East. And

Ashkenazic Jews, distinguished from Sephardic Jews and Falashas ("black" Jews), exhibit a striking difference in their educational, occupational, and income distributions from all other Americans of whatever coloration.[124]

Ethno-racial identities are marked by both continuity and discontinuity; they do not stand still. Indeed, with movements across territories and generations, and with the mixing of flesh-colors, lands of origin, and cultures, religions, tastes, customs, and "thoughtways," affiliation can be lost. In this vein, the South African novelist J. M. Coetzee writes,

> I am one in this country who have become detached from their ethnic roots, whether these roots were in Dutch South Africa or Indonesia or Britain or Greece or wherever, and have joined a pool of no recognisable ethnos whose language of exchange is English.[125]

In similar manner, innumerable Americans become non-ethnic. For one prominent example: During 1997, a young man possessed of tan skin won the U. S. Master's Golf Tournament, and did so in smashing style. Immediately, journalists and ethno-racial "activists" nominated him "African American" and urged him to participate in their group activities as a "role model." However, Tiger Woods declined the invitation.

Stephan and Abigail Thernstrom describe Woods' lineage and the commercial-political advantage of persisting to employ the "one drop of blood" criterion of who one "is":

> Tiger Woods is one-quarter black, one-quarter Chinese, one-quarter Thai, one-eighth white, and one-eighth Native American. But while his "one drop" of black blood would have traditionally made him "black," and while Nike (as a corporate sponsor) had chosen to package him as black, he checked off Asian and African-American on his college application form, and calls himself "Cablinasian"—a contraction of Caucasian, black, Indian, and Asian.[126]

Woods' self-nomination is in the spirit of American individualism. At the same time, it offends the spirit of tribalism or, if you prefer, "communitarianism."

With more people like Coetzee and Woods moving away from conventional categories of "being ," census takers will have increased difficulties with their taxonomies.

Why Categorize?

Beyond what our physiologies do for us (ch. 1), the value of classifying objects and persons depends on one's purpose.

We understand, of course, that a first purpose of a State's census was, and is, to count taxable persons. Latterly, democratic countries enumerate their citizens so as to fairly apportion representatives to their assemblies/ congresses/ parliaments. Neither of these functions requires partitioning populations other than by their age and citizenship. And, on the latter qualification for voting, the U. S. *Census* collects no information, a default that gains importance with notice of widespread fraud in recent elections.

But, as a government begins to pigeonhole its people into narrow slots, it becomes pertinent to ask, "What can we do better with this system of taxonomy than without it, or *cui bono?*—for whose good?" And in an ethico-political setting, this question should be balanced with another: *"Cui malo?*—who is harmed?"

American attempts to count its residents by categories have not addressed these questions openly and clearly. Tallies are confounded by asking adults to identify themselves and their wards by their "ethnicity" (some, but not all, elements of their "culture"), wildly mixed with their "race" (genetic constitution, but principally skin tone), their own and parents' lands of origin (but how far back and under which political regime?), or by some politically constructed and wishfully clean combination of such indicators. But, again, "indicators" of what?

Indeed, some newly invented categories have no relevance to biological-morphological features, lineage, or cultural practices such as language and religion. "Hispanic" is an example. It can refer to people whose skin tones range from "white" to "black," who do not speak Spanish, and who occupy greatly different economic niches.

In the U. S., in particular, but also among many other modern states, political and financial motives, as distinct from any scientific purpose—including any predictive utility—have influenced how governments count and classify their people.[127]

William Petersen records the contest among purposes engaged when a state tries to classify and number its dark-skinned people:

> In the 1990 count the Bureau of the Census offered a choice—black, Negro, African-American—and then coalesced the responses into a single aggregate. When I suggested at an academic conference that it would have been preferable to accept these several group names as indicators of separate ethnicities, my proposal to adjust the standard criterion of race resulted in my being denounced as a racist. Yet in every respect the contrast was sharp between the "black" underclass and the "Negro" middle-class. When *any* attribute of the composite category is given by a median or average figure, this depicts the bottom of a U-shaped curve where the fewest persons are located. There are many with low or very low incomes, but there are fewer between the two extremes. While the change in self-identification (N.B.!) was in process...it might have been possible to catch this distinction statistically by compiling two subcategories separately. It could have been an important measure in lessening the racism implicit in federal data if this distinction were recognized; but the self-appointed spokesmen for blacks, in their fervent opposition to racism, insist on maintaining a racial category.[128]

Here, again, purposes collide and motives are concealed. Maintaining "race" as a marker maintains difference. It permits, and justifies, claims for special privilege. It stimulates the accusation of "racism" when one's aims and means are criticized as inaccurate, unjust, or both.

Much classification of people, both innate and acquired, is performed without thought (ch. 1). But a considerable portion of the taxonomies we employ is, to repeat, generated by purpose. Demographer Petersen's purpose is not that of his race-conscious antagonists; hence their quarrel. Good versus Good.

However, in addition to a state's legitimate interest in identifying taxpayers and apportioning seats in its legislatures, some modern governments claim that commercial and moral concerns justify their categorizing their people by asking them questions about themselves.

Thus, some commercial enterprises find advantage in knowing how many potential customers, with different needs and tastes, reside in particular regions. But a once-every-ten-years census, such as the U. S. conducts, omits much information. And it does so during intervals between decennial tallies as it does with each count. It becomes advisable, then, for corporations to conduct their own market research.

The moral issue that confronts multi-ethno-racial countries concerns fair treatment of their "minorities." It engages the law when states attempt to remedy the conditions deemed to unfairly treat some segments of the population in their access to occupations, residence, education, and justice. This attention, in the context of ideals of "equal opportunity" and freedom from "discrimination," is used to legitimize state action.

However, changes in self-identification between a government's tallies make it questionable whether, and to what extent, differences in "minorities'" variously measured statuses translate into unequal opportunities and unfair treatment.[129]

Debate persists, and we are returned to our initial query, "With what justification do governors assume the right to ask their citizens to identify themselves according to a state's categories?"

This question does not argue that no further justification can be given. It alerts us to the grounds of hostile contest when a central power inquires about who we are and how we are.

Hostile contest is stimulated insofar as a state makes it valuable to list oneself as some kind of "minority." Thus, depending on how one uses language to classify people, the United States may become a land in which everyone can claim that privilege. Indeed, California has probably attained that status now. Ron Unz comments,

The bizarre framework of federal racial [sic!] classification—which divides all mankind into Asians, blacks, Hispanics, and "other" whites—places blond, blue-eyed, third-generation Argentinian Americans, who speak not a word of Spanish, in the category of minorities, while dark-skinned Muslim immigrants from Egypt, speaking not a word of English, are labeled members of the "white" majority. In this Alice-in-Wonderland perspective, the huge inflow into California of hundreds of thousands of Iranians and Armenians and Egyptians had acted to "whiten" the state, partially balancing the huge simultaneous inflow of Vietnamese and Mexicans and Somalis.[130]

Social Science?

The concern of individuals and their governments with ethno-racial identity challenges the utility of a would-be science of the social. It makes dubious the claim that, on this issue, a social science can inform rational decision about State policy. The challenge is technical and moral.

Technically, the difficulty is, again, that of counting "kinds of people" by asking them "who they are." In vast lands, with mobile populations, permutations of identities confound enumerators.

The very people who are to be counted often give up. In Hawaii, for example, individuals derived from varied mixtures of "kinds" are simply termed "Chop Suey." The label is not hostile; it bespeaks indifference.

But social scientists have the job of explaining conduct. To this end, they study variations in actions and situations among aggregates. These collectives are sometimes self-nominated ("ethno-racial identity") and sometimes constructed ("social class"). But whether personally conceived or externally attributed, a science of human action requires clean taxonomies of its categories and accurate tallies of constituents within each type.

This task is particularly sensitive when students of the social wish to make comparisons between the situations and actions of "kinds of people" in their search for the causes and remedies of disapproved conditions/behaviors, including everything from illness and educational failure to crime and success.

To do this requires calculation of rates in which the "classes of people" form the denominator of fractions (ch. 6). Of course, if the tally of any considerable segment of a population is fluid, then the computed rate must also be contestable.

Among large and heterogeneous populations, future censuses will be hard put to ascertain what portion of demand for separate identity represents actual change in a country's coloration, nationalist sentiment, and culture, and what portion represents opportunistic nomination in search of government funds and entrepreneurial profit.

Example: Profit in Identity

With the aid of a government's classification, some "kinds of people" can make money in private industry by obtaining a competitive advantage. Thus, as American Indian tribes were granted the right to construct gambling resorts on their native territories, it became profitable to become "Indian."

In this manner, the Pequot band—the "fox people" of New England legend—gained "members" from "one poor, old woman" in 1972 to some 600 twenty years later. Their Foxwoods Casino in Connecticut is now "the world's biggest gambling operation."[131]

Richard "Skip" Hayward, the tribal chairman who got this industry moving, is "at most 1/16 Pequot. His father's family...arrived on the Mayflower."[132]

Foxwoods pays Connecticut by adding to the state's employment and tax rolls, and contributes to its benefactors in a federal government. Allen Demaree writes,

> Bill Clinton, as governor of Arkansas, led state opposition to Indian gambling and called it "a lousy basis" for building an economy. Once he reached the White House, however, the Pequots gave hundreds of thousands of dollars to the Democratic Party, which listed Mr. Hayward among its "top ten supporters." Soon Mr. Clinton called gambling "a positive economic development tool for Indian tribes."[133]

In short, ethno-racial concern moves money and stimulates moral conflict.

A common justification for State enumeration of "kinds" among its citizenry is, again, the wish to equalize opportunities and correct past and present wrongs. In turn, this justification underwrites a political motive for attending to race and ethnicity: The need in democracies to garner votes by promising privileges.

An opposed morality sees the policies that flow from such justification as threats to rights of privacy, to freedom of speech, movement, and association, and to justice.

This sentiment accords with the Italian proverb, *A chi dici il tuo segreto, doni la tua libertà*—"You give your liberty to the one to whom you tell your secret." This warning gains validity as some legislators wish all their subjects to carry identity cards that show not only their photographs, addresses, drivers' licenses, and blood types, but also, as we've seen, their ethno-racial class.

A secular, "personalist"[134] morality resists the power of central governments to construct taxonomies of their citizen/subjects, and to use tax monies to favor some of its nominated types at the expense of other kinds. Such effort offends a sense of justice.

Political favoritism violates one principle of justice, that of *Pareto optimality*. This argument, proposed by the Franco-Italian mathematician-engineer-economist-sociologist Vilfredo Pareto (1848-1923), holds that resources are "optimally allocated" when it is not possible to make anyone better off without making someone else worse off.[135]

State discrimination among its ethno-racial segments violates this principle. What it awards some is denied others, with the gratuity paid for by taxes extracted from those who are "out of the loop."

Such policy amounts to selective inclusion at the cost of selective exclusion. It changes the role of government from that of impartial referee, enforcing rules of the game, to that of judge and jury who interpret the rules "as they see them," and thereby give one side unearned points.

In this scenario, one group wins *because* others loses. This contest differs from a fair lottery in which unsuccessful gambles are *not caused* by winners' luck.

For the sake of concord, it is important that losers in lotteries understand this. By contrast, losers in government rationing are angered. They perceive injustice, and respond with protests that range from peaceful marching to planting bombs. Public opinion polls indicate that perhaps a majority of adult Americans now *oppose* their government asking them questions about their "race."[136]

Once upon a time, Americans upheld the ideal of assimilation, as emblazoned on our coins: *E pluribus unum*—"Out of many, one." We were to be a "melting pot," and laws mandating difference, such as anti-miscegenation laws, were to be repealed.

This moral objective is now displaced by the ideal of multicultural union, a.k.a. "diversity." Differences among kinds are to be celebrated, with the hope that kinds will nevertheless act in concert for "the common good."

However, prices are paid whichever ideal governments promote. The hazard of assimilation is the possibility that a people will disappear.[137] Multiculturalism allays the anxiety concerning tribal extermination not only by defending the persistence of separate identities, but more, by applauding them and funding them. This policy trusts that a population's distinctive kinds will work in social harmony for socially desirable objectives— separately but equally.

In turn, multiculturalism exacts its own price. It excites tribal passion, accompanied by demand that current governments (i.e., their taxed citizens) pay for past injustices alleged to have been done their forebears, and with threats of expensive litigation and violence if demands are not met.

Thus aboriginal people in Australia claim compensation for the damage presumably inflicted on them over the centuries by the "white" majority. Similarly, Canada's "native" bands sue its major churches— Anglican and United—toward bankruptcy for having practiced "cultural genocide" in their attempts to integrate Indian children into the majority population.[138]

Here again, a moral struggle pits Good versus Good. In such contests, preferences dominate facts, and social science loses relevance.[139]

Legislators and their counselors are in a bind, and their good intentions cannot guarantee happy consequences. On the record, polyethnic harmony has been more a result of partitioned residence and evolved accommodation, as in Switzerland, and less a result of State-coerced congregation.[140] The risk of official recognition of tribal difference is inflammation of it.

Ethno-racial affiliation is suffused with affection. For those who experience it, the sentiment is a source of self-definition: Who one "is."

Lest meliorists forget, no love is more intense than that for one's "kind"—whether it be "family," "village," or "nation."[141] Thus, rulers who disadvantage one of their constituent tribes to favor another stimulate passions that readily turn murderous.

This statement does not merely describe a past from which we've "learned better." It describes a homicidal drama to which we awaken with each morning's news.

The killing is inflamed by differences between "kinds of people" when one or more of these identities regard themselves as unjustly treated. With such regard moral sentiment fortifies hatred and justifies homicide.

Mr. Justice Oliver Wendell Holmes, a thrice-wounded veteran of America's most lethal war—its Civil War or War Between the States— learned this lesson firsthand. In one of his letters to the English socialist theorist Harold Laski, Homes wrote what is often called his "brutal opinion." He remarked that

> Pleasures are ultimates, and in cases of difference between ourself and another there is nothing to do except in unimportant matters to think ill of him and in important matters to kill him.[142]

Today Holmes' "pleasures" translates as "values" and, against his dark view of human nature, it is popular to convert hateful differences to "problems" that therefore must have "solutions." Such optimistic translation yields evangelistic advantage at the expense of accuracy. It denies tragedy, encourages hope, stimulates activism with its perennial possibility of perverse effect, and provides social scientists with license to prescribe questionable means to desired ends.

We are reminded, however, that moral conflicts are not merely quarrels about appropriate means to ends. They are also fights about proper ends[143] (ch. 12).

In Sum

A science of the social is limited by our inability to observe in controlled fashion, most of the events we study. In lieu of this power, we employ intermediaries, often called "indicators" or "tests."

A first question, then, is, "how well do the indicators indicate?" "Do the tests test what we want to measure?"

Some of these proxies are sufficiently distant from the behaviors that concern us as to give pause to consumers of social-science products. In particular, we should be wary of relying on what people *say* as measure of what they *do*.

Inability to observe much that interests us is not the only weakness of an aspiring social science. This deficiency is complemented by disputes about explanation, including contested notions of causation. Chapters 9 and 10 discuss the difficulties of making social events comprehensible.

Part 4

Explanation

9

Empathetic Explanation

*"Disinterested intellectual curiosity is the life
blood of real civilization."*
—*G. M. Trevelyan (1876-1962)*[1]

Curiosity

Explaining is something we do to each other and for ourselves. What we
attempt to explain, and how, are functions of familiarity and strangeness, of
expectation and surprise, of purpose, and of the habits of thinking embedded
in language.

The activity called "explaining" starts with the human propensity to ex-
plore our environs, and then to manipulate parts of it. Curiosity is a physiological function, a built-in feature of our equipment. Evolutionary
psychologists would say it has survival value.

Curiosity expresses itself as a *continuing* need to find-out, and it is, early
on and into late years, an autonomous motive. It is its own "reason-for-ac-
tion," relatively independent of other causes of conduct, and one of the great
engines of science. As such, it is sometimes termed "idle curiosity" and at
other times "disinterested inquiry," a luxury of civilized life, as the English
historian George Trevelyan believed. Inquiry, then, is a pleasure unto itself—
an "itch to be scratched."

For example, John Horgan's interviews with prominent modern scientists
illustrate the self-stimulating motive to inquire. Thus, mathematician Gregory Chaitin tells Horgan, "I think we know very little, and I hope we know
very little because it will be much more fun." And robotics engineer Hans
Moravec claims that curiosity is adaptive, "If you can afford it."[2] He means
that we first have to make a living, and then we can play with ideas.

Acquisition of language—including invented symbol-systems as well as
those that have evolved—enlarges the scope of inquiry. As the human child
learns to think/speak with symbols—signs that stand for something other

than themselves—it begins to ask the awesome "why?" question, and we find ourselves, as adults, asking more "why's?" than we can answer.

We are saved from endless rumination by work, play, and by winnowing questions. We do not attempt to explain everything. In each culture, only certain kinds of behaviors and situations are felt to require those stories regarded as explanations.

We become accustomed to different sorts of explanations for different kinds of events, and for different types of organisms in different conditions. We in the Western world, for instance, usually employ a different set of concepts to explain animate and inanimate "behavior," and to "make sense of" approved and disapproved conduct.

In brief, language stimulates, and allows, exploration of our worlds with ideas, as well as with manual probes, and we soon request explanations in service to motives "less pure" than disinterested finding out.

In the social realm in particular, inquiry is then excited less by what occurs regularly than by what changes unexpectedly and, especially, with undesired effect.

Attachment of curiosity to several different motives means that explanation will not be one kind of activity.

What "Explanation" Means

To explain events is to make them clear. It is to make what happens seem plausible.

We do this in many ways, only some of which are "scientific." The *general* principle by which we explain affairs "connects" the event to be clarified—called the *explanandum* (plural: *explananda*)—to a set of assumptions (prior beliefs) and facts that make the incident comprehensible (a.k.a. "intelligible," "meaningful," "understandable," "sensible").

The mixture of assumption and fact that does the work of making matters clear is called the *explanans*.

The event to be explained (the explanandum) *and* the statements offered to clarify it (the explanans) together constitute the "explanation." That is, an explanation consists of both aspects of understanding the world: Propositions about the activity that interests us *and* propositions advanced to "account" for it.[3]

The popular, but question-begging, adjective, "comprehensible," and its synonyms, require clarification.

What is "intelligible" for individuals depends on the nature of the activity to be explained, their past experience with such an event, their education, and, most important, with that complex of motives that characterizes personalities.

Minds are *not* free-floating abilities. "Will" is *not* free of "Being."[4]

Minds are brain products. Brains are physical organs, affected by body chemistry, and generative of that congeries of distinctive dispositions and actions we call "personality." Personalities select explanations.

Physiology modulates personality. In particular, physiology affects that emotional aspect of our being known as "temperament," and recognized by individual differences in reactivity as early as infancy.

Temperament, in turn, is part of the causal web that selects "philosophy of life," including preference for style of explanation.[5]

Questions, Answers, and Satisfactions

Explanations vary in quality according to the questions they attempt to answer and the satisfactions to be attained by their answers. Most commonly, "satisfaction" refers to what an inquirer wants to *feel/believe* upon receiving an answer. More rarely, satisfaction refers to what the inquirer is better able to *do* with an explanation than without it. ("*Better* able" means "with predictable result"; it does *not* refer to "is stimulated to do.")

Many explanations that allay curiosity have no other use. There is nothing more we can do with them. For example, anthropologist Lawrence Keeley shows how explanations can satisfy curiosity *without* providing any other utility. Toward the end of his fascinating study of *War Before Civilization*, he reviews attempts to explain deadly quarrels, and their absence, and concludes that

> Such simple answers [the explanations] are of little practical use in the complex and highly various social situations in which human beings strive to prevent wars and sustain peace.[6]

How? Why?

After ascertaining "what happened," the explanatory effort addresses two principal questions: "How?" and "Why?" The answer to "how?" can be purely *descriptive*. The answer to "why?" allows a range of *prescription*.

Sometimes, of course, describing how events occur also explains why they occur. This tends to be the case when there is a stable mechanism that causes the occurrence we are trying to explain.

For example, description of the mechanism of an automobile engine tells us something, but not everything, about why it works as it does. Not everything is explained because, after learning the mechanics of the internal combustion engine, we may wish to delve further and inquire about the physics of friction and the chemistry of gases.

However, when we lack such a stable mode of describing how an explanans produces the explanandum, "how?" and "why?" become different questions. This is particularly the case with human action.

Consider, for instance, how we explain many criminal events. We do so, *for some purposes*, by describing *how* they come about. The description includes portraits of the actors, their origins, feelings-thoughts, and situations. Such detail tells us something about the occasions on which certain kinds of events occur.

But this is not the same work as explaining *why* such events occur. We can know how particular offenders feel, think, believe, and act without being given an explanans that assuredly charts the causes of each career.

For some purposes, knowing *how* things occur is valuable. It is useful for constructing forecasts and for self-protection. Knowing *why* events occur as they do is valuable for a different purpose: Temporal, instrumental prediction (TIP).

This kind of prediction, we recall (ch. 3), differs from a forecast in that it states what is likely to happen if we *do* this rather than that—if, for example, we intervene in affairs with a particular program designed to achieve a specific, empirical objective. By contrast, a forecast "merely" indicates what is likely to happen *without* our manipulating the causes of an occurrence, as with our anticipations of earthquakes and changes in the weather.

The Scientist's Satisfaction

Scientists are often satisfied with accurate descriptions of how matters come to be as they are. It is only latterly that they may address the "why?" question. When they do pose this difficult query, their preferred style of answer acquires knowledge that permits them to state a validated empirical rule that, along with a description of initial conditions and some auxiliary assumptions, specifies the *necessary and sufficient* conditions for the production of particular classes of events.

Given the state of our knowledge, and perhaps because of the way Nature works, the best that such empirical rules can achieve are statements of probabilities, not absolutes (ch. 6). Thus, philosopher Wesley Salmon suggests that

> Some of the basic laws of nature may be irreducibly statistical [and] probability relations *may* constitute a fundamental feature of the physical world.[7]

Unfortunately, the citizenry exhibits a shaky understanding of probability, and often demands that their practitioners of science-based skills give them exception-free answers to their "why?" questions.

For example, it is this ignorance that bedevils physicians whose work combines science with art, and whose science, moreover, is incomplete. Physicians continue to confront such mysteries as spontaneous remission and the placebo effect. Their diagnoses and prognoses, with and without treatment, are irremediably contingent, and contingent in contexts where all the possible causes of the course of a disorder are not known.[8]

If this is true of medical practice, that is based on some science of anatomy, physiology, chemistry, and physics, think how damaging it is to an aspiring science of the social where little science underwrites statements of regularities, and where no one explanatory style satisfies all inquirers.

We can categorize these styles by the procedures they invoke to satisfy curiosity. Explicators of social action do this by offering characterizations, arousing empathy, and by nominating numerous candidates as causes of conduct.

Explanation by Characterization

One kind of explanation defines. It states what a thing or event "is," and thereby what it is likely to do or be incapable of doing. This style of explanation indicates what the object or person or event resembles, or what differentiates it, or both. In clarifying human behavior, such definition can take the form of describing individuals' organic constitutions.

Explanation by characterization is most useful when it offers a well-warranted diagnosis that is prognostic. For example, a famous anecdote from the French Revolution has the Duc de la Rochefoucauld-Liancourt advise King Louis XVI of the fall of the Bastille. With this information, the king asks, "Is this a revolt?" And the duke replies, "No, Sire, it is a revolution."[9] The shift of vocabulary tells the king what he can expect.

In making human action seem understandable, definitions often do their work by expressing, *in compressed form*, what is to be expected from kinds of actors in kinds of situations:

> Inquirer: "Why does she do that?"
> Explicator: "She's schizophrenic."

This is a case for which "name-calling" is explanatory. Of course, all such explanation is probabilistic, contingent, and contestable.

Explaining with Empathy ("Understanding")

Without tally of a representative sample of *all* explanations offered of human action, it is likely that the vast majority of attempts to clarify conduct do their work by fitting a story into previously held beliefs allied with an appeal to empathy—commonly called "understanding."

"Understanding" carries great authority. Who can oppose it? But, like other glory-words, this term is used ambiguously, and the ambiguity conceals a false proposition that infects common discourse.

Employers of this concept often confuse comprehending others ("understanding"$_1$) with liking them ("understanding"$_2$). They then assume that U_1 yields U_2 and vice versa. It is this confusion that allows some psychologists and sociologists to believe that "being" of appropriate ethnicity, or race, or social class gives one greater "insight" into the actions of particular kinds of people.

Despite lack of evidence for this assumption, the call to "understand" self and others is popular. It is voiced by journalists, politicians, and theologians, and it is activity that occupies much of sociology, social work, and psychiatry, particularly that school that claims ability to "psychoanalyze," meaning to be able to decipher the codes in which the hidden unconscious speaks.

These vocations exhibit a tendency to assume that "knowing" one's self cures one of whatever discomfort brings a person to a therapist's attention, and that "knowing" others in this manner generates love. These are hypotheses that, if not vague beyond test, remain without warrant.

Those who would explain others' actions by developing empathy for them construct stories that strive to make consumers of their explanations feel-think as the persons being explained presumably felt-thought when they behaved as they did. This is the art of drama; it is the task of playwrights, novelists, and historians. Their tales are effective insofar as they stimulate their audiences to sense *their own possibilities* in the behaviors of others.

To empathize is to "feel-in-with" the persons being portrayed. It requires imagination. Thus, Alfred Schutz, an advocate of this mode of explanation for social science, writes,

> I am able to understand other people's acts *only if* (sic!)
> I can imagine that I myself would perform analogous acts if
> I were in the same situation.[10]

Schutz's necessity puts a bridle on explanation-by-understanding. Its efficacy is limited to "people like us," and, as we shall see, it becomes impossible to apply to those whose conduct is outrageous, heinous, "beyond comprehension."

Despite this limitation, the prescription to "understand" self and others as a way of explaining what we do has reputable forebears who recommend this attribute as a *method* for the social sciences.

The distinguished sociologist Max Weber (1864-1920) is one of the fathers of this style of explanation. He and his disciples claim that *the distinctive objective* of sociology is to construct

> a science (sic!) which attempts the interpretive understanding of social action in order thereby to arrive at a *causal* explanation of its course and effects.[11]

Since Weber and other German theorists gave impetus to this form of comprehension, it is sometimes termed *verstehende* sociology—that is, "understanding" or "interpretive" sociology. Some American followers of such sociology have embraced its attitude in a school known as "Symbolic Interactionism." But whatever its title, no such *science* characterizes sociology and ethnography.

Nevertheless, this effort at clarification appeals to many inquirers because it is commonsensical. It seems obvious and, more than that, this school agrees with Weber that "understanding" self and others yields *causal explanation* of conduct.

The causal engine supposedly exists in "states of mind." The "state of mind" that Weberian explicators seek to understand is the "meaning" actors assign to their activities. *Meaning* is to be found in what actors *intend* and, if we cannot discern intention from what actors *do*, we are told to listen to their *reasons*—that is, to their utterances that express desires and objectives.

This is poor advice. It is poor counsel for personal guidance, but also as a procedure with which to develop a *science* of human action.

Chapters 2 and 6 give reasons—that is, arguments—for doubting that actors' *reasons*—that is, utterances describing purposes— necessarily represent the *causes* of their actions.

Pages to follow supplement these earlier reasons to doubt. Here again, one word can represent several symbols. The same word can indicate more than one referent. Conversely, several words can point to the same referent (chs. 2, 3).

Intention, Purpose, Motive

Would-be interpretive scientists claim that intentions are motives. More than that, they believe that intention describes *all* of motivation. It does not.

Words like "intention," "purpose," and "motive" have evolved with folk psychology. They are therefore at once familiar, congenial, and difficult to de-fine. That is, it's difficult to contain their reference within fixed boundaries. Moreover, these terms are often employed in emotionalized contexts that further fog them.

"Intention" commonly indicates "purpose"—what agents are trying to achieve by their actions. Such acts are "explained," then, by stating the goals toward which they are directed—sometimes obviously, sometimes only purportedly.

By contrast, "motive" most accurately refers to an inferred *drive* that generates intentions. The word describes an imputed organic condition that can impel various activities directed toward more than one intermediate goal. In short, the same drive can stimulate different acts toward its satisfaction.

For example, being thirsty is a psychological state induced by a physiological condition that can be satisfied by several kinds of purposeful acts that lead to the ingestion of some liquid. In addition, whereas actors who intend to gain some objective are deemed to be conscious of their ends, motives can operate unconsciously. Indeed, for some psychologists, motives are more often unconscious than conscious.

Confusion is compounded by lawyer-talk. In criminal trials in particular, lawyers and their audiences characteristically speak of seeking "motives" while they search for them among offenders' purposes. Such language confuses concepts, and thereby discounts other sources of behavior than the immediate intention.

In Sum: What we *intend* to achieve—our purpose—need not describe what *moves* us to act—our motive. This possibility is demonstrated by the many cases in which citing one's purpose does *not* satisfy inquirers who assume they are seeking motives. In such unsatisfactory cases, when the explicator tells us what the actor believed and desired as explanation of his conduct, we regularly ask, "Yes, but what made him want that and believe that?" (Refer, for example, to *The Great Train Robbery*, p. 182).

The distinction becomes more clear as followers of interpretive social studies try to identify others' purposes, not simply by observing their actions, as we do with our animal pets and they do with us, but principally by attending, as Weber advised, to individuals' "*adequate* reasons for the conduct in question."[12]

This advice partakes of the language-proud bias described in the previous chapter and criticized in chapter 2. It is the bias that relies on speech as accurate indicator of cognition to the neglect of other signal systems. It ignores facts: That we recognize intent in the behavior of familiar creatures that can *not* talk; that they reciprocate the inference; that mammals at least, and primates in particular, identify purpose among their conspecifics, and their human friends and enemies, and act to manipulate them.[13]

Notwithstanding its partiality, the empathetic mode of explanation is popular. It satisfies many students of social action while it suffers from major defects. These deficiencies need only be summarized here with some examples added. Detailed criticism is available elsewhere.[14]

Defects of "Understanding"

"Non é vero, é ben trovata." *(It may not be true, but it's a good story.)*
—*Italian proverb*

The proposed "theory" of *verstehende* in explanation of social action conforms to the Italian proverb. It need not be true; it need not, and does not, increase foresight or add to temporal, instrumental predictive power (TIP). It cannot constitute a science because it lacks method and a reliable test of its results.

Everyone engages in the practice of interpreting others' purposes—willy-nilly—and does so without attending university or becoming a scientist. At a primitive level, reading others' intentions is an innate physiological function. Beyond that, it is more art than science.

Understanding others in this empathetic way requires neither truth finding nor truth telling. As a *method*, it has no proven track record in improving forecast or prediction.

Making action seem plausible, comprehensible, reasonable opens doors to "ad-hockery." After events, one can often come up with a description, fit for the occasion, that quiets some peoples' curiosity. All that is required of explicators is that they tell a story that evokes imagery: "How would *you* feel/think, and what would *you* do, in that situation?"

Of course, we cannot know, and can only feebly imagine, what we might do in situations we've never before experienced. Reaction to crisis is a prominent example. So are responses to accumulated insult, to despair, and to a sense of entrapment. Refer below, pages 183-185, to intelligent men's inability to explain their crimes—as per Gary Gilmore and Norman Mailer.

Nevertheless, even psychologists-in-training, who are supposed to be improving their judgment of others—particularly aberrant others—prefer this mode of "making sense" of behavior. Marilyn Freimuth notes that the desiderata of scientific theory—that it be internally coherent, consistent with a body of verified hypotheses, falsifiable, and contribute to novel propositions and predictive power—that these attributes of "good theory" are ignored by her graduate students who evaluate explanations by the *feelings* the induce, by how they "resonate with [their] experiences.[15]

This kind of satisfaction is friendly to "projection," the mistake of assuming that others are like us. It is an error kindly people commit when they confront evil. It is a prejudice that lawyers, social workers, public health nurses, and other unsophisticated judges of human disposition make when they assume, from their limited experience, that strangers must feel-think as they do.

It is, for example, the fault that Jeffrey Toobin attributes to the prosecution in its failed trial of the famous American football star O. J. Simpson.[16] It is recognition of this mistake that has encouraged business among technicians who now advise lawyers how to select juries favorable to their cause.

Note: Criticism of explanations that rely on empathy is not criticism of that sentiment. Empathy constitutes the physiological basis of sociality. It is "built-in" to the human constitution. (Psychopaths, who exist, are an exception.)

Empathy—a.k.a. "fellow-feeling"—is the foundation of mutual aid. It forms the basis of our appreciation of drama, history, biography. Without empathy, we could not cry for others who suffer or rejoice when they prosper.

The defect of empathy when it is employed *as an explanatory tool* is, to repeat, that it promotes projection. Among good people, it is blind to evil.

Wickedness becomes incomprehensible. "Understanding" others from our own inclinations is a limited, and often distorted, way of "knowing" them.

The Great Failure

Interpretive studies fail notably when they attempt to explain acts out-of-the-ordinary. Put the other way about, "understanding" others is easiest when they are "people like us."

Moral evaluation intrudes. We can more readily develop understanding of those who behave well, by our code, than of those who commit "senseless" crimes. In such cases, we are *not* satisfied with actors' statements of their intentions, purposes, reasons.

For example, in his story of *The Great Train Robbery*, Michael Crichton has the Great Robber, played by Sean Connery in the film version, being sentenced for his attempted theft of the Queen's gold. The crown prosecutor, having succeeded in convicting the thief, wants to know *why* an apparent gentleman would commit such a crime. The Great Robber feigns incomprehension; he doesn't understand the question. With that, the venerable judge leans over his elevated desk, and clarifies:

"Why," he asks, "did you conceive, plan and execute this dastardly crime?"

The Great Robber's eyes light up. Now he understands.

"I wanted the money!", he exclaims.[17]

This fictional account parallels that of the famed American bank robber, Willie "The Actor" Sutton, who allegedly responded to an inquisitive journalist who asked him why he stole from banks: "Cause that's where the money is."[18]

Note: What is omitted from both Sutton's explanation and the Great Robber's is the pleasure of risk. This pleasure parallels that of gambling addicts who are stimulated by "the action" as much as, or more than, by the desire to win. "Pleasures are ultimates."

Of course, such statements of purpose do *not* satisfy. They are not what interrogators want to hear, nor is it clear that the inquisitors themselves know what they wish to learn when they ask "why?"[19] They are fishing in the hope that the object of their inquisition will help them with a congenial tale.

Except that some fishing expeditions might, once in a while, catch something, these excursions are futile. The interpretive effort is impotent to clarify the bizarre, horrendous, "incomprehensible" acts that human beings perform.

A brief sample gives the flavor of such conduct. These examples demonstrate the failure of empathetic comprehension—much less any science of human behavior—to explain out-of-the-ordinary events. Nor can such "understanding" help us foretell their occurrence.

A Short List of Empathetically Inexplicable Killers

Failed fishing expeditions for explanation are most apparent when sympathetic inquirers try to understand heinous crimes.

For example, when Gary Gilmore shot to death two unoffending men in once-peaceful Utah, neither he nor any of his friendly interviewers, including the famous novelist Norman Mailer, could "make sense" of the murders.[20]

Mailer and other inquirers continued chatting with Gilmore until the morning of his execution by firing squad. Not one of the conventional, psychosocial roster of plausible causes fit Gary Gilmore: Childhood abuse? A hostile mother? An absent father? Sexual troubles? Low IQ? (On a standard mental test, Gilmore scored an IQ of 130, two standard deviations above the mean.)

During one session, the "wannabe" empathetic Mailer asks,

"Gary, why did you kill those guys?"

"Hey," Gilmore replies, "I don't know. I don't have a reason."

Indeed, this novelist was later to learn the futility of "why?" when he appeared in court and was asked to explain beating his wife. Mailer could not "make sense" of his own violence.

Reviewing the many accounts of Gary Gilmore's crimes, another commentator, Hugh Kenner, concludes,

> All that's to be said is that now and then, under stress (sic!), Gary Gilmore simply killed. That we can explain such matters, which means, express them in terms of something we already know, is a delusion, one of our cheaper delusions.[21]

The parade of inexplicable cruelty appears in other lands than the reputedly homicidal United States. Not for nothing was England the domicile of detective Sherlock Holmes.

On 11 June 1999, four young men, two black and two white, seventeen to twenty-one years of age, kidnapped inoffensive, good-student, eighteen-year-old Jonathan Coles from outside a nightclub in the mid-England city of Milton Keynes. They drove their captive several miles out of town to the Tyringham Bridge over the Great Ouse River where they hoisted him atop the parapet. When Coles pleaded that he didn't know how to swim, his gleeful predators pried his fingers from the railing and allowed him to drop twenty-five feet into the water where they left him to drown.

As is usual with such display of "motiveless malignity," as reporter Justin Marozzi calls the killing, police and populace search in vain for explanation. As Marozzi notes, "eight months after this murder, no one is any nearer understanding why the four youths did what they did that night."[22]

Other Englishmen disagree. Writing independently of one another, they offer a common "understanding" of such purposeless homicide. Tony Häfliger finds its cause in "modern society's moral vacuum."[23] Commenting from far-off Kenya, R. S. Massie-Blomfield agrees that "in a godless society, we should not be surprised when some of its members behave in a godless way."[24] And Charles FitzGerald adds that "where God is absent, why should there be a need for motive?"[25]

Meanwhile, a short distance from the scene of this English crime, God-fearing people in Northern Ireland have been maiming and killing one another, with purpose, for decades. As the following chapter shows, when we attempt to explain human action, affection strongly locates causation.

And horrendous crimes remain nonsensical, although most modern people in rich lands believe there *must be* causes, *satisfying* causes, if only we knew where to look. Thus, when on a May evening in 1989, eight young men savagely beat and raped a twenty-eight-year-old jogger in New York City's Central Park, none of the "official explicators" could answer the awesome "why?" question.*

Journalist Richard Brookhiser summarizes:

> The problem was motive, or lack of it. There were no underlying causes of the sort beloved by sociologists. There were not even plausible personal motives of the kind sought by police. Greed had to be discounted, since only two of the victims were actually robbed. Drugs, the all-purpose urban bogeyman, also did not seem to be a factor....The suspects—at least those arrested on the spot—had been clean and sober at the time of the crime....
>
> Four [of the young men] lived in a building with a doorman, and one went to a parochial school. One received an allowance of $4 a day from his father.... [Their apartment building] was...a moderate-to-middle-income high-rise...at the northeast corner of Central Park—not Park Avenue swank, but not desolation either....Only one of the suspects...had any criminal record. These were not abandoned children.[26]

Badgered by journalists, the city's mayor shouted, "You name me one social reason you can give to explain it!" And commentator Tom Wicker added that his "worst fear" was that the crime was "inexplicable."

If one assumes the role of Weberian "scientist" and asks the predators their reason for rape and mayhem, their reply is that they were out "wilding,"

---

*Qualification: since writing this description, five of the young men convicted of this crime may be exonerated. An older man, serving a life sentence for murder and rape, has confessed to the Central Park attack, and DNA evidence may support his claim. Debate persists concerning the quality of DNA material and its applicability to this crime. But, whatever the result of current appeals, criticism of empathetic explanation remains valid.

meaning "having fun." But the joys of attack, domination, and destruction are beyond the understanding of civilized people like Max Weber and his disciples, and that kind of reason is immediately dismissed as "inadequate." And when we respond, "Inadequate for what?" we confront silence.

Consider the 1990s spate of schoolyard killings that occurred, not in ugly inner cities, but in rural and suburban settings, neither poverty-stricken nor damaged by ethno-racial persecution, and recorded in such distant and different places as Scotland, Alberta, Canada, Tasmania, off the coast of southern Australia, and such American venues as Arkansas, California, Colorado, Kentucky, Michigan, Mississippi, Oregon, and Tennessee.

For example, in an American incident, two schoolboys, ages eleven and thirteen, privileged to attend a middle-school near Jonesboro, Arkansas, prepared to kill their schoolmates and teachers indiscriminately.

Dressed in military camouflage and armed with semi-automatic handguns and rifles, these lads "borrowed" a parent's automobile, loaded it with their weapons, food, sleeping bags, and 200 rounds of ammunition, and drove to within 100 yards of their school. One of them set off the building's fire alarm, causing students and teachers to evacuate the structure and present targets that the boys fired upon. These purposeful youngsters killed four persons and wounded eleven others.

We do not have to ask these assassins what they intended to do. Their intention is plain from their conduct.

But knowing their intention does not "explain" their behavior and, unsatisfied with this "understanding, " citizens ask "why?" They do so more intensely as killers fit no motion-picture image of evil persons. No fangs, no evil eyes, no slavering lips. The most stupid question lawyers and detectives can ask is, "Does he look like a killer to you?"

Prior to their murderous spree, these youngsters seemed "normal." Even the older boy, with a reputation as bully, is not an unheard-of phenomenon on school grounds in Europe and North and South America. Indeed, one of the killer's fathers described his son as "a good boy" who enjoyed his church and singing in its choir.

What the citizenry's "why?" asks for is something like "motive"—*not* the killers' intentions, *not* the reasons they may utter after their arrest—but drive, impetus, cause. *Empathy cannot answer that question.*

However, in the spirit of the citizenry's quest for "understanding," the president of the United States asked the Department of Justice to look for "common elements" that might identify origins of murderous feelings/thoughts/motives that could have "driven" these affluent boys to purposeful killing of their innocent classmates and teachers.

Presumably, the president is not asking for just any correlates common to these many assassins, but only for such associated conditions/experiences/traits as might constitute necessary and sufficient causes of their acts. Such search is apt to be futile.

It is likely to be fruitless because, given such rare deeds, many minatory signals found emanating from these offenders can probably be discovered among other youngsters who provide similar premonitory cues *without* engaging in planned homicide.

False positive signs ordinarily accompany true indicators. Moreover, "confirmation bias" is a constant hazard of research that looks for the origins of unusual action among a welter of causal candidates. This prejudice is notable in a melioristic political climate that seeks *deficiency* as cause of evil activity—particularly something wrongdoers *lack* that governments can provide.

Understanding Others as Predictive Tool

However comforting "understanding" people may be, as a method by which to anticipate what others are apt to do, it is rife with error. More than that, the error tends to be stubborn. Ego is invested in one's intuition. The result is confident assertion based on feel/thinking "insight."

Reams of research in several domains of judgment warn us against assuming that confident argument indicates truthful proposition. Within the limits of our ability to count qualities of assertion, there is *no relationship* between the assurance with which individuals make statements—including statements about what they've done and what they've seen—and the accuracy of their utterances. In some case, the relationship between confidence and validity is *negative*—the more cocksure, the less accurate.[27]

The shape of this association can vary, of course, depending on *what* is examined and *how* confidence and validity are tallied. Thus a meta-analysis of thirty studies confirms a low relationship between assurance and accuracy, but notes that the *strength* of association varies with how it is measured.[28]

Import: The value of this lesson lies in its sensitizing us to bullshit (a.k.a. nonsense, bunkum, hogwash, and more)

Harry Frankfurt, former head of Yale's philosophy department, uses this caustic Americanism to alert us to the difference between liars and bullslingers.[29]

Liars, Frankfurt says, know the difference between what is and what is not so. They assume that there *is* a "fact of the matter" that they are concealing. In this perverse sense, they exhibit a "commitment" to truth.

By contrast, bullshit artists pay no attention to facts. They are free, unhampered by attention to truth. They may, or may not, agree with some modern philosophers who claim that there is no such thing as "fact of the matter," but they don't care. They are insouciant, often brilliantly so. They deceive by writing and talking about what they don't know, and sometimes about what no one can possibly know. And they are simultaneously persuasive and harmful because they exercise their talent for spewing garbage with voices of authority.

They mask their ignorance with confidence. Speaking earnestly, looking directly into our eyes or the camera, they move audiences with their sincerity.

Sincerity is part of the art. It is one of the weapons all fraudsters use. It can even mislead deceivers themselves when they repeat nonsense so often it comes to feel like truth.

Self-deception is a measurable phenomenon.[30] Habituated, lying to oneself becomes "second nature." And it is taught to aspiring professional role-players as "method acting": *Feel* the emotion you wish to portray; practice the masquerade. As the tutor of courtesans advises her whores-in-training in the film, *Dangerous Beauty*, "To give pleasure, you must feel pleasure."

Such double-edged deception raises high the hazards of spreading, and receiving, bunkum. As previously indicated, probably more wealth—money, votes, trust—is stolen by sincere deceivers than by all ordinary thieves combined, with fraudsters' "take" occasionally exceeded only by military looting.

The damage is immense because we are daily immersed in claptrap, and in all domains of personal relations—in commerce, religion, romance, and politics. Indeed, we can propose that it is a principle of effective propaganda that it contain quantities of vak-yak,[31] and that to be successful as a serial lover or chronic politician requires expertise in uttering nonsense with confidence.

The Psychology of Bunkum

At least three processes assure the continuity and efficacy of "talking chaff," or uttering *blague*.

First, in politics and other contentious arenas, confident assertion scores points. Conversely, appearing uncertain often signals being incorrect. Of course, it need not mean this. We should not confuse diffidence with ignorance.

Second, the tendency to evaluate what others tell us by the confidence of their speech and demeanor contributes to the delusion that how others *make us feel* is evidence of the validity of their arguments. Indeed, some people believe confident manner to be a sign of "mental health" (viz., the "self-esteem" movement).

Third, confidence in one's own judgment is friendly to *confirmation bias*. This is the disposition to seek, and to believe, data that favor one's opinions and to ignore contradictory information. "True positives" are remembered; "false positives" and "false negatives" ignored. Social scientists are not immune to this common tendency.

Once more, we confront trade-offs: The pleasure we take from hearing/seeing buoyant personalities versus the accuracy of their judgments, and the need-to-trust versus the prevalence of confident error.

Remedy

An intellectual industry has developed that would improve judgment beyond the frailties of untutored understanding. Clinical psychology is a discipline with which experts are presumed to develop skills in the diagnosis and prognosis of "behavior disorders." However, in 1954, Paul Meehl dropped a bombshell with publication—after several rejections (!)—of his *Clinical versus Statistical Prediction*.

Meehl demonstrated empirically that numerical formulas for *combining cues* allow more accurate forecast of others' actions than do clinicians' judgments. "Objective ordering" of premonitory signs trumps experts' "intuition."

In the almost fifty years since Meehl broadcast his "shocking news," his thesis has been confirmed in a variety of judgmental domains.[32]

Exceptions occur. For example, in the diagnosis of rheumatic diseases, actuarial tables are more accurate than inexperienced physicians, but less accurate than experienced practitioners.[33] Similarly, although *"Past behavior alone* appears to be a better long-term predictor of future [violent] behavior than clinical judgments, [it] may also be a better indicator than cross-validated actuarial techniques."[34]

With few exceptions, then, mathematical weighing of prognostic cues performs better than individual "insight" and "theory-based inference."

Indeed, there is some evidence that the more "theory" one puts into "understanding" others, the more defective one's judgment. For example, Raymond Fancher finds that, for a sample of psychologists, accuracy in judging others is *negatively* associated with "validity in conceptualizing the other." Moreover, while such "conceptual (i.e., theoretical) validity" is positively associated with training in psychology, accuracy in assessing others is *negatively* associated with the number of courses taken in psychology and with course grades in abnormal psychology.[35]

Apropos of the misleading impact of some all-encompassing explanation of human action alleged to have practical application, I discovered years ago that a much-quoted "theory" of embezzlement—theft by "normal," middle-class people "like us"—was not merely descriptively inaccurate, but it also generates poor advice.[36] Nevertheless, the faulty theory is still reprinted and taught.[37] Some professors are "theory-junkies."

Judgment in Interview

Despite accumulated evidence of the defects of personal "understanding" of others, experts in many fields of inquiry continue to believe that their judgments are more valid than any possible "mechanical" formula. For example, the interview persists as a ritual on which parole officers, academics, and industrial-commercial personnel recruiters rely for "information" about the likely success of their applicants.

Probably more than 95 percent of all employers use the interview as an important, if not the most important, "method" of ascertaining the likely performance of candidates on a job.[38] Their faith, obdurate and ignorant, is that they can "tell by looking-listening."[39]

Against this presumption, research indicates that the interview yields *less* predictive value than "track record," and that it "often" produces *worse* judgment.[40]

Detecting Deception

> *"There's no art to find the mind's construction in the face."*
> —*William Shakespeare*, Macbeth[41]

In keeping with excessive reliance on judgment-from-appearance, many individuals—including detectives, customs inspectors, and other citizens—are confident that they can identify who is honest by the "see-hear method." Their assurance is misplaced.

For example, as the impeachment trial of President Clinton began January 7, 1999, a U. S. senator demanded that witnesses be called because he believed he could ascertain from their demeanor whether they were lying.

This false assumption, seconded by some journalists and the general public, indicates either that these self-assured believers have been spared acquaintance with psychopaths or that they can't recognize this kind of callous and consistent prevaricator. Psychopathic deceivers—not unheard of among politicians—lie easily, confidently, and without emotional cost.

Moreover the popular, but baseless, assurance that we can tell who is lying by looking reveals ignorance of fraudsters' skills. Professional con artists are well aware of their victims' folk-beliefs. Their art includes practiced "looking-you-in-the-eye," articulate speech, and serious demeanor as they move their suckers with their sincere lies.

Caution: These comments critical of the likelihood of detecting deception from others' behavior during testimony do not vitiate other reasons for examining witnesses.

Interrogation can be useful to amplify stories—in search of "the whole truth"—and to test the consistency of testimony. Criticism here has to do with one issue only: "Can we detect deceivers by observing them?" The answer is, *not assuredly*. A Russian proverb reminds us, "He lies like an eyewitness."

Review: Years after his "little book" appeared, Meehl offered some causes of evasion of its lessons: Ignorance, reliance on one's favored "theory," dislike of the "dehumanizing flavor" of "tests," mistaken ethical sentiment, and "computer phobia"—more accurately, innumeracy.[42]

To Meehl's list, some additional causes of over-confidence in personal ways of evaluating others are suggested:

1. People are more comfortable with (are habituated to) the see-hear procedure, and hence feel anxious about hiring individuals without "getting to know them."

This common inclination is reinforced by the difficulty many people have in comprehending what *base rates* are and how to use them (cf. pp. 51, 101-102).

When persons who assess others receive "information"—that is, stories—that *individualize* those whom they are judging, they tend to rely on the "personalized case histories" and to ignore what base rates indicate.[43]

2. In the typical interview, "first impressions" count. Employers and other raters tend to form judgments early, and then "find" confirmation of their evaluations in the remainder of the session.[44]

Note: All attempts to improve judgment are conditional. They rest on assumptions.

Thus, the actuarial procedures that would increase foresight assume that prognostic cues have been clearly identified and reliably measured. They assume, too, that "outcomes" can be accurately counted.

Last, nothing stands still. This means that all premonitory signals should be periodically re-evaluated. People change—some of them, some of the time, by degree and department. So, too, do non-human organisms like bacteria and viruses that transform themselves as their hosts are treated.

Therefore, these comments about mathematical methods for reducing error should not be interpreted as making an absolute distinction between actuarial ways of grading cues and "personal knowledge." These comments are intended to moderate arrogance in judging how others are apt to behave, especially the arrogance that comes from affection for, or disaffection from, others.

In "everyday life," it is reasonable to assume that intuition and more rigorous reasoning form a cognitive continuum. "Common sense" probably rests on a variable mixture of these ways of "knowing."[45] The message here is cautionary.

Chapter 10 describes attempts to explain human action by locating its causes.

10

Causal Explanation

"The principle of causality is subject to change, and it will adjust itself to the requirements of physics."
—Richard von Mises[1]

One Word, Many Concepts

The idea of causation is protean; it changes reference with the object of inquiry. Its meaning varies with our affection for the actors being explained and with the purpose of causal assignment. In addition, we are beset by persistent questions:

- Why not abandon such a promiscuous idea? What would happen if we felt-thought without naming causes?
- If we retain causal ideas, where should we look for the causes of human action? This is a query about "causal location"—about *what* causes.
- Since all causal attribution assumes a "system" within which nominated causes do their work, how should we conceive that context?

  This is a *big* quiz. It asks: How can we distinguish cause from coincidence? Where should we set a system's boundaries, and with what justification?

  A version of this query wants to know how to conclude a *causal regression*. Since we can, and do, conceive of chains of causes streaming backwards endlessly in time, with what justification can we stop the regress at one period rather than another?

- How can we measure *causal powers*? Causes are assumed to have "force." How can such impact be known in the social domain and, more troublesome, how can it be measured, given the system assumed?
- In what *style* should we conceive causes to operate, and how can we justify our conception? This is a query about *how* causes, and their inhibitors, arrange themselves.

  Many observed systems of events, organic and inorganic, exhibit varieties of feedback—positive and negative. In such a process, effects influ-

191

ence their causes—"positively" when the "bounce-back" strengthens the original signal, "negatively" when it weakens it.

In human affairs, feedback processes become particularly unpredictable when a cause generates an effect that then stimulates novel intrusions into the previously observed regularity.

Given these likely possibilities, and for the purpose of assigning causes of social events, where should we restrict study of these circulating webs, and with what justification?

Present Purpose

*"Cast aside your allegories and empty
hypotheses! Give us straight answers to the
accursed questions."*
—Heinrich Heine (1797-1856)[2]

No one can give straight answers to these many causal questions and, fortunately, present purpose does not require satisfaction of poet Heine's request.

My intention is to illuminate difficulties in applying the canons of science to study of social action, and thereby to curb fraud and arrogance while promoting a limited competence.

Identifying causes is one of these difficulties. It intrudes upon our inquiries not all the time, but much of the time, and principally when we seek an answer to "why?" in service to rational policy, personal and public. Once we request explanation so as to better address ethico-political concerns, we are drawn into the causal quest.

This chapter argues that a would-be science of the social can neither escape making causal assertions nor justify empirically the choice of any *one* causal location with a determinate causal style and power.

A cause of this double incapacity is, again, the fact that all explanations of social conduct carry ethico-political implication. And, if we cut causal cords with political scissors along moral seams, as is the human habit, we can expect peculiar results, including perverse effects.

Nevertheless, the disposition to inspect worlds for causal connections begins in our physiologies.

Perception and Conception, Again

The concept of causation is saved from absolute vacuity by the fact that our *perceptual apparatus* imputes a primitive notion of something making other things happen. Early on, the human child directly, immediately, and unreflectively "sees" causal connection. When the white billiard ball hits the red one, most children discern that the red ball moves *because* the white ball struck it. This is the "push-pull" concept of causation, so named by psychologist Jean Piaget and later confirmed by others.[3]

More than that, experiments with chimpanzees and bonobos suggest that these primates can discern *intention* in other apes and human beings, and that they make causal assignments.[4]

But, as we've come to expect from the acquisition of language, *conceiving* causation expands its meaning, and thereby blurs it. The idea that some actions generate other events becomes muddled. Philosophers squabble over the ontological status of "causation": Do causes *exist* or are they only creations of our minds? For example, philosopher A. J. Ayer claims that causal analysis is argument about fictions: "In nature one thing just happens after another. Cause and effect have their place only in our imaginative arrangements."[5]

As we shall see, in the very same book and chapter that Ayer writes this disclaimer, he contradicts himself (cf. n.12).

And, as usual, ethico-political preference affects our perspectives on the world, as when some theorists propose that we dispense with the very notion that something produces something else *so that* we can get on with the job of reforming the world.[6] Here, again, a critic of causal reasoning can't avoid invoking causation.

'Tis true; much of the time we get along without causal analysis. Thankfully for our sanity and happiness, we do not incessantly wonder, "Why did she do that?" and "Why am I here?" Healthy physiology spares us.

Then, too, in understanding persons *for the purpose of predicting* their conduct, it is sounder policy, thus far, to ignore the "why?" question in favor of tallies of others' acts. *What* individuals have done, with what frequency, yields greater forecast accuracy than does theorizing about the causes of their behavior (ch. 9). Against the pleasures of theories, this is a difficult lesson to teach.[7]

Those who resist this lesson frequently do so by demanding certainty. They object to tallies of behaviors with the childish "not-all" plaint: "Not all who exhibit X (some past acts) go on to do Y."

But in the social studies we rarely possess certainty. We have to make-do with conditional probabilities (ch. 6). And, apropos of this, we are reminded that individuals who "know for certain" are to be suspected of concealing ignorance under the cloak of confidence (pp. 186-187).

Nevertheless, the idea of causation will not go away. Its questions return in a variety of contexts—medical, legal, marital, military, and more. They occur like a reflex—involuntarily, without our commanding the thought. And its questions persist without our necessarily knowing what kind of information would answer our causal queries.

We're trapped, and even the skeptical David Hume, believed by 250 years of philosophers to have denied the logic of causal assignment, admits the trap.

In his *Abstract* of *A Treatise of Human Nature*, Hume affirms that

[as Resemblance, Contiguity, and Causation] are the only ties of our thoughts, they are really to *us* the cement of the universe, and all the operations of the mind must, in a great measure, depend on them.[8]

Most of the time, most of us assume that there *is* a "cement of the universe," and that the binding element is some kind of causal connection. In recognition of this possibility, and to counter the anarchic hope that we shall rid ourselves of this nagging idea, some causes of causal thinking are listed.

Some Causes of Causal Thinking

*"It is an ancient wisdom that our knowledge
of anything consists in our knowing the causes
of it."*
—Jerome Hall[9]

1. *Perception* of one kind of causation is an innate feature of human physiology. It is a survival device. It occurs unconsciously, without training (p.4).

2. *Language* is saturated with causal terms and, hence, with causal assumptions. Even theorists who would purge our talk of causal notions cannot practice what they preach.
   A short sample from one such author illustrates the difficulty—nay, the impossibility—of thinking-speaking-writing for long without making causal assertions. Thus the anarchist criminologist Bruce DiCristina advises us that

   "...the present social system causes...."
   "...if...it is because...."
   "...an anarchic criminology would promote...."
   "...theoretical anarchism is more likely to encourage progress...."
   "...our cognitive apparatus shapes...."
   "...methodological bondage leads to...."[10]

This sample of inconsistency can be supplemented with statements from other authors who otherwise abjure causal reasoning.
   Assuming causation while denying it is popular. Ordinary language readily corrupts.
   Thus, although social scientists warn introductory students that "correlation does not indicate causation," they search for causes with techniques of correlational analysis. As indicated in chapter 5, this practice subtly conceals causal assumption under a blanket of seemingly innocent technical terms. It

does so, to repeat an example, by the common practice of referring to one of the variables in a co-relation as "dependent."

"Dependent" means "contingent upon," "determined by," or, as one modern statistics textbook puts it, "influenced by."[11] In this fashion, employing a familiar word covertly inserts a causal premise into what is only a statistical artifact.

3. *Beliefs and desires* are regularly named as characteristics of our being, and are given causal roles by popular psychologies:

Q.: "Why did he do that?"

A.: "Because he wanted Y and expected that doing X would obtain it.

4. *Our sense of agency* confirms a "cement of the universe." We produce effects, and we know we do so. Causation is also impressed on us by awareness that external events do things to us.[12]

5. *Our wish to intervene* in lives—our own and others'—often requires causal attribution.

It does so if we are to justify our forecasts as rational and, more strongly, if we are to move beyond forecast of action to its temporal, instrumental prediction (TIP) (cf. pp. 49-51).

6. *Law and religion* incorporate causal assumptions, and so do the moralities on which they rest.

While these institutions employ causal ideas, their causal conceptions are not fixed. Their assignments move with intellectual fashion and moral attitude.[13]

Purposes at Work

This listing is not intended to be exhaustive. My purpose in recording some of the contexts in which causal assignment occurs is to rebut the sophomoric notion that, in the social realm, there is only one determinate conception of how events are produced. To repeat, *purposes move causes, and sympathies form purposes.*

Imperfect Justice

These facts constitute one source, among others, of our lack of perfect justice. Students of jurisprudence have shown repeatedly that similar sets of circumstance, or chains of events, receive different causal interpretations, depending on the affections and preconceptions of judges and juries. Hart and Honoré's work provides numerous examples. Experimental social psychology adds to their inventory.[14]

Perfect justice is missing, too, because ethico-legal purpose separates the idea of "is the cause of" from the idea of "is responsible for." Contrary to some popular opinion and such philosophers as John Searle, it is not necessarily true that, "Causation...is a matter of something being responsible for something else happening."[15]

Searle's choice of words is unfortunate because "responsibility" is a morally laden term. Therefore, those whom the law holds "responsible" need not be those who cause something to happen. And conversely, those who cause something to happen need not be held "responsible."

For example, Western law allows excuses such as "insanity" and "nonage" so that some persons who produce damage may not be deemed responsible for it, that is, they are not regarded as "blameworthy" or "guilty."

But of course, our laws and moralities do not stand still—for long. They, through us, invent categories of culpability.

Thus the laws of many modern lands now recognize a historically novel kind of person called "juvenile." For legal purposes, a "juvenile" is given a moral status between "child" and "adult." Such "intermediate" individuals are then treated as "not fully responsible."

In the United States where, in contrast with Canada and Western Europe, juveniles are disproportionately causes of killings, and where the death penalty is still an option, quarrel ensues concerning the propriety of holding such young persons "fully accountable."

Morals are ultimates (ch. 12). In republics the citizenry is the ultimate source of law, and experiments demonstrate that people often assign responsibility to "locations" different from where they locate causation. Kelly Shaver concludes a detailed review of such research with the comment that "the attribution of causality is substantively different from the attribution of responsibility."[16]

Some observers of the American scene believe the detachment of causation from responsibility is growing, and they suggest at least two likely hypotheses to account for this divorcement.

One possible cause of this separation lies in social scientists' emphasis on the "structural" origins of action, with the associated prescription to seek "root causes" of conduct and to regard at least some persons as "victims of circumstance." With such moral terminology, "victims" are less to be blamed for their misbehavior and more to be helped to escape harmful situations.

In league with this source of looseness between being the cause-of and being responsible-for runs the discovery by lawyers and their clients that money is to be made by shifting the load of responsibility from individuals-as-agents to individuals-as-victims, and thence to "deep pockets" that can be made to pay for injuries, however remote they may have been from immediate, temporo-physical connection to harm.[17]

In the social studies, it is, again, the dual aspiration to develop knowledge *and* to benefit humanity that affects causal nomination. Given the common desire to be useful, and useful as more than entertainers or propagandists, social scientists who wish their research to apply toward reduction of misery confront the necessity to consider not only *what* the relevant causes are— their "location"—but also the *style* in which they presumably operate.

Whether or not one is aware of the issue, causal style is important because, without ability to specify the contexts and patterns in which putative forces do their work, policies can harm rather than help.

Iatrogenic effects are not limited to the practice of medicine. They are at least as likely, and probably more so, in the exercise of state power.

Therefore, some kinds of possible causal connection deserve attention.

Causal Styles

Simple Forms

Among the "simple" ideas of causation, the following styles have been employed:

In a *compound mode*, two or more variables have to occur *in concert* to generate the effect that interests us. The common idea that disposition-in-situation produces a kind of activity is in this style:

$$D \ and \ S \longrightarrow E$$

Plural causation refers to the possibility that several factors, *in varied combinations*, can produce the same result. No particular combination is necessary; several are sufficient.

This is the thesis of "many roads," illustrated by vocational careers, including criminal ones.[18] In short, several combinations of temperament, family nurturing, local circumstance, and luck can produce a successful physicist, a poet, a president of a democracy, a tyrant, or a thief. A few interests may be common within each such career, but no distinctive pattern of possible causes need apply:

$$A, B, C \longrightarrow E; \ A, D, F, G \longrightarrow E; \ B, X, Z \longrightarrow E$$

Multiple causation describes situations in which a host of fluctuating events may be sufficient to yield a particular kind of event, but there is a superfluity of possible generators and their opponents. Some potentially effective factors may not be at work, and counter-productive events may intrude or also be absent. (A minus before a symbol indicates a counter-cause, that is, an inhibitor; a line over a symbol means that a potential cause or counter-cause is absent). For example:

A, B, D, -G, H, J̃, L, P, -Q, R̃, S, -T, X, Z——> E or

B, C, Ẽ, D, -G, H, I, K̃, L, -N, P, R̃, S, X——> E, and so on —

The number of such variable influences, and their relative powers, are *not* assumed to be constant. Therefore, results can be over-determined as well as variously frustrated. For instance, simultaneous over-determination occurs in the action of a firing squad. Any one bullet can be sufficient to produce death, but we have no way of knowing which units in a volley arrived in what series and, hence, which were adequate and which, superfluous—"overkill."

We also conceive of a variant of multiply-phased causation when several causes and counter-causes are *not* independent, but work in linked fashion, producers and inhibitors differentially shaping the course of events. In this style, it is possible that acting to prevent Alpha generates Beta which, in turn, causes the effect we wished to avoid.

With such multiples of producers and inhibitors at work, in varieties of simultaneous and linked arrangements, unexpected happy endings can occur as well as tragedies and double-binds: "Damned if we do, and damned if we don't."

Iatrogenic effects become possible, a likelihood that justifies the school-girl who concludes her essay, "Results are what we expect, and consequences are what we get."

These possibilities lead us to a related quality of causation.

Emergent (Immanent) Causation

Emergence is a system-based idea. Biology, chemistry, and physiology have demonstrated how aggregates, composed of interacting parts, behave as wholes. These composite things and beings perform as "systems," and are regarded as units, with capacities that are independent of their constituents.

Sometimes these aggregates are only *conceived* to be unitary, as are "communities" and "societies." At other times, their separate identities are *observed*, as when we study human physiologies and those of other animals.

Most important, these systems exhibit properties (abilities, powers) *not apparent* in their components. Such units are then said to constitute *in themselves* causal forces.

Note: An implication, disagreeable to meliorists, follows. Insofar as novel systems consist of components that retain powers—that are themselves causes, like bacteria in bodies—the unity of these collectives is never assured.

From this possibility, we have the idea of "immanent" causation. This means that conceived systems are dynamic. They contain *within themselves* the causes of their change. They are the unwitting causes of their own evolution.

In this lies both pleasant and unpleasant surprise. Furthermore, and unhappily for social engineers, this schema indicates our lack of ability to control the causes of large-scale social activities according to plan.

The popular idea of "emergence" is summarized by the slogan, "the whole is more than the sum of its parts." Its common example is the water molecule, H_2O, which, although composed of hydrogen and oxygen atoms, exhibits qualities not apparent in its separable parts.

In this vein, and ignoring the implication noted above, German psychologists during the 1920s and 1930s demonstrated the actuality of the emergent process with small-scale experiments. They called their thesis, *gestalt theory* (*gestalt* = form, figure, pattern), and its English-speaking protagonists adopted the title. This explanatory motif is also recognized as "organicism," "explanatory holism," and "descriptive emergentism."[19]

In the late 1930s, the American psychologist J. F. Brown applied *gestalt* theory to the study of societies. His use of a holistic perspective allowed him to "discover' that the Soviet Union represented the first human aggregate built on *gestaltist* principles, and thereby to have created the first rationally planned productive, happy, and just society.[20] Brown's textbook remained in American use through the 1940s and 1950s.

In the social realm, an emergent is conceived as patterned activity, observable among interacting persons who are said to constitute a "whole," as with the term "society."

Once such a "whole" has been established—whether by an evolutionary process or by the work of Great Leaders and their disciples—the individuals who comprise the society are interpreted as "participants" in the overall schema. However, the actual system, as distinct from its "blueprint," is not the result of Great Leaders' designs. No one acts solely with the intention to produce the society of which s(he) is part; and no individual or group within the whole, knows whether, or how, it contributes to the generation, maintenance, or destruction of the presumed unit.

In Sum: although participants are among the causes that contribute to the society's properties and movements, they are powerless to control qualities of the system or to foresee where the unit is headed.

No person, or cluster of persons, working within the whole, *knows* how to guide it in any particular direction, however much they *intend* to do so. The system, *as an emergent*, is deemed to be a novel composition whose internal processes defy knowledge and control.

This means that, while the emergent properties of a new and unique society are caused, these properties function, in turn, as causes *independent of their origins*.

For the social organicist, the image of human society approximates that of a hive or formicary in which, while individuals are builders, no single one of them, or group of them, is necessary for the system's activities. And this holds even when we outsiders can discern Great Leaders in the system who are causally effective, but, as always, for only a brief span.

Revision

> *"[W]hen philosophers try to become kings*
> *either their philosophy is corrupted, politics is*
> *corrupted, or both."*
> —Mark Lilla[21]

With the development of aspiring sciences of the social in the nineteenth and twentieth centuries, the *gestaltist* idea of emerging patterns of human relations was widely accepted, but with one grand revision.

Many such "systems-theorists" denied that we are powerless to guide "organic wholes" of human beings to desired forms of relationships. Energized by visions of a future in which everyone would be equal and secure, healthy and happy, peaceful and productive, these "communitarians" resented the emergentist idea that systems have their own momentum beyond our knowledge and control.

Those who argued that this limitation was real were deemed "reactionary," and given such additional derogatory titles as "blockheads," "enemies of the people," "lackeys," "dregs," "curs," "hyenas," "cock-roaches," and "insects" that required, and deserved, extermination.

Doubters become obstacles to applications of holists' presumed know-how—a skill allegedly based on "scientific theories" of social relations that would allow them to direct large numbers of persons, and eventually the entire world, to utopia.[22]

The results have been disastrous, as philosopher John Searle notes,

The leading problem in historiography of the twentieth century is why did socialism fail? The combined ideal of state ownership, a classless society, economic equality, and everyone working for the common good has failed everywhere.[23]

Devotees of political holism who can neither admit this phenomenon nor explain it have thereby lost credentials as scientists of the social.

Modern histories of highly abstract theories of human action draw attention to the limits of "social organicism."

Limits

While we recognize that living beings are organisms—composed of distinguishable parts with distinctive functions—and that these components work as separable units interacting with one another, the theoretic effort to transfer this fact, by analogy, to the workings of any defined collective of human individuals runs into difficulties, quite apart from the many troubles of social engineering described throughout these pages.

For starters, at issue is whether, and when, an aggregate of persons constitutes a "whole." This query is particularly appropriate when the unit is to be a "society" composed of thousands or millions of individuals that will be somehow solidary, possessed of harmonious interests (ch. 5).

With this trouble, we encounter another. Is the "social organism" open or closed? Is it permeable by forces external to it or sealed against alien intrusion? Or is its status better regarded as some degree of both? And then, for studies claiming scientific knowledge in a changing world, how can the boundaries of a social unit be identified and the relative impacts of foreign and domestic forces weighed?

These concerns are not impertinent. They return us to questions posed earlier, including where we can reasonably put stop to causal inquiry.

This question occurs, for example, when cosmologists propose that our worlds began with a Big Bang. To this "explanation," skeptics ask, "What came before the Bang? How can something emerge from nothing?"

This kind of question is also raised when criminologists assure us that they know the "root causes" that presumably produce the proximate causes of particular crimes—the proximate causes being, of course, individual actors.[24] Similarly, this question troubles us when economists "explain" inflation, unemployment, and other woes, by referring to "underlying causes."[25]

The Issue: Given the conceivably endless regress of causes that we can extract from history and current research, where should we stop inquiry about sources of today's social events, and with what justification?

Human beings have long put stop to causal regress with religion. God or gods serve as the ultimate cause. Such supernatural agents are defined as Uncaused Causes (ch. 12).

When religions propose moralities, and law evolves to enforce them, it becomes the job of priests and jurists to set limits to causal attribution.

If these customary institutions do not provide answers adequate to one's question about causal limits, then a reply to the query about causal boundaries says, "Everything depends on the 'satisfaction' an inquirer seeks from an explanation."

Whether we need to know causes is a function of what we wish the information to do for us. In particular, with reference to stopping causal regress, the issue is: What can we do better with an explanation that halts at one period in the movement of events rather than another?

In Sum: If the properties of a new whole are themselves products of causes immanent within a system, and if these forces cannot be specified in advance of action, with their powers and directions ascertained, then no social science can rationally propose a politics that promises fulfillment of any large complex of our desires.[26]

Lacking such ability, we dwell in the realm of conceivable possibilities and conjectures. We are left with the necessity of non-scientific judgment, grounded in imperfect social studies and our reading of history.

And then, further to confound a social engineering based on a social science, other styles of causal connection have been proposed.

The INUS Condition

> "We can construct causal concepts as we wish,
> which may be useful for particular purposes."
> —John Mackie[27]

Philosopher John Mackie is concerned with how people characteristically construe causation. He maintains that we ordinarily assign causation in what he calls a "causal field"—an assumed system others denote as "context." This field, he says, "is not itself part of a cause, but is rather a background against which the causing goes on."[28]

Assuming a context, then, *that is itself movable*, Mackie argues that to discern a causal sequence requires consideration of a plurality of causes, among which some *facilitate* and others *inhibit* the events of interest, such that *absence of inhibitory factors* becomes part of the causal schema.

According to this model, we ordinarily select as "cause" of the event or condition we wish to explain some other event or state that is antecedent to the effect that concerns us, but that is *neither necessary nor sufficient to produce it.*

However, the *nominated* cause, Mackie says, "is clearly related [to the] effect in an important way":

> It is an *insufficient* but *non-redundant* part of an *unnecessary* but *sufficient* condition—an INUS condition.[29]

INUS, pronounced, "eye-nus," is, of course, an acronym composed of the four key terms; "insufficient," "non-redundant," "unnecessary," and "sufficient."

The cause we select is *insufficient* to generate the effect we wish to explain because the regularities we discern in Nature, and in the social realm in particular, are known only incompletely, imperfectly. We do not know everything that conceivably enters a causal field or causal mechanism. Thus Mackie argues,

> What we know are certain *elliptical* or *gappy* universal propositions. We do not know [for example] the full cause of death in human beings, but we do know, about

each of a considerable number of items, that it is an inus condition of death, that, as we ordinarily say, it may cause death.[30]

While Mackie offers his proposal as an empirical statement of how we "ordinarily" conceive causation, he provides no test of the frequency or consistency with which either scientists or laypersons employ the INUS tactic. The widespread popularity of superstition questions how "typical" such reasoning may be.

However, laboratory experiment suggests that some individuals approximate Mackie's model when they assess events with *multiple potential* causes. Barbara Spellman's research indicates that, within the limits of select laboratory decisions free of strong emotional import, people act "as intuitive scientists, making contingent judgments while controlling for alternative potential causes."[31]

Implication: With its partial corroboration in experiment, the INUS model describes how individuals select, from a roster of possible generators of events, those factors likely to produce the consequences of interest. For many everyday purposes, we are not bereft of practical, causal judgment.

Such judgment is immediate and local. It receives *prompt feedback* from action that verifies or nullifies causal assignment. But this is a form of cognition distant from the evaluation of events beyond our agency.

Another implication derives from the "US" in INUS. The fact that causes can be "unnecessary but sufficient" allows *many roads* to lead to similar destinations. Contrary to much popular psychology, personal careers need not run in single channels.[32]

In addition, the INUS condition recognizes that the regularities we seek in explanation of human activities are likely to be, as Mackie says, "elliptical and gappy"—that is, open, loose, spaced, holey.

These apertures in our knowledge of ourselves suggest at least one possibility and a lesson. The possibility is that "chance" is an actual part of Nature. The lesson is that we are advised to reason with probabilities rather than with certainties (ch. 6).

Chance

"In vain the sage with retrospective eye
Would from the apparent what conclude the why,
Infer the motive from the deed, and show
That what we chanced was what we meant to do."

—*Alexander Pope*[33]

Aristotle (384-322 BC) called "chance" the absence of cause. But today "chance" has become part of a causal explanation insofar as it is *used* to "explain" some kinds of events regarded as "effects."

Thus, like other oft-used words, "chance" has expanded to serve a variety of employers. With expansion, several synonyms develop, some of which conceal their kinship to "chance"—synonyms such as "luck," "accident," "happenstance," "random event," "fortuitous circumstance," "haphazard occurrence," and more. But, whatever verbal costume "chance" wears, its idea persists, namely, that something unknown and possibly intangible is part of "how things happen," and suffices to "explain" some events.

The promiscuous employment of "chance" is exemplified by at least the following of its services:

1. We assign an event to "chance" when it *conforms* to the *a priori* calculus of probabilities, as with the roll of dice.

This does not mean that such events are uncaused. It means only that we do not know the numerous causes, and their relative forces, that must affect the fall of the cubes. And anyway, for the purpose of gambling, most of us lack the ability to control the "fate" of the dice. (For a possible exception, cf. p. 95). However, we do know the relative probabilities of combinations of faces showing *prior* to tossing "the bones."

2. In the obverse of this usage, we also assign an occurrence to "chance" when it *deviates* from a known frequency of similar events.

Thus we often say that something happened "by chance" when the effect seems "incommensurate' with its putative cause. For example, this is the meaning we give to careers that rise, or fall, in a manner not explicable by recourse to "normal" causes.

3. A congenial, medieval concept of "chance" refers it to activities *not* intended by an actor.

In this Scholastic version of "chance," it is argued that, since our *agency*— our power to produce events—is one guarantor of our belief in causation, any event that occurs without someone's design is attributable to "chance."

Medieval scholars advanced this idea to rationalize belief in God, the Supreme Designer, and hence we have the common "explanation" and proxy for chance, "God's will."

4. We also call an event "chance" when we cannot place it in a course of events bound together by some law-like propositions.

This does not imply that such an event is uncaused, nor that some regularity connecting it with other occurrences will never be discovered. It means only that no such "laws" figure in our accepted system of beliefs today.

In brief, this argument attributes our employment of "chance" to our *igno-rance*. It assumes that "real causes" are there, but that our science has omitted them from our models or that we have yet to find ways to measure them and control them for our studies.

This argument is *epistemic* rather than *ontological*. It concerns what we know rather than how things "really are." It refers, for example, to our inability to explain causally why a particular event, that is itself part of a class of events forming a statistical generalization, does *not* display the property denoted by the general rule. This usage is notable when "chance" ("randomness," "unexplained variance") is brought into play *after* "demographics" fail to explain (predict) some individuals' actions (chs. 6, 11).

5. In contrast to the preceding uses of "chance," an *ontological* thesis proposes that this word refers to an actual openness in the course of events. "Chance" then becomes a feature of Nature, of what we must allow as a possibility about "how things work" rather than of our ignorance. *Tychism* is the title given this argument.

Later pages amplify this usage. Here it is urged that, given the convenience of these multiple uses of the word, "chance," we should be alert to how we employ it.

Examples give the flavor of this concept-in-use. These illustrations can move us toward either the epistemic or ontological attitude.

The American poet Delmore Schwartz illuminates the kinds of happening that encourage appeal to "chance":

> How clearly we see, young man, too late,
> Those mighty world-wide thoughtless causes which
> Suddenly shake a dining room so much,
> Shaking the dining room where a private man
> Sits drinking tea with family and friends,
> And eating fish, swallows a bone and chokes!
> Killed by the quake prepared how many years
> Motiveless in the turning globe's round shelves.
>   AND
> There is a joke which grows within my mind;
> Here is a stadium and cheering crowd,
> Pigeons pass overhead, and one lets go
> (Nature's necessities are all his life),
> The one man wet amid the 70,000
> Cries out, Here are 70,000 faces,
> Why did that pigeon pick on me?
> —The joke of individuality!
> O what a practical joke on everyone,
> Something is always new under the sun!*

And then, life mimics art:

During an otherwise unexceptional week in 1995, a twenty-eight-year-old financial manager, Nicholas William Leeson, *broke* the distinguished 233-year-old British investment bank, Barings PLC, for whom he worked in its Singapore office.

Barings had a solid reputation. It had subsidized England's effort during the Napoleonic Wars and the United States' purchase of the Louisiana Territory. As of March, 1995, its capital was estimated at between US$500 and $550 million. But in short time, one man's judgment had cost it US$1.25 *billion*. (At last information, Barings was in the British equivalent of bankruptcy.)

Leeson, in his legitimate role as arbitrager, had bet that the Nikkei 225, an index of major Japanese stocks, would rise. How was he to foresee the Kobe-Osaka earthquake and Nikkei's consequent fall?

Why did it happen to him, and to Barings?

Oh, the joke of individuality!

Earlier pages describe a similar intrusion of "bad luck" upon the well-laid plan of Long Term Capital Management (ch. 6).

The claim that "chance may be a real part of Nature gains credence as "everyone" experiences surprises that cannot be explained by reference to some known regularity. We notice inexplicable coincidences, happy conjunctions, and fortunate omissions—the Titanic not boarded, the early start that avoids a collision, the delayed bride, the bullet that whizzes past your head and kills the man next to you.

Absent-mindedly, Alexander Fleming leaves a fungus in a petri dish by an open window, and stumbles upon penicillin. This "staggeringly fortuitous" discovery changes medicine and serves as 'template for all subsequent antibiotics."[34]

Richard Horton, editor of the British medical journal, the *Lancet*, concurs:

[M]edicine must pay a great debt to chance. In cancer treatment, for example, virtually all [drugs] owe their origins to chance observation or luck....[As regards] the most impressive achievement of the post-war years [the successful treatment of childhood cancer, 'acute lymphomoblastic leukemia' [ALL], many aspects of the cure remain frankly inexplicable.[35]

In reviewing physician James Le Fanu's criticism of modern medicine, Horton comments,

Drug innovation waned once the limiting effects of burdensome government regulation kicked in after the thalidomide tragedy. A more rational and less random approach to drug discovery was 'much less fruitful than was hoped.' Chance allowed for the unexpected; science did not.[36]

In a parallel argument, Helen Epstein reports,

[Until 1959] ...not a single person is known to have been infected with HIV....now 16,000 people become infected with HIV every day, and 7,000 people die of AIDS.[37]

When Edward Hooper looks for the sources of this scourge, his best guess is that it emerged from a laboratory accident.[38]

Examples multiply. But "chance" is a metaphysical concept. It raises *ontological* questions about how the world works and *epistemological* questions about how we can know it.

These queries ask how to justifiably accord "reality" to phenomena. For many inquirers, giving chance a role in explaining our lives not only commits *ad hockery*—it can be made to fit any hypothesis—but it also seems spooky.

Similarly, to insert chance into explanations means that there are some aspects of natural activities that are not only unknown, but worse for medical and social engineers, beyond our control. In such cases, explanations-with-chance can allay curiosity and satisfy some temperaments but fail to serve meliorists. Explanations, then, can give intellectual pleasure without giving utilitarian advice, and we are returned to Oedipus's complaint that we can have truth *without* utility.

(Recall that Sophocles in his *Oedipus Tyrannus* has the ill-fated Oedipus cry, "How terrible, knowledge of the truth can be, when there is no help in truth.")

In addition, the notion that luck is real—actual—runs counter to the belief in determinism. At least it opposes the determinism called "strict" or "hard."

Hard determinism maintains that everything is caused. It is Albert Einstein's attitude in criticism of quantum mechanics, popularly phrased as "God does not play dice." On this assumption, "free will" becomes a delusion, as Einstein declares, "[H]uman beings, in their thinking, feeling, and acting are not free but are as causally bound as the stars in their motion."[39]

This doctrine follows the teaching of French mathematician-astronomer Pierre Simon Laplace (1749-1827) who believed that, if we had knowledge of all the laws of Nature, and of the initial conditions from which we make statements about the future, then we could not only *foresee* what will occur, we could also instrumentally *predict* it.[40]

Determinists such as Laplace and Einstein argue that we resort to explanation-with-chance to cover our ignorance. And philosophers quarrel about whether the proposals of chance and determinism are contrary or contradictory.

If they were *contrary* to one another, then, while both stories could not be true, they might both be false. However, a sterner attitude claims that these beliefs about how the world works are *contradictory*, meaning that, if one of these conceptions is true, the other must be false.[41]

Tychism

> *"All Nature's but Art unknown to thee,*
> *All Chance,*
> *Direction which thou canst not see."*
> —Alexander Pope[42]

The second possibility is best represented by the American philosopher Charles Sanders Peirce (1839-1914). Peirce (pronounced "Purse") not only invented the important doctrine called "pragmatism," he also gave chance a chance. (Forgive me; the phrase is hard to resist.)

Peirce argued that chance is actual, a part of Nature, and, of course, he lent authority to his claim by giving it the grand title, from the Greek, *Tychism*.

Tychism doubts whether everything that happens can be explained with a description that places an event as part of some regularity. Peirce's conception of evolution requires some looseness in the connections among things and beings. He is therefore friendly to Aristotle's definition of chance as absence of cause and the *contradictory* of hard determinism.

To the deterministic axiom that "every event has a cause," Peirce replies,

> I question whether this is exactly true....may it not be that chance, in the Aristotelian sense, mere absence of cause, has to be admitted to having some place in the universe.[43]

However we notice that, when chance is *employed* as part of an explanatory story, it *serves* as a form of cause. Such service means that, whether or not we're ignorant of some productive force in the web of events in which we are actors, we must expect gaps in our comprehension of the flow of activities.

In particular, Peirce holds that

> In matter's fine grain where molecules are so inconceivably numerous, their encounters so inconceivably frequent, that chance with them is omnipresent...the feature of chance...although it can only work upon the basis of some law or uniformity, or more or less definite ratio towards a uniformity, has the property of being able to produce [sic!] uniformities far more strict than those from which it works.[44]

Here Peirce's qualification—"chance works with more or less definite ratio towards a uniformity"—assimilates his Tychism to a *relative frequency* notion of probability (ch. 6). We are sensitive to Peirce's use of the causal term, "produce," in his application of chance. As *employed*, chance no longer refers to Aristotelian "absence of cause," but is part of the causal-explanatory network.

With such use, Tychism anticipates the twentieth century's twin developments of quantum theory and evolutionary biology-psychology. One hundred years ago, Max Planck (1858-1947) demonstrated that, at the super-atomic level, matter appears to behave as if it were composed of discrete particles—"discrete," "separate," "discontinuous"—providing space for Peirce's loose causal schema.

In parallel, the "new physics" observes how order can arrive out of chaos. It claims that small, apparently chance variations in a current system can generate "self-organized" large-scale effects. In this way, the physical thesis supports the possibility of immanent causation in the biological and social realms as well.

The physicists' idea accords with biologist Jacques Monod's argument that

> chance alone is the source of every innovation, of all the creation in the biosphere. Pure chance, absolutely free but blind, is at the very root of the stupendous edifice of evolution. It is today the sole conceivable hypothesis, the only one that squares with observed and tested fact.[45]

This version of chance comports with Stuart Kauffman and other biologists' themes of "order from chaos" and "complexity catastrophe." It acknowledges that there can be "varied fates from similar states," as Steven Austad phrases the phenomenon. It accords with ideas advanced by mathematically inclined psychologists such as Robyn Dawes, Carl Malmquist and Paul Meehl that "*pure bad luck* may play an important role in the development and course (or even amelioration) of psychopathology." The theme is equivalent to our thesis of "many roads" (p. 197, 203).

Tychism gains credence from geneticist David Stern's comment that "many evolutionarily relevant changes in DNA sequences are probably buried within vast quantities of neutral variation, within both protein-coding sequences and poorly understood regulatory regions." It fits, too, with Caleb Finch and Thomas Kirkwood's proposals. These geneticists show that chance events are inherent in the courses of organisms' lives. Their work joins that of some chemists and zoologists who demonstrate how order can be generated out of disorder, *without human direction*, and how an evolutionary process can reverse.[46]

Indeed, the very idea of "mutation," invoked to explain biological evolution, is based on chance. Zoologist Mark Ridley advises that mutation,

> the raw material for evolution [is] an alteration in the DNA sequence of an organism [that arises mainly] as a copying mistake, but can also arise as *spontaneous* chemical change in a base.[47]

Genes, the information-bearing units in DNA, are "picked at random," Ridley says, as if by lot. It is a basic property of Mendelian inheritance that you cannot predict whether or not a particular gene will be passed on. If it could be predicted which genes were to live on in future generations, and which were to die, natural selection could never have brought complex life forms into existence.[48]

Thus does Tychism persistently enter explanations of our lives, and not just as a restriction on our cognitive powers, but also as a fundamental characteristic of Nature.

Regardless of which side we take in the epistemological-ontological arguments, the fact of such dispute between what we know and how things actually occur has value. It dampens the assumption that we can have error-free knowledge of the courses of human events, and it justifies our reasoning with probabilities rather than with certainties—not that this mode of thinking is easy (ch. 6).

Dissatisfaction and Utility

However plausible chance may be as an intruder upon the course of our lives, it is unsatisfactory as an explanatory device because it gives us no handle with which to intervene rationally to direct patterns of events. Chance cannot be modeled into a forecast, much less a TIP (ch.3). It cannot be assigned a quantity of force nor a time-period within which it will operate.

Nevertheless, Tychism has value. It encourages prudence. It would have told Nicholas Leeson not to put all his eggs in one basket. It would have reminded the modelers of markets at LTCM of Major Warden's warning to Commander Shears about the occurrence of the unexpected (ch. 6). Tychism serves as a weapon against arrogance, the repetitive mother of disaster.

Moreover, living with uncertainty is not all bad. Uncertainty gives hope to those who live in desperate straits. And the possibility that there are gaps in our knowledge, and that Nature may work in loose fashion, cheers lovers of liberty. They fear a determinist social science that, if valid, could give more control to those who hold a monopoly of power.[49]

An additional model of social causation is possible, but neglected.

Systems Conceived

Biologists employ a set of assumptions that differs from those prevalent among social scientists. They are more system-sensitive.

Biologists note that much life feeds on life. Organisms that derive fuel by photosynthesis or chemosynthesis are exceptions. Otherwise the generalization holds, and this process includes omnivorous *Homo sapiens* whether we ingest food while it is alive or after killing it, and with or without cooking it.. (Vegetarians do not escape this necessity; plants, too, are living organisms.)[50]

In this round of activity, biologists view "life" as having neither beginning nor end, although its particular exemplars can be so described.

In addition, and in company with Mackie and many other philosophers, biologists consider events to occur in contexts that are themselves mobile. They assume that these "causal fields" constitute a "web of life" in which every event has many antecedents, and in which, as per immanent change, nothing stands still.[51]

When we adopt this perspective, and assume human action to be generated in a web of causes, we can conceive of such networks as variously stable or fluid, and as sparse, dense, or somewhat in-between. But however we think of causal systems, biologists emphasize contextual effects of our decisions. That's why Hardin's "First Law of Ecology" applies: "We can never do merely one thing."[52]

This rule draws a Grand Circle, and we're probably in it: *Causes change in their identities, numbers, and powers as the systems in which they operate move.*

For example, in an interview with Helen Epstein, cytologist Opendra Narayan explains the *emergence* of AIDS from a heretofore unknown virus by saying, "If you take any virus and 'passage' it through a new species often enough, eventually you get a more pathogenic virus."[53]

Process produces. If we do not get exactly something from nothing, we do get something unthought-of from activity—our own kinds and those of other organisms.

By contrast with such "ecological thinking," social scientists usually conduct research as if we lived in sparse systems—assemblies in which potential producers and inhibitors of action are few and relatively independent of each other. And characteristically, students of the social look at generators of particular kinds of activity without discounting for the inhibitors and counter-generators—factors in the causal schema that stimulate unforeseen effects, some of which are perverse.

Social scientists' models also assume that we *know*, not only the nature of the web of influences within which we function, but also its boundaries.

These are weak assumptions. But journalists and politicians give them credence. Their tendency is to define undesirable social conditions and actions as "problems" that therefore must have "solutions," and this means, in turn, that such "problems" are regarded as though they had few, powerful, and non-interacting causes that can be manipulated without undesirable costs.

Such reasoning is childish but understandable. It's convenient.

Journalists and politicians work in the realm of persuasion. This requires that they simplify. Of necessity in the age of televised "information" and short attention span, rhetoricians must give brief, simple, and convincing answers to causal questions. For persuasive purpose, their replies "explain" when they fit audiences' preconceptions. When they do so, they satisfy. They provide the comfort of confirmation.

Biologists need not be so hurried, and they can communicate through recondite language. Moreover, as distinct from the popular conception of a few causes creating linear effects free of thresholds (dosage effects), biologists are accustomed to considering events as produced in *dense webs* in which the sources of action are *many, interactive, and non-uniform* in their interplay.

"Non-uniform" means that causes need not move at equal pace and with constant power. They can work in cascades, with plateaus between their thresholds of efficacy. Generators can be *allometric; they can change at different rates as the entire system moves.* In such a complex, the respective powers of causes are *not* constant, and what is effect can also be cause.

In Sum

> *"Almost all of the hypotheses of social inquiry are causal..."*
> —*Clark Glymour*[54]

We employ different conceptions of causation in different settings for different purposes.

Given the many complications in applying ideas of causation to the study of social events, we can understand why those who would inform policy under the aegis of a social science assume that we live in a sparse web of causes. This assumption is probably inaccurate.

However, all policies assume some kinds of causation. Everything depends, then, on the purpose for which we gather information and how we intend to use it.

Remembering that no one acts from a single motive, *if* one's principal purpose is to gain and maintain political power, then the kinds of causes sought and the effects desired are different from the models of causation to which independent inquirers attend.

On the other hand, *if* we are uninterested in gaining power over others and less interested in shaping the world according to our desires than in finding out how it is and how it gets that way, then we are free to question current ways of thinking about the social domain. And such curiosity moves us to examine yet other troubles in the way we go about applying what little we know toward the direction of policies, private and public.

Chapters 11 and 12 address these issues.

Part 5

Policy

11

Rationality

Ideal Policy

Rational decision is an *ideal* intellectual performance that weighs Utilities with Probabilities on the supposedly fair scales provided by Reason. A shorthand expression of this difficult balancing act demands, "Know what you're doing!"

As decision theorists use the term, "utilities" refers to the *values* individuals place upon their desires. This means that policy begins with needs and wishes. These are plural and, as per Lasalle, they work in hierarchies that change as we gain and lose in efforts to achieve objectives and weigh their worth against their costs.

This is why formal "decision theory" is tough stuff.[2] It attempts to assign numbers to different arrangements of wants and their movable values—"utilities"—as persons act out of fluctuating balances of expressive and purposive motives.

The other half of the policy-equation—"probabilities"—is also a less-than-exact concept. As chapter 6 demonstrates, the idea of "probability" is employed to describe several ways of disciplining judgment about what has happened and what will happen. We are reminded that, because of the multiplicity of uses for which we judge the likelihood of events—particularly those consequent upon our actions—the late John Mackie concludes that "probability resembles moral concepts such as goodness and obligation."

This is our predicament. Given desires, some of which are infused with moral value, and probabilities calculated from past events projected into futures, the formula for rational policy is to be "solved" with a symbolic manipulation called "reasoning." Unfortunately for rationality, "using our heads" is never a purely distilled process. Reasoning is always saturated with emotions, some of which have moral power.

This fact constitutes a theme of preceding chapters. Our passions, expressed in languages steeped in evaluation, make taxonomies of social activities difficult. This difficulty intrudes upon measurement of human action and, in particular, measurement of "social facts" and activities that cannot be directly observed.

Desire-activated reasoning *selects* the events to be explained, and it affects *how* we explain them. Such affected thinking/feeling assigns causes of conduct differentially, that is, it guides where we look for causes. And it moves our estimates of what is likely to happen if we act, or do not act, in some particular way.

These impediments to knowing our worlds make neither moral terms nor probability concepts useless. These obstacles mean that clear thinking requires clear denotation when we handle such wandering words.

Rational Action and Actors

Clarity is required, then, when we talk of policies being more and less "rational." "Rational" is a glory-word. It is applied to persons and beliefs, and strategies and tactics, and the application usually indicates approval.

Here, however, we attend primarily to the meaning of "rational action," and secondarily to the possibility of "rational actors." And our effort is exercised disinterestedly, without approving or disapproving of agents and actions to which the honorific, "rational," is granted.

For this purpose, the *goodness* of means and ends is not considered. Rationality is concerned with *efficiency of means*. It addresses what is correct, not what is right. We examine the idea, then, to clarify our use of this popular term.

We do so, recognizing that the concepts of a rational person and rational action are employed as ideals. Ideals serve as standards against which to compare our behavior. They perform as guides to policies, *not* as descriptions of what we do.

Since disputes over decisions commonly appeal to rationality, it helps us know the nature of our conduct if we examine this concept. Our analysis acknowledges that the ideal of acting rationally is only one standard with which we assess ourselves. We are aware that, in "real life," what we do is seldom singularly motivated. Efficiency is but one of many tests of the propriety of policy, and conduct is rarely purely rational.

Justifying Social Science

The ideal of rationality has been used to justify a social *science*. Such discipline, it's been promised, would find and verify appropriate means to socially approved ends. With the aid of public education and an agreeable central government, social science would inform policy and serve as guide to our creation of a better world.[3]

Varying with what one thinks would be a better world, and how much a science of the social ought to be able to contribute to it, the enterprise can be judged largely a failure.

Insofar as meliorist social science fails, it does so because it gives Reason a role in social life that exists only in limited, here-and-now, morally neutral, affectionately barren domains—how to bake a cake, build a house, pilot a plane.

It fails because we are passionate creatures, infused with sympathies for and against kinds of people and kinds of acts, and while we often cooperate to attain common goals, we also fight over objectives and the instruments with which to obtain them.

With this understanding, we can describe a concept of "rational act" borrowed, with one addition, from the Franco-Italian economist-sociologist Vilfredo Pareto (1848-1923). Pareto proposed that a rational act has three components:

1. It is purposive, as distinct from expressive or reflective. It aims to achieve an objective.
2. The end sought is empirical. "Pie in the sky" doesn't count.
3. The means chosen to achieve the end must be—for actors—efficient, and knowledgeably so. Lucky success doesn't count.[4]

A strong limitation of this ideal is that, in living with others as opposed to the solitude of the philosopher's den, many activities involve mixtures of the purposive, expressive, and reflexive. We find these moving origins of action in work and play, but not much in labor.

When we engage in sports, for example, we want to win the match, but playing the game, doing the exercise, would be boring if it did not also excite pleasures of the flesh through sight, sound, touch, and movement, and, for many athletes, through the joy of companionship and aesthetics of kinesthetics. In addition, doing sports with skill always requires reflex habits.

Similarly, satisfaction in work also involves some mixture of *purpose* with the *pleasure* of expression. Without delight in the exercise of curiosity and talent, work becomes labor. Converting the expressive-aesthetic delights of action to instrumental-purposive activity destroys pleasure.

In Sum: We define a "rational act" as an ideal—for the purpose of clarity. But we understand that such an ideal never works as a singular motive.

Rationality ≠ Morality

The definition of a "rational act" offered above says nothing about the *goodness* of the ends sought or the means employed. On this issue, rational *decision* departs from rational *action*.

Morality refers to a realm of activity different from purely efficient action (ch. 12). It demands distinctive principles for evaluating conduct. To confuse the moral and the efficient domains is to make a category mistake (pp. 23-27).

However, the confusion is common because the words "rational" and "moral" are both honorific. To repeat, they are "glory words," and unsophisticated persons thereby assume that these terms must refer to correlated acts: "Good is rational; rational is good."

To believe these equations is to muddle concepts. It is to be blind to the possibility of rational evil and moral folly.

Non-Rationality and Irrationality

It is important to distinguish rational activity from that which is non-rational and that which is irrational. The distinctions help us discern which questions are sensible to ask of ourselves and others.

It is *non-rational* to seek non-empirical objectives, although it may be deemed good to do so. Pure play is non-rational activity—for the players—and converting it to rational effort destroys the joy.

People who cannot share the delights of play and aesthetic response, and who believe that every act should be interpretable as rational, ask such unanswerable (silly) questions as "What's the point of skiing deep powder?" or "Why do you enjoy Ravel?"

Queries of this nature do not ask for empirical answers. They are tacit criticisms presented in the guise of "real" questions, and should be treated as such. They deserve Louis Armstrong's reply to the intellectual who asked him to define "jazz" (pp. 11-12). If you can't feel it, you can't "know" it, and defining it won't help.

Darwinians, of course, like to interpret play as rational—from a cosmic perspective. They then impose *functions* upon play that are *not the purposes* of players.

Darwinians do so by describing play as the species' way of preparing organisms for fight, flight, and capture of food and mates. (This comment is of no relevance to the validity of the Darwinian idea of evolution by natural selection.)

But, *for players*, play is its own end. We cannot appreciate the delight of sky-diving by asking fliers why they do it—as if they had a purpose other than the thrill-aesthetic of float.

Pleasures are ultimates. Pleasures are ends in themselves, not to be judged as rational or irrational. The judging cannot appreciate the feeling. Pleasures are outside the spheres of instrumental or lunatic activity. They are non-rational, and open to destructive as well as beneficial results.

Similarly, acting to get to Heaven is non-rational—that is, non-empirical. If individuals believe this is a possible goal, then their believing-acting upon that assumption is neither rational nor irrational. It is beyond the realm of rational decision. It is an article of faith and, by our conception of rational activity, non-rational.

If, on the other hand, individuals adopt such a belief contingently, with the assumption that Heaven may *not* be a real place but that believing the acknowledged myth makes them *feel better*, then such a lukewarm "faith" posits an empirical end: Personal satisfaction.

In this case, belief approximates rational action, and becomes less-than-faith. However, this attitude raises the question of whether *knowing* that one is believing a myth reduces the efficacy of the myth. If myth is to do its work, blind faith is more effective than reasoned belief.

By contrast, action is deemed *irrational* when one's goal is empirical, but one's choice of means is distorted. The common betrayers of rational decision are ignorance, arrogance, and passion.

These nouns refer to capacities and dispositions that are physiologically based, that function by degree, and that work in various combinations with desires and beliefs. They do not, then, describe singular states of organisms.

Additional Distinctions

Our conception of rational action has purposely avoided attaching praise or blame to such conduct. We are thus free to observe that it can be rational to be deceitful. Indeed, many creatures, in addition to humans, protect themselves through fakery.

It can also be rational to be unreasonable. If "being reasonable" means attending to others' reasons, or balancing available reasons before acting, then there are occasions on which obstinacy wins.

Leaders of modern social movements, as well as many of history's heroes and sports stars, have urged toughness, single-mindedness, strength of will as effective means with which to gain power. In our time, this has been the teaching of communism, fascism, Islamism, and Nazism.

Of course, the Will to Power carries costs. One of its major companions is the enthusiasm that blinds. Ignorance is its reliable colleague and error its consequence.

Last, one should not confuse being rational with being logical. There are times when it can be rational to argue illogically. Rhetoricians—those who would move us to action with words—can persuade without adhering to rules of logic.

To repeat, no activity is purely rational, and all action exacts a price.

Expensive Instruments

Acknowledging that the motives that stimulate large-scale social events are multiple, and that they are *changeably interrelated*, it is possible that, for some empirical objectives, the means employed cost more than the ends are worth. And this holds true even when the ends are fully attained, which is rare.

This ever-present possibility underwrites the necessity of *subtracting* from any beneficent results of policies their indirect as well as direct costs. These indirect debits include *opportunity costs*—doing *this* makes it impossible to do *that*—and an assortment of side-effects, ranging from those that are beneficial to those that carry bearable costs (nuisances), to those that are perverse—producing the opposite of what one desires. In medicine, these perverse results are called "iatrogenic," meaning damage done by doctor's prognoses and treatment.

However, some "extraneous" prices of action are always with us. They are expenses that political proponents are loath to consider, much less to calculate.

What political enthusiasts try to do is transfer such inevitable costs to futures or to persons other than their own constituents. That is, they try to protect their kinfolk and their supporters.

This shifting of the prices paid for policies has been observed wherever the State has grown. Thus, in 1764, as France moved toward bankruptcy and a great revolution, the witty Voltaire (1694-1778) declared that "the art of government consists in taking as much money as possible from one class of citizens to give to the other." And after the Revolution, the French economist Frédéric Bastiat (1801-1850) seconded Voltaire. "The state," he wrote, "is that great engine by which everyone seeks to live at the expense of everyone else."

However, when costs are patently greater than achievements, and policymakers seem otherwise sane, then we often attribute such "lack of judgment" to the biasing pull of appetite upon reason.

Love—of people and power—has long been recognized as a powerful seducer of clear thought. We regularly acknowledge this magnet in our attempted explanations of irrational conduct among individuals not obviously lunatic.

Thus the ordinarily reasonable man, desperately in love with "the wrong woman," is said to have "lost his head." And the intelligent woman, excited by her power to propose wild policies, is deemed to be "out of her mind." Lady Macbeth is a model with real-life modern exemplars.

Warring provides additional examples. Although wars seem necessary at their start—at least to some political leaders—their outcomes and costs cannot be foreseen.

Political speech that promises victory "whatever the cost" motivates some followers, but, it is largely fraudulent. People do surrender rather than die, although again, with exceptions. Think of Masada.

Nevertheless, historians recognize "Pyrrhic victories," named after King Pyrrhus of Epirus who defeated the Romans at Asculum, 279 BC, but at "too great" cost. An anonymous wit calls this phenomenon "disastrous success."

The extravagance persists, as when Arthur Wellesley, the Duke of Wellington, expressed mixed feelings about his "success" in defeating Napoleon Bonaparte at Waterloo.

Years after this wavering battle, a lady enthusiast exclaimed to Wellington, "What a glorious thing must be a victory, sir!" To which the Duke is said to have replied, "The greatest tragedy in the world, Madam, except a defeat."[5]

We are left with a reminder provided by an oft-forgotten German proverb: "The broth is never eaten as hot as it is cooked." Success is seldom unadulterated. Costs are unpredictable; gains, impure.

In Sum

Among civic-minded persons in representative democracies, a prime requirement asked of public policy is that it match means to ends, with the important proviso that both ends and means shall satisfy moral demands.

Chapter 12 describes the quality of morality.

12

Morality

Valuing and Knowing

When decision is deliberate, two kinds of consideration come into play. We want to do what is rational within the bounds of what is moral.

The balance between doing what is right and doing what is effective is unstable. It is calibrated, and re-calibrated, by temperaments-in-situations, and by individuals who have been conditioned by, and have affection for, a distinctive people and their way of life with its morally mandated prescriptions and proscriptions.

Moralities do many things, described below, but one of their functions is to define what is important. And when important matters are at stake, when the continuity of a way of life is endangered, moralities characteristically allow, and justify, the ultimate tactic: *Killing enemies* (refer again to Mr. Justice Oliver Wendell Holmes' opinion, p. 169).

At various times, and with various restrictions, moral leaders have recommended murder. Thus, six hundred years ago the Bishop of Verden, Dietrich von Nieheim, demonstrated how what-is-effective can become what-is-good:

> When the existence of the Church is threatened, she is released from the commandments of morality. With unity as the end, the use of every means is sanctified even cunning, treachery, violence, simony, prison, death. For all order is for the sake of the community, and the individual must be sacrificed to the common good.[2]

The Bishop's edict is repeated—without end. Instructions for the self-sacrificing religious warriors who, 11 September 2001, destroyed New York's World Trade Center, bombed the Pentagon, and attempted additional killing, urge them to:

Consider that this is a raid on a path. As the Prophet said, "A raid...on the path of God is better than this World and what is in it.... Smile and feel secure,. God is with the believers, and the angels are guarding you without you feeling them."

The terrorists' manual adds,

If God grants any one of you a slaughter, you should perform it as an offering on behalf of your father and mother, for they are owed by you. Do not disagree amongst yourselves, but listen and obey... If you slaughter, you should plunder those you slaughter, for that is one of the sanctioned customs of the Prophet, on the condition that you do not get occupied with the plunder so that you would leave what is more important....[3]

In response to this morally motivated attack, some teachers of ethics urged that we quell terrorism "with whatever means necessary" while others urged "restraint."

For students of social life who would have their studies perform as sciences useful for decision-makers, the infusion of moral issues into policies further constricts their competence. While many of the disciplines with which we inquire about ourselves have helped eliminate irrationalities—demonstrating defects in means chosen to attain empirical ends—social scientists have no special authority as moral guides. This, despite the fact that some scholars claim to know how to construct a "rational ethic."[4]

If moralities do not prohibit cost-benefit analyses, they make them difficult. Given the impact of morality upon policy, it is important to attend to what moral training and practice are about.

Four Questions

"The nerve of moral judgment is preference;
and preference is a feeling or an impulse to
action which cannot be false or true."
—*George Santayana*[5]

Moral quarrels address four distinct, yet overlapping, issues:

1. A perennial set of questions asks, "What is the good life?" "What should we do?" And, "How can we justify our version of goodness in opposition to other versions?"

This kind of question has troubled philosophers for centuries, and it continues to do so without resolution. Struggles over right and wrong conduct persist, not only because interests differ, but also because *moral questions are not empirical.*

As Santayana declares in the quotation above, matters of fact do not answer moral queries. Moral inquiries ask for prescriptions about *how we should act* and proscriptions about what we should *not* do. They also ask for *justification* of moral mandates.

Such questions do *not* ask for *descriptions* of how we are and what we do. They avoid this task because how we are disposed to act is, by many moral standards, unsatisfactory. Indeed, a major function of moral codes is *to control our inclinations*.

By contrast, science is equipped to answer questions about *what we do* and, within limits, *how* we come to do as we do. But science is *not* equipped to justify a distinctive way of life.

This is one reason why moralities so often appeal to religious authority for approval of their imperatives. It is also a reason why *factual matters do not settle moral quarrels*.

In struggles about answers to our first set of questions, theologians and other philosophers contribute to moral feelings and conduct principally by offering prescription and consolation. These officers of churches assuage curiosity with myth, and provide assurance of relief from our pains and anxieties, if not in this world, then in an unknowable after-world.

But no one acquires morality solely by reading philosophic disquisitions, and people rarely change their ethical stance by attending to others' arguments.

Of course, in a modern world, especially that of "Westernized" people, many individuals are bereft of family and clan. Numbers of persons are detribalized, alienated, without ethnos, and some of these individuals feel "lost."[6]

Some of these persons are "saved" by immersion in one of the many substitute collectives that provide affection and security along with an interpretation of the source and authority of the adoptive community's commandments.

About this, it is worth remembering that converts to a faith are often more zealous than those born into it. But, whether one is a native moralist or an acquired one, moral conflicts persist.

It is also worth noting that this description of moral community says nothing about the legality or criminality of salvatory collectives. Gangsters' "families," Charles Manson's "family," and other such criminal clusters do *the same psychological work* as more peaceful tribes.

They accord honorific difference. They identify "their kind" and its enemies. They justify a way of living. They give "meaning" to being, and they make people happy by turning "nobodies" into "somebodies."

2. A second question asks, "How is morality acquired?" Psychologists have responded to this query with only limited success. Moral careers are various, and variously channeled. Some careers, we've seen, are inexplicable (ch. 9).

We find "bad seeds" in good families, and "good seeds" in bad families. Circumstance is important, but not all-important.

Allowing for individual differences in temperament and talent, becoming a moral kind of person is generated by intimate association with others who reward affiliation. Feeling/thinking/acting in accord with a moral code is an emotional/cognitive/participative product of *reciprocated affection*.

3. A third realm of inquiry is *descriptive*. Ethnographers and historians have worked to show us the many ways in which people have lived, and how they have justified their lives as preferable or despicable, usually the former.

In this domain, study is less concerned with prescription—finding out how we should behave—and more concerned with learning about the range of acts and beliefs others have deemed good and bad. Some moral persons deride, and fear, such inquiry lest description corrupt receptive minds. Censorship for goodness' sake is common. It hangs yet another handicap on liberal education.

4. Compared to the attention paid the first three sets of inquiry, a last question is ignored. And when it is not ignored, it is often misunderstood.

This question asks, "What is the quality of morality?" It wants to know, "What, if anything, distinguishes moral feeling/thought/conduct from 'mere' preference, taste, etiquette?"

Professional inquirers often evade this important request by trying to subsume it under the first set of queries. Experience in academic debate teaches that those who *dislike description of how* we behave are likely to demand that the expositor reveal his/her own preferences. This misses the point, and opens the door to the genetic fallacy.

The genetic fallacy is the error of assuming that, if we know a person's motive for stating a proposition (that is, its source or genesis), we thereby have evidence of its truth or falsity. To the contrary, one's interest in proposing a hypothesis does not constitute evidence of its empirical validity. Knowing "why" a person defends an argument alerts us to the possibility of bias, but by itself this does not provide warrant of its accuracy or inaccuracy.

What evasive debaters wish to quarrel is, again, how we *should* act, and with what justification. But this is not the question.

If, for example, the Yanomamo believe that fighting is fun, honorable, and good, while Christians, despite their homicidal record, deny it, the ethnographers who record these different ethics do not have to approve or disapprove of either way of life.[7]

Against this proposition, some scholars accuse it of the sin of "relativism." They do so on the assumption that *their* moral values are, or should be, universal. However, there are two kinds of relativity to be considered.

One kind is *descriptive*. It is the work of historians and ethnographers to tell us how people in different times and places feel/think morally, and to trace change in moral sentiment.

A second kind of relativism is *prescriptive*. It claims that one morality is as good as another.

It is unfair to confuse the two styles of relativity. For moral actors, *their code is absolute* (cf. below). This provides ground for conflict, but that is not the fault of historians or ethnographers, nor should it distract from their work.

Given that there is a domain of moral action, we should be able to describe it. And description, if it is to be accurate, should not project our ethics upon exotic others.

In describing the distinctive features of moral feeling/belief/action, we are portraying a social fact—namely, what people commonly recognize as constituting moral sentiment and conduct. The description offered below distinguishes, by shifting degrees perhaps, moral demands from manners and other less important preferences.

Moreover, this description is *neutral as to content*. That is, description of the quality of morality says nothing about what we *should* feel moral about.

The definition to follow borrows from philosopher-ethnographer John Ladd's thoughtful work, with apologies for any abuse I may perpetrate by a brief exposition of his detailed argument.[8]

Differentiae

> "A moral code is a collection of ...rules and
> principles relating to what ought or ought not
> to be done—what is right and wrong."
> —John Ladd[9]

After a comprehensive review of earlier philosophers' attempts to find the distinctive features—the *differentiae*—of a moral code, and a probing quest for such distinctions among a band of Navajo in the southwestern United States, Ladd proposes that moral codes can be distinguished from other preferences by two categories of pre- and proscription: Moral mandates are regarded by their carriers as *superior* and *legitimate*.

The *superiority* of a moral command is evident in two of its distinctive qualities: Its autonomy and its priority.

The *autonomy* of a moral demand refers to its function as an *ultimate*. A moral mandate constitutes *in itself* sufficient reason for doing or not doing. It does not require further justification, although Man, the talking animal, usually gives reasons when challenged. But we do *not* acquire a morality by weighing the reasons given during the process of our being trained.

For example, award-winning actor and devout Roman Catholic Mel Gibson was once asked why he was not "particularly broad-minded" about celibacy and abortion, to which Gibson unhesitatingly replied, "Those are unquestionable. You don't even argue those points."[10] Similarly, Orthodox Jews regard their moral precepts as absolute and ultimate. Thus physician Fred Rosner describes his nation's attitude toward life and death:

> Judaism ascribes a supreme value to life. Therefore...suicide is morally and legally forbidden, refusal of life-saving treatment is not respected, and active euthanasia is strictly prohibited.[11]

Secular preferences can also be organized as moral codes. Not all moralities are legitimized by religion, and atheists can behave ethically. Indeed, when atheistic ideologies have gained political power, their proponents have assumed moral status for their preferred ways of life. Recall the Soviet Union, Mao's China, and other subscribers to Marxist-Leninist ethical principles. (Cruelty toward infidels—non-believers—does not distinguish atheistic from religious moralists.)

A moral stance, with or without religious justification, is apparent, too, when people fight for limited resources in situations that are zero-sum contests: What one side wins, the other loses. The repeated battles for water in America's West represent such a continuing struggle. In a recent instance, drought in Oregon's Klamath River Basin made demand for water a matter of survival: fish versus human beings.

Compromise, a favored way of resolving conflict, is not available. Equal division of water, or proportional shares (which units count?), allows both species to suffer. The struggle becomes intractable—good versus good. Moral attitudes harden, and the side one takes is regarded as autonomous and deserving precedence.

For example, in the general context of "protecting the environment," David Graber, a biologist with the U. S. National Park Service, expresses the ultimate quality of a moral attitude:

> We are not interested in the utility of a particular species, or free-flowing river, or ecosystem to mankind. They have intrinsic value, more value—to me—than another human body, or a billion of them.[12]

Moral rights and wrongs are ultimates. Autonomy means independence of consequence, other than the moral objective. A moral command operates to halt the endless regress of justification. It says, in effect, "If you cant's *sense* the wrongness (or rightness) of this demand, additional argument will not convince you."

We know we've touched another person's moral sense when, after lengthy debate and exchange of "good reasons," our opponent insists, "Nevertheless, it's our duty to...." or, "It's still wrong (or right) regardless...."

This test is easily applied to those who believe that the consequences of an act are *sufficient* to determine its goodness (or wickedness). A fragment from an actual debate between an anthropological moralist and a utilitarian philosopher illustrates the point:

(After two hours of inconclusive dispute):

Anthro: "Would it be right for you to have sexual intercourse with your mother?"

Philo: "No!" (without hesitation).

Anthro: "Why not?"

Philo: "Because consanguineous reproduction has maleficent genetic consequences."

Anthro: "We're not talking about reproduction, only about sexual congress."

Student #1 (from the audience): "Maybe it's not as pleasurable." (Sic!)

Anthro: "That's just a prejudice."

Student #2:   "Don't you recognize that all acts have consequences?

Anthro: "Yes."

Student #2:   "Then that's how you know what's right and wrong."

Anthro: "Which consequences count? By what criteria ought we to assess them, and since consequences have consequences, how are we to know where to stop in counting them?"

To repeat, the *superiority* of a morality lies in its work as an *ultimate*. It puts "stop" to quarrel, at least *within a community of its practitioners*.

Superiority is a matter, too, of a moral code's being accorded *precedence*. It has *priority*. It demands "come before" other considerations that might affect action. Once imbued, moral training overrides other reasons for acting, such as pleasure or immediate practical ends.

In some circumstances, moral priority trumps survival. Ethics have been known to require self-sacrifice, and upholders of a moral way of life honor their martyrs as exemplars of right conduct.

Among Muslims for example, *jihad* means "struggle." It is the constant effort to obey the decrees of Islam against the corrupting influence of the passions and of the infidel world. In defense of this faith, it becomes the *duty*, not an option, for all believers to fight evil.

Legitimacy: The second distinguishing mark of a moral code is its claim to legitimacy. This claim is sustained by three linked characteristics.

The first guarantor of legitimacy is the possibility of *justifying* one's moral beliefs and practices. Under challenge, moral persons can offer "good reasons" for holding their creed, but it should not be assumed that these justifications are the causes of their coming to their faith. They function as rationalizations after the fact of acquisition.

Second, within the band of believers, the moral code is *binding*. In this sense, it is impersonal, disinterested, and applicable to all the congregation, with the possible exception of children and the mentally incompetent.

However, this sense of what Ladd calls "intersubjective validity" does *not* require that a morality apply to outsiders. In practice, as opposed to Kantian prescription, a moral doctrine need not be universal.

Indeed, it cannot be universal for those who believe God selected them as special bearers of His wishes or who assume that their faith is "true" while others live "in error" and are thereby damned to Hell.

Last, the claim that a morality is legitimate is made reasonable by its practitioners' faith that their sense of right and wrong derives from *the way the world works*—from human nature, or "natural law," or "the cosmic scheme of things," or from a divine Creator's plan.

Indeed, some modern students of science attempt to reason from their sought-for Theory of Everything to a design for "the good society." Thus Danah Zohar and Ian Marshall seek to

> draw on the principles and dynamics of quantum reality to derive a whole new model for our social and political relations [and to] extend this model to a new vision of social reality that embraces every aspect of our daily lives—our sense of personal identity, our relationships to others and to nature, our political and moral decisions, the manner in which we design our cities and educate our children, the management practices with which we run our industries, and the fundamental values and goals that inspire our actions.[13]

This search for foundations of morality in science is not new. For example, in the 1920s and 1930s Pascual Jordan, one of the early interpreters of quantum mechanics, believed that National Socialism ("Nazism") was "rooted" in Nature, as quantum physics describes it.[14] Of course, contrary moralists find a different "nature" with which to legitimize their preferred morality.

Confusing "what science finds" (facts) with what we want (ideals) persists. For example, the United Nations produces a *World Social Science Report, 1999*[15] that sociologist Irving Louis Horowitz describes and criticizes:

> With rare exceptions, the *Report*...fails to take account of the ambiguous response of the social sciences to the normative goals of free societies. From Auguste Comte's sociology as the religion of humanity and Marx's inexorable stages in class evolution and revolution, to Durkheim's solution of the division of labor in a corporatist set-up, the prescriptive collectivist ethos provided a steady drum-beat for rule *of* the people, not *by* the people... The unwelcome fact is that for every example of social science as handmaiden to social democracy, there are an equal number of examples of social science in the service of totalitarianism. But it seems that this hard lesson has yet to penetrate the purveyors of bureaucratic administrative social research.[16]

In the Western World, attempts to find ground for a preferred way of life in Nature are as old as pre-Socratic philosophers in sixth-century BC Greece, and as recent as neurobiologists' efforts to rationalize their hopes with an evolutionary story about how life has been generated.[17] But, in opposition to such endeavor, a moral code's claim to legitimacy does *not* require that the sense of reality used to validate its mandates must be the *source* of a tribe's ideals for the good life. The causal arrow probably points in the opposite direction.

The morality that orders our relations with others and our conceptions of ourselves is *not* learned from perceiving the "real" world correctly and then deriving ethical principles from this information. At least among people we've been able to study, moral preference is acquired by individuals with selective constitutions who live among others who *practice a morality* in word and deed.

Reasons given to legitimize a morality, like those that accord it superiority, *work independently* of how things "really are." Indeed, they function to combat how we ordinarily would act if our dispositions were not bridled with ethical restraints. And they work to inhibit how we would behave if we were purely rational agents, perceiving the world accurately and acting only to use efficient means toward the attainment of individual or collective ends.

Among other implications, this means that moral doctrines can be suicidal (pp. 126-131). Contrary to biologists who assume that the ultimate end of action is survival—if not of persons, then at least of their genes—moral actors often do *not* accept endurance on earth—either individual or collective—as the validating test of the superiority and legitimacy of their preferred way of life.

Many moralities command death of self, as well as death of others, as duty. They do so in requiring sacrifice of self *for* others and in the maintenance of honor upon one's breach of a community's code. In the latter example, honorable suicide has the silent function of deterring others from failing to fulfill a moral assignment.

This instruction is found among Christian, Muslim, Samurai, and other moral practitioners. In this spirit, the Roman Catholic moralist, Daniel Callahan, declares, "An ethic of survival, at the cost of other basic human values, is not worth the cost."[18]

Emotional Fuel: Morality has yet another quality, not emphasized by Ladd. Moral demand is charged with emotion. Therein lies its force.

The emotional charge borne by moral persons is cause of their being so often dangerous. Criticism of their moral precepts insults them and enrages them. It stimulates hatred, and provides repeated occasion for killing non-believers.[19]

For a recent example, recall the unhappy consequence of a United Nations conference called to end "Racism, Racial Discrimination, Xenophobia, and Related Intolerance," 2001, that served as a forum for racism, racial discrimination, xenophobia, and related intolerance (ch. 8, n. 111).

A moral sense is a matter of *feeling*. Reasoning comes later. The emotional fuel of moral sentiment is a function, in part, of a human nature that is tuned to detect imminent danger and, in part, a result of the manner in which a distinctive morality is acquired.

Acquiring Morality: We imbibe the morals of our "tribe," if we have one, *not* by reciting lessons, or by performing logical exercise, or by reasoning things out—although these practices can accompany acquisition. Moral feeling-belief-action develops as we live with caring intimates who demonstrate particular ways of being and doing. And this living-with-others that embeds moral attitude does its formative work not so much by teaching as by training.

Training differs from teaching in that it molds the behavior of organisms without either trainer or trainee necessarily knowing what is occurring. Of course, there are also formal training regimes, consciously applied, as when we housebreak pets, toilet-train infants, and propagandize adults.

But formal training practices are only a small part of the training we receive—without trainers, teachers, or parents and their "subjects" knowing that they are involved in affecting one another. Parents and other intimates train offspring by the way *they themselves behave*. Children are "adhesive." They imitate. They pick up moral sentiment and moral habit without being aware that they are doing so. In short, insofar as we acquire a morality, we do so as we acquire our native tongues—*un*self-consciously.

Moreover, just as children do not learn to speak—and read, write, and cipher—with equal facility, so too they exhibit individual differences in amenability to training. These differences are largely constitutional—a function of genetic material affected by intrauterine and perinatal environments. We do not enter this world innocent of a nature (ch. 1).

This is not to deny the importance of training, but to indicate the mysteries of human development. The social environment is important, but it is not a stamping mill that makes equal impression upon uniform material.[20]

This means, too, that what has been acquired by the training of individual constitutions is not readily changed by teaching. *Teaching* is a conscious process in which skills are demonstrated and symbols manipulated according to rules. Teaching is time-consuming, error-prone, and expensive. By contrast with the ubiquity and automaticity of training, teaching is far less effective in moral transmission than is consistent training in an environment of rewarding elders.

Discontent

Some philosophers are unhappy with this conception of morality *as it is acquired, felt, believed, and practiced.* They complain that such a description is circular, in the style of anthropologist-sociologist W. I. Thomas's famous dictum, "The mores can make anything right."[21]

As noted earlier, these inquirers are dissatisfied because they want an answer to a different question: not what moral attitude is like, but what it *should* consist of. They seek a foundation with which to validate *their* moral sense, and that can thereby legitimize *their* claim to universal application.

By contrast, and unpleasantly, an anthropological attitude is non-parochial. It permits one to argue that some people whose practices offend us nevertheless constitute moral units. And, of course, one's choice of offensive moral competitor is wide and forever refreshed with new candidates: fascists, National Socialists, communists, Mormon polygamists, Mafiosi, secular humanists, Jews (Hasidim v. secular), gypsies, pagans, papists, Muslims (Shia v. Sunni), Buddhists, Hindus, Kurds, Pushtun and Tajik, Serbs and Kosovars, Turks and Armenians, Russians and Chechens, Christians (Protestants v. Roman Catholics), and more.

All these believers, and others, regard their doctrines as Right. At the same time, they have themselves been objects of obloquy according to other tribes' conceptions of good behavior.

History is a record of lethal struggle between groups defending, and promoting, their preferred ways of living. The morality that unifies a people is also stimulant to homicidal enthusiasm.

The engine of moral action is reciprocating. It "pushes" with hatred of evil, and "pulls" with love of the good. "The good" can be empirical— realizable—or inspirational—hoped for. Enthusiasm makes no distinction between the possible and the imagined.

In modern times, all morally inspired large-scale social movements have justified fights to the death. This is true of Japanese Bushido, Italian Fascism, German National Socialism, Chinese and Russian Communism, Christian, Muslim, and Hindu contestants in Africa and across Asia, and combatants in the fifty-year struggle between Muslim and Jew in the Middle East. The killing goes on.

Stating this truth does not apologize for the practices associated with any of these passions. But, to deny this truth is to assume that only people who share our image of the good life can be moral—in the manner of *Gott mit uns*—"God's on our side." And, if one's faith expels god, then "History is on our side." "Same difference," as the American folkway puts it.

Moreover, to deny this truth is to make incomprehensible the magnetism of visionaries. Both denials reinforce ignorance of *how we are.*

Since many American readers did not experience, directly or indirectly, the fervor with which their forefathers, and some mothers, engaged in their nineteenth-century Civil War, the Spanish-American War, and the wars with Mexico, and in the twentieth century's Spanish (actually international) Civil War, and its World Wars I and II, it deserves reminding that the combatants in these fierce fights believed Right was on their side.[22] (U. S.'s warring in Korea, Vietnam, and Yugoslavia is more ambiguous.)

By their nature, moralities excite sympathies. They draw loyalties, so that when English-speaking peoples entered their major wars from the late eighteenth into the twenty-first centuries, respectable citizens have been divided by moral issues as well as by economic interests.

Then as now, a *moral sense* encourages sacrifice for the defense of one's country. At the same time, among citizens with a contrary morality, it encourages allegiance to the enemies of one's country.[23] In earlier wars in particular, considerable numbers of Britons and Americans argued for the *goodness* of enemy objectives, some to the extent of committing espionage and treason.

Of course, lust for money and power also drives individuals to take sides in fights, but love of *a Good*—promised as well as actual—forcefully moves individuals to risk their lives in betrayal of their homelands as it does in defense of them.

Against enthusiasm for promissory, but murderous, regimes, neither academic intelligence nor scientific expertise provides immunity. Indeed, scholarly authority has often operated perversely. It has encouraged the folly of believing that, if one knows a few things well, one knows larger things as well.

For example, during the 1930s and into the 1980s, many English-speaking voices praised *The Wave of the Future* that they saw coming in communism, fascism, or National Socialism.[24] They commended these *moral movements* for producing full employment and ending class exploitation. They cited favorably central powers' repair of their countries' "infrastructures," getting railroads to run on time, and building super-highways, large dams, and gigantic factories.

They praised these regimes for restoring national dignity and ennobling art and literature. They enthused when their favored states exterminated prostitution and "sexual perversion" and required "national service" from all, beginning in childhood.

They lauded these commanding governments for protecting their subjects' physical and mental health not only with "free" medical care, but also with such devices as "educational" campaigns against smoking and "noise pollution." In addition, dictatorial powers promised to extinguish interpersonal violence, self-abuse, and dissolute idleness.

In Nazi Germany programs to eliminate "useless" leisure were given the self-refuting title, *Freizeitgestaltung*, "free time organization." This *morally motivated* concept was promoted with bureaucratic enthusiasm and without a sense of horror, contradiction, or humor.[25]

In the Soviet Union, where the British intellectuals Beatrice and Sidney Webb had seen "the future that works,"[26] subjects were punished for "using impolite language," "traveling on street cars in dirty clothes," and "wearing a hat in the wrong place." It became a criminal offense to refer to the USSR as "Russia" or to say "Russian" instead of "Soviet." And to these prohibitions more serious crimes were added, many of them arbitrarily defined and painfully penalized.[27]

Cruelty accompanied these "progressive" reforms but, we were assured, "The evils we deplore in these systems are not in themselves the future, they are the scum on the wave of the future.[28]

We are advised to beware of monolithic power and of confident futurists and their seductive figures of speech. The gentle, kind Anne Morrow Lindbergh who foresaw a better world in Nazi Germany could not know what policies and instruments could produce her envisioned happy ending, and at what cost.[29]

Added Caution: We are also advised against confusing what succeeds short-term with what produces good long-term. The quotation from Arthur Koestler with which this chapter began is intended to alert us to the danger of fusing morality with rationality.

Novelist-journalist Koestler wrote his story, *Darkness at Noon*, from his experience with a rationalist regime that converted might into right for "a noble enterprise." Koestler addresses us with the authority of an insider. He had been a communist. He fought in the Spanish Civil War, 1936-1939, was captured by the rebels, sentenced to death, and reprieved.

His tale depicts the Moscow "purge trials" of 1936, and explains the inexplicable: how a good man, a devoted party member and original Bolshevik, N. S. Rubashov in the book, could be reasoned into confessing crimes against the State he had not committed, and allow himself to be executed "for the good of the movement."

In the foreword to this tale, Koestler tells us that the fictional persons he describes are based on people he's known. He puts the proposition about ends justifying means in the mouth of Rubashov's prosecutor, Examining Magistrate Ivanov. Appropriately, the ethic that Ivanov expresses mimics that of a leading Marxist theorist, Nikolai Bukharin (1888-1938) who wrote,

> "Ethics" transforms itself for the proletariat, step by step, into simple and comprehensible rules of conduct necessary for communism, and, in point of fact, ceases to be ethics.[30]

Bukharin was more prophetic than he knew. George Walden writes,

Before having him shot after a show trial, Stalin told his former friend [Bukharin] that, should it come to execution, it would be "nothing against you personally."[31]

In Sum

Moral conflicts need not be considered to be of one kind. From the viewpoint of moral persons who fight one another, each is struggling against evil. The attitude is Manichean. Right versus Wrong; Light versus Darkness: *Good Versus Evil.*

From an anthropological perspective, warfare between moralists is better conceived as *Good versus Good.* In this kind of struggle, demands are "nonnegotiable," and fighting, intractable.

A third category of moral conflict is seldom mentioned. It sees *Evil versus Evil.* For example, prior to America's entry into World War II, 1939-1941, some of us regarded the slaughter between Hitler's Germany and Stalin's USSR as this type of killing.

However, in whichever manner a moral conflict is interpreted, social scientists have nothing to say. They take sides, of course, but they have *no special competence* to determine the ends of public policy, nor are they equipped to prescribe policies for the efficient attainment of peace, justice, prosperity, and happiness.

Social scientists have a limited competence to assess what works. But the question persists: How much of this talent, based on hindsight, improves foresight, and of what?

Summing Up

"You can do everything with your bayonets, sire, except sit on them."
—Talleyrand to Napoleon, 1805, or Prudence
speaking to Arrogance.

Rationalism

An excess of rationalism misleads would-be scientists of social action. Rationalists seek regularity, pattern, structure in explanation of whatever concerns them. Where they find some such order in social life, they assume that their yield gives power—to themselves or to those they advise.

Preceding chapters describe major obstacles to such ambition. Describing such obstacles does not deny the enlargement of knowledge about ourselves to which biological and social studies have contributed. Indeed, earlier pages refer to many such improvements.

However, mischief intrudes when curiosity about our nature—what we do and why—is directed toward practice and, in particular, toward practice that would produce particular kinds of good among masses of anonymous persons who attempt to live civilly under one set of tranquillizing customs.

Compound ambition—to know correctly and to do good with that knowledge—moves rationalists to illegitimately translate information as knowledge, and knowledge as know-how.

Our long exercise shows that such twinned aspiration largely fails both objectives. The failure starts with feeble conceptualizing. In turn, porous concepts generate fickle classification, unreliable observation, and inaccurate measurement. These foibles are exacerbated by the meliorist impulse that selects causes for their ethico-political congeniality rather than their efficacy.

In addition, such selectivity ignores those major motors of action: The Passions. It is prone to rationalize emotions and intellectualize pleasures. It is, in brief, half-bodied.

As a consequence of these many debilities, the regularities we find in social activities are always time-and-space-bound. They are hedged about with contingencies, including the popular *ceteris paribus* clause—"other things being equal." This convenient apology is useful for thought-experiments, but is never known to be true.

Rationalists' "laws" of human action are further constricted by their attempts to extend a partial knowledge to large, novel spheres of activities. "Large" refers to numbers of actors in social dramas and to spans of time. "Novel" refers to situations different from those of the original inquiries.

Most of us live among, and are affected by, large masses of strangers in circumstances that change drastically within lifetimes. Eighty years ago, philosopher George Santayana reminded us that "every generation is born as ignorant and willful as the first man." He was, and is, correct.

The transmission of lessons learned is fragile; bonds of affiliation, slippery. Given the history of great transformations of ideas and practices, no one can foresee the direction or scope of social movements across generations.

None of these cautionary comments is likely to distress social theorists. In rich lands, numerous persons are employed to be vocationally thoughtful and called "intellectuals." I'm one.

Our tendency is to work with high-level abstractions with which we construct models of how things happen. In the social realm, these pictures are frequently converted into blueprints for better worlds. We read, then, of designs by which the vast majority of humanity will become happy, healthy, wealthy (by current Western European/American standards), and cooperative and peaceful, because equal.

Equality in the distribution of these desiderata is to be gained, and then ensured, by release of opportunities for talented, good persons who will, as far as possible, share their products with individuals who are less well equipped. In this new global community, sharing will occur either voluntarily or through state coercion by law. And this law will presumably be well articulated, coherent, efficiently administered, and morally validated.[1]

Such aspiration is not new. It has been approximately attained by small religious bands that limit their units to around 150 individuals, unified by uncomplicated modes of production and rules of conduct.

But what is at issue for rationalists is the road to be taken to such utopia among large populations of strangers with diverse histories and cultures and changing ways of making a living.

Briefly, we attend to five suggested routes to a planned, better world. For example, classicist Peter Jones describes one ancient prescription:

> [E]arth, Gaia, was thought to have been in existence from the very beginning of time...[therefore] ancients argued that it must be a god. Many concluded from this that man could have been permitted existence on it only if he were somehow at one with it and worked closely together with it. But nature was not always friendly. Ancients got around this by crediting it with moral purpose.[2]

With such belief, one's meliorist objective should be either to understand Nature's purpose—if it has one—and align oneself with it, or to transcend Nature. And we can transcend some aspects of Nature by retreating from earthly pursuits, which usually means having others support us, or by improving upon Nature as scientists have done in some domains of biology.

The great monotheisms paved a parallel road. These faiths taught thoughtful persons that desirable objectives of human action will be achieved by following the edicts of an inspired teacher. Such an instructor's words are believed to have been authorized by a supernatural agent who, although different from us in His omnipotence, omniscience, and all-loving nature, is conveniently possessed of the human attributes of purpose, plan, and preference.

Beneficent social change can be attained, then, by living in accord with the divine plan. This prescription is urged not only upon individuals, but, for greater efficiency, upon the tribes to which they adhere.

Alternatively, and principally within the last two centuries, secular teachers have taken the place of divine authority. But they, too, have often been revered, and accorded semi-divine status.

The most popular of these earthly instructors are assumed to have power to read History "correctly." Their power is allegedly warranted by well-reasoned theories of how we are and come to be. Such right reading of History tells disciples "what must be done" to fulfill Clio's design, a course which, if faithfully followed, assures "progress." Secular teachers such as Marx and Engels, Lenin and Stalin, Mao Tse-tung and Pol Pot, and younger epigoni, profess a "historical materialism" according to which all social events are caused and all actors are social products.

However, despite such determinism, it is assumed, not only that History reveals a causal pattern, but also that knowledge of this schema allows leaders to construct programs, enforced with a monopoly of power, that will steer social change in a preferred course with a desired "outcome."

A different road to the "good society," and possibly to a better world, would be educational—or more accurately, propagandistic. As earlier pages show, some scholars claim that they know how to devise a "rational ethic." Given instruction in its principles and the satisfaction of worldly needs, it is assumed that the logic of the new morality will suffice to persuade people to live in accord with its reason-justified habits.

Thus biochemist, and Nobel-laureate, Jacques Monod, calls for "an ethic of knowledge" [to] save us from our "deepening spiritual malaise [and] from the new age of darkness" that he sees coming.[3] His rational morality "defines a *value*: that value is objective knowledge itself."[4]

According to Monod, such a rational morality

is the only ethic compatible with the modern world [that knowledge has created]...The ethic of knowledge is...the one at once rational and resolutely idealistic attitude upon which a real socialism might be built...[and rhetorically he asks] Where then shall we find the source of truth and moral inspiration for a really *scientific* socialist human- ism, if not in the sources of science itself, in the ethic upon which knowledge is founded, and which by free choice makes knowledge the supreme value—the mea- sure and warrant for all other values?[5]

Philosophers like Gilbert Ryle and George Santayana would find Monod's logic faulty. His reasoning, they'd say, makes a category mistake (pp. 23-27). It confuses wish with fact or, in another guise, it tries to derive an ought from an is.

But, whether or not we agree with these doubters, Monod does not, and probably could not, answer Lassalle's compound question (p. 215): How shall we find the road to this lovely land; how shall we build it once it is envisioned, and at what cost?

By contrast with either strongly deterministic or voluntaristic ideologies, other modern inquirers believe that social change is better described as a process to which we contribute, but over which we have only limited control. This process is called "evolution."

In its Darwinian form, evolution diminishes the role of Man as master of all we survey, including our own destiny as well as that of other forms of life.[6] We are not surprised, then, when contemporary interpreters of Darwin's "dangerous idea"[7] translate his hypothesis to yield a prophetic, hopeful message.

Theory-Poaching

Inventors of seminal ideas frequently become victims of poachers who borrow original arguments for conversion to their own evangelical use. Hav- ing been such a victim, Karl Marx is reported to have complained, *Je ne suis pas Marxiste* ("I'm not a Marxist").

In similar vein, Charles Darwin and his disciples have suffered illicit trans- lation of his original thesis. "Ideological trespassers" have borrowed the naturalist's conception of evolution, and have converted it to suit their own ethico-political preferences—usually a happy ending to the human story.[8]

Contrary to optimistic destinies accorded humanity, and stories that *know* "the purpose of it all," the Darwinian conception of biological evolution by natural selection does not allow a telic interpretation of the evolutionary process. In Darwin's schema, Nature exhibits neither purpose nor ultimate objective. It offers no pleasing "end-in-view."

In addition, the Darwinian story rejects supernatural causes of our condi- tion and it denies "essentialism." That is, it opposes the notion that varieties of organisms exist as immutable kinds.[9]

Nothing stands still. Classification of living things—from viruses to whales to Man—change with human knowledge and purpose. Taxonomies are not fixed "in the cosmic scheme of things." Geneticist Steve Jones affirms that:

> Individuality is everywhere....Chromosomes vary in shape, size, and arrangement; and the proteins themselves are filled with difference....Species can, in the new world of molecules, no longer be seen as absolutes. They are not units, but groups of individuals, each with a biological personality of its own.[10]

We are returned to Delmore Schwartz's "joke of individuality" (pp. 205-206).

Furthermore, Darwinian theory does not regard evolution as deterministic. Students of evolution acknowledge the work of chance. For them, haphazard events occur repeatedly and universally. Nature appears to be a bit loose, and Tychism is a viable hypothesis.

Depending on whether one's attitude is ontological or epistemological, not all events are effects or not all events have known, or knowable, causes. For present purpose, the difference makes no difference because all we can know is through exercise of our neurological apparatus. We can never *know* how Nature "really is" apart from our thoughts about it and tests of it. What we believe is a different matter.

In Sum: The results of reasoning are imperfect. Even educated reason provides little defense against the fleshly passions and none against neurosis and psychosis. Informed judgment does not answer all questions nor does it guarantee a particular future beyond our current horizon.

Nevertheless, prudential reasoning, empirically informed, is the best device we have for testing reality. Given our mixed nature, and the conflicting demands made of brainwork, clear thought and empirically grounded belief are apt to remain minority attributes, and even minority aspirations. But, as objectives, they constitute major justifications of liberal education and reasons for writing a book.

Notes

Preface

1. This is part of the definition of "sociology" given by *The Random House Dictionary of the English Language, The Unabridged Edition, 1966.*
2. "Rhetoric...the art of using language so as to persuade or influence others...." *Oxford English Dictionary, 1993.*
3. I employ "ethico-political" to emphasize the infusion of political ideas and actions with moral passion. Political policies are concerned with the distribution of powers. They are emotionally fortified as well as rationally directed. Chapters 11 and 12 describe the distinctive qualities of moral feelings and rational acts.
4. "Iatrogenic"—a disease or disorder caused by physician's diagnosis or treatment.

Chapter 1: Primal Knowledge

1. Holmes, 1881/1991.
2. Bouissou, 1942; Brain, 1950; Pitts and McCulloch, 1947; Schusterman, Thomas, and Wood, 1986; Reichmuth and Kastak, 2000.
3. Weiskrantz, 1985, p. 10.
4. Amos et al., 1995; J. M. Black, 1996, Field and Fox, 1985, Godard, 1991; Hearne, 1987; Insley, 2000; Restak, 1982; 1984, 1988; Smuts et al., 1987; Spelke et al., 1982, 1993a, 1993b, 1995; Weiskrantz, 1985.
5. Savage-Rumbaugh et al., 1985, p. 181. Cf. also her work with Shanker and Taylor, 1998, esp. pp. 65-99.
6. Azar, 2000; Gopnik, Meltzoff, and Kuhl, 1999; Hoffman, 1983.
7. Restak, 1988, p. 46.
8. Ibid., pp. 49-50.
9. Eimas, 1985.
10. Restak, *op.cit.*, 1988, pp. 48-51; D. Stern, 1977.
11. Restak, 1998a, pp. 46-57.
12. *Ibid.*
13. Tarabulsy *et al.*, 1996
14. Spelke et al., 1992, 1993, 1995.
15. Hood et al., 1996; Leslie, 1982, 1986, 1987; Leslie and Keeble, 1987; Rochat, 2001; Woodward, 1998.
16. Edelman, 1987, 1989, 1992; Furth, 1986; Michotte, 1963; Piaget, 1930, 1969, 1973; Restak, 1982, 1988; Spelke et al., *op. cit.*
17. Furth, op. cit., p. 38.

18. Bates and Elman, 1996; Jusczyk, 1998; Saffran et al., 1996.
19. Saffran et al., op. cit., p. 1996.
20. Einstein, A., 1931/1982.
21. Furth, op. cit. p. 38 and *passim.*
22. Piaget, J., 1969.
23. Hockett, 1968.
24. A current quarrel among long-schooled individuals about the actuality of UFOs and "alien" abduction of Americans vindicates philosopher George Santayana who believed that lunacy is normal among human beings (cf. n. 25 below). A recent debate between literate men about the reality of invaders from space substantiates Santayana (Crews et al., 1998).
25. During the twentieth century, mass suicides stimulated by religious faith bewildered less homicidal believers who attempted to distinguish sane faith from lunacy. For example, in 1997, thirty-nine sober, apparently happy persons residing in rich, quiet Rancho Santa Fe, an enclave near San Diego, California, joyously killed themselves so that their souls could board a spaceship they believed trailed comet Hale-Bopp en route to Heaven. Christian commentators were at a loss to understand this event. Wrestling with this consequence of faith, British journalist Matthew Parris (1997) argued that these nice suicides were "deluded" but not "mad," as though individuals could be in one such state without being in the other. Eight decades ago philosopher George Santayana (1926) described "normal madness" and held the condition to be a persistent characteristic of the human creature. He claimed, therefore, that identifying who is crazy is only a matter of majority vote.
26. Freud, 1958, p. 61.
27. Mackie, 1973, p. 155.
28. E.g., Quinney (1970, p. 4), "We cannot be certain of an objective reality beyond man's conception of it. Thus, we have no reason to believe in the objective existence of anything." More recently, DiCristina (1995, p. 105) celebrates the same skepticism and urges that, "If all knowledge about the social world is subjective and conjectural...why not just select a goal (a vision of an ideal world), and try to reach it?" On this premise, how could we know whether we were moving toward the goal or away from it?
29. Lenin, 1902/1969. See also Feuer, 1970; Malia, 1994, 1999; A. Meyer, 1957; Service, 2000, p. 193.
30. Some American college students believe that the Scottish verdict, "not proven," means either "hung jury" or "acquitted." Not so. It means that available evidence does not allow a judgment pro or con.
31. C. I. Lewis, 1962, p. 167. For a contrary thesis, read Stroud, 2000.
32. Ibid. Refer also to Lewis's 1956.
33. Ibid., 1962.
34. Einstein, cited by Calaprice, p. 224.
35. Restak, 1988; Sapolsky, 1992.
36. James, 1890.
37. Hearne, op. cit.
38. Concerning zeal in the marketplace, read Mayer, 2001, and Shiller, 2000.

Chapter 2: Linguistic Follies

1. Not all evidence of conceptualization depends on ability to use symbols. Cf. Furth, 1966.

2.   A. Burgess, 1992.

3.   Churchland and Churchland, 1998; P. M. Churchland, 1981, 1988, 1989, 1995;
       P. S. Churchland and Sejnowski, 1992; Crick, 1994; Edelman and Tononi, 2000;
       Greenwood, 1991; Marcel and Bisiach, 1988; Metzinger, 1995; Stich, 1989,
       1993; Tononi and Edelman, 1998.

4.   "Abuse" is a pejorative label. It indicates disapproval of many changes and the
       deceptions associated with them. For example, consider how "parameter" has
       become a signal of ostentatious learning divorced from its pristine reference. And
       notice how far from their original reference newly invented terms wander. Trace
       the vagaries of concepts such as "disability," "discrimination," "genocide," "hate
       crime," "sexual harassment," "terrorist," "freedom fighter," and many similarly
       socially stretched terms.
           We can't do science with such rubbery concepts.

5.   See Raphael's 1998 review of four new "authoritative" dictionaries of the En-
       glish language. He titles his essay, "Equaller, Hopefully," in disgust with the
       ugly, and sometimes illogical, transformations offered.
           In addition, academics, legislators, and lexicographers are currently besieged by
       interested persons who wish words they deem insulting to be deleted from
       common use and even from dictionaries. Cf. Dooling, 1999.

6.   Einstein's 1905 paper was titled, "On the Electrodynamics of Moving Bodies."
       Many American high-school diplomates do not know who Einstein was, much
       less how he changed their world.

7.   John von Neumann was a child prodigy who helped advance game theory, the
       modern computer, the hypothesis of nuclear deterrence, and other seminal ideas.
       Cf. Macrae, 1992, p. 226.

8.   Macrae, 1992, p. 264.

9.   This question is asked repeatedly about many conflicts, but especially about the
       "First World War," a.k.a. "The Great War." Cf. Ferguson, 1998; M. Howard,
       1996, 1998, 2001; Keegan, 2001. This question is difficult because the term,
       "necessary," is asked with the gift of hindsight, usually in a moral context, and
       with nominated causes conceived as interlocked and saturated with contingen-
       cies—"if only's."...

10.   Nobel laureate physicist Richard Feynman was asked this question by orthodox
       religionists for whom it had important implications. The physicist's reply could
       not satisfy the religious motive. Cf. Feynman, 1985, pp. 253 ff.

11.   The U. S. Constitution, Article II, Section 4.

12.   Cf. Turley, 1998, and Holmes, p.550, n. 1. And concerning the murderous struggle
       between Palestinians and Israelis in The Holy Land, cf. Halkin, 2000; Karsh,
       2000; Pipes, 2000; Podhoretz, 2000.
           We have an American example in the fight over the impeachment of U. S.
       President Bill Clinton. During this largely verbal battle, actor Alec Baldwin was
       quoted as having urged his television audience, "If we were in other countries,
       we would all right now, all of us together would go down to Washington and
       we would stone Henry Hyde to death! We would stone Henry Hyde to death
       and we would go to their homes and we'd kill their wives and children. We
       would kill their families...." (Editors, *Wall Street Journal*, 1998; Weissman,
       1998). Congressman Hyde was chairman of the House Judiciary Commit-
       tee that recommended that the full House of Representatives send four
       articles of impeachment to the Senate for trial. The House sent two of these
       charges to the Senate where the president was acquitted. However, after the
       Senate's decision, a federal judge found the president guilty of contempt of court,

a charge involving some of the same accusations passed by the House. Cf. Turley, 1999.

13. L. Carroll, 1872.
14. Hobbes, 1651/1994.
15. Stove, 1991.
16. Blackburn, 1991.
17. For some horror stories chronicling the emission and consumption of nonsense by "learned" persons, read Sokal and Bricmont, 1998. In particular, see the reprint in this book of Sokal's notorious spoof in which, by writing modern jabberwocky, he is able to publish an essay in a scholarly journal promising such silliness as "liberatory science," "emancipatory mathematics," and "a transformative hermeneutics of quantum gravity." Twenty-five years before Sokal's exposé of semantic lunacy among intellectuals, Donald Naftulin, John Ware, and Frank Donnelly, 1973, demonstrated how audiences of university instructors could be influenced by the *form* of a lecture as much, or more, than by its *content*. These psychologists hired a professional actor to rehearse a nonsensical, presumably scholarly, lecture, and deliver it dramatically to three different academic audiences. The lecture was laced with double-talk, jabberwocky, and contradictions, but its delivery was sincere, warm, and lightened with humor. The performance of this fake "Dr. Myron L. Fox" was well received.
18. H. McCord, 1951.
19. Bishop et al., 1980; I. A. Lewis and W. Schneider, 1982; Schuman and Presser, 1980.
20. Chapter 9 describes conditions under which people's statements of their desires and beliefs are accepted as answers to "why?" It is shown that acceptance of others' verbalizations as explanations is not so much a matter of their being answers that increase the predictability of their conduct, but more a function of providing conventionally comfortable *reasons* that need say nothing about the *causes* of the behaviors being "explained."
21. Nisbett, R. E. and T. DeC. Wilson, 1977; Nisbett and L. Ross, 1980; T. DeC. Wilson et al., 1989.
22. Connes, 1995, p. 30.
23. Frege. 1892/1972.
24. Staats and Staats, 1952. "Implicit learning" is now recognized as actual. A large inventory of research describes the conditions that affect such unconscious acquisition of attitudes and feelings. Cf. Reber, 1993.
25. Nettler, 1972. Tests of "comparative syllogisms" ask persons to judge whether conclusions are logically valid. That is, whether conclusions are warranted by premises. Individuals are not asked whether the conclusions are true. This task becomes more difficult as the verbal content of syllogisms becomes more "meaningful." Such tests were used during the 1930s through the 1950s as unobtrusive probes of ethno-racial prejudice. However, in today's sensitive academic climate, experiments of this nature would be both impolitic and forbidden. By necessity, these tests use hostile language.
26. Winner, 1988.
27. L. Carroll, 1872.
28. Furst, 1952, terms these specialists in ideas, "professionally thoughtful persons."
29. Sokal and Bricmont, 1998 and n. 17 above.
30. Ryle, 1949.
31. Bleuler, 1911, 1912.

32. Meehl, 1990.
33. Santayana, 1926.
34. The idea of a "right" to be guaranteed by a State or a World Government (i.e., by force) has its own history. It is a notion unknown in some cultures and one that, like all words promiscuously used, is stretched toward absurdity. For example, the Brazilian Constitution includes a right to be happy. Less irrationally, but yet frightening to individualists, is the demand of a Swedish leader of the Social Democratic Party to nullify a current practice. Appalled by "urban sprawl" and the flight of affluent citizens to suburbs outside Stockholm, this meliorist claims, "Suburbs with private houses mean social segregation....We cannot allow people to preserve their differences. People will have to give up their right to choose their own neighbors." F. Siegel, 1998, citing P. Hall, 1998.   Claims to rights are moral claims (ch. 12). Moralists regularly justify their demands. They have done so by citing divine authority, the nature of human nature, the consensus of a people, and, more recently, by referring to what everyone in the world *needs*. Cf. *The Universal Declaration of Human Rights*, 1947.
35. Shakespeare, *Hamlet*, Act 2, Scene 2, ¶381. The biographies of some wildly insane individuals reveal some kinds of inexplicable—i.e., un-treated, hence "miraculous"—returns from madness to sanity. Read Sylvia Nasar's story, 1998, about the Nobel laureate in economics and long-time schizophrenic John Nash, and the remarkable tale of "Anna O" (Bertha Pappenheim) as abstracted by Nettler, 1989, p. 295. Nasar's book, *A Beautiful Mind*, is the basis of a popular motion picture, 2002.
36. Neuroscientists show that much more goes on in brains that affects action than actors are aware of. Such processing is called *anoetic*, meaning that "highly automated routines that make it possible to talk, listen, read, write, and so forth, in a fast and effortless way, do not appear to contribute directly to conscious experience, although they are essential in determining its content." (Tononi and Edelman, 1998, p. 1849; see also J. D. Cohen and Schooler, 1997; Baddeley and Weiskrantz, 1993).

    In brief, we can *do* much that requires "thinking" without having to "take thought." Reasoning is an effort-full conscious process that depends on an unconscious neural substrate.
37. Koestler, 1945b, p. 117, emphasis his.
38. Blackburn, 1994a, p. 58.
39. Hausman, 1998, p. 201.
40. Informal questioning of California high school diplomates and college undergraduates suggests that their understanding of the word, "average," is often confused. For many of these adults, "average" signifies "the most" or "a majority." This is one common sense of "average." However, Hausman's usage refers to an arithmetic mean, a measure of central tendency that need not yield a typical object, person, or activity.
41. Savage-Rumbaugh et al., 1993, and Savage-Rumbaugh, Shanker, Taylor, 1998, provide evidence that species of ape—bonobo and chimpanzee—*act with intent*, and transmit their "plans" to others of their species and humans. Such action underwrites assignment of "belief," and it does so for both ape and human. That is, *purposeful* activities can be said to be produced with the "belief" that others will *contingently act* upon one's signals.
42. Changeux, 1995, pp. 92-97; P. M. Churchland, 1995; P. S. Churchland, 1995; P. M. and P. S. Churchland, 1998; Crick, 1994; Delbrück, 1986; Flanagan, 1991.
43. Quine, 1987, p. 21.

44. One way of denying the falsifying effect of facts (events) employs the unbeatable argument, "Is all the evidence in?" Of course, all *conceivable* evidence is never in.
45. Blackburn, 1994c.
46. For studies demonstrating the limits of parental influence on children's personalities and behaviors, cf. Bouchard, 1997a, 1997b, 1997c, 1997d, and with others, 1990; Colapinto, 2000; Harris, 1998; Minnesota Center, 1990; Segal et al., 1990; L. Wright, 1997.
47. Sampson and W. J. Wilson, 1995, p. 44, emphasis theirs.
48. Larceny, for example, is a BIG word that covers a great variety of theft. The stealing that Sampson and Wilson have in mind does not include the lucrative kinds of theft by fraud and embezzlement. Of course, *how* one steals is a mixed function of opportunity, talent, and personality.
49. Gustav Bergmann, 1968, provides a coherent conception of "ideology." For him, an ideology is a mixture of facts, preferences, and a third category that is neither the one nor the other, but consists of *value judgments masquerading as facts*. He reserves the term, "ideology," for preferences that wear such disguise.

    Economist Joan Robinson agrees, 1962, and adds that ideologies are necessary for social control. Economics, she claims, is saturated with ideology that is part of a regulatory process. In service to this function, Robinson argues that these sets of economic beliefs are not testable, and therefore not refutable. They need not be factual because their job is not so much to describe truths, but to express values, to reinforce them, and thus to serve as guides to conduct.

    On the record, Robinson may be correct in saying that myth is necessary for social life. But neither myth-making nor myth-spreading is supposed to be the occupation of scientists of social action.

    For other valuable descriptions of "ideology," read Lichtheim, 1968, and Shils, 1968.

Chapter 3: Varieties of Knowing

1. Diderot, 1752/1966.
2. Eriksen, 1960, critically summarizes research on this possibility. A large library of research addresses the issue of "implicit learning and tacit knowledge," as per Arthur Reber's thesis, 1993. He and other investigators examine conditions under which we acquire skills, attitudes, and bits of information without being aware that we're learning. They also show that we acquire abilities to discriminate and categorize without being able to put the process into words. Refer to Berry, 1984, 1991; Bowers and Meichenbaum, 1984; de Sousa, 1991; Seamon *et al.*, 1983; Uleman and Bargh, 1989.
3. Hockett, 1968.
4. J. C. Scott, 1998, pp. 6, 315-316.
5. *Ibid.*, pp. 315-316.
6. *Ibid,*
7. Glass, McGaw, M. L. Smith, 1981.
8. Wachter, 1988, p. 1408.

9. *Explanans*, that which does the explaining. *Explanandum*, that which is to be explained. A conditional that repeats a proposal is a statement in which the protasis is contained within the apodosis. *Protasis*, the first or conditional clause in a sentence—"If." *Apodosis*, the consequent asserted by a sentence—"then."
10. Goethe, 1808/1987.

11. Cicero, ca. 50 B.C./1950. I:58.
12. Mitchell, 1966.
13. Bok and Jerome, 1975; Culver and Ianna, 1984, I. Kelly, 1979; Thagard, 1978; Wedow, 1976.
14. Dean and Mather, 1977.
15. Bloodworth, 1980; J. C. A. Cohen, 1968.
16. S. Carlson, 1985; G. A. Tyson, 1984.
17. Festinger, 1956.
18. J. S. Armstrong, 1978.
19. Einhorn, 1986.
20. Useful forecasting tools need not include the causes of the events being antici-pated, and this, in turn, means that we lack control of those events. Lack of control assures error. Our intellectual task is to minimize error and admit it when we produce it. Our moral task is to live with the possibility of mistake, an acknowledgment that should reduce arrogance and induce modesty.
21. Chapter 10, "Causation," discusses the meanings of terms such as "necessary," "sufficient," "efficient." It also describes contests about whether the worlds of action are determined, chaotic, or can be known only probabilistically. And, if events appear to be random, is it because of our ignorance or because Nature works with spaces among its causes?
22. Lao Tzu, trans., 1973.
23. As with many of the more interesting generalizations—those that depart from the obvious—there are exceptions to this one. Cf. McNees and Ries, 1983; M. B. Smith, 1978.
24. Swets, Dawes, Monahan, 2000a, 2000b.
25. *Ibid.*, 2000a, pp. 8-9.
26. Mayer, 2001.
27. Arendt, 1969.
28. Nettler, 1989, ch. 11.
29. Dawes 1993a, 1993b, 1994.
30. Dawes, 1993a, p. 1. Bracketed phrases added.

Chapter 4: Measurement

1. Colleagues tell me that the economist-financier Josiah Stamp (1880-1941) ac-quired this "information" from a Hindu scholar, but who knows? In any event, to ignore his advice is now called *the Watchman's Error*. See Stamp's essays, 1929.
2. Alonso and Starr, 1987; Cooke, 1991; Feynman, 1988, McGinley, 1997; Morgenstern, 1963; Nettler, 1994; Porter, 1996; Wildavsky, 1995.
3. Connes, 1995, p. 7.
4. Connes, 1995, p. 5.
5. Lichter and Rothman, 1999, Cf. Also Fumento, 1999. In the United States, for example, state and federal legislators regularly propose laws to "address" rare risks that have affected a few of their constituents and that have received persua-sive dramatization on television. Such legislation has received the sneering title, "60 Minutes' bills." Boaz, 2000.
6. Cited by Herbert Stein, 1995.
7. McLeish, 1991.
8. Cooke, 1991; Gullberg, 1997; Porter, 1995.
9. Blair, 1956, p. 87; Desrosières, 1998.
10. Desrosières, 1998, p. 85.

11. United Nations, 2000. Cf. also *Economist*, 2000a.
12. For propagandistic purpose, "poverty" is a stronger word than "inequality." It has more image-making force. This is an empirical proposition, open to test.
13. Morgenstern, 1963, p. 244.
14. M. Black, 1963.
15. Cohen and Nagel, 1934, p. 291, emphasis theirs.
16. Stevens, 1959, p. 24.
17. Hempel, 1952, p. 49.
18. I've had students and neighbors look at me with glazed eyes when I've asked them the simple question, "Are vehicle crashes of one kind?" In addressing a facet of this query, a large library of research criticizes the public numbers advertised as having *fairly tested* the efficacy of safety devices. For a start, cf. B. J. Campbell, 1990; L. Evans, 1991; Garbacz, 1990; 1991, 1992a, 1992b; Garret and Braunstein, 1962; Huelke, 1987, Huelke, et al., 1987; Huelke, 1987, E. Levine and Basilevsky, 1990, 1991, 1992, 1993; Levine and Basilevsky, 1990, 1992, 1993; Levine et al., 1999; Semmens, 1991, 1992; Tourin and Garrett, 1962; Van Laningham, 1986.
19. Silverman, 1980.
20. Rateson, 1979; Russell, 1979.
21. Silverman, 1980, p. 272.
22. Guttman, 1976, p. 25, brackets added.
23. Reber, 1985.
24. Suen, 1990, p. 7, emphasis added.
25. Guaranty of reliability is one, among several, good reasons for examining students, and other kinds of candidates, frequently. The lazy practice of sampling students' performance once or twice a term is not likely to yield as reliable a final grade as a succession of tests.
26. Originating with Cronbach et al., 1972, and popularized by Shavelson and Webb, 1991.
27. Shavelson and Webb, 1991, p. 1.
28. Guttman, 1976, pp. 32 and 39, emphasis his.
29. Meier, 1994; Schwarz, 1999.
30. Alsop 1986; Edwards, 1957; Ferber, 1986; Johnson, 1974; I. Lewis and Schneider, 1982; Peterson, 1985; Schwarz, 1999; *Wall St. J.*, 1999.
31. Nettler, 1989, pp. 108n.20. 144, 145, and ch. 8 below.
32. Campbell and Fiske, 1959.
33. Harrington, 1999; Kirsch, 1999.
34. Bean, 1906.
35. Mall, 1909.
36. With a limited amount of material, I found the "evil eye" to be as acute, and in some domains more so, than the "beneficent eye." This study should be expanded with different kinds of data. Nettler, 1961.
37. Recording and reporting are different practices. Interested parties do not always report what they have recorded. This occurs in laboratory research and medical practice, as well as in finance and social studies. Nettler, 1961.
38. For the Enron story, read K. Brown, 2002; K. Brown, G. Hill, Liesman, J. Weil, 2002; K. Brown and Sender, 2002; Cummings, Hamburger, Kranhold, 2002; Editors, *Wall St. J.*, 2002; Emshwiller, Raghaven, Sapsford, 2002; Glassman, 2002; Liesman, Weil, Paltrow, 2002; Malkiel, 2002.

Chapter 5: Units and Correlates

1. Cited by M. R. Cohen, 1931, p. 91, n.4.
2. Mould, 1990, p. 787.
3. Bishop, J., 1993.
4. The United States' shameful experience with counting votes in its presidential election, 2000, is but one forceful example.
5. Einstein, 1950, p. 43.
6. For a dramatic illustration, read Groopman, 2000.
7. Alker, 1969, pp. 82-82; see also Hogben, n.d., ca. 1957.
8. Cleveland, 1985, 1993; Tufte, 1974, 1983, 1997. Refer also to R. A. Cook, 1989; Hankins, 2000; Hayes, 2000; Wainer, 2000.
9. Monmonier, 1991.
10. Tufte, 1997, p. 45, emphasis his.
11. Bauer, 2000, p. 19.
12. Glymour, 1998, p. 1.
13. Historian Kenneth Clark, a student of "civilizations," tells us that, while he cannot define "civilization," he know one when he sees one, 1999. However, he agrees with art critic and social theorist John Ruskin (1819-1900) that of the three indicia of a civilization—deeds, words, and art—the only trustworthy one is the latter" (K. Clark, 1999, ch. 1).
14. At eighty-nine years of age, I sometimes wonder in what sense I am the same "person" as I was at nineteen or thirty-nine years. Name and government-as-signed "social security" number remain the same, but flesh and bone, "mind" and behavior have changed. Therefore, in what way(s) does the abstract "I" refer to the same "me" in its earlier "Selves"?

    This question gains significance in the era of miraculous surgery that alters the sexual apparatus of persons and hence their gender. In what sense is a transsexual individual the same person pre- and post-surgery? Perhaps we are better described as existing as "personality fragments" or in "personality states," as Philip Coons, 1984, suggests. For a detailed consideration of changing ideas of "the self," see Ian Hacking, 1995.
15. Rector and Hederman, 1999, p 2.
16. Lynch, 2000; Rector and Hederman, 1999, p. 11.
17. Rector and Hederman, 1999, p. 19.
18. Blackburn 1999, p. 65. In this example, the word "average" can refer to an arithmetic mean or to that which is "typical."
19. Haeckel, 1867. Cf. also Stauffer, 1952.
20. Alihan, 1939; Faris, 1964; Hawley, 1950; McKenzie, 1933; Park and Burgess, 1921; Theodorsen, 1961.
21. Alker, 1969; Allardt, 1969; D.C. Gottfredson et al., 1991; Gupta, 1969; J. L. Hammond, 1973; J. M. Richards, et al., 1991a, 1991b.
22. W. S. Robinson, 1950.
23. Epstein, S., 1990, p. 98.
24. Murray, 1996, p. 110, emphasis his.
25. Zajonc and Mullaly, 1997, p. 688. Note again the use of causal language—"strong consequence"—when all that is observed is correlation.
26. My inquiry of Professor Zajonc for evidence of his assertion went unanswered (7 July 1997). However, Dr. Elizabeth Whelan, president of the American Council on Science and Health (9 July 1997) and Dr. Eugenia McCall, director of Analytic Epidemiology with the American Cancer Society (4 August 1997), kindly provided me with extensive bibliographies of research that report associations between *degrees* of tobacco-smoke inhalation and risk of lung cancer, *individual by individual*.

27. For instruction, cf. Abelson, 1995; Giere, 1984; 1988; Tufte, 1974.
28. Holmes, 1921.
29. Kirsch, 1999, brings together current research on this tendency.
30. This is an empirical hypothesis for which we have some limited evidence. Cf. Nettler, 1961.
31. B. J. Taylor, 2000.
32. Horton, 1999.
33. Horton, 1999, p. 8, emphasis his.
34. A short sample of evidence includes Balch, 1986; Balch and London, 1986; Grenier, 1984; E. B. Hook, 1996; S. Hook, 1984; S. Keeley, 1971; Ladd and Ferree, 1982; Lichter and Rothman, 1981, 1982, 1984; S. Miller, 1982; M. Novak, 1982; Riesman, 1969; Rothman, 1986; Rothman and Lichter, 1982; Schneider and Lewis, 1985; D. Seligman, 1982; O. Stone, 2000; J. Weiner, 1986; Wooster, 1991.
35. To repeat an earlier comment on "professionalism," these workers do not merit the title, "professional," because, for the most part, they do not depend for their livelihoods upon sales of their services to those who consume them. Most of their work is subsidized by strangers.
36. Since editorial work is private, this quantity cannot be measured. However, personal experience suggests the likelihood of such loss. But, of course, individual experience is limited, and it is itself open to the charge of bias. However, privately I can offer convincing tales of the ideologically driven refusal of editors to accept reasoned dissent. In at least two cases, editors have justified their censorship with lies. I don't name names because I have neither the time nor the money to defend against lawsuits.

Chapter 6: Probabilities

1. Einstein, n.d./1993, 369.5.
2. Of course, there are "flat-earthers" who deny this. But outside their superstition, the regularity we currently depend on with certainty is itself relative to the time span conceived. In sidereal time (star time), cosmologists reckon that our long-lived stability of nights and days will end as our aging star, Sun, becomes more luminous. In about one billion years, this change will make life on Earth difficult, if not impossible (Garlick, 2001).
3. John Barrow presents a brief, clear description of quantum theory in his 2001, pp. 195-204.
4. Rubin, 2000, p. 91.
5. Hume, 1739-1740, Book I.
6. David Stove gives a strong defense of induction, 1965, 1973, 1986, 1991. D. C. Williams, 1947, provides a balanced analysis of "the grounds of induction." Ian Hacking, 2001, describes uses of different kinds of inference drawing.
7. The fictional British Major Warden (played by Jack Hawkins) puts this question to the fictional American Major Shears (William Holden) in the motion picture, *The Bridge on the River Kwai*, as they prepare to destroy the bridge.
8. Beckmann, 1967, p. 2.
9. "meliorism...n...The doctrine that the world may be made significantly better by rightly-directed human effort." Meliorist *n. & a.* (a) an adherent of meliorism; (b) *adj.* of or pertaining to meliorists or meliorism.... Reproduced from *The New Shorter Oxford English Dictionary*, Lesley Brown, editor, 1993, by permission of Oxford University Press.
10. L. J. Cohen, 1989.
11. Feller, 1957, v. 1, p. 39.

12. Diaconis, cited by Kolata, 1986, p. 1070.
13. Ibid, emphasis added.
14. Cattell, 1979; Matthews and Deary, 1998; Petrie, 1967.
15. Kahneman, Slovic, Tversky, 1982.
16. Farber and Sherry, 1997; Howson, 1997; Jasanoff, 1997. It deserves reminder that "justice" is a many-splendored word, variously defined and employed rhetorically because of the emotional force invested in its use. Notice, then, that scholars frequently use the qualifier, "sense of justice," a phrase that allows more than one kind of justice. Cf. pp. 97-98.
17. Bayes, 1875/1970; Carnap, 1950.
18. Savage, 1954, p. 3.
19. L. J. Cohen, 1977.
20. Ayer, 1972, 1973.
21. Mackie, 1973, p. 167.
22. Mackie, ibid.
23. For one recent example, recall the shock "white" Americans expressed when a predominantly "black" jury (8/12) acquitted the "black" football star, O. J. Simpson, of murdering his "white" former wife and her "white" male friend. Toobin, 1996a, 1996b.
24. Nettler, 1979, and n. 16 above.
25. Ortega, 1946, p. 29.
26. Alschuler, 2000; Ayala and Black, 1993; S. Goldberg, 1987.
27. Jasanoff, 1997.
28. Thus Ortega argues (1946, p. 26), "In his book *De Legibus* Cicero enunciates solemnly that 'without government existence is impossible for a household, a city, a people, the human race, physical nature and the universe itself.' But government and consequently the state, in the last instance, spell violence, mitigated in prosperous times, formidable in times of crisis."
29. Milton, 1996; D. Robinson, 1985.
30. Jasanoff, 1997, p. 11.
31. Law is always infused with morality—supportive and challenging. In applying the law, justice is also a moral concept. These emotionalized dispositions move— with time and circumstance. During such movement, law loses moral sanction, as when Ortega writes that "[we are]...born into a time that has minced law with the extrajuridical chopper of justice...." (1946, p. 29).
32. D. J. Bennet, 1998, p. 155.
33. Mackie, 1973, p. 154.
34. Wildavsky, 1979, 1995.
35. Matt Ridley, 1999, p. 63.
36. Ibid.
37. Lindh, 1992.
38. Parsons et al., 2000, p. 663.
39. Rial, 2001, pp. 187-188, emphasis added. See also Alley, 2000, and Lean and Rind, 2001.

40. U. S. Surgeon General, 1999.
41. *Wall Street Journal*, 2000b.
42. Barrow, 1998; Cooke, 1999; Feynman, 1988; Shrader-Frechette, 1991; Wildavsky, 1979, 1995.
43. Cited by Barrow, 1998, p. 248.
44. May and Zelikow, 1997.
45. F. B. Smith, 2000.

46.   A facet of the art of politics is to design the application of one's policies so that their costs (errors) are paid for (blamed on) others—especially one's opponents. California's ongoing energy debacle, 2000-2002, provides an example of such tactic. Shifting the load of responsibility is an ancient and current practice. Nettler, 1982b; *Wall Street Journal*, 2001.
47.   For recent descriptions of the harm that results from misplaced confidence, read Derek Freeman, 1998, on how an excess of cultural determinism promises "idyllic sex" without side effects. And refer to John Colapinto, 2000, on the damage done by trying to force sex to conform to gender.
48.   Wittgenstein, 1983, I: 55-57.
49.   Merton, 2000.
50.   The unexpected is always to be expected. That's why we insure. It also justifies the Boy Scout motto, "Be prepared." Of course, what we would like to know is how much to pay for preparation-insurance, and for what.
51.   Scholes, 2000.
52.   *Economist*, 2000b, p. 79.
53.   Melloan, 1998. For amplification, read Lowenstein, 2000, and Malkiel and Mei, 1998.
54.   M. Clark, S. Holt et al., 2000.

Chapter 7: Social Facts

1.   This is physicist John Wheeler's way of describing knowledge of quantum phenomena as proposed by his teacher, Niels Bohr. Physicist Jeremy Bernstein, 1991, p. 96, uses this anecdote to illustrate the debate about reality between Albert Einstein (Umpire #2) and Niels Bohr (Umpire #3).
2.   Gillan, 1999, p. 15, trying to find truth during the international warring in the Balkans, 1990s.
3.   Searle, 1999a, p. 37. Cf. also his 1999c.
4.   I was born in the United States, 1913. This is the same year that our Constitution was amended to give power to Congress to tax our "incomes." Among colleagues and students much younger than I, many assume that the "income tax" has "always" existed, like a force of Nature or at least since the founding of the Republic.
5.   Biologist Lee Dugatkin, 1990, describes such processes. Cf. also Ball, 1999.
6.   For fiction about such self-organization *de novo*, cf. Golding, 1997.
7.   *Surprise*: In the aftermath of several schoolyard murders by armed youngsters in Canada, the United Kingdom, and the United States, 1998-2000, criminologists, psychologists, and sociologists have been unable to explain such attacks. In these instances, the correlates that experts usually nominate as causes of such killing do not apply.
8.   Ch. 12 describes the meaning of "morality."
9.   In this relativistic vein, a recent dean of a College of Humanities in a large American university calls for a "family friendly campus" where the definition of "family" will differ from today's conventional meaning. Annette Kolodny writes, 1991, that "the family of the twenty-first century will no longer be identified solely by blood ties, by legalized affiliations, by cohabitation, or by heterosexual arrangements." Kolodny adds that it may also include people who are only occasionally or temporarily "associated with" the family.
10.   Koestler, 1945a, p. 227. Confusion between what is *useful* for ethico-political purpose and what is *truthful* is common. Koestler's Gletkin is but a fictionalized

characterization of how real people behave when they become inflamed with political ideals. Desire then bends Truth to Power.

11. Earlier chapters have urged that these powers can be delusive as well as prescient.

12. The histories of the sciences, physical and social, are pocked with fights about ownership of data. In my own attempts to find out "whether and how" in several realms of social action, I have encountered both openness and resistance to inquiry.

Given journalists' distortion of some scientific reports, researchers' caution is justified. But some obstruction, and outright hostility, are patently self-protective, lest an "external auditor" find error.

13. Meehl, 1990, p. 3.

14. "Less than half of American adults understand that the Earth orbits the Sun yearly," Norman Augustine writes, citing a National Science Foundation survey, 1999. Augustine is chairman of the Lockheed Martin Corporation and professor of engineering, Princeton University.

Despite this ignorance of a brute fact, most American adults probably can read our calendar, tell time, and recognize seasons. What proportions know that other modern people employ different calendars is another question.

15. Clark Blaise (2001) tells the story in his biography of Fleming.

16. Amis, 1985.

17. Cf. P. Bernstein, 2000; Buchan, 1997, 2000; M. Friedman, 1992, Grant, 1992, Seabrook, 2001.

18. Bannock, et al., 1987; Melloan, 1998.

19. There's neat etymological significance here. "Currency" is what is "current"— temporary. It is also that which, like a current, flows and changes in quantity and force as it moves.

20. Dietrich, 1961-1962, p. 57.

21. This qualification is inserted because individuals differ in their appreciation of time. Temperaments decide, and what might be called "appetite-for-life" assigns different values to time. Age is also a strong conditioner of the worth of each day. In turn, these different evaluations of time affect persons' objectives. Cf. Carstensen, Isaacowitz, and Charles, 1999.

22. Chapter 8 gives reasons for distinguishing between what people *say* they prefer and what they *do* with their opportunities.

23. Economist Roy Jastram, 1977, shows that, for some Western lands, a quantity of gold had retained a constant relationship to wealth, when wealth is measured as gold's exchange value for a bundle of goods and services. This is a fidelity that cannot be expected of currency. But it is also a fidelity that is subject to change. What Jastram discovered need not hold forever. Cf. P. Bernstein, 2000.

24. Economist Martin Hollis, 1998, wrestles with two of economists' basic assumptions: That trust is a lubricant of exchange and rationality is a desirable attribute of individuals. While some minimum of trust is essential for civil life, individual rationality sometimes justifies wariness and deception. That is, it is often rational for individuals to distrust others (*caveat emptor*), and it can also be rational to deceive others. "Rational action" is defined in chapter 11.

25. M. Friedman, 1992, p. xii.

26. In Latin, *credit* means "he trusts."

27. Grant, 1992, pp. 432-433. For description of how Charles Ponzi performed his amazing swindle, see D. H. Dunn, 1975.

28. To repeat, "ontology" derives from the Greek for "being"; hence it is the study of what exists. "Epistemology" also derives from the Greek in which it refers to "knowledge." Hence, it is the study of "knowing" in its several senses described in chapter 3.

29. Lohse and Pacelle, 1999; Pacelle, Pollock, and Lohse, 1999; Pollock, Lohse, and Pacelle, 1999a, 1999b; Pollock, Lohse, and Paltrow, 1999.

30. McKinnon and Hitt, 2002.

31. Pap, 1958; 1962.

32. B. Gray, 1978, p. 129. Ability to keep dying individuals alive has heightened moral-medical debate about when a person is "as good as dead" for the purpose of extracting his/her organs that other persons can use. Gary Greenberg, 2001, tells the story.

33. Shneidman, 1973, esp., Ch. 7; Youngner, Arnold, and Schapiro, 1999.

34. According to the Holy Bible, murder was the third social act among humans. The first act had Eve tempting Adam with the fruit of "the tree of knowledge." The second act involved Adam "knowing" Eve. In the third act, Cain killed his brother, Abel (*Genesis* 4:8).

    Apropos of early killing, anthropologist Lawrence Keeley, 1996, p. 39, writes, "the archaeological evidence indicates...that homicide has been practiced since the appearance of modern humankind and that warfare is documented in the past 10,000 years in every well-studied region."

    In continuity of Keeley's story, a short list of historical accounts of intentional killing of human beings by humans on large scale can be read in Gay, 1992; Grossman, 1995; D. Kagan, 1995; Keegan, 1993; and Polk, 1997. The difficulty of employing a newly named and morally saturated kind of murder called "genocide" (a.k.a. Holocaust) can be read in Alan Rosenbaum's edited work, 1998. See also R. W. Smith, 1998a, 1998b.

34. Bierce, 1911/1958.

35. Koestler, 1982.

36. Durkheim, 1897/1951.

37. Buruma, 1984; Netanyahu, 2001; R. J. Smith, 1983; J. Stern, 1999.

38. Attributed to Disraeli by Mark Twain in his *Autobiography*, 1924. Disraeli was prime minister of Great Britain, 1868-1880.

39. Descriptions of the process can be read in Alvarez, 1971; J. Douglas, 1967; Farberow, MacKinnon, Nelson, 1977; Nelson, Farberow, MacKinnon, 1978; I. Ross, 1981; Shneidman, 1968, 1973. For a history of the meanings of suicide in Western culture, cf. Minois, 1998. Approved suicide is, of course, commonly called "martyrdom."

40. I. Ross, 1981, p. 20, emphasis added.

41. J. Douglas, 1967, p. 193.

42. Schneider, 1954.

43. F. L. Nelson et al., 1978, p. 75. Cf. also N. L. Farberow et al., 1977.

44. Lichtenberg, 1765-1799.

45. This fact helps explain why statistical (actuarial) modes of forecasting others' likely conduct have proved more accurate than "insight." Cf. pp. 119-126.

46. For those who read suicide notes, a declaration of intention need not be explanatory. My collection of such farewells includes this one: "So damn tired of buttoning and unbuttoning." This example of synechdoche—a little stands for much—was written before the age of zippers.

47. I. Ross, 1981, pp. 250-259.

48. J. Douglas, 1967, p. 205; cf. Also p. 213.

49. P. H. Brown and P. B. Barham, 1992; Summers, 1985.
50. Ruddy, 1997.
51. O. Morgenstern, 1965, p. 23, n. 15.

Chapter 8: Vicarious Observation

1. Wittgenstein, 1964, p. 209.
2. Bacon, 1697-1725.
3. Conrad, 1911/1991.
4. Brown and Gilmartin, 1969.
5. J. Kagan, 1988. Raymond Cattel's studies of personality types is unique in correlating self-reports with others' reports and test scores, 1979.
6. Babor, et al., 1990. No one has counted this practice across wide ranges of inquiry that would evaluate the efficacy of medical interventions. However, it is probable that many "compliance studies" depend on patients' self-reports. For suggestions in this regard, cf. Thomas Moore, 1989, and James Le Fanu, 1999.
7. James, 1890.
8. Reminder: There is a difference. Some people can lie consistently. Reliability does not guarantee validity, and validity cannot be known from unreliable information (ch. 4).
9. Burgess, 1992, p. 119.
10. A short sample of reports of slippage between the ethics people speak and the ethics they display in action includes: A. Bennett, 1995; Blasi, 1980; Hartshorne and May, 1928-1930; Hetherington and Feldman, 1964; Lord, 1955; M. Meyers, 1999; S. Robinson, 1992; Sackett, 1994; Wills, 1992a.
11. Harding, 1948; T. W. Smith, 1981; Winthrop, 1946.
12. A sample of studies includes Bauer, et al., 1949, Gilovich, 1991; Gur and Sackeim, 1979; Sackeim and Gur, 1979; Skinner, 1945; Tanur, 1992.
13. Slovic, 1995.
14. Krosnick, 1999; Tanur, 1992.
15. Bass, 1956; Husek, 1961; Krosnick, 1999, Lenski and Leggett, 1960; Ross and Mirowsky, 1984.
16. Edwards, 1957; Granberg and Holmberg, 1991; Krosnick, 1999. *Examples*: When American university professors rate themselves in comparison with their colleagues, 94 percent find that they are "better than average." So, too, when one million high school seniors compare themselves with their peers on "ability to get along with others," ALL believe they're "above average" and one-fourth rank themselves in the top 1 percent (Gilovich, 1991).
17. For one such technique, cf. Nettler, 1946a, Nettler and Golding, 1946b. For definitions of other kinds of "validities," cf. Reber, 1985; Suen, 1990.
18. Cited by Johnson's biographer, J. Boswell, 1791, Comment: 3 April 1775.
19. Sadly, this insertion is required because even professors certified with Ph.D.'s have tried to deflect criticism with the all-or-none fallacy.
20. Connes, 1995, p. 30.
21. Anders, 1996; Barnes, 1995; Schneiders and Livingston, 1999; Schwarz, 1999.
22. Bishop, et al., 1980; Lewis and Schneider, 1982; H. McCord, 1951; Schuman and Fresser, 1980.
23. Valuable analyses of the phenomenon of self-deception can be read in Lockard and Paulhus, 1988, and Mele, 2001. Cf. also n. 12 above.
24. Gurstein, 1996; S. E. Taylor, 1989.

25. Feige, 1980; Jencks, 1989; Kennickell and McManus, 1993; McKenney et al., 1993; Melis-Wright et al., 1993; Queen, 1993; Stearns et al., 1993; K. F. Thomas and Dingbaum, 1993.
26. Harwood and Crossen, 2000.
27. Cooper, 1999. In a comparable embarrassment, French pollsters and pundits were surprised and alarmed when a widely disapproved outsider, Jean-Marie Le Pen, beat fourteen candidates in its first round voting, April 2002, to become one of two finalists for the presidency.
28. Melis-Wright et al., 1993, p. 425, emphasis added.
29. Toobin, 1996a, p. 27.
30. Meyers, 1999, cf. also Cose, 1999.
31. Guttman, 1976, pp. 25, 33, 38, and his 1977, pp. 58-61, and our chapter 4 above.
32. Hobbes, 1651.
33. "Neuroticism" is one of the five major dimensions of personality. Costa and McCrae, 1985, 1992; Digman, 1990.
34. Hahn, 1999.
35. S. Porter et al., 2000.
36. The literature on sources of variation in memory is huge. An informative sample includes J. Alper, 1986; Conway and Ross, 1984; Grady et al., 1995; Kirsch, 1999; Norman, 1976; S. Porter, 1998; S. Porter and Marxsen, 1998; S. Porter, Yuille, Lehman, 1999; Schacter, 1996, 1999, 2000; Schacter, Norman, Koutstaal, 1998; Schacter, Israel, Racine, 1999; Schacter and Scarry, 2000; Schmolck, Buffalo, Squire, 2000; Shiffman et al., 1997; Squire and Kandel, 1999.
37. Lewinsohn and Rosenbaum, 1987.
38. Bahrick et al., 1996; Steinweg, 1993.
39. Marcus, 1986.
40. Tanur et al., 1994.
41. Taubes, 1995.
42. Kuyken et al., 1995.
43. Cited by Taubes, 1995. See also Wildavsky, 1995.
44. In re diet, cf. Taubes, 1995, p. 167. In re implants and breast cancers, cf. Angell, 1996; Bandow, 1998; Levitt, 2000.
45. Shiffman et al., 1997.
46. Fendrich and Vaughn, 1994; Fendrich and Warner, 1994; Fendrich and Xu, 1994; Fendrich and Mackesy-Amiti, 1995.
47. Neisser and Harsch, 1992.
48. Neisser and Harsch, pp. 18-19, emphasis added.
49. Wells and D. M. Murray, 1994; Wells et al., 2000.
50. Ceci and Bruck, 1996; Crews, 1994a, 1994b, 1995; C. G. Garry et al., 1996; Lindsey and Reed, 1995; Loftus, 1997; Loftus and Ketcham 1994; Nathan and Snedeker, 1995; Ofshe and Watters, 1994; Payne et al., 1996; Rabinowitz, 1990, 1995, 2000; Schacter et al., [???]; Zaragoza et al., 2001.
51. Clancy et al., 2000.
52. M. Garry and Polaschek, 2000, p. 6.
53. Brainerd, Reyna, Brandes, 1995; Hirt et al., 1999.
54. Burtt, 1932, 1937, 1941. Reprinted in Dennis, 1963.
55. De Santis, 1996.
56. Jencks, 1997, p. 106.
57. Card and Krueger, 1994.
58. Neumark and Wascher, 1996, emphasis theirs.
59. Harding, 1948; T. W. Smith, 1981; Winthrop, 1946.

60. Mason et al., 1976.
61. Broom, et al., 1978.
62. Neimi, 1974.
63. Christensen, Margolin, and Sulloway, 1992.
64. Quarm, 1981.
65. "Power" is a word that symbolizes more than one kind of relationship. Unless a particular quality of connection between persons can be specified and observed, scientists should refrain from using it in social settings.
66. Booth and Welch, 1978.
67. J. J. Card, 1978.
68. Szinovacz, 1983.
69. Dobash et al., 1992. Concerning "known-group" validation, cf. Nettler, 1946a, and Nettler and Golding, 1946b.
70. Personal correspondence, 10 April - 20 April 1999. The advertisement appears in Transaction Publishers, *New Book Catalog*, Fall/Winter, 2000, #55:12.
71. Lykken, 1997, shows why polygraph interpretation is not a valid "lie-detector." The quantity of false-positive verdicts suggests that innocent individuals should not submit to it.
72. Laumann, Gagnon, Michael, and Michaels, 1995.
73. Laumann, et al., 1995, p. 284.
74. Laumann, et al., 1995, p. 94, table 3.5.
75. Geneticist Richard Lewontin has been a notably caustic critic, 1995, 1997, 2000.
76. Laumann, et al., 1995, pp. 38-39, 79, 107.
77. These include the U. S. Census Bureau's 1991 survey (CPS91), the National Opinion Research Center's 1991 General Social Survey (GSS91), and the University of Wisconsin's and Temple University's 1986-1987 National Survey of Families and Households (NSFH). Appendix B of Laumann, et al., 1995. Reference is also made to data from the earlier Kinsey studies, 1948, 1953.
78. Laumann, et al., 1995, pp. 603-604.
79. Laumann, et al., 1995. Appendix C, Section 4.
80. Laumann, et al., 1995, p. 91, Figure 3.1.
81. Mead, 1928, p. 261.
82. Blazer et al., 1988, p. 395.
83. Mead, 1967.
84. Freeman, 1999a, p. 2. Many academics, hampered by a restricted range of experience, do not understand a joking relationship as practiced by alien peoples, including some "tribes" within their own jurisdictions. "Jiving" strangers who inquire seriously about our lives is great sport. Some of us train for it, that is, we rehearse fables to feed naive outsiders. The joking relationship can be friendly as well as hostile.
85. For parts of the furious debate about sexual liberty in 1920s Samoa, cf. American Anthropological Association, 1983; Coté, 1998, 1999; Freeman, 1983, 1996, 1998, 1999a, 1999b, 1999c, 2000; Mead, 1967, Orans, 1996, 1999; Shankman, 1998.
86. Freeman, 1999a, pp. 187-188, 206.
87. MacDonald, 1999; Newman, 1999.
88. Cox and Alm, 1999; Dalrymple, 1999; DiIulio, 1996; Feldstein, 1999; Foreman, 1997; Freeman and Holzer, 1996; Jencks and Peterson, 1991; C. Murray, 1996; Sheehan, 1976; W. J. Wilson, 1997.
89. Maguire, Pastore et al., 1995; Major 1995. For the nation's capital, see Gearey, 1997.

90. Ethnographers who live with isolated peoples often report high homicide rates among them. Friedrich, 1962, calculates that the Tarascans with whom he lived were killing each other at a rate that came to 250 victims per 100,000 population per year. Nash, 1967, tallies a similar rate in his Mayan village. L. R. Schwartz, 1972, counts homicides in her central Mexican mestizo community that range between 250 and 800 per 100,000 per annum. Such rates contrast with annual figures of about 2 per 100,000 for Western European nations, Canada, and Japan, and between 8.5 and 10 per 100,000 for the United States.

91. DiIulio and Piehl, 1997.

92. La Rochefoucauld, 1878.

93. For description of some of the "tricky ways" of discerning who is honest, cf. Nettler, 1994, ch. 4.

94. This is an update of David Hume's 1758 comment that, "A man who at noon leaves his purse full of gold on the pavement at Charing Cross may as well expect that it will fly away like a feather as that he will find it untouched an hour later."

95. Hindelang, Hirschi, Weis, 1978.

96. Petersilia et al., 1977, 1978.

97. Peterson and Braiker, with Polich, 1981.

98. An old inmates' saw is, "Everyone in here is innocent." Cf. *The Shawshank Redemption*, motion picture and book.

99. Chaiken and Chaiken, 1982.

100. Visher, 1984, pp. 170, 173.

101. Caspi, et al., 1994.

102. Elliott et al., 1983.

103. Wolfgang, 1974.

104. Ibid., p. 246. This is Wolfgang's language, referring to Chambliss and Nagasawa, 1969.

105. The unpublished questions asked, "Have you done these things? If so, how often?—Drive a car without a driver's license. Skip school without an excuse. Defy parents' authority (to their face). Take little things that do not below to you (worth less than $2). Buy or drink beer, wine, or liquor (including drinking at home). Run away from home. Purposely damage or destroy public or private property that does not belong to you. Take things of medium value that do not belong to you (between $2 and $50)?"
     After responding to this set of peccadilloes, subjects were asked, "Do you think you might do any of these in the future? How often?"
     Professor F. D. Cousineau kindly provided me with a copy of this foolish questionnaire.

106. Like humans, some birds paint themselves. See David Attenborough's documentary film, *The Life of Birds*, especially episode Six, "Signals and Songs."

107. "Fundamental" here is intended to mean "worth our attention." The adjective serves as a prescription for conduct. It is not a description of how human beings regard one another.

108. Morrison, 1995.

109. Matt Ridley, 1999, p. 28.

110. Psychologist Paul Meehl provides procedures for discerning taxa (types, classes, categories) that may be hidden in continuous distributions. His work has long been neglected. It is ignored, I believe, because it is mathematical and graphic, and because of the quarrels about the reliability-validity of the "indicators" used in taxonomic formulas. Cf. Meehl, 1965, 1968, 1973b, 1992, 1995, 1999, and with Golden, 1982, with Yonce, 1996, and Waller and Meehl, 1998.

111. Such confusion raises the perennial question: What purpose is served by classifying individuals? Recent advances in genetic tracing give different, and more biologically exact, pictures of our lineage. Read Colin Renfrew, 2001, Mark Ridley, 2001.

   Moreover, "racism" is a recently invented word, and one so abused for political purpose as to be useless for scientists. Illustratively, the United Nations shamed itself by convening a meeting, 2001, ostentatiously titled the *World Conference Against Racism, Racial Discrimination, Xenophobia, and Related Intolerance* that became a congress for expression of ethnic hatred. For one account, read Arch Puddington, 2001.

112. Tell, 1999, *Wall St. J.*, 2000c. See also Kulish, 2001a, 2001b.

113. Lewontin, Rose, and Kamin, 1984, preface. See also Gould, 1984.

114. Bureau of the Census, 2000.

115. E. Porter, with R. S. Greenberger, 2001.

116. Bleakley, 1997.

117. Office of Management and the Budget, 1994; D. Seligman, 1995; Wynter, 1995.

118. Moffett, 1996.

119. Grimond, 2001.

120. C. E. Johnson, 1964.

121. Petersen, 1985.

122. T. W. Smith, 1989.

123. Fay, Morrissey, Smyth, 2000; heath, Breen, Whelan, 2000; O'Doherty, 2000; O'Toole, 2000.

124. Lipset and Raab, 1995, esp., pp. 7, 22-27.

125. Coetzee, 1997. On this historical movement and mixture of kinds of human beings, see the issue of *Science, "Human evolution: Migration."* v. 291, #5509, 2 March 2001, and Tattersall and J. Schwartz, 2000.

126. S. Thernstrom and A. Thernstrom, 1997, p. 527.

127. Recent demonstrations of political intrusion upon tallies of kinds of people within sovereign jurisdictions include Alonso and Starr, 1987; Anderson and Fienberg, 1999; Derosières, 1998; Peterson, 1997, 2000a, 2000b; Satel, 2000; Skerry, 1999, 2001; Skrentny, 2002; Zuriff, 2002.

128. Petersen, 1999. See also his works in 1997 and 2000a, 2000b. From Petersen's description of the numbers of "black underclass" and "middle-class Negroes" in America, it should not be assumed that the "median or average" necessarily "depicts the bottom of a U-shaped curve." His statement assumes information not given his readers concerning the shape of the distribution of cultural attributes within this colored population.

129. "Minorities" is placed in quotation marks because not all ethno-racial clusters are accorded this title, and particularly not those that are deemed successful, but also because females are often included despite their constituting a majority among many populations. Such inconsistencies mean that "minority" becomes inexact and inexact because it is used as a moral term.

130. Unz, 1999.

131. Demaree, 2001. See also K. I. Eisler, 2001.

132. Demaree, ibid.

133. Ibid.

134. *Personalist*: "...any philosophy according to which the individual person or thinker is the starting point of theory" (Blackburn, 1994, p. 284).

135. "Optimally allocated" is usually translated as "fairly distributed." It also means "least distressing to those affected."

136. A Zogby poll, April 2000, asked, "Do you feel the government should require you to disclose your race?" Seventy-seven percent of respondents answered, "No." Among "Blacks," 64 percent replied in the negative; among "Asians," 81 percent did so." *Wall St. Jour.*, 2000d.
137. Jews are particularly sensitive to the threat of disappearance through assimilation. They have endured history's longest record of survival despite persecution, a history in which many have vanished through integration and others through extermination. On the tension between the maintenance of Jewish identity and its erosion through assimilation, see Ginzberg, 1999; Lipset and Raab, 1995; Wertheimer, 2001.
138. Duffy, 2000; Steyn, 2000.
139. For a taste of this conflict, see Twight, 1999, versus Etzioni, 1999a, 1999b.
140. The American practice of enforcing "congregation" and calling it "integration" is inaccurate. It represents the triumph of hope over reality.
141. "Nation," from the Greek "ethnos," meaning "a people," "a culture." Proper nouns like "Belgium," "Canada," and "The United States of America" do not describe nations.
142. Holmes, 1926. In keeping with Holmes' opinion, studies of the "statistics of deadly quarrels" (Nettler, 1976, ch. 14), brought up to date, find that *none* of the conditions conventionally nominated as causes of war explains such large-scale killing. Brian Hayes, 2000, p. 14, summarizes: "the one social factor that does have some detectable correlation with war is religion. In the Richardson data set nations that differ in religion are more likely to fight than those that share the same religion. Moreover, some sects seem generally to be more bellicose. (Christian nations participated in a disproportionate number of conflicts). But these effects are not large." Hayes reports that, to date, wars are like "randomly distributed accidents" (p. 13).
143. People do not fight only as tribes, nations, and sovereign states. They also identify with sports teams, wear their colors, copy their uniforms, and sometimes enjoy violent action against emissaries from opposing teams. In both rich and poor countries, devotees riot—riot happily when their teams win as well as when their athletes seem unfairly treated. For one account of the pleasures of fighting and destruction, read Bill Buford's European story, 1991. It accords with Edward Banfield's earlier American report, *"Rioting Mainly for Fun and Profit,"* 1968, 1974.

Chapter 9: Empathetic Explanation

1. Trevelyan, 1942/1976.
2. Horgan, 1996, pp. 240 and 251, respectively.
3. Salmon, 1994.
4. Double, 1991; Kim, 1999.
5. Damasio, 1999a, 1999b; Moravec 1999a, 1999b; Sheldon, 1940, 1942.
6. Keeley, 1996, p. 161.
7. Salmon, 1994, p. 20, emphasis his.
8. Harrington, 1999; Kirsch, 1999; Nuland, 1999. Dr. Nuland shows how it is that medical diagnoses and prognoses, with and without treatment, are necessarily probabilistic. There is no such thing as risk-free attention.
9. Schama, 1989, p. 420.
10. Schutz, 1960, p. 220, emphasis added.
11. Weber, 1947, p. 88, emphasis added.

12. Weber, ibid., emphasis added.
13. De Waal, 1996; Dunbar, 1996; Gardner and Gardner, 1985; Griffin, 1976, 2000; Kummer and Goodall, 1985; Romanes, 1910; Savage-Rumbaugh, Shanker and Taylor, 1998; Schusterman, J. A. Thomas and F. G. Wood, 1985; Weiskrantz, 1985; E. M. Thomas, 1993.
14. F. Collin, 1985; Nettler, 1970, ch. 3.
15. Freimuth, 1992.
16. Toobin, 1996a, 1996b.
17. Crichton, 1975.
18. In his autobiography, 1976, Sutton denies that he ever said this and suggests that some journalist invented this quip. However, Sutton adds, "If anybody had asked me, I'd have probably said it" (p. 120).
19. When interrogating suspected or convicted felons, it is seldom advisable to ask them "why" they did it. (An exception occurs when one wants to elicit confession by assuming that one knows guilt.) Otherwise, after rapport has been established, one can ask, "What happened?" or "How did it happen?" This mode of inquiry takes heat from the question and respondent. It eliminates blame and stimulates storytelling.
20. Mailer, 1986.
21. Kenner, 1980, p. 231.
22. Marozzi, 2000.
23. Häfliger, 2000.
24. Massie-Blomfield, 2000.
25. FitzGerald, 2000.
26. Brookhiser, 1989, p. 51.
27. Chapman and Chapman, 1967, 1969; Cook, 1991; Dawes, 1993b, 1994; DePaulo, 1994; Einhorn and Hogarth, 1976; Einborn and Schacht, 1977; Faust, 1991; Garry et al., 1996; Hogarth, 1987; Kassin and Kiechel, 1996; Loftus, 1997; Meehl, 1954, 1973, 1983, 1986; Meier, 1994, pp. 73, 85; Nickel, 1994; Oskamp, 1965, 1976; Uelman, 1989; Wells, 1979, 1980, 1980a, 1980b.
28. Sporer et al., 1995.
29. Frankfurt, 1988. Read also philosopher Max Black's 1985 analysis of the maleficent effects of bullshit.
30. Gur and Sackeim, 1979; Sackeim and Gur, 1979; Ainslie, 2001, *passim.*
31. "Vac-yak" is Glen Newey's expressive neologism, 2001, p. 26.
32. Dawes, Faust, Meehl, 1989; Faust, 1991; Forst, 1984; L. R. Goldberg, 1968, 1970, 1991; L. R. Goldberg and Werts, 1986, 1991; S. D. Gottfredson 1986, 1987; Grove and Meehl, 1996; Kleinmuntz, 1991; Sawyer, 1966; Swets, Dawes, Monahan, 2000a, 2000b; Wiggins and Kohen, 1971.
33. Shapiro, 1977.
34. Mossman, 1994, p. 783, emphasis added.
35. R. E. Fancher, Jr., 1965, 1967.
36. Nettler, 1974a, 1989, pp. 42-53.
37. Cressey, 1950, 1953, 1964, 1971.
38. Guion, 1976; Miner and Miner, 1870; Murphy and Davidshofer, 1988.
39. My informal, untallied observations of interviewers' conduct in universities and industries suggest that "too many" employers do "too much" of the talking. They tend to approve of those candidates who are attentive auditors and who are "socially compatible" with those who might hire them. Cf. note 43 below.
40. Murphy and Davidshofer, 1988.

41. Shakespeare, ca. 1600-1608, reprint, 1988. This is King Duncan's response to his, and others', inability to detect a traitor by his appearance in *The Tragedy of Macbeth*.
42. Meehl, 1986.
43. J. S. Carroll, 1977.
44. Berman, 1997; Dabbs, 1969, Gada, 1999; Gifford, Ng, Wilkinson, 1985; Lydon, Jamieson, Zanna, 1988; Prickett, Gada-Jain, Bernieri, 2000; Webster, 1964.
45. K. R. Hammond, 1996, particularly chapter 6.

Chapter 10: Causal Explanation

1. Von Mises, 1957, p. 211.
2. Heine, 1827/1982.
3. Kun, 1978; Michotte, 1963; Piaget, 1930; White, 1988.
4. J. L. Marx, 1980; D. Premack, 1988; Savage-Rumbaugh, Shanker, Taylor, 1998.
5. Ayer, 1973, p. 181.
6. DiCristina, 1995.
7. Dawes, 1991, 1994, and the preceding chapter 9, pp. 188-189.
8. Hume, 1739, 1740, emphasis his.
9. J. Hall, 1947, p. 248.
10. DiCristina, 1995, pp. 84, 89-90, 102, 80, 89, respectively.
11. Iversen and Gergen, 1997, p. 323.
12. Ayer, 1973, pp. 172 ff. Cf. Also O'Connor, 2001.
13. J. Hall, 1947; Hart, 1965, Hart and Honoré, 1959; Shavell, 1980.
14. Avison, 1980; J. L. Evans, 1968, 1974; Hart and Honoré, 1959, Regan, 1974; Schiffman and Wynne, 1963; Shaver, 1985.
15. Searle, 1999c, p. 59.
16. Shaver, 1985, p. 132.
17. Huber, 1998; Huber and Litan, 1991; Nettler, 1972b; Olson, 1991.
18. Nettler, 1982b.
19. Addis, 1995, Kim, 1999. While it is popular to spell this philosophic enterprise "holism," it is more accurately identified as "wholism."
20. J. F. Brown, cf. also p. 00, n.23.
21. Lilla, 1999, p. 28. See also his 2001a, 2001b.
22. "Utopia," from the Greek *ou* (not) and *topos* (a place) is not what people have in mind when they use that word. What they hope for is "eutopia," from the Greek *eu* (good) and *topos*, hence a place of "ideal happiness or good order," as the *Oxford English Dictionary* instructs. It is also accurate to call that imagined society of large numbers of individuals, "no place."
23 Searle, 1999a; Cf. also Billington, 1982; Conquest, 1987, 1990, 2000, Courtois et al., 1999; Lasky, 1978; Malia, 1994, 1999; Pipes, 1990, 1994, 1996, 1999a; Ulam, 1976, 1989. Robert Service, 2000, provides an illuminating biography of Vladimir Ilich Lenin—né Ulyanov, 1870-1924—arguably the most important protagonist of an idealized social order the world has ever suffered. Lenin was a bibliophile and fervent social theorist. In league with his contemporary Bolsheviks and disciples, his teaching and practice encouraged other modern tyrants-for-humanity's-sake. At one time, these wholists dominated about a third of Earth's population. Their legacy is the impoverishment and slaughter of more human beings than any political movement in history.
24. Currie, Curtis et al., 1999.
25. *Economist*, 1999.

26. Kelly, 1999; Letwin, 1999; Oakeshott, 1962/1991, 1966, 1983; Rosenblueth, Wiener, and Bigelow, 1943.
27. Mackie, 1974, p. 58.
28. Mackie, 1974, p. 62.
29. Mackie, 1974, p. 62, emphasis his.
30. Mackie, 1974, p. 66, emphasis his.
31. Spellman, 1996, p. 337.
32. Nettler, 1989.
33. Pope, 1751/1967.
34. Bamforth, 1999, p. 3.
35. Horton, 2000b, p. 43.
36. Ibid.
37. H. Epstein, 1999, p. 14.
38. Hooper, 1999. Others question Hooper's hypothesis, Cf. Weiss, 1999.
39. Calaprice, 1996, p. 148, and her pp. 172, 178, 189. Cf. also Jammer, 1999; Pais, 1994. Einstein did not use "god" to refer to an anthropomorphic agent such as that to whom billions of people pray. For Einstein, "God," whom he also called "the old one," was only the order apparent in Nature. His oft-quoted quip about "God playing dice" appears in his letter to Max Born, December 1926, in which Einstein objects to the Born-Heisenberg statistical interpretation of quantum states. He wrote, "Quantum mechanics is certainly imposing. But an inner voice tells me that it is not yet the real thing. The theory says a lot, but does not really bring us any closer to the secret of the 'old one.' I, at any rate, am convinced that *He* is not playing dice" (Pais, 2000, p. 42, emphasis Einstein's).
40. Laplace, 1796.
41. See "the square of opposition" in Boh, 1995.
42. Pope, 1751/1967, Epistle I.
43. Cited by Brent, 1993, p. 174.
44. Brent, 1993, p. 175.
45. Monod, 1971, pp. 113-114, emphasis his.
46. Austad, 2000; Barrow, 1991b; Bull, 2000; Bullock, 1955; Dawes, 1991; Dawkins, 1986; *Economist*, 2000c; Finch and Kirkwood, 2000; Gleick, 1987; Kauffman, 1993, 1995; Malmquist and Meehl, 1978; Prigogine and Stengers, 1989; D. L. Stern, 2000; The quotation about "bad luck" and psychopathology is from Dawes, 1991, pp. 249-250, emphasis his.
47. Mark Ridley, 2001, p. 281, emphasis added.
48. Ridley, 2001, p. ix.
49. We distinguish between uncertainty and risk. Uncertainty refers to lack of knowledge of probable causes and their timing and powers. Risk refers to action taken when there is some knowledge of possibilities, as with classical and relative frequency probabilities, but no certainty. Recall that taking risks, and watching others do so, is pleasurable.
50. For a detailed history of the variety of materials human beings have drunk and eaten, cf. Kiple and Ornelas, 2000.
51. Hardin, 1972, pp. 43-49.
52. Hardin, 1972, 18.
53. H. Epstein, 1999, p. 18.
54. Glymour, 1998, p. 2.

Chapter 11: Rationality

1.   Lassalle, 1919-1920. Ferdinand Lassalle (1825-1864) helped establish Prussia's first workers' political party, 1863, that later became Germany's Social Democratic Party. He died young, killed in a lovers' duel.
2.   Resnik, 1987.
3.   Concerning this ambition, refer to DeLeon, 2000; Horowitz, 2000; Kazancigil and Makinson, 1999; Kruskal, 1982; Lundberg, 1961; Mills, 1956; M.E.P. Seligman and Csikszentmihalyi, 2000; Simon, 1982.
4.   This description of "rational act" follows Pareto, 1916/1935 with a qualification added to his item 3. We wish the means to be "knowledgeably selected," not a matter of lucky choice. Furthermore, the idea of "rational act" is not to be confused with the idea of "rational belief," about which philosophers continue to quarrel. For example, cf. G. A. Cohen, 2000, especially his chapter 1, "Paradoxes of Conviction."
5.   Hibbert, 1997, p. 184.

Chapter 12: Morality

1.   Koestler, describing a Communist commissar's ethic, 1945a, p. 145. Apropos, read Koestler's contribution to *The God That Failed*, edited by Crossman, 1950, and reprinted with Engerman as editor, 2000.
2.   Von Nieheim, 1411, cited by Koestler, 1945a, p. 95.
3.   The FBI found three handwritten copies of instructions for Muslim raiders on the U. S. (Makiya and Mneimineh, 2002).
4.   Cantril, 1948; Chein, 1948; Nozick, 2000.
5.   Santayana, 1937, p. 471.
6.   For an attempt to measure such sentiment among a time-and-place-bound set of Americans, cf. Nettler, 1957. Also review Coetzee, pp. 372-373.
7.   Chagnon, 1977.
8.   Ladd, 1957.
9.   Ladd, 1957, p. 9.
10.   Cited by Meroney, 1999.
11.   Rosner, 1999, p. 214.
12.   Graber, 1989. Glen Woiceshyn kindly provided this reference.
13.   Zohar and I. Marshall, 1994, p. 33.
14.   Jordan, 1934/1993.
15.   Kazacingil and Makinson, 1999.
16.   Horowitz, 1993, p. 28, emphasis his.
17.   Classicist Peter Jones, 2001, argues that many ancient Greek philosophers "thought there was a crucial connection between the way the world was constructed and the best way to live...." In sympathy with this idea, neuroscientist Jean-Pierre Changeux and philosopher Paul Ricoeur, 2000, rationalize this thesis with a depiction of how the human brain works. From this foundation, they foresee the possibility of a new eutopia in which "citizens" will be "free and equal," living "joyously" in a "universal civilization" cleansed of a market economy and therefore (?) "peaceful, stable, and just" (pp. 311-312). Unfortunately for this dream, and as far as we now know, evolution is not a process that has an ending so that, even if a universal, serene civilization were to evolve (or be created?), we can have no faith in its continuity. Cf. also notes 3 and 4 above.
18.   Callahan, 1972.
19.   As Easter approached in the new millennium, 12 March 2000, Pope John Paul II asked publicly for forgiveness for his Church's role in murdering infidels during Crusades and Inquisitions. He sought pardon for his organization's maltreatment

of Jews, heretics, women, and indigenous peoples. Whether this confession will reduce in any degree the quantity of morally motivated killing remains to be recorded. Refer also to Cornwell, 1999, and remember 11 September 2001.

Apropos of the impulse to destroy those who refuse to believe secularly, as well as religiously, justified ethics, refer, *inter alia*, to Courtois et al., 1999; Gay, 1993; Mayer, 2000; Zheng, 1996.

20. Concerning this variability, individual careers are instructive. For example, if one were to read the life of Winston Churchill, without knowing how he "turned out," the ready socio-psychological expectation would be that he'd "come to no good." But William Manchester's biography of this leader, 1983, reveals how greatly Churchill's career diverged from such expert expectation.

21. W. I. Thomas, 1937. "Mores" (more-âze) is the plural of the Latin, *mos*, meaning "custom." It is therefore a population term, like the relative frequency concept of probability. Properly speaking, "moral," our English derivative, refers to a person's character or behavior *regarded by some community* as good or bad. "Ethical," from the Greek, is often used as a synonym. However, some English-speakers prefer to use "ethical" to refer to a profession's special standards of practice or to an individual who acts from his or her own conscience. In the latter usage, a person could be deemed "ethical" while behaving immorally. Here I avoid such fine distinction and use the words interchangeably to refer to conduct deemed good or bad according to some community's norms.

22. This is not "just history" put behind us. It is history as we live it. After 11 September 2001, both the Christian American president and his Muslim antagonists called upon God and Allah, respectively, to justify their policies and to fortify their resolve.

23. For one brief catalogue of American professors who defended opponents of the United States in its New War, read James Bowman, 2001.

24. Lindbergh, 1940.

25. The notion that "free time" can be organized reminds us of Curzio Malaparte's definition of a totalitarian state as, "One in which everything that is not required is forbidden" (Malaparte, 1964, my paraphrase).

26. B. P. Webb, 1935; S. and B. P. Webb, 1941.

27. Fitzpatrick, 1999; Getty, 2000; Gordievsky, 2000.

28. Lindbergh, 1940, pp. 18-19. Reminder: Metaphors are useful, but dangerous. They draw vivid pictures in minds, but portraits can be false.

29. Of course, there is never a final terminus to some kind of social arrangement. Nothing social stands still—forever. As Mrs. Slade, citing Tennyson, taught us in eighth grade, "The old order changeth, giving place to new."

30. Pipes, 1994, p. 320, emphasis in the original.

31. Walden, 2000, p. 6. Apropos, cf. Remnik, 1993.

Summing Up

1. For some recent proposals that partake of these assumptions, read Changeux and Ricoeur, 2000, esp., their "Fugue"; Dworkin, 2000; Monod, 1971; Nozick, 2001; Rawls, 1971; Sen, 1992; van Parijs, 1991, 1992, 1995; and van Parijs, Cohen, Rogers, 2001.

2. P. Jones, 2000.

3. Monod, 1971, jacket.

4. Monod, 1971 p. 176, emphasis his.

5. Monod, 1971, pp. 179-180, emphasis his.

6.   "Destiny" is a fateful, deterministic word. It not only attributes purpose to all action, but it also posits an *end* to which change inevitably leads.
7.   Dennett, 1995.
8.   Nozick, 2001; P. Singer, 2000; R. Wright, 2000.
9.   Dawkins, 1986; Mayr, 2000; Tattersall and Schwartz, 2000.
10. S. Jones, 2000, pp. 44-45. Richard Horton, 2000b, p. 40. seconds this thesis. Horton argues that "finding the pattern for the ways genes and proteins are expressed in each disease state will enable much more precise classification of diseases....Currently accepted disease classifications will soon be torn up."

References

Aaron, R. I., 1971. *Knowing and the Function of Reason*. New York: Oxford U. P.

Abelson, R. P., 1995. *Statistics as Principled Argument*. Hillsdale, NJ: Erlbaum.

Addis, L., 1995. "Holism." In R. Audi (ed.), *the Cambridge Dictionary of Philosophy*. New York: Cambridge U. P.

Adelson, J., 1995a. "Sex Among the Americans," *Commentary*, 100: 26-30.

——, 1995b. "Sex in America," *Criminologist*, 20: 1-16.

Aeppel, T, 1998. "Losing faith: Personnel disorders sap a factory owner of his early idealism," *Wall St. J.*, 138: A1, A14 (Jan.14.)

Ainslie, G., 2001. *Breakdown of Will*. New York: Cambridge U. P.

Alihan, J., 1939. *Social Ecology*. New York: Columbia U. P.

Alker, H. R., 1969. A typology of ecological fallacies." In M. Dogan and S. Rokkan (eds.), *Quantitative Ecological Analysis in the Social Sciences*. Cambridge, MA: MIT Press.

Allardt, R. B., 1969. "Aggregate analysis: The problem of its informative value." In Dogan and Rokkan (eds.), *Quantitative Ecological Analysis in the Social Sciences*. Cambridge, MA: MIT Press.

Alley, R. B., 2000. *The Two-Mile Time Machine: Ice Cores, Abrupt Climate Change, and Our Future*. Princeton, NJ: Princeton U. P.

Alonso, W. and P. Starr (eds.), 1987. *The Politics of Numbers*. New York: Russell Sage Foundation.

Alper, J., 1986. "Our dual memory: It turns out the brain stores skills and facts differently," *Science 86*, 44-49.

Alschuler, A. W., 2000. *Law Without Values: The Life, Work, and Legacy of Justice Holmes*. Chicago: U. Chicago Press.

Alsop, R., 1986. "People watchers seek clues to consumers' true behavior," *Wall St. J.*, 115:29 (Sept. 4).

Alvarez, A., 1981. *The Savage God: A Study of Suicide*. New York: Norton.

Amis, M., 1985/. In J. Haffenden (ed.), *Novelists in Interview*. London: Routledge, Chapman & Hall.

Amos, B. *et al.*, 1995. "Evidence for mate fidelity in the gray seal," *Science*, 268:1897-1899.

Anders, G., 1996. "Polling quirks give HMOs healthy ratings," *Wall St. J.*, 135:B1, B7 (Aug. 27).

Anderson, C. A. and K. Gunderson (eds.), 1991. *Paul E. Meehl: Selected Philosophical and Methodological Papers*. Minneapolis: U. Minnesota Press.

Anderson, M. J. and S. R. Fienberg, 1999. *Who Counts? The Politics of Census-Taking in Contemporary America*. New York: Russell Sage Foundation.

Angell, M., 1996. *Science on Trial: The Clash of Medical Evidence and the Law in the Breast Implant Case*. New York: Norton.

Arendt, H., 1967. "Reflections: Truth and politics," *New Yorker*, 43:49-88 (Feb. 25).

Armstrong, J. S., 1978. *Long-Term Forecasting: From Crystal Ball to Computer.* New York: Wiley.

Asberg, M., 1982. "Mind and Body." Paper read at the Stone House Conference on *Mind and Body: Global Enigma and Opportunity.* Bethesda, MD: National Institutes of Health. (Dec. 3-5).

Attenborough, D., 1998. *The Life of Birds.* Los Angeles and London: CBS/Fox and BBC.

Augustine, N., 1999. "What we don't know does hurt us: How scientific illiteracy hobbles society," *Science,* 279:1640-1641.

Austad, S., 2000. "Varied fates from similar states," *Science,* 290:944. (Nov. 3).

Austin, H. L. 1981. *Philosophical Papers.* Oxford: Clarendon Press.

Avison, W. R., 1980. "Liking and the attribution of causation for success and failure," *J. Gen. Psychol.,* 102:193-209.

Ayala, F. H. and B. Black, 1993. "Science and the courts," *Amer. Scientist,* 81:230-239.

Ayer, A. J., 1946. *Language, Truth, and Logic.* New York: Dover.

——, 1972. *Probability and Evidence.* London: Macmillan.

——, 1973. *The Central Questions of Philosophy.* London: Weidenfeld and Nicolson.

Ayre, R. V. and A. Anton, 1977. *What Is Crime?: Marxist Ethical Theory in the Construction of Revolutionary Criminology.* Paper read at the annual meeting of the Soc. For the Study of Soc. Problems, Chicago.

Azar, B., 2000. "Monkeying around with numbers," *Monitor on Psychol.,* 3:69

Babor, T. F., J. Brown, F. K. Del Boca, 1996. "Validity of self-reports in applied research in addictive behaviors: Fact or fiction?" *Beh. Assess.,* 12:5-31.

Bacon, F., 1597-1625/1970. *The Advancement of Learning.* Reprint, 1970. Norwood, NJ: W. J. Johnson.

Baddeley, A. D. and L. Weiskrantz (eds.), 1993. *Attention, Selection, Awareness, and Control.* Oxford: Clarendon Press.

Bahrick, H. P., L. K. Hall, S. A. Berger, 1996. "Accuracy and distortion in memory for high school grades," *Psychol. Sci.,* 7:265-271.

Baker, G. P. and P. M. S. Hacker (eds.), 1983. *Wittgenstein: Meaning and Understanding.* Chicago: U. Chicago Press.

Baker, L. R., 1995. *Explaining Attitudes: A Practical Approach to the Mind.* New York: Cambridge U. P.

Balch, S. H., 1986. "Radical delusions," *Society,* 23:3.

——, and I. London, 1988. "The tenured left," *Commentary,* 82:41-51.

Balkwell, J. W., 1990. "Ethnic inequality and the rate of homicide," *Soc. Forces,* 69:53-70.

Ball, P., 1999. *The Self-Made Tapestry: Pattern Formation in Nature.* New York: Oxford U. P.

Bamforth, I., 1999. "Are we really what we eat?" *Times Lit. Supp.,* 5048:3-4. (Dec. 31).

Bandow, D., 1998. "Many torts later, the case against implants collapses," *Wall St. J.,* 139:A23 (Nov. 30).

Banfield, E. C., 1958. *The Moral Basis of a Backward Society.* New York: Free Press.

——, 1968. "Rioting mainly for fun and profit." In his *The Unheavenly City: The Nature and Future of the Urban Crisis.* Boston: Little, Brown.

——, 1974. *The Unheavenly City Revisited.* Boston: Little, Brown.

Bannock, G. et al., 1987. *Dictionary of Economics.* London: Hutchinson Bus. Books.

Barkow, J. R., L. Cosmides, J. Tooby (eds.), 1992. *The Adapted Mind: Evolutionary Psychology and the Generation of Culture.* New York: Oxford U. P.

Barnes, F., 1995. "How to rig a poll," *Wall St. J.,* 132:A16 (June 14).

Barrow, J. D., 1989. "Longing for reality," *Times Higher Educ. Supp.,* March 3, p. 25.

——, 1991a. "What is mathematics?" In T. Ferris (ed.), *the World Treasury of Physics, Astronomy, and Mathematics*. Boston: Little, Brown.

——, 1991b. *Theories of Everything: The Quest for Ultimate Explanation*. New York: Oxford U. P.

——, 1998. *Impossibility: The Limits of Science and the Science of Limits*. New York: Oxford U. P.

——, 2000. *The Book of Nothing: Vacuums, Voids, and the Latest Ideas About the Origins of the Universe*. New York: Pantheon.

Barrow, S. B., 1997. Interview. *Arts & Entertainment TV*. (Jan. 29).

Bartlett, B., 1989. "The world-wide tax revolution," *Wall St. J.*, 121:A16 (Aug. 29).

Bass, B. M., 1956. "Development and evaluation of a scale for measuring social acquiescence," *J. Ab. Soc. Psychol.*, 52:296-299.

Bastiat, F., 1860/1956. *Harmonies of Political Economy*. G. B. de Huszar (ed.). New York: Foundation for Economic Education.

Bates, E. and J. Elman, 1996. "Learning rediscovered," *Science*, 274:1849-1850. (Dec. 13).

Bateson, G., 1979. *Mind and Nature*. New York: Dutton.

Bauer, P., 1997a. *Class on the Brain: The Cost of a British Obsession*. London: Centre for Policy Studies.

——, 1996b. "Class dismissed," *Spectator*, 279:14 (Sept. 27).

——, 2000. *From Subsistence to Exchange and Other Essays*. Princeton, NJ: Princeton U. P.

Bauer, R. A., R. W. Riechen, J. S. Bruner, 1949. "An analysis of the stability of voting intentions, Massachusetts, 1948," *Int. J. Opin. Att. Res.*, 3:169-192.

Bayes, T., 1765. "An essay towards solving a problem in the doctrine of chances," *Philosophical Transactions of the Royal Society of London*. 53:370-418. Reprinted, 1970, in E. S. Pearson and M. G. Kendall (eds.), *Studies in the History of Statistics and Probability*. London: Charles Griffin.

Baynes, K., J. Bohman, and T. McCarthy (eds.), 1993. *After Philosophy: End or Transformation?* Cambridge, MA: Blackwell.

Bean, R. B., 1906. "Some racial peculiarities of the Negro brain," *Amer. J. Anatomy*, 5:353-432.

Beauchamp, T. L. (ed.), 1974. *Philosophical Problems of Causation*. Encino, CA: Dickenson.

——, and A. Rosenberg, 1981. *Hume and the Problem of Causation*. New York: Oxford U. P.

Becker, G. S., 1996. "Government and the market," In J. Pavlik (ed.), *Gary Becker in Prague*. Prague: Centre for Liberal Studies.

——, 1968. "Crime and punishment: An economic approach," *J. Pol. Econ.*, 78:169-217.

——, 1976. *The Economic Approach to Human Behavior*. Chicago: U. Chicago Press.

Beckmann, P., 1967. *Elements of Applied Probability Theory*. New York: Harcourt, Brace, & World.

Bell, D., 1980. *The Winding Passage*. Cambridge, MA: Harvard U. P.

——, 1996. *The Cultural Contradictions of Capitalism*. New York: Basic Books.

Bell, R. Q., 1979. "Parent, child, and reciprocal influences," *Amer. Psychol.*, 34:821-826.

——, and L. V. Harper (eds.), 1977. *The Effects of Children on Parents*. Hillsdale, NJ: Erlbaum.

Benda, J., 1928. *The Great Betrayal*. (R. Aldington, Trans.). London: Routledge & Kegan Paul.

Bennett, A., 1994. "Numbers game: Half-million people are 'lost' from work force in survey," *Wall St. J.*, 132:B1 (Jan. 18).

Bennett, W. J., J. J. DiIulio, J. P. Walters, 1996. *Body Count: Moral Poverty and How to Win America's War Against Crime and Drugs*. New York: Simon & Schuster.

Bergmann, G., 1968. "Ideology." In M. Brodbeck (ed.), *Readings in the Philosophy of the Social Sciences*. New York: Macmillan.

Berlin, I., 1955/1979. *Against the Current: Essays in the History of Ideas*. London: Hogarth.

——, 1957. *The Hedgehog and the Fox*. New York; Mentor.

——, 1959/1990. *The Crooked Timber of Humanity: Chapters in the History of Ideas*. New York: Vintage.

——, 1969. *Four Essays on Liberty*. London: Oxford U. P.

Berman, J. A., 1997. *Competence-Based Employment Interviewing*. Westport, CT: Quorum.

Bernstein, J., 1991. *Quantum Profiles*. Princeton, NJ: Princeton U. P.

Bernstein, P., 2000. *The Power of Gold: The History of an Obsession*. New York: Wiley.

Berridge, K. C. and T. E. Robinson, 1995. "The mind of an addicted brain: Neural sensitization of wanting versus liking," *Curr. Direcs. Psychol. Sci.*, 4:71-78.

Berry, DC and D. E. Broadbent, 1984. "On the relationship between task performance and associated verbalizable knowledge," *Quart. J. Exper. Psychol.*, 39A:585-609.

——, and Z. Dienes, 1991. "The relationship between implicit memory and implicit learning," *Br. J. Psychol..*, 82:359-373.

Bertrand, A., 1892. "Cours municipal de sociologies: Lecon d'ouverture," *Archives d'Anthropologie criminelle de Medicine Legale et de Psychologie normale et pathologique*, 7:677.

Bierce, A., 1911/1958. *The Devil's Dictionary*. New York: Boni. Reprint 1959. New York: Dover.

Billington, J. H., 1980. *Minds of Men: Origins of the Revolutionary Faith*. New York: Basic.

Bishop, G. P. et al., 1980. "Pseudo-opinions on public affairs." *Pub. Opin. Quart.*, 44:198-209.

Bishop, J., 1993. "Medical studies' claims irk professions' skeptics," *Wall St. J.*, 129:B1 (July 12).

Black, J. M., 1996. *Partnership in Birds: The Study of Monogamy*. New York: Oxford U. P.

Black, M., 1963. "Reasoning with loose concepts." *Dialogue*, 2:1-12.

——, 1969. "Some half-baked thoughts about induction." In S. Morgenbesser, P. Suppes, M. White (eds.), *Philosophy, Science, and Method: Essays in Honor of Ernest Nagel*. New York: St. Martin's.

——, 1985. *The Prevalence of Humbug*. Ithaca, NY: Cornell U. P.

Blackburn, S., 1991. "The ways of going wrong." *Times Lit. Supp.*, 21 (Feb. 22).

——, 1994a. "Equivocate." In his *The Oxford Dictionary of Philosophy*. New York: Oxford U. P.

——, 1994b. "Moore." In ibid.

——, 1994c. "Culture." In ibid.

——, 1999. *Think*. New York: Oxford U. P.

Blair, S., 1956. *Measurement of Mind and Matter.* New York: Philosophical Library.

Blaise, C., 2001. *Time Lord: Sir Sandford Fleming and the Creation of Standard Time*. New York: Pantheon.

Blake, W., 1977. In G. Keynes (ed.), *The Portable Blake*. New York: Viking/Penguin.

Blasi, A., 1980. "Bridging moral cognition and moral action: A critical review of the literature," *Psychol. Bull.*, 88:1-45.

Blau, J. R. and P. M. Blau, 1982. "The costs of inequality: Metropolitan structure and violent crime," *Amer. Sociol. Rev.*, 471: 114-129.

Blazer, S. E. et al., (eds.), 1993. *The Dictionary of Cultural Literacy*. 2/e. Boston: Houghton, Mifflin.

Bleakley, F. R., 1997. "Appalachian clan mines web sites for ancestral clues," *Wall St. J..*, 136:B1, B5 (April 14).

Bleuler, P. E., 1911. *Dementia Praecox*. Reprinted 1950. Trans., J. Zinkin. New York: International Universities Press.

——, 1912. *Theory of Schizophrenic Negativism*. Trans. W. A. White. New York: Jr. Nervous Mental Disease Publishing Co.

Blight, J. G., 1987. "Toward a policy-relevant psychology of avoiding nuclear war: Lessons for psychologists from the Cuban crisis," *Amer. Psychol.*, 42:12-29.

Block, J., 1971. *Lives Through Time*. Berkeley, CA: Bancroft.

Bloodworth, D., 1980. "New freedoms in old China," *Edmonton J.*, A-6 (Feb. 29).

Blumberg, M. S. and E. A. Wasserman, 1995, "Animal mind and the argument from design," *Amer. Psychol.*, 50:133-144.

Blumenthal, W. H., 1954. *Rendezvous with Chance: How Luck Has Shaped History*. New York: Exposition Press.

Blumer, H., 1969. *Symbolic Interactionism: Perspectives and Method*. Englewood Cliffs, NJ: Prentice-Hall.

Boaz, D. (ed.), 1997. *The Libertarian Reader*. New York: Free Press.

——, (ed.), 2000. "To be governed...," *Cato Policy Report*, 22:16.

Boehm, C., 1997. *American Naturalist*, 150: S (100).

Boh, I., 1995. "The square of opposition." In R. Audi (ed.), *The Cambridge Dictionary of Philosophy*. New York: Cambridge U. P.

Bok, B. J. and L. E. Jerome, 1975. *Objections to Astrology*. Buffalo, NY: Prometheus Books.

Booth, A. and S. Welch, 1978. "Spousal consensus and its correlates," *J. Marr. Family*, 40:23-34.

Boskin, M. J. and C. E. McClure, 1990. *Worldwide Tax Reform*. San Francisco, CA: ICS Press.

Boswell, J., 1791/1981. Rev. by Frank Morley (ed.), 1981. *Everybody's Boswell: Being the Life of Samuel Johnson*. Columbus: Ohio State U. P.

Bouchard, T. J., Jr., 1997a. "IQ similarity in twins reared apart: Findings and responses to critics." In R. J. Sternberg and E. Grigorenko (eds.), *Intelligence, Heredity, and Environment*. New York: Cambridge U. P.

——, 1997b. "Genetic influences on mental abilities and work attitudes." In C. L. Cooper and J. T. Robertson (eds.), *International Review of Industrial and Organizational Psychology*. New York: Wiley.

——, 1997c. "The genetics of personality." In K. Blum and P. Noble (eds.), *Handbook of Psychiatric Genetics*. Boca Raton, FL: CLC Press.

——, 1997d. "Experience producing drive theory: How genes drive experience and shape personality," *Acta Paediatr. Supp.*, 422:50-64.

——, *et al.*, 1990a. "Sources of human psychological differences: the Minnesota study of twins reared apart," *Science*, 250:223-228 (Oct. 2).

——, N. L. Segal, and D. T. Lykken, 1990b. "Genetic and environmental influences on special mental abilities in the sample of twins reared apart," *Acta Genet. Med. Gemellol.*, 39:193-206.

Bouissou, R., 1942. *Essai sur l'Abstraction et Son Role dans la Connaissance*. Paris: Librairie Hachette.

Bovard, J., 1990. "Welfare for millionaire farmers," *Wall St. J.*, 122:A14 (May 22).

——, 1995a. *Shakedown: How Government Screws You From A to Z*. New York: Viking.

——, 1995b. "The lame game," *Amer. Spectator*, 28:30-31.

——, 1995c. *Lost Rights: The Destruction of American Liberty*. New York: St. Martin's Griffin.

——, 2000. *Feeling Your Pain: The Explosion and Abuse of Government Power in the Clinton-Gore Years*. New York: St. Martin's Press.

Bowers, K. S. and D. Meichenbaum, (eds.), 1984. *The Unconscious Reconsidered*. New York: Wiley.

Bowlby, J., 1990. *Charles Darwin: A Life*. New York: Norton.

Bowman, J., 2001. "Towers of intellect," *Wall St. J.*, 238:W17 (Oct. 5).

Brain, R., 1950. "The cerebral basis of consciousness," *Brain*, 73:465-470.

Brainerd, C. J., V. P. Reyna, and E. Brandes, 1995. "Why are children's false memories more persistent than their true memories?" *Psychol. Sci.*, 6:359-364.

Brent, J., 1993. *Charles Sanders Peirce: A Life*. Bloomington: Indiana U. P.

Bricmont, J. and A. Sokal, 1997. "What is all the fuss about?" *Times Lit. Supp.*, #4933:17 (Oct. 17).

Brinkley, D., 1995. "The long road to tax reform," *Wall St. J.*, 133:A10 (Sept. 18).

Brookhiser, R., 1989. "Public opinion and the jogger," *Commentary*, 88:50-55.

Broom, L. *et al.*, 1978. "Is it true what they say about Daddy?" *American J. Sociol.*, 84:417-426.

Brown, J. and B. G. Gilmartin, 1969. "Sociology today: Lacunae, emphases, and surfeits," *Amer. Sociol.*, 4:283-291.

Brown, J. F., 1938. *Psychology and the Social Order*. New York: McGraw-Hill.

Brown, P. H. and P. B. Barham, 1995. *Marilyn: The Last Take*. New York: Dutton.

Browne, J., 1996. *Charles Darwin: Voyaging*. New York: Knopf.

Browning, E. S., 1997. "Will Asia crisis keep down U. S. stocks?" *Wall St. J.*, 1317:C1, Ca (Pct/24).

Brumm, H. J. and D. O. Cloninger, 1995. "The drug war and the homicide rate: A direct correlation?" *Cato J.*, 14:509-517.

Buchan, J., *Frozen Desire: The Meaning of Money*. New York: Farrar, Straus, Giroux.

——, 2000. "Only a hop and a skip to money," *London Rev. Books*, 22:28-29 (Nov. 16).

Buchanan, J. M., 1979. *What Should Economists Do?* Indianapolis, IN: Liberty Press.

Buford, B., 1991. *Among the Thugs: The Experience and Seduction of Crowd Violence*. New York: Norton.

Bull, J. J., 2000. "Deja vu," *Nature*, 408:416-417. (Nov. 23).

Bullock, A., 1955. *Men, Chance, and History*. London: Lindsey Press.

Bunge, M., 1979. *Causality and Modern Science*. 3/e. New York: Dover.

Burgess, A., 1992. *A Mouthful of Air: Language, Languages...Especially English*. New York: Morrow.

Bureau of Indian Affairs, 1981. *Information About the Indian People*. Washington, DC: U. S. Government Printing Office.

Burtt, H. E., 1932, 1927, 1941. "The retention of early memories." *J. General Psychol.*, 1932, 40:287-295; 1937, 50:187-192; 1941, 58:435-439. Reprinted and abridged in W. Dennis, 1963. *Readings in Child Psychology*. 2/e. Englewood Cliffs, NJ: Prentice-Hall.

Buruma, I., 1984. *Behind the Mask*. New York: Pantheon Books.

Cairncross, F., 1997. *The Death of Distance*. Cambridge, MA: Harvard Business School Press.

Calaprice, A. (ed.), 1996. *The Quotable Einstein*. Princeton, NJ: Princeton U. P.

Callahan, D., 1972. "Ethics and population limitation," *Science*, 175:494, n. 25. (Feb. 4).

Campbell, B., 1985. *Human Evolution: An Introduction to Man's Adaptation*. 3/e. Hawthorn, NY: Aldine.

Campbell, B. J., 1990. Personal correspondence (July 30). Campbell was Director, Highway Safety Research Center, Univ. of North Carolina. Chapel Hill, NC.

Campbell, D. T. and D. W. Fiske, 1959. "Convergent and discriminant validation by the multitrait-multimethod matrix," *Psychol. Bull.*, 56:81-105.

Cantril, H., 1949. "Toward a scientific morality," *Jour. Psychol.*, 27:262-276.

Card, D. and A. B. Krueger, 1994. "Minimum wages and employment: A case study of the fast-food industry in New Jersey and Pennsylvania," *Amer. Econ. Rev.*, 84:772-783.

Card, J. J., 1978. "The correspondence of data gathered from husband and wife: Implications for family planning studies," *Soc. Biol.*, 25:196-204.

Carley, W. M. and T. L. O'Brien, 1995. "Cypher caper: How Citicorp system was raided and funds moved around the world," *Wall St. J.*, 133:A1, A6 (Sept. 12).

Carlson, S., 1985. "A double-blind test of astrology," *Nature*, 318:419-423.

Carlsson, G., 1977. "Crime and behavioral epidemiology: concepts and applications to Swedish data." In S. Mednick and K. O. Christiansen (eds.), *Biosocial Bases of Criminal Behavior*. New York: Gardner.

Carnap, R., 1950. *Logical Foundations of Probability*. Chicago: U. Chicago Press.

Carroll, J. S., 1977. "Judgments of recidivism risk: Conflicts between clinical strategies and base-rate information," *Law Hum. Beh.*, 1:191-209.

Carroll, L., 1872. *Through the Looking Glass*. Reprint, n.d., the Modern Library.

Caspi, A. et al., 1994. "Are some people crime-prone?" Replications of the personality-crime relationship across countries, genders, races, and methods," *Criminology*, 32:163-183.

Cassidy, J., 1997. "Bear headed," *New Yorker*, 73:37-41 (July 28).

Cattell, R. B., 1979. *Personality and Learning Theory: Vol. 1: The Structure of Personality in Its Environment*. New York: Springer.

——, 1980. *Personality and Learning Theory. Vol. 2: A Systems Theory of Maturation and Structured Learning*. New York: Springer.

——, and H. J. Butcher, 1968. *The Prediction of Achievement and Creativity*. Indianapolis: Bobbs-Merrill.

Cavalli-Sforza, L. L., P. Menozzi, and A. Piazza, 1994. *The History and Geography of Human Genes*. Princeton, NJ: Princeton U. P.

Ceci, S. and M. Bruck, 1995. *Jeopardy in the Courtroom*. Washington, DC: Amer. Psychol. Assoc.

Central Intelligence Agency, 1993. *The World Factbook, 1993-1994*. Washington, DC: Brassey's.

Chagnon, N. A., 1977. *Yanomamo: the Fierce People*. 2/e. New York: Holt, Rinehart, & Winston.

Chai, C. and W. Chai (eds.), 1964. *I Ching: Book of Changes*. (Trans. By J. Legge). New Hyde Park, NY: University Books.

Chaiken, J. M. and M. Chaiken, 1982. *Varieties of Criminal Behavior*. Santa Monica, CA: Rand.

Chamberlain, J., 1980. "Robber governments," *Nat. Rev.*, 32:1449-1452 (Nov. 18).

Chambliss, W. J., 1964 and R. H. Nagasawa, 1969. "On the validity of official statistics: A comparative study of white, black, and Japanese high-school boys," *J. Res. Crim. & Delinq.*, 6:71-77.

Chang, L., 1995. "In Taiwan, unofficial postal services often deliver the goods," *Wall St. J.*, 133:A18 (Nov. 8).

Changeux, J-P. And A. Connes, 1995. *Conversations on Mind, Matter, and Mathematics.* M. B. DeBevoise, trans. Princeton, NJ: Princeton U. P.

——, and P. Ricoeur, 2000. *What Makes Us Think?* M. B. DeBevoise, trans. Princeton, NJ: Princeton U. P.

Chapman, L. J. and J. P. Chapman, 1967. "Genesis of popular but erroneous psychodiagnostic observations," *J. Ab. Psychol.*, 72:193-204.

——, 1969. "Illusory correlation as an obstacle to the use of valid psychodiagnostic signs," *J. Ab. Psychol.*, 74:271-280.

Chein, I., 1947. "Towards a science of morality," *J. Soc. Psychol.*, 25:235-238.

Chipello, C. J., 1998. "Francophones struggle outside Quebec," *Wall St. J.*, 138:A12 (Feb. 26).

Christensen, A., G. Margolin, and M. Sulloway, 1992. "Interpersonal agreement on child behavior problems," *Psychol. Assess.*, 4:419-425.

Churchland, P. M. 1981. "Eliminative materialism and the propositional attitudes," *Jr. Phil.*, 78:67-90.

——, 1988. "Folk psychology and the explanation of human behavior," *Proc. Aristot. Soc.*, Supp., #62:209-221.

——, 1989. *A Neurocomputational Perspective: The Nature of Mind and the Structure of Science.* Cambridge, MA: MIT Press.

——, 1995. *The Engine of Reason, the Seat of the Soul.* Cambridge, MA: MIT Press.

——, and P. S. Churchland, 1998. *On the Contrary: Critical Essays, 1986-1997.* Cambridge, MA: MIT Press.

Churchland, P. S., 1995. *Neurophilosophy: Toward a Unified Science of Mind/Brain.* Cambridge, MA: MIT Press.

——, and T. J. Sejnowski, 1992. *The Computational Brain.* Cambridge, MA: MIT Press.

Cicero, M. T., ca 50 B.C./1950. *De Divinatione, I;118.* In his *Collected Essays.* H. M. Poteat, trans. Chicago: U. Chicago Press.

Clancy, S. A., *et al.*, 2000. "False recognition in women reporting recovered memories of sexual abuse," *Psychol. Sci.*, 11:26-31.

Clark, H. H. and M. F. Schober, 1994. "Asking questions and influencing answers." In J. M. Tanur (ed.), *Questions about Questions: Inquiries into the Cognitive Bases of Surveys.* New York: Russell Sage.

Clark, K., 1999. *Civilization.* 5 Vols. London: BBC.

Clark, M., S. Hold *et al.*, 2000. *Trillion Dollar Bet.* Boston: Nova TV.

Clarke, B., 1975. "The causes of biological diversity," *Sci. Amer.*, 225:50-60.

Cleveland, W. S., 1985. *The Elements of Graphing Data.* Summit, NJ: Hobart Press.

——, 1993. *Visualizing Data.* Summit, NJ: Hobart Press.

Coetzee, J. M., 1997. |*Boyhood Scenes from Provincial Life.* London, UK, Secker.

Cogan, J. F., 1981. *The Decline in Black Teenage Employment, 1950-1970.* Stanford, CA: The Hoover Institution.

Cohen, G. A., 2000. *If You're an Egalitarian: How Come You're So Rich?* Cambridge, MA: Harvard U. P.

Cohen, J. A., 1968. *The Criminal Process in the People's Republic of China.* Cambridge, MA: Harvard U. P.

Cohen, J. D. and J. W. Schooler (eds.), 1997. *Scientific Approaches to Consciousness.* Mahwah, NJ: Erlbaum.

Cohen, J. E., 1995a. "Population growth and the earth's carrying capacity," *Science*, 269:341-346 (July 21).

——, 1995b. *How Many People Can the Earth Support?* New York: Norton.

Cohen, L. J., 1977. *The Probable and the Provable.* Oxford: Clarendon Press.

——, 1989. *The Philosophy of Induction and Probability.* Oxford: Clarendon Press.

Cohen, M. R., 1931. *Reason and Nature.* New York: Harcourt, Brace.

——, 1944. *A Preface to Logic.* New York: Holt.

——, and E. Nagel, 1934. *Introduction to Logic and Scientific Method.* New York: Harcourt, Brace.

Colapinto, J., 2000. *As Nature Made Him: The Boy Who Was Raised as a Girl.* New York: Harper/Collins.

Collin, F., 1985. *Theory and Understanding: A Critique of Interpretive Social Science.* New York: Blackwell.

Connes, A., (with J-P Changeux), 1995. *Mind, Matter, and Mathematics.* Princeton, NJ: Princeton U. P.

Conquest, R., 1987. *The Harvest of Sorrow: Soviet Collectivization and the Terror-Famine.* New York: Oxford U. P.

——, 1990. *The Great Terror: A Reassessment.* New York: Oxford U. P.

——, 2000. *Reflections on a Ravaged Century.* New York: Norton.

Conrad, J., 1911/1991. *Under Western Eyes.* New York: Knopf

Conway, M. and M. Ross, 1984. "Getting what you want by revising what you had," *J. Person. Soc. Psychol.*, 47:738-748.

Cook, R. D., 1989. *Regression Graphics: Ideas for Studying Regression through Graphics.* New York: Wiley.

Cook, W. L. *et al.*, 1991. "Parental affective style, risk, and the family system: A social relations model analysis," *Jr. Ab. Psychol.*, 100:492-501.

Cooke, R. M., 1991. *Experts in Uncertainty: Opinion and Subjective Probability in Science.* New York: Oxford U. P.

Coombs, C. H., 1952. "Psychological scaling without a unit of measurement," *Psychol. Rev..*, 57:145-158.

Coons, P. M., 1984. "The differential diagnosis of multiple personality: A comprehensive review," *Psychiatric Clinics of North America*, 7:51-67.

Cooper, A., 1999. "Pointless polls," *Spectator*, 283:27 (July 24).

Cornwell, J., 1999. *Hitler's Pope: The Secret History of Pius XII.* New York: Viking.

Cose, E., 1999. "In defense of busing," *Wall St. J.*, 141:A23 (Aug. 4).

Costa, P. T., Jr. and R. R. McCrae, 1985. *NEO PI: Professional Manual.* Odessa, TX: Psychol Assessment Resources.

——, 1992. *NEO: PI-R.*

Coté, J. E., 1998. "Much ado about nothing: The 'fateful hoaxing' of Margaret Mead," *Skeptical Inquirer*, 29-34.

——, 1999. "The fateful hoaxing of Margaret Mead: Review," *Pacific Affairs*, 72:308-320.

——, "Was *Coming of Age in Samoa* based on a 'fateful hoaxing'?" Forthcoming *Current Anthropology*, 2000.

Courtois, S. *et al.*, 1999. *The Black Book of Communism: Crimes, Terror, Repression.* Trans. By J. Murphy and M. Kramer. Cambridge, MA: Harvard U. P.

Cox, W. M. and R. Alm, 1999. *Myths of Rich and Poor: Why We're Better Off than We Think.* New York: Basic Books.

Cressey, D. R., 1950. "The criminal violation of financial trust," *Amer. Sociol. Rev.*, 15:738-743.

——, 1953. *Other People's Money: A Study in the Social Psychology of Embezzlement.* 2/e, 1971. Belmont, CA: Wadsworth.

——, 1964. *Causes of Employee Dishonesty.* Paper presented at the Top Management Business Security Seminar. East Lansing, MI. (April 16)

Crews, F., 1994a. "The revenge of the repressed, Part I," *NY Rev. Books*, 41:54-60 (Nov. 17).

——, 1994b. "The revenge of the repressed, Part II," *NY Rev. Books*, 41:49-58 (Dec. 1).

——, 1995. *The Memory Wars: Freud's Legacy in Dispute*. New York: New York Review.

——, 1998. "The mindsnatchers," *NY Rev. Books*, 48:14, 16-18 (June 25).

Crichton, M., 1975. *The Great Train Robbery*. Boston, MA: G. K. Hall.

Crick, F., 1994. *The Astonishing Hypothesis: The Scientific Search for the Soul*. New York: Scribner's.

Cronbach, L. J. et al., 1972. *The Dependability of Behavioral Measurements: Theory of Generalizability of Scores and Profiles*. New York: Wiley.

Crossman, R., (ed.), 1950. *The God That Failed*. London: Hamilton.

Crutchfield, J. O. et al., 1986. "Chaos," *Sci. Amer.*, 255:46-57.

Culver, R. B. and P. A. Ianna, 1984. *The Gemini Syndrom: A Scientific Evaluation of Astrology*. Buffalo, NY: Prometheus Books.

Currie, E., L. A. Curtis *et al.*, 1999. *To Establish Justice and Insure Domestic Tranquility: A Thirty-year Update of the National Commission on the Causes and Prevention of Violence*. Washington, DC: The Milton S. Eisenhower Foundation.

Dabbs, J. M., Jr., 1968. "Similarity of gestures and interpersonal influence," *Proceedings*, 77th Annual Convention, Amer. Psychol. Assoc., 337-338.

Dalrymple, T., 1995. "A cage gilded with fool's gold," *Spectator*, 275:11-14 (Oct. 7).

——, 1999. "What is poverty?" *City J.*, 9:106-111.

Damasio, A. R., 1994. *Descartes' Error: Emotion, Reason, and the Human Brain*. New York: Grosset/Putnam.

——, 1999a. "How the brain creates the mind," *Sci. Amer.*, 281-:112-117.

——, 1999b. *The Feeling of What Happens: Body and Emotion in the Making of Consciousness*. New York: Harcourt, Brace.

Dancy, J., 1985. *Introduction to Contemporary Epistemology*. New York: Blackwell.

Dawes, R. M., 1988. *Rational Choice in an Uncertain World*. New York: Harcourt, Brace, Jovanovich.

——, 1991. "Probabilistic versus causal thinking," In D. Cicchetti and W. M. Grove (eds.), *Thinking Clearly About Psychology: Essays in Honor of Paul E. Meehl*. Minneapolis: U. Minnesota. Press.

——, 1993a. "Prediction of the future versus understanding of the past: A basic asymmetry," *Amer. J. Psychol.*, 106:1-24.

——, 1993b. "Cognitive bases of clinicians' overconfidence." Paper read at the April *Conference on Memory and Reality: Emerging Crisis*. Philadelphia: The False Memory Syndrome Foundation.

——, 1994. *House of Cards: Psychology and Psychotherapy Built on Myth*. New York: Free Press.

——, D. Faust, and P. E. Meehl, 1989. "Clinical versus actuarial judgment,": *Science*, 243:1668-1674 (March 31).

Dawkins, R., 1986. *The Blind Watchmaker*. New York: Norton.

——, 1995. *River out of Eden*. New York: Basic Books.

Dean, G. and A. Mather, 1977. *Recent Advances in Natal Astrology: A Critical Review, 1900-1976*. Subizco, Australia: Analogic.

Delbrück, M., 1986. *Mind from Matter*. Palo Alto, CA: Blackwell Scientific.

DeLeon, P. H., 2000. "The critical importance of public policy involvement," *Monitor on Psychol.*, 31:5.

Demaree, A. T., 2001. "Betting on a casino, and winning big," *Wall St. J..*, 237:A20 (Feb. 12).

DeMuth, C., 1997. "The new wealth of nations," *Commentary*, 104:23-28.

Dennett, DC, 1987. *The Intentional Stance*. Cambridge, MA: MIT Press.

——, 1991. *Consciousness Explained*. Boston: Little, Brown.

——, 1995. *Darwin's Dangerous Idea: Evolution and the Meaning of Life*. New York: Simon & Schuster.

Dennis, W. (ed.), 1963. *Readings in Child Psychology*. 2/e. Englewood Cliffs, NJ: Prentice-Hall.

Denton, M., 1986. *Evolution: A Theory in Crisis*. Bethesda, MD: Adler & Adler.

Denzin, N. K., 1982. "Note on criminology and criminality." In H. E. Pepinsky (ed.), *Rethinking Criminology*. Beverly Hills: Sage.

DePaulo, B. M., 1994. "Spotting lies: Can humans learn to do better?" *Curr. Direcs. Psychol. Sci.*, 3:83-86.

De Santis, S., 1996. "Canada modified 1996 census form after angry homemaker's campaign," *Wall St. J.*, 135:A5C (Aug. 9).

Desrosières, A., 1998. *The Politics of Large Numbers: A History of Statistical Reasoning*. Cambridge, MA: Harvard U. P.

De Sola Pool, J., (ed.), 1967. *Contemporary Political Science: Toward Empirical Theory*. New York: McGraw-Hill.

de Sousa, R., 1991. *The Rationality of Emotion*. Cambridge, MA: MIT Press.

de Waal, F., 1996. *Good Natured: The Origins of Right and Wrong in Humans and Other Animals*. Cambridge, MA: Harvard U. P.

Diamond, B. L., 1961-1962. "Criminal responsibility of the mentally ill," *Stanford Law Rev.*, 14:59-68.

Diamond, J., 1992. *The Third Chimpanzee: The Evolution and Future of the Human Animal*. New York: Harper/Collins.

DiCristina, B., 1995. *Method in Criminology: A Philosophical Primer*. New York: Harrow & Heston.

Diderot, D., 1752/1966. *Selected Writings*. L. G. Crocker, trans. & ed. New York: Macmillan.

Dietrich, M., 1961-1962. *Marlene Dietrich's ABC*. New York: Doubleday.

DiIulio, J. J., Jr., 1996. "My black crime problem, and ours," *City J.*, 6:14-28.

——, and A. M. Piehl., 1997. "What the crime statistics don't tell you," *Wall St. J.*, 136:A18 (Jan. 8).

Dobash, R. P. et al., 1992. "The myth of sexual symmetry in marital violence," *Soc. Problems*, 39:79-91.

Dohrenwend, D. R. et al., 1980. "Epidemiology and genetics of schizophrenia," *Soc. Bio.* 26:142-153.

Dooling, R., 1999. "What a niggling offense? Oops. We mean....," *Wall St. J.*, 140:A14 (Jan. 29).

Double, R., 1991. *The Non-Reality of Free Will*. New York: Oxford U. P.

——, 1997. *Metaphilosophy and Free Will*. New York: Oxford U. P.

Douglas, J. D., 1967. *The Social Meaning of Suicide*. Princeton, NJ: Princeton U. P.

Douglas, M., 1983. *Rules and Meanings*. Harmondsworth, UK: Penguin Books.

Drucker, P., 1987. Cited by Editors of *Fortune*, "Now hear this!" 115:16 (Aug. 31).

Duffy, M., 2000. "The world's next white pariah," *Spectator*, 284:14-15. (April 15).

Dugatkin, L, 1999. *Cheating Monkeys and Citizen Bees: The Nature of Cooperation in Animals and Humans*. New York: Free Press.

Dunbar, R., 1996. *Grooming, Gossip, and the Evolution of Language*. London: Faber.

Dunn, D. G., 1975. *Ponzi! The Boston Swindler*. New York: McGraw-Hill.

Durkheim, E., 1897/1951. *Suicide: A Study in Sociology*. Trans. by J. A. Spaulding and G. Simpson. New York: Free Press.

——, 1958. *The Rules of Sociological Method*. Trans. by S. Z. Solvay and J. H. Mueller. Glencoe, IL: Free Press.

Dworkin, R., 2001. *Sovereign Virtue*. Cambridge, MA: Harvard U. P.

Eaves, L. J., H. J. Eysenck, and N. G. Martin, 1989. *Genes, Culture, and Personality*. New York: Academic Press.

Eberstadt, N., 1998. "Prosperous paupers and affluent savages," *Society*, 35:393-401.

Eco, U., 1990. "Some paranoid readings," *Times Lit. Supp.*, 4552:694-706. (June 29).

Economist, 1982. "Spanners in the clockwork," 283:62-63 (April 17).

——, 1990. "Money and mayhem," 315:83 (April 21).

——, 1995a. "America and religion," 336:19-21 (July 8).

——, 1995b. "Urban crime: From Rio...." 337:37-38.

——, 1996. "Treating blood disease," 340:60.

——, 1997a. Policing for profit: Welcome to the new world of private security." 343:21-24.

——, 1997b. "Light on the shadows...look at the growth of the underground economy and think again about taxes." 343:63-64 (May 3).

——, 1997c. "Mexico: Criminal neglect." 345:56 (Nov. 1).

——, 1979d. "Canada." 345:55 (Nov. 15).

——, 1998a. "Giving the customer what he wants." 346:21-23 (Feb. 14).

——, 1998b. "When the shooting is child's play." 346:27 (March 28).

——, 1998c. "Blinded by the dark." 347:15 (April 4).

——, 1999. "German hyperinflation: Whose fault?" 353:92 (Dec. 31).

——, 2000a. "Child poverty." 355:57-58 (June 17).

——, 2000b. "Wall Street dreams: Lessons learned?" 356:79 (Sept. 2).

——, 2000c. "Just thanck Planck.: 357:88-89 (Dec. 9).

Edelman, G. M., 1987. *Neural Darwinism: The Theory of Neuronal Group Selection*. New York: Basic Books.

——, 1989. *The Remembered Present: A Biological Theory of Consciousness*. New York: Basic Books.

——, 1992. *Bright Air, Brilliant Fire: On the Matter of Mind*. New York: Basic Books.

——, and G. Tononi, 2000. *A Universe of Consciousness: How Matter Becomes Imagination*. New York: Basic Books.

Edwards, A. L., 1957. *The Social Desirability Variable in Personality Assessment and Research*. New York: Dryden.

Edwards, R., 1989. *Life Before Birth: Reflections on the Embryo Debate*. London: Hutchinson.

Eimas, P. D., 1985. "The perception of speech in early infancy," *Sci. Amer.*, 252:46-52.

Einhorn, H. J., 1986. "Accepting error to make less error," *J. Person. Assess.*, 50:387-395.

——, and R. M. Hogarth, 1978. "Confidence in judgment: Persistence of the illusion of validity," *Psych. Rev.*, 85:395-416.

——, and S. Schacht, 1977. "Decisions based on fallible clinical judgment." In M. F. Kaplan and S. Schwartz (eds.), *Human Judgment and Decision Processes in Applied Settings*. New York: Academic Press.

Einstein, A., 1931. "The world as I see it." *Forum and Century*. Reprinted, 1982, in his *Ideas and Opinions*. New York: Crown.

——, 1950. *Out of My Later Years*. New York: Wisdom Library.

——, 1962. In P. Michelmore, *Einstein: Profile of the Man*. New York: Dodd.

——, 1979. In H. Dukas and B. Hoffman, *Albert Einstein: The Human Side*. Princeton, NJ: Princeton U. P.

——, 1993. In R. Andrews (ed.), *The Columbia Dictionary of Quotations*. New York: Columbia U. P.

——, 1996. In A. Calaprice (ed.), *The Quotable Einstein*. Princeton, NJ: Princeton U. P.

Eisler, K. I., 2001. *Revenge of the Pequots*. New York: Simon & Schuster.

Eisner, R. A., 2000. "Abused accountants?" *Wall St. J.*, 142:A27 (Feb. 2).

Elliott, D. *et al.*, 1983. *The Prevalence and Incidence of Delinquent Behavior, 1926-1980*. Boulder, CO: The National Youth Survey. Project Report #25. Behavioral Research Institute.

Ellis, L., 1993. Preface to Vol. 1 of his (ed.), *Social Stratification and Socioeconomic Inequality*. Westport, CT: Praeger.

Elman, J. L., 1996. *Rethinking Innateness: A Connectionist Perspective on Development*. Cambridge, MA: MIT Press.

Emsley, C. and L. A. Knafla (eds.), 1995. *Crime History and Histories of Crime: Studies in the Historiography of Crime and Criminal Justice in Modern History*. Westport, CT: Greenwood.

Engerman, DC, 2001. "Foreword" to Crossman (ed.), *The God That Failed*. Reprint. New York: Columbia U. P.

Epstein, H., 1999. "Something happened," *NY Rev. Books*, 46:14-18 (Dec. 2).

Epstein, R. A., 1985. *Takings: Private Property and the Power of Eminent Domain*. Cambridge, MA: Harvard U. P.

——, 1995. *Simple Rules for a Complex World*. Cambridge, MA: Harvard U. P.

——, 1992. *Forbidden Grounds: The Case Against Employment Discrimination Laws*. Cambridge, MA: Harvard U. P.

Epstein, S., 1990. "Comment on the effects of aggregation across and within occasions on consistency, specificity, and reliability," *Methodika*, 4:95-100.

Eriksen, S. W., 1960. "Discrimination and learning without awareness: A methodological survey and evaluation," *Psychol. Rev.*, 67:279-300.

Etzioni, A., 1999a. "Identification cards in America," *Society*, 36:70-76.

Evans, J. L., 1968. *Affect and the Attribution of Causation*. MA. Dissertation. Edmonton, Canada: Univ. of Alberta, Dep't. of Sociology.

——, 1974. *Attribution Theory and Information Search*. Ph.D. dissertation. Edmonton, Canada: Univ. of Alberta, Dep't. of Sociology.

Evans, L., 1991. *Traffic Safety and the Driver*. New York: Van Nostrand Reinhold.

Fancher, R. E., Jr., 1965. "Explicit personality theories and accuracy in person perception," *J. Person.*, 34:252-261.

——, 1967. "Accuracy vs. validity in person perception," *J. Consult. Psychol.*, 31:264-269.

Farber, D. A. and S. Sherry, 1997, *Beyond All Reason: The Radical Assault on Truth in American Law*.

Farberow, N. L., D. R. MacKinnon, F. L. Nelson, 1977. "Suicide: Who's counting?" *Pub. Health Reports*, 92:223-232.

Faris, R. E. L. (ed.), 1964. *Handbook of Modern Sociology*. Chicago: Rand McNally.

Farrington, D., 1973. "Self-reports of deviant behavior: Predictive and stable?" *J. Crim. Law & Crim.*, 64:99-110.

——, et al., 1996. "Self-reported delinquency and a combined delinquency seriousness scale used on boys, mothers, and teachers: Concurrent and predictive validity for African-Americans and Caucasians," *Criminology*, 34:493-517.

Faust, D., 1984. *The Limits of Scientific Reasoning*. Minneapolis: U. Minnesota Press.

——, 1991. "What if we had really listened?" In D. Cicchetti and W. M. Grove (eds.), *Thinking Clearly About Psychology: Essays in Honor of Paul E. Meehl*. Vol. 1. Minneapolis: U. Minnesota Press.

Fay, M. T., M. Morrissey, M. Smyth, 2000. *Northern Ireland's Troubles: The Human Costs*. London: Pluto Press.

Feige, E., 1980. *A New Perspective on Macroeconomic Phenomena: The Theory and Measurement of the Unobserved Sector of the United States Economy: Causes, Consequences, and Implications.* Madison: Department of Economics, Univ. of Wisconsin.

Feldstein, M., 1981. "Retreat from Keynesian economics," *Pub. Interest*, 64:92-105.

——, 1999. "Reducing poverty, not inequality," *Pub. Interest*, 137:33-41.

Feller, W., 1957. *An Introduction to Probability Theory and Its Applications.* 2 vols. 2/e. New York: Wiley.

Fendrich, M. and C. M. Vaughn, 1994a. "Diminished lifetime substance use over time: An inquiry into differential underreporting," *Pub. Opin. Quart.*, 58:96-123.

——, and V. Warner, 1994b. "Symptom and substance use reporting consistency over two years for offspring of high and low risk for depression." *J. Child Psychol.*, 22:425-439.

——, and Y. Xu, 1994c. "The validity of drug use reports from juvenile arrestees," *Inter. J. of the Addictions*, 29:971:985.

——, and M., Mackesy-Amiti, 1995. "Inconsistencies in lifetime cocaine and marijuana use reports: Impact on prevalence and incidence," *Addiction*, 90:111-118.

Ferber, R., 1966. *The Reliability of Consumer Reports of Financial Assets and Debts.* Urbana: U. Illinois Press.

Ferguson, N., 1998. *The Pity of War.* New York: Basic Books.

Festinger, L, 1956. *When Prophecy Fails.* Minneapolis: U. Minnesota Press.

Feuer, L. S., 1970. "Lenin's fantasy," *Encounter*, 35:22-35.

Feyerabend, P., 1987. *Farewell to Reason.* London: Verso.

Feynman, R. P., 1985. *Surely You're Joking, Mr. Feynman: Adventures of a Curious Character.* New York: Bantam.

——, 1988. *What Do YOU Care about What Other People Think?* New York: Norton.

Field, T. M. and N. A. Fox (eds.), *Social Perception in Infants.* Norwood, NJ: Ablex.

Finch, C. and T. B. J. Kirkwood, 2000. *Chance, Development, and Aging.* New York: Oxford U. P.

Fisher, J., 1959. "The twisted pear and the prediction of behavior," *J. Consult. Psych.*, 23:400-405.

——, *et al.*, 1955. "The Rorschach and central nervous system pathology: A cross-validation study," *Amer. J. Psychiat.*, 3:487-492.

——, and T. A. Gonda, 1955. "Neurologic techniques and Rorschach test in detecting brain pathology: A study of comparative validities," *AMA Arch. Neurol. Psychiat.*, 74:117-124.

Fisher, R. A., 1958. *Statistical Methods for Research Workers.* 13/e. New York: Hafner.

——, 1971. *The Design of Experiments.* 9/e. New York: Hafner.

——, 1974. *Collected Papers of R. A. Fisher.* Adelaide, Australia: Univ. of Adelaide.

Fiske, D. W., 1979. "Two worlds of psychological phenomena," *Amer. Psych.*, 34:733-739.

FitzGerald, C., 2000. "Godless criminality," *Spectator*, 284:29 (March 11).

Fitzpatrick, S., 1999. *Everyday Stalinism: Ordinary Life in Extraordinary Times: Soviet Russia in the 1930s.* New York: Oxford U. P.

Flanagan, O., 1991. *The Science of the Mind.* 2/e. Cambridge, MA: MIT Press.

Follman, J., 1984. "Cornucopia of correlations," *Amer. Psych.*, 40:701-702.

Foreman, J., 1997. "Bombay on the Hudson," *City J.*, 7:14-27.

——, 1998. "Toward a more civil society," *City J.*, 8:56-64.

Forst, B., 1984. "Selective incapacitation: A sheep in wolf's clothing," *Judicature*, 68:153-160.

Frankfurt, H. G., 1988. "On bullshit." In his *The Importance of What We Care About: Philosophical Essays.* New York: Cambridge U. P.

Freeman, D., 1983. *Margaret Mead and Samoa: The Making and Unmaking of an Anthropological Myth.* Cambridge, MA: Harvard U. P.

——, 1996. *Margaret Mead and the Heretic.* New York: Viking/Penguin.

——, 1998. "On the ethics of skeptical inquiry," *Skeptical Inquirer*, 60:21.

——, 1999a. *The Fateful Hoaxing of Margaret Mead: A Historical Analysis of Her Samoan Research.* Boulder, CO: Westview.

——, 1999b. "Margaret Mead in Samoa," *Science*, 285:49 (July 2).

——, 1999c. "Margaret Mead, Samoa, and the sexual revolution," *News Weekly*, 12:188. Sydney, Australia. (Aug. 14).

——, 2000. "Statement from Derek Freeman," *Newsletter*, Australian Anthrop. Soc., #79-80:36-37.

Freeman, R. B., and H. J. Holzer (eds.), 1986. *The Black Youth Unemployment Crisis.* Chicago: U. Chicago Press.

Frege, G., 1892/1964. *Über Sinn und Bedeutung.* Reprint, 1964. I. Angelelli (ed.), *Begriffschrift und Andere Aufsätze*, 2/e. Munchen: Lubrecht & Cramer.

——, 1972. Trans. By T. W. Bynum as *Conceptual Notation and Related Articles.* New York: Oxford U. P.

Freimuth, M., 1992. "Is the best always preferred?" *Amer. Psychol.*, 47:673 674.

Freud, S., 1958. *Civilization and Its Discontents.* Garden City, NY: Doubleday/Anchor.

Friedman, M., 1975a. *There Is No Such Thing as a Free Lunch.* LaSalle, IL: Open Court.

——, 1975b. *An Economist's Protest: Columns on Political Economy.* 2/e. Sun Lakes, AZ: Tomas Horton and daughters.

——, 1992. *Money Mischief: Episodes in Monetary History.* New York: Harcourt, Brace, Jovanovich.

——, and R. Friedman, 1980. *Free to Choose.* New York: Avon.

——, and ——, 1984. *Tyranny of the Status Quo.* New York: Harcourt, Brace, Jovanovich.

Friedrich, P., 1962. "Assumptions underlying Tarascan political homicide," *Psychiat.*, 25:315-327.

Fumento, M., 1999. "Science reporting under a microscope," *Wall St. J.*, 140:A16 (Feb. 24).

Furst, T. M., Jr., 1952. *Unifying Theory and Practice: The Pragmatic Program.* Doctoral candidacy paper. Los Angeles: U. Calif., Dept. of Pol. Sci.

Furth, H. G., 1966. *Thinking Without Language: Psychological Implications of Deafness.* New York: Free Press.

Gada, N., 1999. *Beyond the Handshake: Intentional Synchrony Effects on Job Interview Evaluation.* M.S. dissertation. Dept. of Psychology, Univ. of Toledo.

Garbacz, C., 1990. "Seat-belts don't necessarily save lives," *Commentary*: St. Louis Dispatch. (Oct. 30).

——, 1991. "Impact of the New Zealand seat-belt law," *Econ. Inquiry*, 29:310-316.

——, 1992a. "More evidence on the effectiveness of seat-belt laws," *Appl. Econ.*, 24:313-315.

——, 1992b. "Do front seat-belt laws put rear-seat passengers at risk?" *Pop. Res. & Policy Reviews*, #8872.

Gardner, B. T. and R. A. Gardner, 1985. "Signs of intelligence in cross-fostered chimpanzees." In L. Weiskrantz (ed.), *Animal Intelligence.* Oxford: Clarendon Press.

Garlick, M. A., 2001. "Save the earth: Delaying our planet's ultimate demise," *Sci. Amer.*, 284:240.

Garrett, J. W. and P. W. Braunstein, 1962. "The seat belt syndrome," *J. Traffic*, 2:220-237.

Garry, C. G. et al., 1996. "Confidence that it occurred," *Psychonomic Bull. & Rev.*, 3:208-214.

Garry, M. and D. L. L. Polaschek, 2000. "Imagination and memory," *Curr. Directions Psychol. Sci.*, 9:6-8.

Garside, W. R., 1981. *The Measurement of Unemployment: Methods and Sources in Great Britain*. Oxford: Blackwell.

Gay, P., 1993. *The Cultivation of Hatred: The Bourgeois Experience: Victoria to Freud*. New York: Norton.

Gazzaniga, M. S., 1985. *The Social Brain: Discovering Networks of the Mind*. New York: Basic Books.

Gearey, R., 1997. "A Capital Crime," *New Republic*. 216:12-13 (Jan., 20).

Gehlke, C. and R. Riehel, 1934. "Certain effects of grouping upon the size of the correlation coefficient in census tract material," *Jour. Amer. Stat. Assoc.*, Supp. #29:169-170.

——, 1973b. *Cause and Meaning in the Social Sciences*. London: Routledge & Kegan Paul.

——, 1979. *Spectacles and Predicaments: Essays in Social Theory*. Cambridge, UK: Cambridge U. P.

Getty, J. A., 2000. "Palaces on Monday," *London Rev. Books*, 22:23-27. (March 2).

Giere, R. N., 1984. *Understanding Scientific Reasoning*. 2/e. New York: Holt, Rinehart, Winston.

——, 1988. *Explaining Science: A Cognitive Approach*. Chicago: U. Chicago Press.

Gifford, R., C. Ng, M. Wilkinson, 1985. "Nonverbal cues in the employment interview: Links between qualities and interviewer judgments," *J. Appl. Psychol.*, 70:729-736.

Gillan, A., 1999. "What's the story?" *London Rev. Books*, 21:5-16 (May 27).

Gillispie, C. c., 1998. *Pierre-Simon Laplace, 1749-1827: A Life in Exact Science*. Princeton, NJ: Princeton U. P.

Gilovich, T., 1991. *How We Know What Isn't So*. New York: Macmillan.

Ginzberg, E., 1980. "Youth unemployment," *Sci. Amer.* 242-:43-49.

——, 1999. "Letter to editor," *Society*, 36:2.

Glass, G. V., B. McGaw, M. L. Smith, 1983. *Meta-Analysis in Social Research*. Beverly Hills, CA: Sage.

——, "The hard questions: Money isn't everything," *New Republic*, 216:29 (Mar. 3).

Gleick, J., 1987. *Chaos: Making a New Science*. New York: Viking.

Glymour, C., 1998. "What went wrong? Reflections on science by observation and *The Bell Curve*," *Phil. Sci.*, 65:1-32.

Godard, R., 1991. "Long-term memory of individual neighbors in a migratory songbird," *Nature*, 350:228-229.

Godfrey-Smith, P., 1998. *Complexity and the Function of Mind in Nature*. New York: Cambridge U. P.

Goethe, J. W. v., 1808/1987. *Faust*. F. D. Luke, trans. New York: Oxford U. P.

Goldberg, B., 2002. *Bias: A CBS Insider Exposes How the Media Distort the News*. Chicago: Regnery.

Goldberg, L. R., 1968. "Simple models or simple processes?: Some research on clinical judgments," *Amer. Psychol.*, 23:483-496.

——, 1970. "Man versus model of man: A rationale plus some evidence for a method of improving on clinical interference," *Psychol. Bull.*, 73:422-432.

——, 1991. "Human mind versus regression equation: Five contrasts." In D. Cicchetti and W. R. Grove (eds.), *Thinking Clearly About Psychology: Essays in Honor of Paul E. Meehl*. Vol. 1. Minneapolis: U. Minnesota Press.

——, and C. E. Werts, 1966. "The reliability of clinicians' judgments: A multitrait-multimethod approach," *J. Consult. Psychol.* 30:199-206.

Goldberg, S., 1987. "The reluctant embrace: Law and science in America," *Georgetown Law J.*, 75:1345.

——, 1993. *Why Men Rule: A Theory of Male Dominance*. La Salle, IL: Open Court.

Goldhagen, D. J., 1996a. *Hitler's Willing Executioners: Ordinary Germans and the Holocaust*. New York: Knopf.

——, "Motive, causes, and alibis," *New Republic*, 215:37-45 (Nov. 23).

Golding, W., 1959/1997. *Lord of the Flies*. New York: Viking/Penguin.

Goldsmith, D., 1995. *Einstein's Greatest Blunder: The Cosmological Constant and Other Fudge Factors in the Physics of the Universe*. Cambridge, MA: Harvard U. P.

Goldstein, K., 1995. *The Organism: A Holistic Approach to Biology Derived from Pathological Data in Man*. New York: Zone Books, reissue of original, 1963.

Gopnik, A., A. N. Meltzoff, P. KI. Kuhl, 1999. *The Scientist in the Crib: Minds, Brains, and How Children Learn*. New York: Morrow.

Gordievsky, O., 2000. "My country and I," *Spectator*, 287:47-50. (Dec. 16/23).

Gottfredson, DC, R. J. McNeill, and G. D. Gottfredson, 1991. "Social area influences on delinquency: A multi-level analysis," *Jour. Res. Crime & Delinq.*, 28:197-226.

——, and J. C. Sharf, 1988. "Fairness in employment testing," *Jour. Voc. Beh.*, 33:225-463.

——, 1997. "Why g matters: the complexity of everyday life," *Intelligence*, 34:79-132.

Gottfredson, S. D., 1986. "Statistical and actuarial considerations." In F. Dutile and C. Foust (eds.), *The Prediction of Criminal Violence*. Springfield, IL: Thomas.

——, 1987. "Prediction: An overview of selected methodological issues." In D. M. Gottfredson and M. Tonry (eds.), *Prediction and Classification: Criminal Justice Decision Making*. Chicago: U. of Chicago Press.

Gould, S. J., 1984. "Between you and your genes," *NY Rev. Books,* 31:30-32 (Aug. 16).

——, 1997. "Evolutionary psychology: An exchange," *NY Rev. Books*, 44:56-58 (Oct. 9).

Graber, D. M., 1989. "Mother Nature as a hothouse flower," *L. A. Times Book Review.* (Oct. 22).

Grady, C. L. et al., 1995. "Age-related reductions in human recognition memory due to impaired encoding," *Science*, 269:218-223 (July 14).

Grainger, R., 1980. *Unemployment and Crime: A Critique of Methodology*. Ottawa: Solicitor General, Canada.

Granberg, G. and S. Holmberg, 1991. "Self-reported turnout and voter validation," *Amer. J. Pol. Sci.*, 35:448-459.

Grant, J., 1992. *Money of the Mind*. New York: Farrar, Straus, Giroux.

Gratzer, W., 1997. "In the hands of any fool," *London Rev. Books*, 19:24 (July 3).

Gray, B., 1978. "The semiotics of taxonomy," *Semiotics*, 22:127-149.

Gray, J. A., 1971. "The mind-brain identity theory as a scientific hypothesis," *Phil. Quart.*, 21:247-252.

Green, A. and R. P. Wakefield, 1979. "Patterns of middle and upper-class homicide," *J. Crim. Law & Crim.*, 70:172-181.

Green, B. F., 1990. "Comprehensive assessment of measurement," *Contemp. Psychol.*, 38:850-851.

Greenberg, G., 2001. "As good as dead," *New Yorker*, 36-41. (Aug. 13).

Greenberg, M., 1995. "What connects thought and action?" *Times Lit. Supp.*, #4812:7-8 (June 23).

Greenwood, J. B. (ed.), 1991. *The Future of Folk Psychology: Intentionality and Cognitive Science*. New York: Cambridge U. P.

Grenier, R., 1984. "The hard left and the soft," *Commentary*, 77:56-61.

Griffin, D. R., 1976. *The Question of Animal Awareness*. New York: Rockefeller U. P.

——, 2000. *Animal Minds*. Chicago: U. Chicago Press.

Grimond, J., 2001. "Africa's great black hope," *the Economist Supplement*, "South Africa." 258 (Feb. 24).

Groopman, J., 1998. "Decoding destiny," *New Yorker*, 73:42-47 (Feb. 9).

——, "Second opinion," *New Yorker*, 75:40-49 (Jan. 24).

Grossman, D., 1995. *On Killing*. Boston: Little, Brown.

Grove, W. M. and P. E. Meehl, 1996. "Comparative efficiency of informal (subjective, impressionistic) and formal (mechanical, algorithmic) prediction procedures: The clinical-statistical controversy," *Psychol., Pub. Policy, and Law*, 2:293-323.

Groves, R. M., N. H. Fultz, and E. Martin, 1994. "Direct questioning about comprehension in a survey setting." In J. M. Tanur (ed.), *Questions about Questions: Inquiries into the Cognitive Bases of Surveys*. New York: Russell Sage Foundation.

Grünbaum, A., 1993. *Validation in the Clinical Theory of Psychoanalysis: A Study in the Philosophy of Psychoanalysis*. Madison, CT: International Universities Press.

Guion, R. M., 1976. "Recruiting, selection, and job placement." In M. D. Dunnette (ed.), *Handbook of Industrial and Organizational Psychology*. Chicago: Rand McNally.

Gullberg, J., 1992. *Mathematics: From the Birth of Numbers*. New York: Norton.

Gupta, K. L., 1969. *Aggregation in Economics: A Theoretical and Empirical Study*. Rotterdam: Rotterdam U. P.

Gur, R. C. and H. A. Sackeim, 1979. "Self-deception: A concept in search of a phenomenon?" *Jour. Person. Soc. Psychol.*, 37:147-169.

Gurstein, R., 1996. *The Repeal of Reticence*. New York: Hill & Wang.

Gutin, J. C., 1994. "The end of the rainbow," *Discover*, 15:70-75.

Guttman, L., 1976. "What is not what in statistics," Reprinted 1981 in I. Borg (ed.), *Multidimensional Data Representations: When & Why*. Ann Arbor, MI: Mathesis Press.

——, 1977. "What is not what in theory construction." Reprinted 1981 in I. Borg (ed.), *Multidimensional Data Representations: When & Why*. Ann Arbor, MI: Mathesis Press.

Haber, R. N., 1970. "How we remember what we see," *Sci. Amer.*, 222:104-112.

Hacking, I., 1990. *The Taming of Chance*. Cambridge, UK: Cambridge U. P.

——, 1995. *Rewriting the Soul: Multiple Personality and the Sciences of Memory*. Princeton, NJ: Princeton U. P.

——, 2001. *An Introduction to Probability and Inductive Logic*. New York: Cambridge U. P.

Haeckel, R. H., 1867/1991. *Naturliche Schöpfungsgesichte*. Trans. J. McCabe, 1991. *The Riddle of the Universe*. Buffalo, NY: Prometheus Books.

Häfliger, T., 2000. "Godless criminality," *Spectator*, 284-:29 (Mar. 11).

Hagan, J. et al., 1989. *Structural Criminology*. New Brunswick, NJ: Rutgers U. P.

——, and R. D. Peterson (eds.), 1995. *Crime and Inequality*. Stanford, CA: Stanford U. P.

Hahn, R. A., 1999. "Expectations of sickness: Concept and evidence of the nocebo phenomenon." In I. Kirsch (ed.), *How Expectations Shape Experience*. Washington, DC: Amer. Psychol. Assoc.

Halkin, H., 2000. "Intifada II: Israel's nightmare," *Commentary*, 110:44-48.

Hall, J., 1947. *General Principles of Criminal Law*. 2/e. Indianapolis, IN: Bobbs-Merrill.

Hamilton, R. F., 1996. *The Social Misconstruction of Reality: Validity and Verification in the Scholarly Community*. New Haven, CT: Yale.

Hammond, J. L., 1973. "Two sources of error in ecological correlations," *Amer. Sociol. Rev.*, 38:764-777.

Hammond, K. R., 1996. *Human Judgment and Social Policy: Irreducible Uncertainty, Inevitable Error, Unavoidable Injustice.* New York: Oxford U. P.

Hankins, T. L., 2000. "Blood, dirt, and nomograms," *Chance*, 13:26-37.

Hannan, M. T., 1971. *Aggregation and Disaggregation in Sociology.* Lexington, MA: Lexington.

Hardin, G., 1972. *Exploring New Ethics for Survival: The Voyage of the Spaceship Beagle.* New York: Viking.

——, 1985. *Filters Against Folly: How to Survive Despite Economists, Ecologists, and the Merely Eloquent.* New York: Penguin.

Harding, L., D. Leigh, and D. Pallister, 1997. *The Liar: The Fall of Jonathan Aitken*, London, U. K.: Penguin.

Harding, L. W., 1948. "Experimental comparisons between generalizations and problems as indices of value," *Jour. Gen. Psychol.*, 38:31-50.

Harper's Index, 1996. "U. S. intelligence agencies spending on psychics," *Harper's*, 292:11.

Harrington, A. (ed.), 1999. *The Placebo Effect: An Interdisciplinary Exploration.* Cambridge, MA: Harvard U. P.

Harris, J. R., 1998. *The Nurture Assumption: Why Children Turn Out the Way They Do.* New York: Free Press.

Hart, H. L. A., 1965. *The Morality of the Criminal Law.* London: Oxford U. P.

——, and A. M Honoré, 1959. *Causation and the Law.* Oxford: Clarendon Press.

Hartigan, J. A. and A. K. Wigdor (eds.), 1989. *Fairness in Employment Testing: Validity, Generalization, Minority Issues, and the General Aptitude Test Battery.* Washington, DC: National Academy Press.

Hartshorne, C. and M. A. May, 1928-1930. *Studies in the Nature of Character.* 3 Vols. New York: Macmillan.

Harwood, J. and C. Crossen, 2000. "Head counting: Why many new polls put different spins on presidential race," *Wall St. J.*, 236:A1, A8 (Sept. 29).

Hausman, D. M., 1998. "Problems with realism in economics," *Econ. And Phil.*, 14:185-213.

Hawley, A., 1950. *Human Ecology: A Theory of Community Structures.* New York: Ronald.

Hawthorn, G., 1989. "Informals of the world unite," *London Rev. Books*, 11:8-9 (Sept. 8).

Hayes, B., 2000. "Graph theory in practice: Part II," *Amer. Sci.*, 88:104-190.

——, 2002. "Statistics of deadly quarrels," *Amer. Sci.*, 90:10-15.

Health and Human Services, USA, 1996. *The National Survey on Drug Abuse and the Drug Abuse Warning Network Report.* Washington, DC: Dept. of Health and Human Services.

Hearne, V., 1987. *Adam's Task: Calling Animals by Name.* London: Heinemann.

Heath, A. F., R. Breen, C. T. Whelan, 2000. *Ireland North and South: Perspectives from Social Science.* London: Oxford U. P.

Hebb, D., 1980. *Essay on Mind.* Hillsdale, NJ: Erlbaum.

Heertje, A., Ied.), 1982. *Schumpeter's Vision: Capitalism, Socialism, and Democracy after 40 Years.* Eastbourne, UK: Praeger/Holt-Saunders.

Heine, J., 1847/1982. *Zum Lazarus.* In *The Complete Poems.* Hal Draper, trans., Munich: Suhr Verlag.

Hempel, C. G., 1952. *Fundamentals of Concept Formation in Empirical Science.* Chicago: U. Chicago Press.

Henderson, D. R., 1996. "If Quebec separates, almost everybody wins," *Wall St. J.*, 134:A9 (Jan. 19).

Hetherington, M. and S. E. Feldman, 1964. "College cheating as a function of subject and situational variables." Unpublished study, cited by L. Berkowitz, *The Development of Motive and Values in the Child*, p. 87. New York: Basic Books.

Hibbert, C., 1997. *Wellington: A Personal History*. Reading, MA: Addison-Wesley.

Highfield, R. and P. Carter, 1994. *The Private Lives of Albert Einstein*. New York: St. Martin's Press.

Hindelang, M. J., T. Hirschi, and J. G. Weis, 1981. *Measuring Delinquency*. Beverly Hills, CA: Sage.

Hirt, E. R. et al., 1999. "Expectancies and memory: Inferring the past from what must have been." In I. Kirsch (ed.), *How Expectancies Shape Experience*. Washington, DC: Amer. Psychol. Assoc.

Hobbes, T., 1651/1994. *Leviathan*. Reprint, 1994, K. Minogue (ed.). Boston: Tuttle.

Hockett, C. F., 1968. *The State of the Art*. The Hague: Mouton.

——, 1973. *Man's Place in Nature*. New York: McGraw-Hill.

Hoffman, D. D., 1983. "The interpretation of visual illusions," *Sci. Amer.*, 249:154-162.

Hogarth, R. M., 1987. *Judgement and Choice*. 2/e. New York: Wiley.

——, and M. W. Reder (eds.), 1987. *Rational Choice: the Contrast Between Economics and Psychology*. Chicago: U. Chicago Press.

Hogben, L., n.d., ca. 1957. *Statistical Theory: The Relationship of Probability, Credibility, and Error.* New York: Norton.

Holden, C., 1991. "New center to study therapies and ethnicity," *Science*, 251:748 (Feb. 15).

——, 1995. "Jewish breast cancer gene?" *Science*. 269:1819 (Sept. 29).

——, 1996. "Wiley drops IQ book after public furor," *Science*, 272:644 (May 3).

Holland, B., 1995. "Do you swear that you will well and truly tell...?" *Smithsonian*, 25:108-117.

Holmes, O. W., Jr., 1881/1991, *The Common Law*. Reprint 1991 by Dover, New York.

——, 1921/1991. "Natural law," in R. A. Posner (ed.), 1991. *The Essential Holmes*. Chicago: U. Chicago Press.

——, 1926. Unpublished letter (Aug. 5) collected by his biographer, Mark DeWolfe Howe, and reprinted in Edmund Wilson, *Patriotic Gore: Studies in the Literature of the American Civil War*. New York: Oxford, 1962.

——, 1931. Radio address on his 90th birthday, (March 8.).

Homans, G. C., 1984. *Coming to My Senses: The Autobiography of a Sociologist*. New Brunswick, NJ: Transaction.

Honderich, T., 1989. *Violence for Equality: Inquiries in Political Philosophy*. New York: Routledge.

Hood, B. M. et al., 1996. "Habituation changes in early infancy: Longitudinal measures form birth to 6 months," *J. Repro. & Infancy Psychol.*, 14:177-185.

Hook, E. B., 1996. "Affirmative action," *Science*, 272:336-337.

Hook, S. 1962. *From Hegel to Marx: Studies in the Intellectual Development of Karl Marx*. Ann Arbor: U. Michigan Press.

——, 1975. *Revolution, Reform, and Social Justice: Studies in the Theory and Practice of Marxism*. New York: New York U. P.

——, 1982. *Marx and Marxists: the Ambiguous Legacy*. New York: Krieger.

——, 1984. "Memories of the Moscow trials," *Commentary*, 77:57-63.

——, 1987. *Out of Step: An Unquiet Life in the 20th Century*. New York: Harper and Row.

Hooper, E., 1999. *The River: A Journey to the Source of HIV and AIDS*. Boston: Little, Brown.

Horgan, J., 1993. "A splendid anachronism," *Sci. Amer.*, 169:94.

——, 1995. *The End of Science: Facing the Limits of Knowledge in the Twilight of the Scientific Age*. Reading, MA: Addison-Wesley.

Horowitz, I. L., 1993. *The Decomposition of Sociology*. New York: Oxford U. P.

——, 2000. "Whose handmaiden?" *Times Lit. Supp.*, 5056:28-29 (March 10).

Horton, R., 1999. "Secret society: Scientific peer review and Pusztai's potatoes," *Times Lit. Supp.*, #5046:8-9 (Dec. 17).

——, 2000a. "In the danger zone," *NY Rev. Books*, 47:30-34 (Aug. 10).

——, 2000b. "How sick is modern medicine?" *NY Rev. Books*, 47:46-50 (Nov. 2).

Howard, M., 1996. *The Crisis in Anglo-German Antagonism, 1916-1917*. London:

——, 1998. "Out of the trenches," *Times Lit. Supp.*, #4989:3-4 (Nov. 13).

——, 2001. "The Great War: Mystery or error?" *Nat. Interest*, 64:78-84.

Howson, C., 1997. "Logic and probability," *Brit. J. Phil. Sci.*, 48:517-531.

Huber, P. W., 1988. *Litigation: The Legal Revolution and Its Consequences*. New York: Basic Books.

——, 1991. *Galileo's Revenge: Junk Science in the Courtroom*. New York: Basic Books.

——, and R. E. Litan, 1991. *The Liability Maze: The Impact of Liability Law on Safety and Innovation*. Washington, DC: the Brookings Institution.

Huelke, D. F., 1987. "Seat-belt effectiveness: Case examples from real-world crash investigations. *J. Trauma*, 27:750-753.

——, et al., 1987. "Effectiveness of current and future restraint systems in fatal and serious injury automobile crashes. *SAE paper #790323*. Warrendale, PA: Society of Automotive Engineers.

Huizinga, D. and D. S. Elliott, 1986. "Reassessing the reliability and validity of self-report measures," *J. Quant. Crim.*, 2:293-327.

Hume, D., 1739-1740/1978. *Treatise of Human Nature*. L. A. Selby-Bigge and F. H. Nidditch (eds.). New York: Oxford U. P.

——, 1751-1757/1999. *Enquiry Concerning Human Understanding*. T. L. Beauchamp (ed.). New York: Oxford U. P.

Hunter, G. P. and R. F. Hunter, 1984. "Validity and utility of alternative predictors of job performance," *Psychol. Bul.*, 96:72-98.

——, F. L. Schmidt, and M. K. Judeisch, 1990. "Individual differences in output as a function of job complexity," *J. Appl. Psychol.*, 78:28-42.

Huntington, M., 1997. *The Warrior's Honor*. New York: Metropolitan Books.

Husek, T. R., 1961. "Acquiescence as a response set and as a personality characteristic," *Educ. Psychol. Meas.*, 21:295-307.

Hutchins, D., 1987. "Dennis Levine: Where the scam faltered," *Fortune*, 115:49-50 (Jan. 3).

Hutchison, T. W., 1977. *Knowledge and Ignorance in Economics*. Chicago: U. Chicago Press.

Huxley, A., 1932. *Brave New World*. London: Chatto & Windus. Reprinted 1942, New York: Harper.

Insley, S. J., 2000. "Long-term vocal recognition in the northern fur seal," *Nature*, 406:404-4-6.

International Labour Office, 1966. *Year Book of Labour Statistics*, 25th issue. Geneva: The Office.

——, 1971. *Year Book of Labour Statistics*. 31st issue. Geneva: The Office.

Iversen, G. R. and M. Gergen, 1997. *Statistics: The Conceptual Approach.* New York: Springer-Verlag.

Jackman, M. E. and M. S. Senter, 1980. "Images of social groups: Categorical or qualified?" *Pub. Opin. Quart.*, 44:341-361.

Jackson, J. S., L. M. Chatters, and H. W. Neighbors, 1986. "The subjective life quality of black Americans," In F. M. Andrews (ed.), *Research on the Quality of Life.* Ann Arbor, MI: Institute for Social Research.

Jackson, P. G., 1988. "Assessing the validity of official data on arson," *Criminology*, 26:181-195.

James, W., 1890. *Principles of Psychology.* New York: Dover.

——, 1906. *Pragmatism: A New Name for Some Old Ways of Thinking.* Reprinted in B. Kuklick (ed.), 1987. *Williams James: Writings 1902-1910.* New York: Library of America.

Jammer, M., 1999. *Einstein and Religion: Physics and Theology.* Princeton, NJ: Princeton U. P.

——, 1975. "Cultural relativism again," *Phil. Soc. Sci.*, 5:343-353.

Jasanoff, S., 1997. *Science at the Bar: Law, Science, and Technology.* Cambridge, MA: Harvard U. P.

Jastram, R., 1977. *The Golden Constant.* New York: Wiley.

Jencks, C., 1985. "How poor are the poor?" *NY Rev. Books*, 32:41-49.

——, 1987. "The politics of income measurement." In W. Alonso and P. Starr (eds.), *The Politics of Numbers.* New York: Russell Sage Foundation.

——, 1994. "The homeless," *NY Rev. Books*, 41:20-27 (April 21).

——, and P. W. Peterson (eds.), 1991. *The Urban Underclass.* Washington, DC: The Brookings Institution.

Jerome, L. E., 1977. *Astrology Disproved.* Buffalo, NY: Prometheus Books.

——, 1981. "Eysenck's astrology," *Encounter*, 56:103-104.

Johnson, C. E., Jr., 1974. *Consistency of Reporting of Ethnic Origin in the Current Population Survey.* Washington, DC: U. S. Bureau of the Census Technical Paper #31.

Jones, P., 2000. "Ancient and modern," *Spectator*, 284:18 (May 27).

——, 2001. "Ancient and modern," *Spectator*, 286:23 (Jan. 20).

Jones, S., 1999. *Almost Like a Whale: The Origin of Species Updated.* New York: Doubleday.

Jordan, P., 1933/1974. *Science and the Course of History.* Ralph Manheim, trans., Westport, CT: Greenwood Press.

Kagan, D., 1995. *On the Origins of War and the Preservation of Peace.* New York: Doubleday.

Kagan, J., 1988. "The meanings of personality predicates," *Amer. Psychol.*, 43:614-620.

——, 1994. *Galen's Prophecy: Temperament in Human Nature.* New York: Basic Books.

Kahneman, D., P. Slovic, A. Tversky, 1982. *Judgment under Uncertainty.* New York: Cambridge U. P.

Kalow, W. and H. Kalant, 1997. "Evolutionary psychology: An exchange," *NY Rev. Books*, 44:56 (Oct. 9).

Kamen, A., 1994. "For Gore, It's all in the translation," *Washington Post*, Section 1:A13 (Jan. 10).

Kant, I., 1790/1990. *The Critique of Pure Reason.* Reprint, 1990. Buffalo, NY: Prometheus Books.

Karsh, E., 2000. "Intifida II: the long trail of Arab anti-Semitism," *Commentary*, 110:49-53.

Kassin, S. M. and K. L. Kiechel, 1996. "The social psychology of false confessions: Compliance, internalization, and confabulation," *Psychol. Sci.*, 7:125-128.

Kauffman, S. A., 1993. *Origins of Order: Self-Organization and Selection in Evolution.* London: Oxford U. P.

——, 1995. *At Home in the Universe: The Search for the Laws of Self-Organization and Complexity.* New York: Oxford U. P.

Kazincigil, A. and D. Makinson (eds.), 1999. *World Social Science Report, 1999.* Paris: UNESCO Publishing.

Keegan, J., 1993. *A History of Warfare.* New York: Knopf.

Keeley, J., 1971. *The Left-Leaning Antenna: Political Bias in Television.* New Rochelle, NY: Arlington House.

Keeley, L. H., 1996. *War Before Civilization: The Myth of the Peaceful Savage.* New York: Oxford U. P.

Kelly, I., 1979. "Astrology and science: A critical examination," *Psychol. Reports*, 44:1231-1240.

Kelly, R., 1999. "Is civilization the only value?" *Times Lit. Supp.*, 5045:27 (Dec. 10).

Kelner, K. and J. Benditt (eds.), 1994. "A special report: Genes and behavior," *Science*, 264:1685-1739 (June 17).

Kenner, H., 1980. "To die in Deseret," *Nat. Rev.*, 32:230-231 (Feb. 12).

Kennickell, A. B., 1997. Staff researcher, Federal Reserve Board, cited by Wessel, 1997, q.v.

——, and D. A. McManus, 1993. "Sampling for household financial characteristics using information on past income." In American Statistical Association, *1993 Proceedings* of the Section on Survey Research Methods. Vol. I.

Keyfitz, N., 1987. "The social and political context of population forecasting." In W. Alonzo and P. Starr (eds.), *The Politics of Numbers.* New York: Russell Sage Foundation.

Kim, J., 1999a. "Making sense of emergence," *Phil. Studies*, 95:3-36.

——, 1999b. *Mind in a Physical World.* Cambridge, MA: MIT Press.

Kiple, K. F. and K. C. Ornelas (eds.), 2000. *The Cambridge World History of Food.* 2 vols. Cambridge, U. K.: Cambridge U. P.

Kirsch, I. (ed.), 1999. *How Expectancies Shape Experience.* Washington, DC: Amer. Psychol. Assoc.

Kleinmuntz, B., 1991. "Recent developments in computerized clinical judgment." In D. Cicchetti and W. M. Grove (eds.), *Thinking Clearly About Psychology: Essays in Honor of Paul E. Meehl.* Vol. 1. Minneapolis: U. Minnesota Press.

Koestler, A., 1941. *Darkness at Noon.* New York: Macmillan.

——, 1945a. "The yogi and the commissar." In his *The Yogi and the Commissar and Other Essays.* New York: Macmillan.

——, 1945b. "Anatomy of a myth." In his *The Yogi and the Commissar.* New York: Macmillan.

——, 1982. Suicide Note. Cited by G. Steiner, "Le Morte d'Arthur," *New Yorker*, 60:121-124. (June 11).

Kolata, G., 1986. "What does it mean to be random?" *Science*, 231:1068-1070 (Mar. 7).

Kolodny, A., 1999. *Failing the Future: A Dean Looks at Higher Education in the Twenty-First Century.* Durham, NC: Duke U. P.

Kontorovich, E. V., 1995. "Business owner or race inquisitor?" *Wall St. J.*, 133:A14 (Dec. 1).

Krosnick, J. A., 1999. "Survey research," *Ann. Rev. Psychol.*, 50:537-567.

Kruskal, W. H., (ed.), 1982. *The Social Sciences: Their Nature and Uses.* Chicago: U. Chicago Press.

Kulish, N., 2001a. "Wrong pigeonhole? Chaldeans, Assyrians, are vexed with census," *Wall St. J.*, 237:A1, A10 (March 12).

——, 2001b. "Population of Asian-Americans surges, 1 of 4 persons is minority, census shows," *Wall St. J.*, 237:A28 (March 13).

Kummer, R. and J. Goodall, 1985. "Social and non-social knowledge in vervet monkeys." In L. Weiskrantz (ed.), *Animal Intelligence*. Oxford: Clarendon Press.

Kun, A., 1978. "Evidence for preschoolers' understanding of causal direction in extended causal sequences," *Child Develop.*,49:218-222.

Kuyken, W. et al., 1995. "The World Health Organization Quality of Life (WHOQOL) position paper from the World Health Organization," *Soc. Sci. Med.*, 41:1403-1409.

Kyburg, H. P., Jr., 1987. "Probabilistic metaphysics," *J. Phil.*, 84:45-49.

Ladd, E. C., 1995. "The Clinton-Dole polls," *Weekly Standard*, 1:14-15 (Dec. 25).

——, and G. B. Ferree, Jr., 1982. "The politics of an American theology faculty," *This World*, 2:6-13.

Ladd, J., 1957. *The Structure of a Moral Code: A Philosophical Analysis of Ethical Discourse Applied to the Ethics of the Navaho Indians.* Cambridge, MA: Harvard U. P.

Lambro, D., 1986. *Land of Opportunity: The Entrepreneurial Spirit in America.* Boston: Little, Brown.

Lao Tzu, 1973. *The Canon of Reason and Virtue.* P. Carus and D. T. Suzuki (eds.). LaSalle, IL: Open Court.

Laplace, P. S., 1814/1994. 1796. *Exposition de System du Monde.* Paris: Gaillard.

——, 1994. *Philosophical Essays on Probability.* G. J. Toomer (ed.). Trans. By A. J. Dale. New York: Springer-Verlag.

La Rochefoucauld, F., Duc de, 1678/1961. *Sentences et Maximes Morales*, #89. Reprint, 1961. Paris: Garniere Freres.

Lasky, M. J., 1976. *Utopia and Revolution.* Chicago: U. Chicago Press.

Lassalle, F., 1919-1920. *Gesammelte Reden und Schriften.* E. Bernstein (ed.) 12 vols. Berlin.

Laumann, E. O. et al., 1995. *The Social Organization of Sexuality.* Chicago: U. of Chicago Press.

——, 1995. With Gina Kolata, an abbreviated version published as *Sex in America: A Definitive Survey.* Boston: Little, Brown.

Lean, J. and D. Rind, 2001. "Earth's response to a variable sun," *Science*, 292:234-236. (April 13).

Le Fanu, J., 1999. *The Rise and Fall of Modern Medicine.* New York: Carroll and Graf.

Lenin, V. I., 1902/1969. *What Is to Be Done? Burning Questions of the Moment.* J. S. Allen (ed.), New York: International Publishers.

Lenski, G. and J. Leggett, 1960. "Case, class, and difference in the research interview," *Amer. J. Sociol.*, 65:463-467.

Leslie, A. M., 1982. "The perception of causality in infants," *Perception*, 11:173-186.

——, 1986. "Getting development off the ground." In P. L. C. von Geert (ed.), *Theory Building in Developmental Psychology.* Amsterdam: Elsevier Science.

——, 1987. "Pretense and representation: The origins of 'theory of mind,'" *Psych. Rev.*, 94:412-426.

——, and S. Keeble, 1987. "Do six-month-old infants perceive causality?" *Cognition*, 25:265-288.

Letwin, O., 1999. *The Purpose of Politics.* London: Social Market Foundation.

Levine, A., 1995. "Fairness to idleness: Is there a right not to work?" *Econ. and Phil.*, 11:255-274.

Levine, E. and A. Basilevsky, 1990. "In-vehicle fatalities, seat belts, and compulsory seat-belt legislation: The Manitoba experience," *Soc. Indicators Res.*, 22:287-297.

——, 1992. "Isolating the seat belt virus: In-vehicle automotive seat belt use: Assembly and initial examination of a multi-source counterfactual data base." Washington, D.C.: Transportation Res. Board and Nat. Res. Council, Pre-print #920665 (Jan. 14).

——, 1993. "Canadian seat belt research," (April 1).

Levine, E. et al., 1999. "Determinants of driver fatality risk in front impact fixed object collisions," *Mature Medicine*, 2:239-242.

Levitt, J. L., 2000. "The truth about implant study," *Wall St. J.*, 236:A31 (Oct. 30).

Lewin, R., 1984. "Practice catches theory in kin recognition: Burgeoning laboratory and field studies are beginning to focus on the mechanisms by which even the lowliest animals recognize their kind," *Science*, 223:1049-1051.

Lewinsohn, P. M. and M. Rosenbaum, 1987. "Recall of parental behavior by acute depressives, remitted depressives, and nondepressives," *J. Person. Soc. Psychol.*, 52:611-621.

Lewis, C. I., 1929/1956. *Mind and the World Order: Outline of a Theory of Knowledge*. New York: Dover.

——, 1946/1962. *An Analysis of Knowledge and Valuation*. La Salle, IL: Open Court.

Lewis, I. and W. Schneider, 1982. "Is the public lying to the pollsters?" *Pub. Opin.*, 5:42-47.

Lewontin, R. C., 1995. "Sex, lies, and social science," *NY Rev. Books*, 42:24-29 (April 20).

——, 1997. "Letter to editor," *NY Rev. Books*, 44:51 (March 6.)

——, 2000. *It Ain't Necessarily So: The Dream of the Human Genome and Other Illusions*. New York: NY Rev. Books.

——, S. Rose, L. J. Kamin, 1984. *Not in Our Genes: Biology, Ideology, and Human Nature*. New York: Pantheon.

Lichtenberg, G. C., 1765-1799. My paraphrase from one of his aphorisms cited by R. Andrews (ed.), *Columbia Dictionary of Quotations*, 1993, p. 287:#17. New York: Columbia U. P.

Lichter, S. R. and S. Rothman, 1984. "Media and business elites," *Pub. Opin.*, 4:42-46, 59-60.

——, 1982. 'Media and business elites: Two classes in conflict?" *Pub. Interest.*, 69:117-125.

——, 1984. "Watching the media watchdog," *Pub. Opin.*, 7:19-20, 59-60.

——, 1999. *Environmental Cancer: A Political Disease?* New Haven, CT: Yale.

Lichtheim, G., 1967. *The Concept of Ideology*. New York: Random House.

Lilla, M., 1999. "The perils of friendship," *NY Rev. Books*, 46:25-29 (Dec. 2).

——, 2001a. *The Reckless Mind: Intellectuals and Politics*. New York: NY Rev. of Books.

——, 2001b. The lure of Syracuse," *NY Rev. Books*, 48:81-86.

Lindbergh, A. M., 1940. *The Wave of the Future*. New York: Harcourt, Brace.

Lindemann, A. S., 1997. *Esau's Tears: Modern Anti-Semitism and the Rise of the Jews*. New York: Cambridge U. P.

Lindesmith, A. R. and A. L. Strauss, 1956. *Social Psychology*. New York: Holt, Rinehart, Winston.

Lindh, A. G., 1992. Personal correspondence (Oct. 22 and 30).

Lindsay, D. S. and J. D. Read, 1995. "'Memory work' and recovered memories of childhood sexual abuse: Scientific evidence and public, professional, and personal issues." In G. L. Wells (ed.), Special issue of *Psychology, Public Policy, and Law*. 1:#4 (Dec.).

Lipset, S. M. and E. Raab, 1995. *Jews and the New American Scene*. Cambridge, MA: Harvard U. P.

Lockard, J. and D. Paulhus (eds.), 1988. *Self-Deception: An Adaptive Mechanism?* Englewood Cliffs, NJ: Prentice-Hall.

Loehlin, J. C. 1989. "Partitioning environmental and genetic contributions to behavioral development," *Amer. Psychol.*, 44:1285-1292.

——, J. M. Horn, and L. Willerman, 1997. "Heredity, environment, and IQ in the Texas Adoption Project." In R. J. Sternberg, and E. Grigorenko (eds.), *Intelligence, Heredity, and Environment.* New York: Cambridge U. P.

Loftus, E. F., 1997. "Creating false memories," *Sci. Amer.*, 277:70-75.

Lohse, D. and M. Pacelle, 1999. "The case of the vanishing manager and missing millions," *Wall St. J.*, 140:C1, C6 (June 21).

Lord, W., 1955. *A Night to Remember.* New York: Bantam Books.

Lowenstein, R., 2000. *When Genius Failed: The Rise and Fall of Long-Term Capital Management.* New York: Random House.

Luce, E. D. and L. Narens, 1987. "Measurement scales on the continuum," *Science*, 236:1527-1532.

Lukacs, J., 1997. *The Hitler of History.* New York: Knopf.

Lundberg, G. A., 1961. *Can Science Save Us?* New York: Longman, Green.

Lydon, J. E., D. W. Jamieson, M. P. Zanna, 1988. "Interpersonal similarity and the social and intellectual dimensions of first impressions," *Soc. Cognition*, 6:269-286.

Lykken, D. T., 1981. *A Tremor in the Blood: Uses and Abuses of the Lie Detector.* New York: McGraw-Hill.

——, 1982. "Research with twins: The concept of emergenesis," *Psychophysiology*, 19:361-373.

——, 1987. "Genes and the mind," *the Harvard Med. School Mental Health Letter*, 4:4-8.

——, 1991. "What's wrong with psychology anyway?" In D. Cicchetti and W. M. Grove (eds.), *Thinking Clearly About Psychology: Essays in Honor of Paul E. Meehl.* Minneapolis: U. Minnesota Press.

——, et al., 1992. "Emergenesis: Genetic traits that may not run in families," *Amer. Psychol.*, 47:1565-1577.

Lynch, M. W., 2000. "Info gap," *Reason*, 31:17.

Lyons, A. and M. Truzzi, 1991. *The Blue Sense.* New York: Warner Books.

MacDonald, H., 1999. "Impoverished theories of the working poor," *Pub. Interest*, 137:116-120.

MacKay, D. G., 1988. "Under what conditions can theoretical psychology survive and prosper?: Integrating the rational and empirical epistemologies," *Psychol. Rev.*, 95:559-565.

Mackie, J. L., 1973. *Truth, Probability, and Paradox: Studies in Philosophical Logic.* Oxford: Clarendon Press.

——, 1974. *The Cement of the Universe: A Study of Causation.* Oxford: Oxford U. P.

Macrae, N., 1992. *John von Neumann.* New York: Pantheon.

Maguire, K., A. L. Pastore et al., 1995. Bureau of Justice Statistics *Sourcebook of Criminal Justice Statistics - 1994.* Washington, DC: Dept. of Justice.

Mailer, N., 1986. *The Executioner's Song.* New York: Warner Books.

Major, V., 1995. Telephonic report (August 16), U. S. Dept. of Justice, Fed. Bureau of Investigation.

Makiya, K. and H. Mneimineh, 2002. "Manual for a 'raid,'" *NY Rev. Books*, 49:18-21 (Jan. 17).

Malaparte, C., 1964. *The Skin.* New York: Avon.

Malia, M., 1994. *The Soviet Tragedy: A History of Socialism in Russia.* New York: Free Press.

——, 1998. "The lesser evil?" *Times Lit. Supp.*, 4956:3-4 (March 27).

——, 1999. *Russia Under Western Eyes: From the Bronze Horseman to the Lenin Mausoleum*. Cambridge, MA: Harvard U. P.

Malkiel, B. G. and J. P. Mei, 1998. "Hedge funds: The new barbarians at the gate." *Wall St. J.*, 139:A22 (Sept. 29).

Mall, F. P., 1909. "On several anatomical characters of the human brain, said to vary according to race and sex, with especial reference to weight of the frontal lobe," *Amer. J. Anatomy*, 9:1-32.

Malmquist, C. E. and P. E. Meehl, 1978. "Barbaras: A study in guilt-ridden homicide," *Internat. Rev. Psychoan.*, 5:149-174.

Manchester, W., 1982. *The Last Lion: Winston Spencer Churchill, Visions of Glory, 1874-1932*. Boston: Little, Brown.

Marcel, A. J. and E. Bisiach (eds.), 1988. *Consciousness in Contemporary Sciences*. Oxford: Clarendon Press.

Marcus, G. B., 1986. "Stability and change in political attitudes: Observe, recall, and 'explain,'" *Pol. Behavior*, 8:21-44.

Marozzi, J., 2000. "Monsters of motiveless malignity," *Spectator*, 284:12-13 (March 11).

Marx, J. L., 1980. "Ape-language controversy flares up," *Science*, 207:1330-1333 (March 20).

Marx, K. and F. Engels, 1976. *Marx-Engels Collected Works*. New York: International Publishers.

Mason, W. M. et al., 1976. "Models of response error in student reports of parental socioeconomic characteristics." In W. H. Sewell et al. (eds.), *Schooling and Achievement in American Society*. New York: Academic.

Massie-Blomfield, R. A., 2000. "Godless criminality," *Spectator*, 284:29 (March 11).

Masters, B., 1990. *Gary*. London: Cape.

Mattaini, M. A. and B. A. Thyer (eds.), 1996. *Finding Solutions to Social Problems: Behavioral Strategies for Change*. Washington, DC: Amer. Psychol. Assoc.

Matthews, G. and I. J. Deary, 1998. *Personality Traits*. Cambridge, UK: Cambridge U. P.

May, E. R. and P. D. Zelikow, (eds.), 1997. *The Kennedy Tapes: Inside the White House During the Cuban Missile Crisis*. Cambridge, MA: Balknap Press at Harvard U. P.

Mayer, A. J., 2000. *The Furies: Violence and Terror in the French and Russian Revolutions*. Princeton, NJ: Princeton U. P.

Mayer, M., 2001. *The Fed: The Inside Story of How the World's Most Powerful Financial Institution Drives the Markets*. New York: Free Press.

Mayr, E., 2000. "Darwin's influence on modern thought," *Sci. Amer.*, 283:78-83.

McCloskey, D. N., 1994. *Knowledge and Persuasion in Economics*. New York: Cambridge U. P.

——, 1995. "The Gulliver effect," *Sci. Amer.*, 273:44.

McCord, H., 1951. "Discovering the 'confused' respondent: A possible projective method," *Pub. Opin. Quart.*, 15:363-366.

McGinley, L., 1997. "How sweet it is: Saccharin's presence on list of carcinogens may be near an end," *Wall St. J.*, 137:A1, A10 (Oct. 29).

McGowan, W., 2002. *Coloring the News: How Crusading for Diversity Has Corrupted American Journalism*. San Francisco: Encounter.

McKean, K., 1987. "The orderly pursuit of pure disorder," *Discover*, 8:72-87.

McKenney, N. et al., 1993. "Evaluating racial and ethnic reporting in the 1990 census." In Amer. Stat. Assoc., *1993 Proceedings* of the Section on Survey Research.

McKenzie, R. D., 1933. *The Metropolitan Community*. New York: McGraw-Hill.

McKinnon, J. D. and G. Hitt, 2002. "Double play: How Treasury lost in battle to quash a dubious security," *Wall St. J.*, 239:A1, A8 (Feb. 4).

McLeish, J., 1991. *Number: The History of Numbers and How They Shape Our Lives.* New York: Fawcett.

McNees, R. and J. Ries, 1983. "The track record of macroeconomic forecasts," *New Eng. Econ. Rev.*, 16:5-17.

Mead, M., 1928. *Coming of Age in Samoa.* Reprint, 1971. New York: Morrow.

——, 1930. *Growing Up in New Guinea.* New York: Morrow.

——, 1967. Letter to S. E. Blazer, editor of the Dell 1968 paperback edition of *Coming of Age in Samoa.* In papers of Margaret Mead, Washington, D.C.: Manuscript Division, Library of Congress. Cited by D. Freeman, 1999, p. 235.

Meehl, P. E., 1954. *Clinical vs. Statistical Prediction: A Theoretical Analysis and a Review of the Evidence.* Minneapolis: U. Minnesota Press.

——, 1971. "Law and the fireside inductions: Some reflections of a clinical psychologist." Originally published as part of J. I. Tapp (ed.), "Socialization, the law, and society," *J. Soc. Issues*, 27, and reprinted in C. A. Anderson and Gunderson (eds.), 1991. *Selected Philosophical and Methodological Papers: Paul E. Meehl.* Minneapolis: U. Minnesota Press.

——, 1973. "Why I do not attend case conferences." In his *Psychodiagnosis: Selected Papers.* Minneapolis: U. Minnesota Press.

——, 1978. "Theoretical risks and tabular asterisks: Sir Karl, Sir Ronald, and the slow progress of soft psychology," *J. Consult. Clin. Psych.*, 46:806-834. Reprinted, 1991, in Anderson and Gunderson (eds.), *Paul E. Meehl.*

——, 1983. "Subjectivity in psychoanalytic inference: The nagging persistence of Wilhelm Fliess's *Achensee* question." In J. Earman (ed.), *Testing Scientific Theories.* Minnesota Studies in the Philosophy of Science. Vol. X. Minneapolis: U. Minnesota Press.

——, 1986. "Causes and effects of my disturbing little book," *J. Person. Assess.*, 50:370-375.

——, 1990. *Toward an Integrated Theory of Schizotaxia, Schizotypy, and Schizophrenia.* New York: the Guilford Press.

——, 1999. "Clarification about taxometric method." *Appl. And Prev. Psychol.*, 8:165-174.

——, and R. R. Golden, 1982. "Taxometric methods." In P. C. Kendall and J. R. Butcher (eds.), *Handbook of Research Methods in Clinical Psychology.* New York: Wiley.

——, and L. J. Yonce, 1996. "Taxometric analysis; II: Detecting taxonicity using covariance of two quantitative indicators in successive intervals of a third indicator (MaxCov procedure)," *Psychol. Reports*, Monograph Supplement, 1-V78.

Meier, S. I., 1994. *The Chronic Crisis in Psychological Measurement and Assessment: A Historical Survey.* New York: Academic Press.

Mele, A. R., 2001. *Self-Deception Unmasked.* Princeton, NJ: Princeton U. P.

Melis-Wright, N. V., D. Stone, and M. Miller, 1993. "Psychological variables associated with respondent sensitivity to the income question and a measure of their willingness to give financial information on government surveys." *1993 Proceedings* of the Section on Survey Research Methods. Vol. 1. Alexandria, VA: Amer. Stat. Assoc.

Melloan, G., 1996. "Who's right? Greenspan, Matsushita, or both?" *Wall St. J.*, 134:A19 (June 24).

——, 1997. "Germany's 'flagship' casts off as Kohl fiddles," *Wall St. J.*, 136:A17 (Jan. 13).

——, 1998. "Best laid plans go awry when currencies fail," *Wall St. J.*, 139:A23 (Sept. 29).

Meroney, J., 1999. "The ultimate unmade war movie," *Amer. Enterprise*, 10:77.

Merton, R. C., 2000. Interview for *Trillion Dollar Bet*. Boston: Nova TV.

Merton, R. K., 1957. *Social Theory and Social Structure*. Revision of 1949 edition. Glencoe, IL: Free press.

Metzinger, T. (ed.), 1995. *Conscious Experience*. Thorverton, UK: Imprint Academic.

Meyer, A., 1957/1967. *Leninism*. Reprint, New York: Praeger.

Meyers, M., 1999. "In defense of busing," *Wall St. J.*, 141:A23 (Aug. 4).

Michotte, A., 1963. *The Perception of Causality*. New York: Basic Books.

Miller, S., 1982. Commerce and the literary culture," *Pub. Opin.*, 5:6-9.

Millikan, R. G., 1993. *White Queen Psychology and Other Essays for Alice*. Cambridge, MA: MIT Press.

Mills, C. W., 1959. *The Sociological Imagination*. New York: Oxford U. P.

Milton, J., 1996. *Tramp: The Life of Charlie Chaplin*. New York: Harper/Collins.

Miner, C. G. and J. B. Miner, 1979. *Employee Selection Within the Law*. Washington, DC: Bureau of National Affairs.

Minois, G., 1998. *A History of Suicide: Voluntary Death in Western Culture*. Baltimore, MD: Johns Hopkins U. P.

Minnesota Center for Twin and Adoption Research, 1990. *Bibliography of Scientific Papers*. Minneapolis: U. Minnesota, Dept. of Psychology.

Mitchell, J., 1966. "Women–the longest revolution," *New Left Rev.*, (Nov.-Dec.).

Moffett, M., 1988. "Safety net: In depressed Mexico, families pull together to make ends meet," *Wall St. J.*, A1, A14 (July 28).

——, 1996. "Seeking equality: A racial 'democracy' begins painful debate on affirmative action," *Wall St. J.*, 135:A1, A6 (August 6).

Moffitt, T. E., D. R. Lynam, and P. A. Silva, 1994. "Neuropsychological tests and predicting persistent male delinquency," *Criminology*, 32:277-300.

Monmonier, M., 1991. *How to Lie with Maps*. Chicago: U. Chicago Press.

Monod, J., 1971. *Chance and Necessity: An Essay on the Natural Philosophy of Biology*. New York: Knopf.

Moore, M., 1997. "Looking backward to look forward: The 1967 Crime Commission Report in retrospect," *Nat. Inst. of Justice J.*, 234:24-30.

Moore, T. J., 1989. *Heart Failure: A Critical Inquiry into American Medicine and the Revolution in Heart Care*. New York: Random House.

Moravec, H., 1999a. "Rise of the robots," *Sci. Amer.*, 281:124-135.

——, 1999b. *Mere Machines to Transcend Mind*. New York: Oxford U. P.

Morgenstern, O., 1963. *On the Accuracy of Economic Observations*. 2/e. Princeton, NJ: Princeton U. P.

——, 1965. Personal correspondence (November 5).

Morrison, P., 1995. "Genetic distance," *Sci. Amer.*, 273:102-103.

Mossman, D., 1994. "Assessing predictions of violence: Being accurate about accuracy," *J. Clin. Consult. Psych.*, 62:783-792.

Mould, D. E., 1990. "A reply to Page: Fraud, pornography, and the Meese commission," *Amer. Psychol.*, 45:777-778.

Murphy, E. A., 1978. "Some epistemological aspects of the model in medicine," *J. Med. Phil.*, 3:273-292.

Murphy, K. R. and C. Davidshofer, 1988. *Psychological Testing*. Englewood Cliffs, NJ: Prentice-Hall.

Murray, C., 1990. *The Emerging British Underclass*. London: Institute of Economic Affairs.

——, 1996. "Underclass: The crisis deepens." In R. Lister (ed.), *Charles Murray and the Underclass: The Developing Debate*. London: Institute of Economic Affairs.

Naftulin, D. H., J. E. Ware, Jr., F. A. Donnelly, 1973. "The Doctor Fox lecture: A paradigm of educational seduction," *J. Med. Educ.*, 48:630-635.

Nagel, E., 1961. *The Structure of Science: Problems in the Logic of Scientific Explanation*. New York: Harcourt, Brace, and World.

Nasar, S., 1998. *A Beautiful Mind: Genius and Schizophrenia in the Life of John Nash*. London: Faber.

Nash, J., 1967. "Death as a way of life: The increasing resort to homicide in a Maya Indian village community," *Amer. Anthro.*, 69:455-470.

Nathan, D. and M. Snedeker, 1995. *Satan's Silence: Ritual Abuse and the Making of a Modern American Witch Hunt*. New York: Basic Books.

Neisser, U. and N. Harsch, 1992. "Phantom flashbulbs: False recollections of hearing the news about *Challenger*." In E. Winograd and U. Neisser (eds.), *Affect and Accuracy in Recall: Studies of "Flashbulb" Memories*. New York: Cambridge U. P.

Nelson, F. L., N. L. Farberow, D. R. MacKinnon, 1978. "The certification of suicide in eleven Western states: An inquiry into the validity of reported suicide rates," *Suicide and Life-Threatening Beh.*, 8:75-88.

Netanyahu, B., 2001. "This is Israel's fight too," *Wall St. J.*, 238:A14 (Oct. 26).

Nettler, G., 1945. *The Relationship Between Attitude and Information Concerning the Japanese in America*. Stanford: Ph.D. dissertation, Stanford University, Departments of Psychology and Sociology. Reprinted, 1980, in H. Zuckerman and R. K. Merton (eds.), *Dissertations on Sociology*. New York: Arno Press.

——, 1946a. "The relationship between attitude and information concerning the Japanese in America," *Amer. Sociol. Rev.*, 11:177-191.

——, 1961. "Good men, bad men, and the perception of reality," *Sociometry*, 24:279-294.

——, 1970. *Explanations*. New York: McGraw-Hill.

——, 1972a. "Knowing and doing," *Amer. Sociol.*, 7:307-313.

——, 1972b. "Shifting the load: Changing conceptions of personal responsibility," *Amer. Beh. Sci.*, 17:2-5.

——, 1974a. "Embezzlement without problems," *Brit. J. Crim.*, 14:70-77.

——, 1974b. *Explaining Crime*. 2/e. New York: McGraw-Hill.

——, 1976. *Social Concerns*. New York: McGraw-Hill.

——, 1978. "Description, prescription, and science: On differences between knowing something and knowing enough, promising, and predicting." In M. Yinger and S. Cutler (eds.), *Major Social Issues: A Multi-Disciplinary View*. New York: Basic Books.

——, 1979. "Criminal justice." In R. H. Turner and A. Inkeles (eds.), *Annual Review of Sociology*. Vol. 5. Palo Alto: Annual Reviews.

——, 1982a. *Lying, Cheating, Stealing*. Cincinnati, OH: Anderson.

——, 1982b. *Killing One Another*. Cincinnati, OH: Anderson.

——, 1984. *Explaining Crime*. 3/e. New York: McGraw-Hill.

——, 1989. *Criminology Lessons*. Cincinnati, OH: Anderson.

——, 1994. "Trafficking in numbers," *Liberty*, 7:33-42.

——, 1995. "Sex in America," *Commentary*, 100:14.

——, and E. R. Danzig, 1960. *Sanitary Practices of Mexican Women in the Federal District*. Neenah, WI: The Kimberly-Clark Corp., and Mexico City, Mexico: Dando S.A.

——, and E. H. Golding, 1946b. "The measurement of attitudes toward the Japanese in America," *Amer. J. Sociol.*, 52:31-39.

Neumark, D. and W. Wascher, 1995. *The Effect of New Jersey's Minimum Wage Increase on Fast-Food Employment: A Re-evaluation Using Payroll Records*. East Lansing, MI: Employment Policies Institute.

Newey, G., 1999. "Effing the ineffable," *London Rev. Books*, 232:25-27. (Jan. 25).

Newman, K. S., 1999. *No Shame in My Game: The Working Poor in the Inner City*. New York: Russell Sage Foundation/Knopf.

Nickel, J. (ed.), 1994. *Psychic Sleuths*. Buffalo, NY: Prometheus Books.

Niemi, R. G., 1974. *How Family Members Perceive Each Other*. New Haven, CT: Yale U. P.

Nisbett, R. E. and L. Ross, 1980. *Human Inference: Strategies and Shortcomings*. Englewood Cliffs, NJ: Prentice-Hall.

——, and T. DeC. Wilson, 1977. "Telling more than we can know: Verbal reports on mental processes," *Psychol. Rev.*, 84:231-259.

Norman, D. A., 1976. *Memory and Attention: An Introduction to Human Information Processing*. 2/e. New York: Wiley.

Novak, M., 1982. "A stunning survey: Notes and comments," *This World*, 2:101-108.

Nozick, R., 2001. *Invariances: The Structure of the Objective World*. Cambridge, MA: Harvard U. P.

Nuland, S. B., 1999. "The hazards of hospitalization," *Wall St. J.*, 141:A22 (Dec. 2).

Oakeshott, M., 1962/1991. *Rationalism in Politics*. London: Methuen. Reprinted, 1991, in T. Fuller (ed.), *Rationalism in Politics and Other Essays*. Indianapolis, IN: Liberty Press.

——, 1966. "Historical continuity and causal analysis." In W. H. Dray (ed.), *Philosophical Analysis and History*. New York: Harper & Row.

——, 1983. *On History and Other Essays*. Oxford: Blackwell.

O'Connor, T., 2001. *Persons and Causes*. London: Oxford U. P.

O'Doherty, M., 2000. *The Trouble with Guns: Republican Strategy and the Provisional IRA*. Belfast: Blackstaff.

Office of Management and the Budget, 1994. *Standards for the Classification of Federal Data on Race and Ethnicity*. Washington, DC: The Office (June 8).

Ofshe, R. and E. Watters, 1994. *Making Monsters: False Memories, Psychotherapy, and Sexual Hysteria*. New York: Scribner's.

Olson, W. K., 1991. *The Litigation Explosion: What Happened When America Unleashed the Lawsuit*. New York: Penguin Books.

Orans, M., 1996. *Not Even Wrong: Margaret Mead, Derek Freeman, and the Samoans*. Novato, CA: Chandler and Sharp.

——, 1999. "Mead misrepresented," *Science*, 293:1649-1650. (March 12).

Ortega y Gasset, J., 1946. *Concord and Liberty*. New York: Norton.

——, 1955. "Conversation with a friend, reported by *Time*, "Death of a philosopher." (Oct. 31).

Orwell, G., 1949. *Nineteen Eighty-Four*. London: Secker & Warburg.

Osgood, C. E. *et al.*, 1987. *The Measurement of Meaning*. Urbana: U. Illinois Press.

Oskamp, S., 1965. "Overconfidence in case study judgments," *J. Consult. Clin. Psych.*, 29:261-265.

O'Toole, F., 2000. "Are the troubles over?" *NY Rev. Books*, 47:10-13 (Oct. 5).

Owens, D., 1992. *Causes and Coincidences*. New York: Cambridge U. P.

Pacelle, M., E. J. Pollock, D. Lohse, 1999. "Some firms saw red flags about Frankel," *Wall St. J.*, 140:C1, C14 (June 24).

Pagels, E., 1995. *The Origin of Satan*. New York: Random House.

Pais, A., 1983. *Subtle Is the Lord: The Science and Life of Albert Einstein*. Oxford: Oxford U. P.

——, 2000. *The Genius of Science: A Portrait Gallery of Twentieth-Century Physicists.* New York: Oxford U. P.

Pap, A., 1958. *Semantics and Necessary Truth.* New Haven, CT: Yale U. P.

——, 1962. *An Introduction to the Philosophy of Science.* San Francisco: W. H. Freeman.

Pareto, V., 1916/1935. *Trattato di Sociologia Generale.* Trans. 1935, as *Mind and Society*, Arthur Livingston (ed.), 4 vols. New York: AMS Press.

Park, R. E. and E. W. Burgess, 1921. *Introduction to the Science of Sociology.* Chicago: U. Chicago Press.

Parke, R. D. and S. R. Asher, 1983. "Social and personality development," *Ann. Rev. Psychol.*, 34:465-509.

Parris, M., 1997. "They really believe it–these death-cults," *Spectator*, 278:10 (April 5).

Parsons, T. et al., 2000. "Heightened odds of large earthquakes near Istanbul: An interaction-based probability calculation," *Science*, 288:661-665. (April 28).

Patterson, J. E., 1996. *Grand Expectations: The United States, 1945-1974.* New York: Oxford U. P.

Payne, D. G. et al., 1996. "Memory illusions: Recalling, recognizing, and recollecting events that never occurred," *J. Memory Lang.*, 35:261-285.

Peirce, C. S., 1885. "Design and chance." Reprinted in H. Hartshorne and P. Weiss (eds.), 1931-1935. *Collected papers of Charles Sanders Peirce.* Vols. I-IV. Cambridge, MA: Harvard U. P.

——, 1891. "The architecture of theories," *Monist*, 1:161-176.

——, 1892. "The law of mind," *Monist*, 2:533-559.

——, 1898. *Reasoning and the Logic of Things.* Reprinted in H. L. Ketner (ed.), 1992. Cambridge, MA: Harvard U. P.

Petersen, W., 1985, "Who's what? 1790-1980," *Wilson Quart.*, 9:97-120.

——, 1987. "Politics and the measurement of ethnicity." In W. Alonso and P. Starr (eds.), *The Politics of Numbers.* New York: Russell Sage Foundation.

——, 1997. *Ethnicity Counts.* New Brunswick, NJ: Transaction.

——, 1999. "Population: The Fundamentals," *Society*, 37:48-55.

——, 2000a. *From Birth to Death: A Consumer's Guide to Population Studies.* New Brunswick, NJ: Transaction.

——, 2000b. "Counting heads," *Pub. Interest*, 141:116-120.

Petersilia, J. R., 1977. *The Validity of Criminality Data Derived from Personal Interviews.* Santa Monica, CA: Rand Report P-5890.

——, 1978. "The validity of criminality data derived from personal interviews." In C. Wellford (ed.), *Quantitative Studies in Criminology.* Newbury Park, CA: Sage.

——, and M. Lavin, 1978. *Targeting Career Criminals: A Developing Criminal Justice Strategy.* Santa Monica, CA: Rand.

Peterson, M. A. and H. B. Braiker with S. M. Polich, 1981. *Who Commits Crimes?: A Survey of Prison Inmates.* Cambridge, MA: Oelgeschlager, Gunn, and Hain.

Petrie, A., 1967. *Individuality in Pain and Suffering.* Chicago: U. Chicago Press.

Phillipson, N., 1989. *Hume.* New York: St. Martin's Press.

Piaget, J., 1930. *The Child's Conception of Physical Causality.* New York: Harcourt, Brace.

——, 1969. *The Mechanisms of Perception.* New York: Basic Books.

——, 1973. *The Psychology of Intelligence.* Lanham, MD: Littlefield, Adams.

Pietroski, P. and G. Rey, 1995. "When other things aren't equal: Saving *ceteris paribus* laws from vacuity," *Brit. Jour. Phil. Science*, 46:81-110.

Pinker, S., 1997. "Evolutionary psychology: An exchange," *NY Rev. Books*, 44:55-56 (Oct. 9).

Pipes, R., 1990. *The Russian Revolution.* New York: Knopf.
——, 1994. *Russia Under the Bolshevik Regime.* New York: Knopf.
——, 1996. *The Unknown Lenin: From the Secret Archive.* New Haven, CT: Yale.
——, 1999a. *Property and Freedom.* New York: Knopf.
——, 1999b. "Life, liberty, and property, *Commentary,* 107:17-21.
——, 1999c. "Response to critics," *Commentary,* 107:10-11.
——, 2000. "Intifada II: What should the U. S. do?" *Commentary,* 110:39-48.
Pitts, W. and W. S. McCulloch, 1947. "How we know universals: the perception of auditory and visual forms." *Bull. Math. Biophysiology,* 9:127-147.
Plomin, R. (ed.), 1998. "Current directions in behavioral genetics; Special issue. *Current Directions in Psychological Science,* 6, #4.
——, and J. C. DeFries, 1985. *Origins of Individual Differences in Infancy: The Colorado Adoption Project.* New York: Academic Press.
——, and G. E. McClearn, 1990. *Behavior Genetics: A Primer.* 2/e. New York: Freeman. And with M. Rutter. 3/e, 1997. New York: Freeman.
Podhoretz, N., 2000. "Intifada II: Death of an illusion," *Commentary,* 110:27-38.
Poincaré, J. H., 1913. *Science and Method.* Reprinted 1996. London: Thoemmes Press.
Polk, W. R., 1997. *Neighbors and Strangers: The Fundamentals of Foreign Affairs.* Chicago: U. Chicago Press.
Pollock, E. J., D. Lohse, M. Pacelle, 1999a. "For regulators, Frankel's past has similarities to current case," *Wall St. J.,* 140:C1, C12 (June 23).
——, 1999b. "Portrait of Frankel: Cocky, ambitious, insecure," *Wall St. J.,* 140:C1, C11 (June 25).
——, and S. J. Paltrow, 1999c. "At heart of Frankel's insurance plan: A prominent Tennessee businessman," *Wall St. J.,* 140:C1, C11 (June 29).
Pope, A., 1751/1967. *Moral Essays.* Reprinted 1967, J. W. Croker (ed.), *Pope, Works.* London: Gordian.
Porter, E. with R. S. Greenberger, 2001. "Even 126 sizes don't fit all," *Wall St. J.,* 237:B1, B4 (March 2).
Porter, S. and D. Marxsen, 1998. "Challenging the eyewitness expert: An update considering memory for trauma and created memories." In J. Ziskin (ed.), *Supp.* To *Coping with Psychiatric and Psychological Testimony,* 1997. 5/e. Los Angeles: Law and Psychol. Press.
Porter, S., J. C. Yuille, and D. R. Lehman, 1999. "The nature of real, implanted, and fabricated childhood events: Implications for the recovered memory debate," *Law & Hum. Beh.,* 23:517-537.
——, et al., 2000. "Negotiating false memories: Interviewer and rememberer characteristics relate to memory distortion," *Psychol. Sci.,* 11:507-510.
Porter, T. M., 1995. *Trust in Numbers: The Pursuit of Objectivity in Science and Public Life.* Princeton, NJ: Princeton U. P.
Premack, D., 1988. "Does the chimpanzee have a theory of mind?" Revisited in R. Byrne and A. Shiten, (eds.), *Machiavellian Intelligence.* Oxford, U. K.: Oxford U. P.
Prickett, T. J., N. Gada-Jain, F. J. Bernieri, 2000. "The importance of first impressions in a job interview." Paper in submission from the Dept. of Psychology, Univ. of Toledo.
Prigogine, I. and I. Stengers, 1989. *Order Out of Chaos: Man's New Dialogue with Nature.* New York: Viking.
Puddington, A., 2001. "The wages of Durban," *Commentary,* 112:29-34.
Quarm, D., 1981. "Random measurement error as a source of discrepancies between the reports of wives and husbands concerning marital power and task allocation," *J. Marr. And Family,* 43:521-535.

Queen, S. G., 1993. "Comparability between items reported on the death certificate and informants on the 1993 national mortality followback survey," *1993 Proceedings* of the Section on Survey Research Methods, Vol. I. Arlington, VA: Amer. Stat. Assoc.

Quine, W. V., 1987. *Quiddities: An Intermittently Philosophical Dictionary.* Cambridge, MA: Harvard U. P.

Quinney, R., 1974. *Critique of Legal Order: Crime Control in Capitalist Society.* Boston: Little, Brown.

Rabinowitz, D., 1990. "Out of the mouths of babes and into a jail cell," *Harper's Magazine*, 278:52-63.

——, 1995. "A darkness in Massachusetts, II.," *Wall St. J.* 132:A18 (March 14).

——, 2000. "The hate-crimes bandwagon," *Wall St. J.*, 142:A30 (June 27).

Raphael, F., 1998. "Equaller, hopefully," *Times Lit. Supp.*, 4985:7-8 (Oct. 16).

Rawls, J., 1971. *A Theory of Justice.* Cambridge, MA: Harvard U. P.

Reber, A. S., 1985. *Dictionary of Psychology.* New York: Viking/Penguin.

——, 1996. *Implicit Learning and Tacit Knowledge: An Essay on the Cognitive Unconscious.* New York: Oxford U. P.

Rector, R. and R. S. Hederman, 1999. *Income Inequality: How Census Data Misrepresent Income Distribution.* Washington, DC: The Heritage Center for Data Analysis.

Regan, D. T. *et al.*, 1974. "Liking and the attribution process, *J. Exper. Soc. Psych.*, 10:385-397.

Remnick, D., 1993. *Lenin's Tomb: Last Days of the Soviet Empire.* New York: Random House.

Renfrew, C., 2001. "Mother of all mankind," *Times Lit. Supp.*, 4152:4-5 (Oct. 19).

Rescher, N., 1995. *Luck: The Brilliant Randomness of Everyday Life.* New York: Farrar, Straus, Giroux.

Resnik, M. D., 1987. *Choices: An Introduction to Decision Theory.* Minneapolis: U. Minnesota Press.

Restak, R. M., 1982. "Newborn knowledge: Infants arrive less wet behind the ears than we thought," *Science 82*, 3:58-65.

——, 1984. *The Brain.* New York: Bantam Books.

——, 1988. *The Mind.* New York: Bantam Books.

Reynolds, A., 1997. "The lessons of Black Monday," *Wall St. J.*, 137:A22 (Oct. 17).

Rial, J. A., 2000. "Time travel on ice," *Amer. Sci.*, 89:187-188.

Rice, S. A., 1926. "Stereotypes," *J. Person. Res.*, 5:266-276.

Richards, J. M., DC Gottfredson, and G. D. Gottfredson, 1991a. "Units of analysis and item statistics for environmental assessment scales," *Current Psychol.*, 9:407-413.

——, 1991b. "Units of analysis and the psychometrics of environmental assessment scales." *Environ. and Beh.*, 23:423-437.

Richardson, L. F., 1960a. *Arms and Insecurity.* Chicago: Quadrangle Books.

——, 1960b. *Statistics of Deadly Quarrels.* Chicago: Quadrangle Books.

Ridley, Mark, 2000. *The Cooperative Gene: How Mendel's Demon Explains the Evolution of Complex Beings.* New York: Free Press.

——, 2001. "Near the end of the line?" *Times Lit. Supp.*, 5142:3-4 (Oct. 19).

Ridley, Matt, 1999. *Genome: The Autobiography of a Species in 23 Chapters.* New York: Harper/Collins.

Riesman, D., 1969. "The young are captives of each other," *Psychol. Today*, 3:28-33, 43-67.

——, and N. Glazer, 1948-1949. "The meaning of opinion," *Pub. Opin. Quart.*, 12:633-648.

Robinson, A. L., 1986. "What does it mean to be random?" *Science*, 231:1068-1070. (March 7).

Robinson, D., 1985. *Chaplin: His Life and His Art*. New York: McGraw-Hill.

Robinson, G., "Cultural contradiction," *Encounter*, 62:80.

Robinson, J., 1962. *Economic Philosophy*. Chicago: Aldine.

Robinson, S., 1992. "Periodic fits of morality," *Spectator*, 9-10 (Feb. 8).

Robinson, W. S., 1950. "Ecological correlation and the behavior of individuals," *Amer. Sociol. Rev.*, 15:351-357.

Rochat, P., 2001. *The Infant's World*. Cambridge, MA: Harvard U. P.

Romanes, G. J., 1910. *Animal Intelligence*. London: Kegan, Paul, Trench, Trubner.

Rosenbaum, A. S., (ed.), 1997. *Is the Holocaust Unique?: Perspectives on Comparative Genocide*. New York: Oxford U. P.

Rosenberg, A., 1992. *Economics–Mathematical Politics or Science of Diminishing Returns?* Chicago: U. Chicago Press.

Rosenblueth, A. N., J. B. Wiener, J. Bigelow, 1943. "Behavior, purpose, and teleology," *Phil. Sci.*, 10:18-24.

Rosner, F., 1999. "The definition of death in Jewish law." In S. J. Youngner, R. M. Arnold, and R. Schapiro (eds.), *The Definition of Death: Contemporary Controversies*. Baltimore, MD: Johns Hopkins.

Ross, C. E. and J. Mirowsky, 1984. "Social-desirability response and acquiescence in a cross-cultural survey of mental health," *J. Health & Soc. Beh.*, 25:189-197.

Ross, I., 1981. *Medicolegal Categories of Death: Taxonomic Problems*. Ph.D. Dissertation, Dept. of Sociology, Univ. of Alberta, Edmonton, Canada.

Rothman, S., 1986. "Academics on the left," *Society*, 23:4-8.

——, and S. R. Lichter, 1982. *Roots of Radicalism: Jews, Christians, and the New Left*. New York: Oxford U. P.

Rottschaefer, W. A., 1998. *The Biology and Psychology of Moral Agency*. New York: Cambridge U. P.

Royce, W. S. and R. L. Weiss, 1975. "Behavioral cues in the judgment of marital satisfaction: Linear regression analysis," *J. Consult. Clin. Psychol.*, 43:816-824.

Rubin, V., 2000. "Dark matter in the universe." In D. R. Levy (ed.), *The Scientific American Book of the Cosmos*. New York: St. Martin's Press.

Rucker, R., 1985. "Puzzles in thoughtland: The powers of coincidence," *Science 85*, 6:54-57.

Ruddy, S., 1997. *The Strange Death of Vincent Foster: An Investigation*. New York: Free Press.

Rummel, R. J., 1994. *Death by Government: Genocide and Mass Murder Since 1900*. New Brunswick, NJ: Transaction.

Russell, J. C., 1979. "Perceived action units as a function of subjective importance," *Person. Soc. Psychol.*, 5:206-209.

Ryle, G., 1949. *Concept of Mind*. Reprint, 1984. Chicago: U. Chicago Press.

Sackeim, H. A. and R. C. Gur, 1979. "Self-deception, other-deception, and self-reported psychopathology," *Jour. Consult. Clin. Psychol.*, 47:213-215.

Sackett, P. R., 1994. "Integrity testing for personnel selection," *Curr. Directions Psychol.*, 3:73-76.

Salmon, T. N. and A. F. Blakeslee, 1935. "Genetics and sensory thresholds: Variations within single individuals in taste sensitivity for PTC," *Proceedings* of the National Academy of Science, 21:78-83.

Salmon, W. C., 1984. *Scientific Explanation and the Causal Structure of the World*. Princeton, NJ: Princeton U. P.

Sampson, R. J. and W. J. Wilson, 1995. "Toward a theory of race, crime, and urban inequality." In J. Hagan and R. D. Peterson (eds.), *Crime and Inequality*. Stanford: Stanford U. P.

Santayana, G., 1905-1906. *The Life of Reason*. Reprinted in 3 volumes, 1980-1983. New York: Dover.

———, 1923. *Skepticism and Animal Faith*. New York: Scribner's. Reprinted, 1955. New York: Dover.

———, 1926. "Normal Madness" from *Dialogues in Limbo*. New York: Scribner's.

Sapolsky, R. M., 1992. *Stress: The Ageing Brain and the Mechanism of Neuron Death*. Cambridge, MA: MIT Press.

Satel, S., 1996. "Psychiatric apartheid," *Wall St. J.*, 134:A14 (May 8.)

———, 2000. *PC M.D.: How Political Correctness Is Corrupting Medicine*. New York: Basic Books.

Sattath, S. and A. Tversky, 1987. "On the relation between common and distinctive feature models," *Psych. Rev.*, 94:16-22.

Savage, L., 1954. *The Foundations of Statistics*. New York: Wiley.

Savage-Rumbaugh, E. S. et al., 1985. "The capacity of animals to acquire language: Do species differences have anything to say to us?" In L. Weiskrantz (ed.), *Animal Intelligence*. Oxford: Clarendon Press.

———, S. G. Shanker, T. J. Taylor, 1998. *Apes, Language, and the Human Mind*. New York: Oxford U. P.

Sawyer, J., 1966. "Measurement and prediction: Clinical and statistical," *Psychol. Bull.*, 66:278-300.

Schacter, D. L., 1996. *Searching for Memory: The Brain, the Mind, and the Past*. New York: Basic Books.

———, 1999. *The Cognitive Neuropsychology of False Memories*. Philadelphia: Psychology Press.

———, 2000. *The Seven Sins of Memory*. Boston: Houghton, Mifflin.

———, K. A. Norman, W. Koutstaal, 1998. "The cognitive neuroscience of constructive memory," *Ann. Rev. Psychol.*, 49:289-318.

———, L. Israel, C. Racine, 1999. "Suppressing false recognition in younger and older adults: The distinctiveness heuristic," *J. Memory and Lang.*, 40:1-74.

———, and E. Scarry, Ieds.), 2000. *Memory, Brain, and Belief*. Cambridge, MA: Harvard U. P.

Schama, S., 1989. *Citizens: A Chronicle of the French Revolution*. New York: Knopf.

Schelling, T. C., 1978. *Micromotives and Macrobehavior*. New York: Norton.

Schiffman, H. and R. Wynne, 1963. *Causation and Affect*. Princeton, NJ: Educational Testing Service, RM-63-7.

Schmidt, F. L. and J. E. Hunter, 1981. "Employment testing: Old theories and new research findings," *Amer. Psychol.*, 36:1128-1137.

———, 1993. "Tacit knowledge, practical intelligence, general mental ability, and job knowledge," *Curr. Directions Psychol. Sci.*, 1:8-9.

Schmolck, H., E. A. Buffalo, L. R. Squire, 2000. "Memory distortions develop with time: Recollections of the O. J. Simpson trial verdict after 15 and 32 months," *Psychol. Sci.*, 11:39-45.

Schneider, P-B, 1954. *Tentative de Suicide*. Neuchatel: Delauchaux et Nestlé.

Schneider, W. and I. A. Lewis, 1985. "Views on the news," *Pub. Opin. Quart.*, 8:6-11, 58.

Schneiders, G. and J. E. Livingston, 1999. "Can you trust the polls? Well, sometimes," *Wall St. J.*, 146:A22 (Feb. 8).

Scholes, M., 2000. Interview for *Trillion Dollar Bet*. Boston: Nova TV.

Schuman, H. and S. Presser, 1980. "Public opinion and public ignorance: The fine line between attitudes and non-attitudes," *Amer. J. Sociol.*, 85:1214-1225.

Schumpeter, J. A., 1947. *Capitalism, Socialism, and Democracy*. 2/e. New York: Harper & Brothers.

Schusterman, R. J., J. A. Thomas, F. G. Wood (eds.), 1998. *Dolphin Cognition and Behavior: A Comparative Approach.* Hillsdale, NJ: Erlbaum.

——, G. J. Reichmuth, D. Kastak, 2000. "How animals classify friends and foes," *Curr. Dir. Psychol.*, 9:1-6.

Schutz, A., 1960. "The social world and the theory of social action," *Soc. Res.*, 27:203-221.

Schwartz, D., 1943. *Genesis.* New York: New Directions.

Schwartz, L. R., 1972. "Conflict without violence and violence without conflict in a Mexican village." In J. F. Short, Jr., and M. E. Wolfgang (eds.), *Collective Violence.* Chicago: Aldine.

Schwarz, N., 1999. "Self-reports: How the questions shape the answer," *Amer. Psychol.*, 54:93-105.

Scott, J. A., 1998. *Seeing Like a State: How Certain Schemes to Improve the Human Condition Have Failed.* New Haven, CT: Yale.

Seabrook, J., 2001. "Soldiers and spice," *New Yorker*, 60-69 (Aug. 15).

Seagle, W., 1932. "Homicide." In E. R. A. Seligman and A. Johnson (eds.), *Encyclopedia of the Social Sciences.* New York: Macmillan.

Seamon, J. G., N. Brody, D. M. Kauff, 1983. "Affective discrimination of stimuli that are not recognized: Effects of shadowing, masking, and cerebral laterality," *J. Exper. Psychol.: Learning, Memory, Cognition*, 9:544-555.

Searle, J. E., 1995a. *The Construction of Social Reality.* New York: Free Press.

——, 1995b. "The mystery of consciousness," *NY Rev. Books*, 42:60-66 (Nov. 2).

——, 1999a. "I married a computer," *NY Rev. Books*, 46:34-38 (April 8).

——, 1999b. "Contribution to "International books of the year–and the millennium." *Times Lit. Supp.*, 5044:6 (Dec. 3).

——, 1999c. *Mind, Language, and Society: Philosophy in the Real World.* London: Weidenfeld & Nicolson.

Segal, N. L. et al., 1990. "Psychiatric investigations and findings from the Minnesota study of twins reared apart." In M. Tsuan, K. Kendler, and M. Lyons (eds.), *Genetic Issues in Psychosocial Epidemiology.* New Brunswick, NJ: Rutgers U. P.

Seligman, D., 1979. "The non-working class," *Fortune*, 100:33 (Sept. 24).

——, 1982. "Seminarian economics," *Fortune*, 106:27.

——, 1992. *A Question of Intelligence: The IQ Debate in America.* New York: Birch Lane Press.

——, 1996. "Mystical moments in Columbus Circle," *Fortune*, 133:208-210 (May 27).

Seligman, M. E. P., 1991. *Learned Optimism.* New York: Knopf.

——, and J. L. Hager, 1972. *Biological Boundaries of Learning.* New York: Appleton-Century-Crofts.

——, and M. Csikszentmihalyi, 2000. "Positive psychology." In their edited, *Special Issue on Happiness, Excellence, and Optimal Human Functioning. Amer. Psychol.*, 55:#1.

Semmens, J., 1991. "Hawaii's 'successful' seat-belt law," *Heartland Perspective*, 7889-7999. (Oct. 11).

——, 1992. "Do seat belts work?" *Freeman*, 124:280-281.

Sen, A., 1992. *Inequality.* New York: Oxford U. P.

Service, R., 2000. *Lenin: A Biography.* Cambridge, MA: Harvard U. P.

Shankman, P., 1998. "Margaret Mead, Derek Freeman, and the issue of evolution," *Skeptical Inquirer*, 35-390.

Shapiro, A., 1977. "The evaluation of clinical prediction: A method and initial application," *New Eng. J. Med.*, 296:1509-1514.

Shavell, S., 1980. "An analysis of causation and the scope of liability in the law of torts," *J. Legal Studies*, 9:463-518.

Shavelson, R. J. and N. M. Webb, 1991. *Generalizability Theory: A Primer*. Thousand Oaks, CA: Sage.

Shaver, K. G., 1985. *The Attribution of Blame: Causality, Responsibility, and Blameworthiness*. New York: Springer-Verlag.

Sheehan, S., 1976. *A Welfare Mother*. Boston: Houghton, Mifflin.

Sheldon, W. H., 1940. *Varieties of Human Physique*. New York: Harper & Bros.

——, 1942. *Varieties of Temperament*. New York: Harper & Bros.

Shiffman, S., et al., 1997. "Remember that? A comparison of real-time vs. retrospective recall of smoking lapses," *J. Consult. Clin. Psychol.*, 65:292-300.

Shiller, R. J., 2000. *Irrational Exuberance*. New York: Broadway Books.

Shils, E., 1968. "Ideology: the concept and function of ideology." In D. L. Sills (ed.) *International Encyclopedia of the Social Sciences*, v. VII:66-75. New York: Macmillan.

——, 1972. *The Intellectuals and the Powers and Other Essays*. Chicago: U. Chicago Press.

——, 1987. "The ways of sociology," *Encounter*, 24:84-93.

Shkilnyk, A., 1985. *A Poison Stronger Than Love: The Destruction of an Ojibwa Community*. New Haven, CT: Yale.

Shneidman, E. S., 1968. "Orientation toward cessation: A reexamination of current modes of death," *J. Forensic Sci.*, 13:330-345.

——, 1973. *Deaths of Man*. New York: Quadrangle Books.

Shrader-Frechette, K. S., 1991. *Risk and Rationality: Philosophical Foundations for Populist Reforms*. Berkeley, CA: U. Calif. Press.

Siegel, F., 1998. "What matters in the metropolis," *Wall St. J.*, 139:A20 (Dec. 9).

Silverman, R. A., 1980. "Measuring crime: More problems," *J. Police Sci. and Admin.*, 8:265-274.

Simon, H. A., 1968. "Causation." In D. L. Sills (ed.), *The International Encyclopedia of the Social Sciences*. New York: Macmillan.

——, 1982. "Are social problems problems that social science can solve?" In W. H. Kruskal (ed.), *The Social Sciences: Their Nature and Uses*. Chicago: U. Chicago Press.

——, and N. Rescher, 1966. "Cause and counterfactual," *Phil. Sci.*, 33:323-340.

Singer, P., 1994. *Rethinking Life and Death: The Collapse of Our Traditional Ethics*. New York: St. Martin's Press.

——, 2000. *A Darwinian Left: Politics, Evolution, and Cooperation*. New Haven, CT: Yale.

Skemp, R. R., 1983. "Mathematics." In R. Harré and R. Lamb (eds.), *The Encyclopedic Dictionary of Psychology*. Cambridge, MA: MIT Press.

Skerry, P., 1999. *Counting on the Census: Race, Group Identity, and the Evasion of Politics*. Washington, DC: Brookings Institution Press.

Skinner, B. F., 1945. "On the accuracy of introspective reports." Cited by P. E. Meehl, 1992. "Needs and state variables," *Psychol. Reports*, 70:407-450.

——, 1987. "What religion means to me," *Free Inquiry*, 7:12.

Skrentny, J. D., 2002. "Inventing race," *Pub. Interest*, 146:97-113.

Slovic, P., 1995. "The construction of preference," *Amer. Psychol.*, 50:364-371.

Smith, F. B., 2000. "Big Nanny is watching your house," *Wall St. J.*, 236:A23 (July 31).

Smith, J. M., 1982. *Evolution and the Theory of Games*. Cambridge: Cambridge U. P.

Smith, M. B., 1978. "Psychology and the future," *Amer. Psychol.*, 33:644-646.

Smith, R. J., 1983. *Japanese Society: Tradition, Self, and the Social Order*. New York: Cambridge U. P.

Smith, R. W., 1998a. "The meaning of 'genocide,'" *Times Lit. Supp.*, 4954:17 (March 11).

——, 1998b. "The meaning of 'genocide,'" *Times Lit. Supp.*, 4967:18 (June 12).

Smith, T. W., 1981. "Qualifications to generalized absolutes: 'Approval of hitting' questions on the GSS," *Pub. Opin. Quart.*, 45:224-230.

——, 1989. *Problems of Ethnic Measurement: Over-, Under-, and Misidentification*. Washington, D.C.: General Social Survey Project, Technical Report, #29.

Smuts, B. et al. (eds.), 1997. *Primate Societies*. Chicago: U. Chicago Press.

Sokal, A., 1996. "A physicist experiments with cultural studies," *Lingua Franca*, 6:62-64.

——, and J. Bricmont, 1998. *Fashionable Nonsense: Postmodern Intellectuals' Abuse of Science*. New York: Picador.

Sowell, T., 1985. *Marxism: Philosophy and Economics*. New York: Morrow.

——, 1994. *Race and Culture: A World View*. New York: Basic Books.

——, 1995. *The Vision of the Anointed: Self-congratulation as a Basis for Social Policy*. New York: Basic Books.

Spelke, E. et al., 1982. "Origins of knowledge," *Psychol. Rev.*, 99:605-632.

——, 1993a. "Gestalt relations and object perception: A developmental study," *Perception*, 22:1483-1501.

——, 1993b. "Early knowledge of object motion: Continuity and inertia," *Cognition*, 31:131-176.

——, 1995. "Infants' knowledge of object motion and human action." In D. Sperber, D. Premack, and A. Premack (eds.), *Causal Cognition: A Multi-disciplinary Debate*. Oxford: Clarendon Press.

Spellman, B., 1996. "Acting as intuitive scientists: Contingency judgments are made while controlling for alternative potential causes," *Psychol. Sci.*, 7:337-342.

Spitzer, N. C. and T. J. Sejnowski, 1997. "Biological information processing: Bits of progress," *Science*, 277:1060-1061 (Aug. 22).

Sporer, S. L. *et al.*, 1995. "Choosing, confidence, and accuracy: A meta-analysis of the confidence-accuracy relation in eyewitness identification studies," *Psychol. Bull.*, 118-:315-327.

Staats, C. K. and A. W. Staats, 1957. "Meaning established by classical conditioning," *J. Exper. Psychol.*, 54:74-80.

Stamp, J. C., 1929. *Some Economic Factors in Modern Life*. London: P. S. King and Son.

Stearns, S. C. et al., 1993. "Reconciling respondent reports and Medicare claims for national estimates of hospital use," *1993 Proceedings* of the Section on Survey Research Methods. Vol. I. Arlington, VA: Amer. Stat. Assoc.

Stein, H., 1991. "My price-control days with Nixon," *Wall St. J.*, 115:A15 (Aug. 16).

——, 1995. "The consumer price index: Servant or master?" *Wall St. J.*, 133:A14 (Nov. 1).

——, 1998. "Bottom rung: A German who offers low-pay service work dismays countrymen," *Wall St. J.*, 138:A1, A10 (Mar. 3).

Steinweg, D. A., 1993. *The Influence of Naturally Occurring Non-Pathological Fluctuations of Mood on Recall*. Ph.D. dissertation. Buffalo: State Univ. of New York, Dept. of Psychology.

Stern, D., 1977. *The First Relationship: Infant and Mother*. Cambridge, MA: Harvard U. P.

Stern, D. L., 2000. "The problem of variation," *Nature*, 408:529-531. (Nov. 30).

Stern, J., 1999. *The Ultimate Terrorists*. Cambridge, MA: Harvard U. P.

Stevens, S. S., 1959. "Measurement." In C. W. Churchman and P. Ratoosh (eds.), *Measurement*. New York: Wiley.

Steyn, M., 2000. "All Canadians are guilty," *Spectator*, 284:16-17. (June 24).

Stich, S., 1983. *From Folk Psychology to Cognitive Science: The Case Against Belief*. Cambridge, MA: MIT Press.

——, 1990. *The Fragmentation of Reason*. Cambridge, MA: MIT Press.

Stiglitz, J., 1993. *Economics*. New York: Norton.

——, 1996. "I changed my mind, what's the big deal?" *Wall St. J.*, 134:A21 (April 17).

Stinchombe, A. L., 1995. "Sex, lies, and sociology: A response to Lewontin, *NY Rev. Books*, 42:68 (June 8).

Stokols, D., 1995. "The paradox of environmental psychology," *Amer. Psychol.*, 50:821-837.

Stone, A. A. and S. Shiffman, 1994. "Ecological momentary assessment (EMA) in behavior medicine," *Annals Beh. Med.*, 16:199-202.

Stove, DC, 1965, "Hume, probabilities, and induction," *Phil. Rev.*, 74:#2.

——, 1973. *Probability and Hume's Inductive Skepticism*. Oxford: Oxford U. P.

——, 1986. *The Rationality of Induction*. Oxford: Clarendon Press.

——, 1991. *The Plato Cult, and Other Philosophical Follies*. Oxford: Blackwell.

Stroud, B., 2000. *The Quest for Reality: Subjectivism and the Metaphysics of Colour*. New York: Oxford U. P.

Suen, H. K., 1990. *Principles of Test Theories*. Hillsdale, NJ: Erlbaum.

Sulloway, F., 1996. *Born to Rebel*. Westminster, MD: Random House.

Summers, A., 1985. *Goddess: The Secret Lives of Marilyn Monroe*. New York: Macmillan.

Sutton, W., 1976. *Where the Money Was: The Memoirs of a Bank Robber* (with E. Linn). New York: Viking.

Swets, J. A., R. M. Dawes, J. Monahan, 2000a. "Psychological science can improve diagnostic decisions," Supplement to *Psychol. Sci. in Pub. Interest*, 1:#1.

——, 2000b. "Better decisions through science," *Sci. Amer.*, 283:82-87.

Sykes, B., 2001. *The Seven Daughters of Eve*. New York: Bantam.

Szinovacz, M. E., 1983. "Using couple data as a methodological tool: The case of marital violence," *J. Marr. Fam.*, 45:633-644.

Tanur, J. M. (ed.), 1994. *Questions About Questions: Inquiries into the Cognitive Bases of Surveys*. New York: Russell Sage Foundation.

Tarabulsy, G. M., R. Tessier, and A. Kappas, 1996. "Contingency detection and the contingent organization of behavior in interactions: Implications for socio-emotional development in infancy," *Psychol. Bull.*, 120:25-41.

Tattersall, I. and J. H. Schwartz, 2000. *Extinct Humans*. Boulder, CO: Westview.

Tatum, B. D., 1997. *Why Are All the Black Kids Sitting Together in the Cafeteria? And Other Conversations about the Development of Racial Identity*. New York: Basic Books.

Taubes, G., 1995. "Epidemiology faces its limits," *Science*, 269:164-169 (July 14).

Taylor, A. J. P., 1995. *From the Boer War to the Cold War: Essays on Twentieth Century Europe*. London: Allen Lane/ Penguin.

Taylor, B. J., 2000. "Bak to skool," *Reason*, 31:16-17.

Taylor, S. E., 1989. *Positive Illusions: Creative Self-Deception and the Healthy Mind*. New York: Basic Books.

Tell, D., 1999. "Hawaii's Nuremberg laws," *Weekly Standard*, 4:9-10 (Oct. 4).

Terman, L. M. and M. H. Oden, 1947. *Genetic Studies of Genius, Vol. IV: The Gifted Child Grows Up: Twenty-five Years' Follow-up of a Superior Group*. Stanford: Stanford.

——, 1959. *Genetic Studies of Genius: Vol. VI. The Gifted Group at Mid-Life: Thirty-five Years' Follow-up of the Superior Child.* Stanford, CA: Stanford U. P.

Thagard, P. R., 1979. "Why astrology is a pseudo-science." In P. D. Asquith and I. Hacking (eds.), *PSA 1978.* East Lansing, MI: Phil. Sci. Assoc.

Theodorsen, G. A. (ed.), 1961. *Studies in Human Ecology.* Evanston, IL: Row.

Thernstrom, S. and A. Thernstrom, 1997. *America in Black and White: One Nation, Indivisible: Race in Modern America.* New York: Simon & Schuster.

Thomas, K. F. and T. L. Dingbaum, 1993. "Data quality in the 1990 census–the content reinterview survey." In *1993 Proceedings* of the Section on Survey Research Methods. Vol. 1. Arlington, VA: Amer. Stat. Assoc.

Thomas, W. I., 1937. *Primitive Behavior.* New York: McGraw-Hill.

——, and D. S. Thomas, 1928. *The Child in America: Behavior Problems and Programs.* New York: Knopf.

Tononi, G. and G. M. Edelman, 1998. "Consciousness and complexity," *Science,* 282:1846-1851 (Dec. 4).

Toobin, J., 1996a. "The Marcia Clark verdict," *New Yorker,* 72:57-71 (Sept. 9).

——, 1996b. *The Run of His Life.* New York: Random House.

Tourin, B. and J. W. Garrett, 1962. *Safety belt effectiveness in rural California automobile accidents: A comparison of injuries to users and non-users of safety belts.* Ithaca, NY: Cornell U., Automotive Crash Injury Research.

Trevelyan, G. M., 1942/1976. *A Shortened History of England.* New York: Viking/Putnam.

Tufte, E. R., 1974. *Data Analysis for Politics and Policy.* Englewood Cliffs, NJ: Prentice-Hall.

——, 1983. *The Visual Display of Quantitative Information.* Cheshire, CT: Graphics Press.

——, 1990. *Envisioning Information.* Cheshire, CT: Graphics Press.

——, 1997. *Visual Explanations: Images and Quantities, Evidence and Narrative.* Cheshire, CT: Graphics Press.

Turley, J., 1998. "High crimes and misdemeanors, according to the Framers," *Wall St. J.,* 139:A23 (Nov. 9).

——, 2000. "What's wrong with Wright?" *Wall St. J.,* 140:A23 (April 19).

Twight, C., 1999. "Watching YOU: Federal surveillance of ordinary Americans," *Independent Rev.,* 4:165-200.

Tyson, G. A., 1984. "An empirical test of the astrological theory of personality," *Person. Individual Diffs.,* 5:247-250.

Uelman, G. F., 1980. "Testing the assumptions of Neil v. Biggers: A classroom experiment," *Crim. Law Bull.,* 16:28-39.

Ulam, A. B., 1975. *A History of Soviet Russia.* New York: Harcourt, Brace.

——, 1989. *Stalin: the Man and His Era.* Boston: Beacon Press.

Uleman, J. S. and J. A. Bargh, 1989. *Unintended Thought.* New York: Guilford.

United Kingdom, Office of Population Censuses and Surveys, 1995. *1991 Census Users' Guide: Topic Statistics: Ethnic Group and Country of Birth.* Foreham, Hants, U.K.

United Nations Children's Fund (UNICEF), 2000. *State of the World's Children, 2000.* United Nations Publications.

U. S. Surgeon General, 1999. *Mental Health: A Report of the Surgeon General.* Rockville, MD: U. S. Dept. of Health and Human Services.

Unz, R., 1999. "California and the end of white America," *Commentary,* 108:17-28.

Van Laningham, J. G., 1986. "The making of the 1986 Florida safety belt law: Issues and insight," *Florida State Univ. Law Rev.,* 14:685-717. Tallahassee, FL.

Van Parijs, P., 1991. "Why surfers should be fed: The liberal case for a basic income," *Phil. and Public Affairs*, 20:101-131.

——, 1992. "Basic income capitalism," *Ethics*, 102:465-484.

——, 1997. *Real Freedom for All: What If Anything Can Justify Capitalism?* New York: Oxford U. P.

——, Joshua Cohen, Joel Rogers (eds.), 2001. *What's Wrong with a Free Lunch?* Boston: Beacon Press.

Visher, C., 1984. *The RAND Second Inmate Survey: A Reanalysis*. Washington, DC: Panel on Research on Criminal Careers. National Res. Council.

Von Mises, R., 1956. *Positivism: A Study in Human Understanding*. New York: Braziller.

——, 1957. *Probability, Statistics, and Truth*. 2/e. London: George Allen & Unwin.

Von Neumann, J. and O. Morgenstern, 1944. *Theory of Games and Economic Behavior*. Princeton, NJ: Princeton U. P.

Wachter, K. M., 1988. "Disturbed by meta-analysis?" *Science*, 241:1047-1048 (Sept. 16).

Wainer, H., 2000. "Visual revelations," *Chance*, 12:47-48.

Walden, G., 2000. "Thunder in the air," *Times Lit. Supp.*, 5060:6-8 (March 24).

Walinsky, A., 1995. "The crisis of public order," *Atlantic Monthly*, 276:39-54.

Wall Street Journal, Editors, 1991. "Fight on, Exxon," *Journal*, 124:A14 (May 2).

——, 1995a. "The breast implant tragedy," 132:A10 (May 19).

——, 1995b. "Higginbotham v. Thomas," 133:A14 (Dec. 1).

——, 1996. "Stiglitz v. Clinton," 134:A14 (April 12).

——, 1999. "The Broadrick polls," 140:A18 (March 13).

——, 2000a. "Judicial discretion," 142:A18 (Feb. 4).

——, 2000b. "ADD a campaign issue," 142:A48 (March 27).

——, 2000c. "Goodbye to Fiji," 236:A22 (July 19).

——, 2000d. "Race counts," 236:A26 (May 30).

——, 2001. "Governor chicken," 238:A18 (Oct. 21).

Waller, N. G. and P. E. Meehl, 1998. *Multivariate Taxometric Procedures: Distinguishing Types from Continua*. Newbury Park, CA: Sage.

Webb, B. P., 1935. *Soviet Communism: A New Civilization?* London: Gollancz.

Webb, S. and B. P. Webb, 1941. *Soviet Communism: A New Civilization*. London: Gollancz.

Weber, M., 1947. *Gesammelte Aufsätze zur Wissenschaftslehre*. Tübingen, Germany: Siebeck. Portions are reprinted in A. M. Henderson and T. Parsons (eds.), *Max Weber: The Theory of Social and Economic Organization*. New York: Oxford U. P.

Webster, E. C., 1964. *Decision Making in the Employment Interview*. Montreal: McGill Univ., Industrial Relations Centre.

Wedow, S. M., 1976. "The strangeness of astrology: An ethnography of credibility processes." In W. Arens and S. P. Montague (eds.), *The American Dimension: Cultural Myths and Social Realities*. Port Washington, NY: Alfred.

Weiskrantz, L., 1985. "Categorization, cleverness, and consciousness." In his edited volume, *Animal Intelligence*. Oxford: Clarendon Press.

Weismann, K., 1998. "Violent, hate-filled speech," *Wall St. J.*, 139:A19 (Dec. 21).

Weiss, R. A., 1999. "Is AIDS man-made?" *Science*, 286:1305-1306 (Nov. 12).

Wells, G. L., 1979. "Accuracy, confidence, and juror perceptions in eyewitness identification," *J. Appl. Psych.*, 64:440-448.

——, et al., 1980a. "Effects of expert psychological advice on human performance in judging the validity of eyewitness testimony," *Law and Human Beh.*, 4:386-406.

——, 1980b. Editor, Special Issue, "On eyewitness behavior," *Law and Human Beh.*, Vol. 4.

——, and D. M. Murray, 1984. "Eyewitness confidence." In G. L. Wells and E. F. Loftus (eds.), *Eyewitness Testimony: Psychological Perspectives*. New York: Cambridge U. P.

——, et al., 2000. "From the lab to the police station: A successful application of eyewitness research," *Amer. Psychol.*, 55:561-598.

Wertheimer, J. 2001. "Surrendering to intermarriage," *Commentary*, 111:25-32.

Wessel, D., 1997. "America's wealth is being distributed a bit more evenly, Fed survey shows," *Wall St. J.*, 136:A1 (Jan. 24).

——, and B. Davis, 1998a. "Crisis crusaders: Would-be Keyneses view over how to fight globe's financial woes," *Wall St. J.*, 139:A1, A6 (Sept. 25).

——, 1998b. "Limits of power: How global crisis grew despite efforts of a crack U. S. team," *Wall St. J.*, 139:A1, A10. (Sept. 24).

White, P. A., 1988. "Causal processing: Origins and development," *Psychol. Bull.*, 104:36-52.

Whyte, L. L., 1948a. *The Next Development in Man*. New York: Holt.

——, 1948b. *Everyman Looks Forward*. New York: Holt.

Wiggins, N. and E. S. Kohen, 1971. "Man versus model of Man revisited: The forecasting of graduate school success," *J. Person. Soc. Psych.*, 19:100-106.

Wildavsky, A., 1979. *Speaking Truth to Power: The Art and Craft of Policy Analysis*. Boston: Little, Brown.

——, 1995. *But Is It True? A Citizen's Guide to Environmental Health and Safety Issues*. Cambridge, MA: Harvard U. P.

Williams, B. 1993. *Morality: An Introduction to Ethics*. New York: Cambridge U. P.

——, 1995. *Making Sense of Humanity and Other Papers*. New York: Cambridge U. P.

——, 1996. "On hating and despising philosophy," *London Rev. Books*, 18:17-18 (April 18).

Williams, D.C., 1947. *The Ground of Induction*. Cambridge, MA: Harvard U. P.

Williams, R. J., 1956. *Biochemical Individuality*. New York: Wiley.

——, 1979. *Free and Unequal: The Biological Basis of Individual Liberty*. Indianapolis, IN: Liberty Press.

Wills, G., 1992a. "H. R. Clinton's case," *NY Rev. Books*, 39:3-5 (March 5).

Wilson, D. S., 1997. "Human groups as units of selection," *Science*, 276:1816-1817.

Wilson, E. O., 1976. *Sociobiology: The New Synthesis*. Cambridge, MA: Harvard U. P.

——, 1995. *Naturalist*. Washington, DC: Island Press/Clearwater Books.

Wilson, J. Q., 1996. *Moral Judgment*. New York: Basic Books.

——, and G. Kelling, 1982. "Broken windows: The police and neighborhood safety," *Atlantic Monthly*, 249:29-38.

Wilson, W. J., 1997. *When Work Disappears: The World of the New Urban Poor*. New York: Knopf.

Wilson, W. K., 1995. "Equivocation." In R. Audi (ed.), *The Cambridge Dictionary of Philosophy*. New York: Cambridge U. P.

Winner, E., 1988. *The Point of Words: Children's Understanding of Metaphor and Irony*. Cambridge, MA: Harvard U. P.

Winthrop, H., 1946. "Semantic factors in the measurement of personality integration," *J. Soc. Psychol.*, 24:149-175.

Wittgenstein, L., 1921. *Tractatus Logico-Philosophicus*. Trans. and edited, 1961, by D. F. Pears and B. F. McGuinnes. London: Routledge & Kegan Paul.

——, 1930-1933. "Wittgenstein's lectures." G. E. Moore, original editor. In J. C. Klagge and A. Nordmann (eds.), *Ludwig Wittgenstein: Philosophical Occasions, 1912-1951*. Indianapolis, IN: Hackett.

——, 1953. *Philosophical Investigations*. 3/e. G. E. M. Anscombe (ed.). New York: Macmillan.

——, 1958. *The Blue and Brown Books*. Reprinted 1964. New York: Harper and Row.

Wolfgang, M. E., 1974. "The social scientist in court," *J. Crim. Law & Criminology*, 65:239-247.

Woodward, A. L., 1998. "Infants selectively encode the goal of an actor's reach," *Cognition*, 69:1-34.

Wooster, M. M., 1992. "Campus followers," *Reason*, 23:52-55.

Wright, L., 1995. "Double mystery," *New Yorker*, 71:45-62 (Aug. 7).

Wright, R., 2000. *Non Zero: The Logic of Human Destiny*. New York: Pantheon.

Wynne, K., 1995. "Infants possess a system of numerical knowledge," *Current Directions in Psych. Sci.*, 4:172-177.

Wynter, L. E., 1995. "Business and race: Groups want census to expand race choices," *Wall St. J.*, 133:B1 (Sept. 13).

Youngner, S. J., R. M. Arnold, R. Schapiro (eds.), 1999. *The Definition of Death: Contemporary Controversies*. Baltimore, MD: Johns Hopkins.

Zajonc, R. B. and P. R. Mullaly, 1997. "Birth-order: Reconciling conflicting effects," *Amer. Psychol.*, 52:685-699.

Zaragoza, M. S. et al., 2001. "Interviewing witnesses: Forced confabulation and confirmatory feedback increase false memories," *Psychol. Sci.*, 12:473-477.

Zedlewski, F. W., 1983. "Deterrence findings and data sources: A comparison of Uniform Crime Reports and National Crime Surveys," *J. Res. Crime and Delinq.*, 20:262-276.

Zheng, Y., 1996. *Scarlet Memorial: Tales of Cannibalism in Modern China*. Boulder, CO: Westview Press.

Zohar, D. and I. Marshall, 1994. *The Quantum Society: Mind, Physics, and a New Social Order*. New York: Morrow.

Zuckerman, M., 1995. "Good and bad humors: biochemical bases of personality and its disorders," *Psych. Sci.*, 6:325-332.

Zuriff, G. E., 2002. "Inventing racism," *Pub. Interest*, 146:114-128.

Index

abstraction, x, 27-34, 81-86
  levels of, 78-81, 238
Achensee question, 129-130, 256.n.45
acquiescence bias, 56, 136
actuarial procedure, 188-189
ad hockery, 14, 181, 207
agency, 27, 195, 204
aggregation, 50, 58, 80-81
aggregative error, 81-86
Alice-in-Wonderland, 16-17
Alker, H., Jr., 76
Allen, W. R., 41-42
allometry, 212
animal cognition, Ch. 1, 180, 263.n.13
anoetic process, 247.n.37
anthropology, cultural, *see* ethnography
anticipation, 12, 34, 44-50
apotropaic ritual, 74
Aristotle, 42, 204, 208
Armstrong, L., 11, 12
assimilation, 108
astrology, 46, 74
atheism, 228
attention deficit disorder (ADD), 107
attitude, 136
Austad, S., 209
Australia, 168
average, 28, 63, 247.n.41, 21.n.18, 261.n.128
awareness, *see* consciousness
Ayer, A. J., 193, 264.n.5, n.12

Babor, T. F., 134
Bacon, F., 133
Bakunin, M., 12
Baldwin, A., 245.n.12
Barings LPC, 206
Barry, J., 98
base rate, 101-102
Bastiat, F., 220
Bayes, T., 96

Bean, R. B., 70
beauty as power, 120
Beckmann, P., 92
belief, 20, 28-32, 74, 204
  as cause, 194-195
  confidence ≠ accuracy, 74, 95, 108, 145, 190, 210, 237
  and knowledge, 26-34, 61, 63-68, 108, 241, 246.n.25, 247.n.37, 247-248.n.42
  as predictive, 219
  and probability, 95
  reasons for, 95, 246.n.21
Benedict V, Pope, 7
Bennett, D., 98
Berger, P., 42
Bergmann, G., 248.n.50
Bias, 54, 61, 88, 138, 180, 248.n.50
  antidote to, 69-71
  good and evil, 70
Bierce, A., 125-126
bigotry for goodness's sake, 70, 87
biology, 210-211
Bishop, J., 74
Blackburn, S., 19-20, 27, 31, 262.n.134
Bleuler, E., 25
blind test, 70
bolshevik, 235
Bonaparte, N., 7, 27, 306, 221, 237
bonobo, 3, 193, 247.n.42; *see* also chimpanzee
Booth, A., 146-147, 259.n.66
Brookhiser, R., 184
Broom, L., 43
Brown, J., 134
Brown, J. F., 199
Bruce, L., 23
Buddhism, 288-289
Bukharin, N., 235
bullshit, 117, 186
  antidote for, 158-160

For Product Safety Concerns and Information please contact our EU
representative GPSR@taylorandfrancis.com Taylor & Francis Verlag GmbH,
Kaufingerstraße 24, 80331 München, Germany

Batch number: 08153774

Printed by Printforce, the Netherlands